Grimm Fairy Tales presents:

Vampires & Werewolves

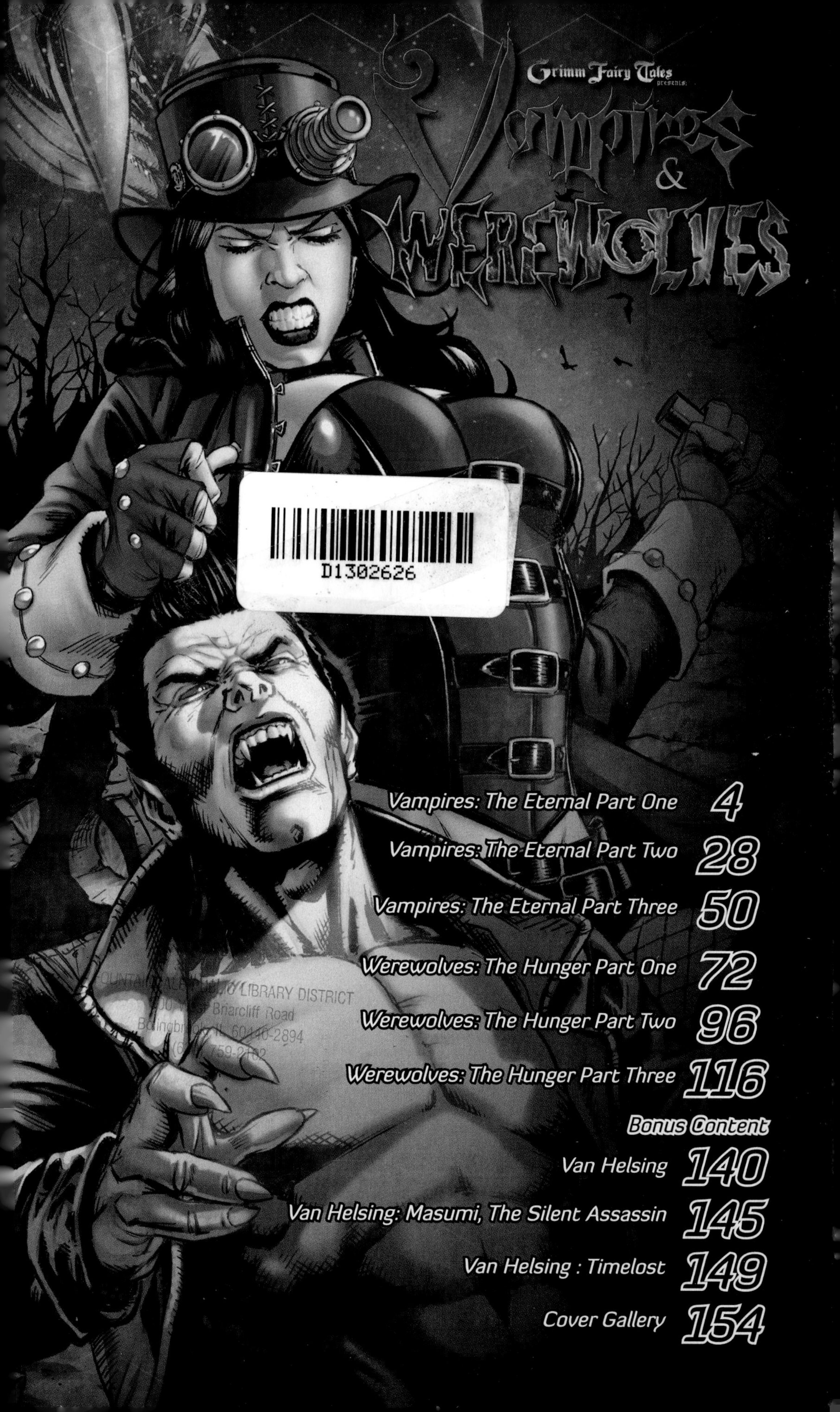

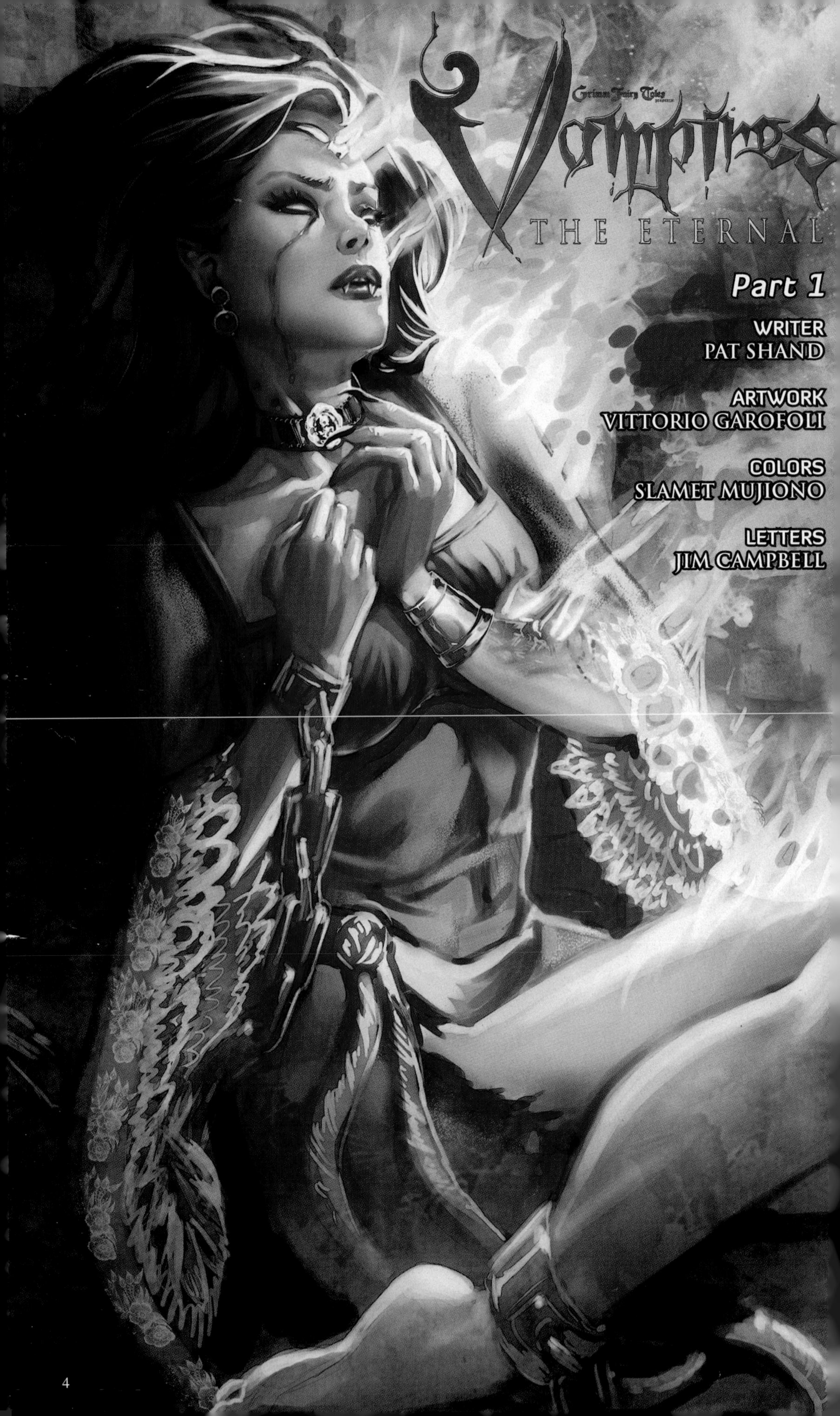
Grimm Fairy Tales presents
Vampires
THE ETERNAL
Part 1
WRITER
PAT SHAND
ARTWORK
VITTORIO GAROFOLI
COLORS
SLAMET MUJIONO
LETTERS
JIM CAMPBELL

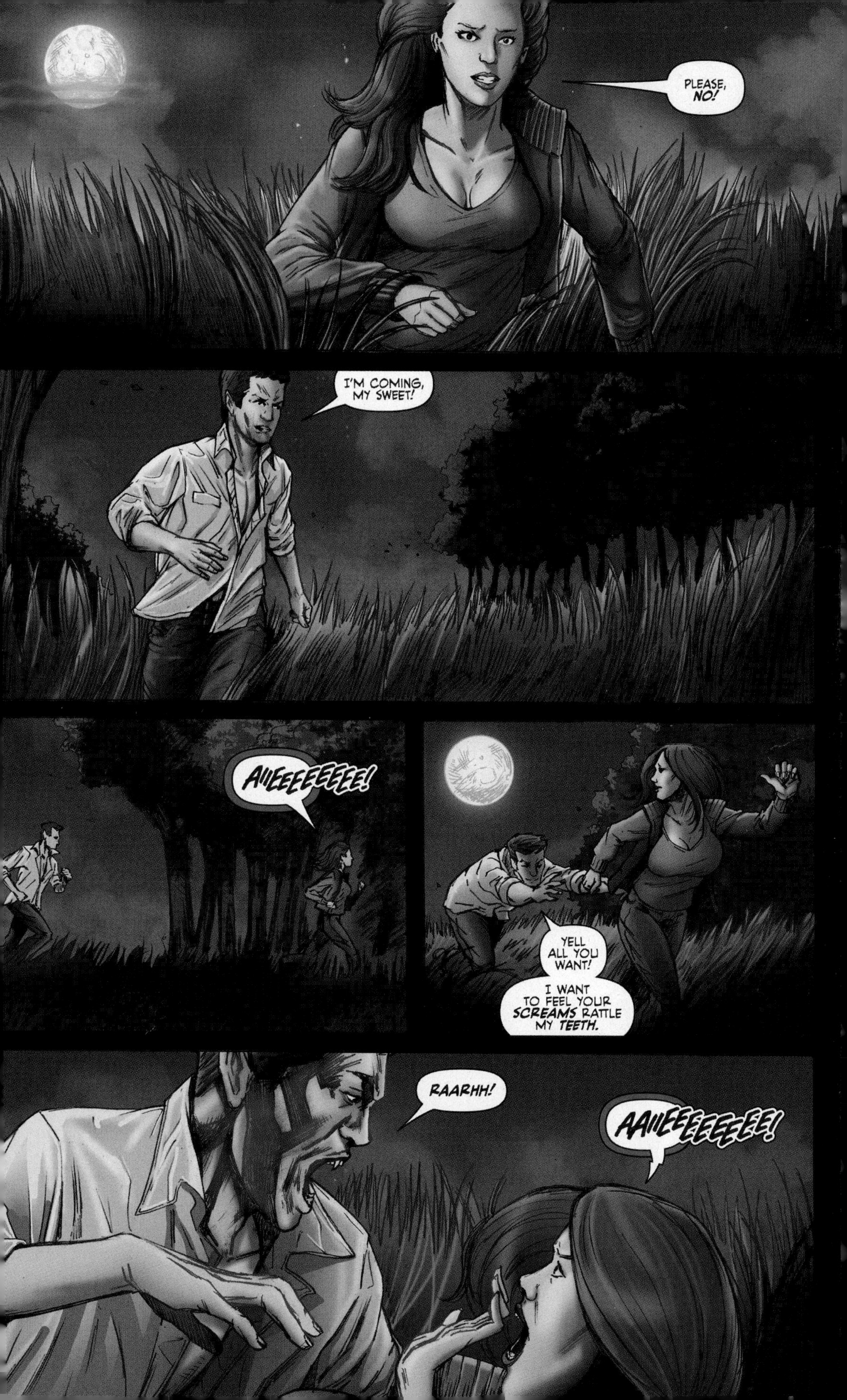
PLEASE, NO!
I'M COMING, MY SWEET!
AIIEEEEEEEE!
YELL ALL YOU WANT!
I WANT TO FEEL YOUR SCREAMS RATTLE MY TEETH.
RAARHH!
AAIIEEEEEEEEE!

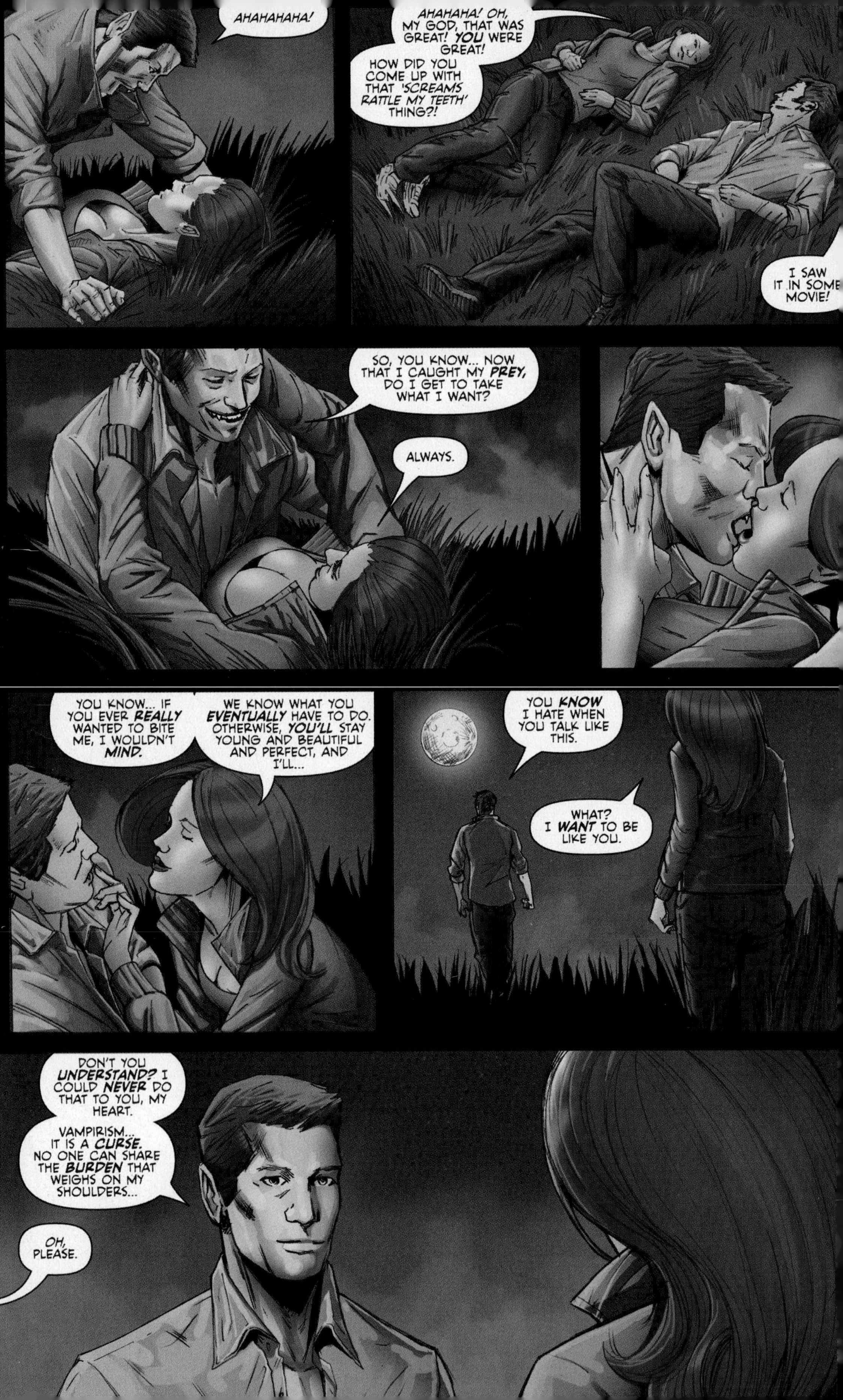
AHAHAHAHA!
AHAHAHA! OH, MY GOD, THAT WAS GREAT! YOU WERE GREAT!
HOW DID YOU COME UP WITH THAT 'SCREAMS RATTLE MY TEETH' THING?!
I SAW IT IN SOME MOVIE!
SO, YOU KNOW... NOW THAT I CAUGHT MY PREY, DO I GET TO TAKE WHAT I WANT?
ALWAYS.
YOU KNOW... IF YOU EVER REALLY WANTED TO BITE ME, I WOULDN'T MIND.
WE KNOW WHAT YOU EVENTUALLY HAVE TO DO. OTHERWISE, YOU'LL STAY YOUNG AND BEAUTIFUL AND PERFECT, AND I'LL...
YOU KNOW I HATE WHEN YOU TALK LIKE THIS.
WHAT? I WANT TO BE LIKE YOU.
DON'T YOU UNDERSTAND? I COULD NEVER DO THAT TO YOU, MY HEART.
VAMPIRISM... IT IS A CURSE. NO ONE CAN SHARE THE BURDEN THAT WEIGHS ON MY SHOULDERS...
OH, PLEASE.

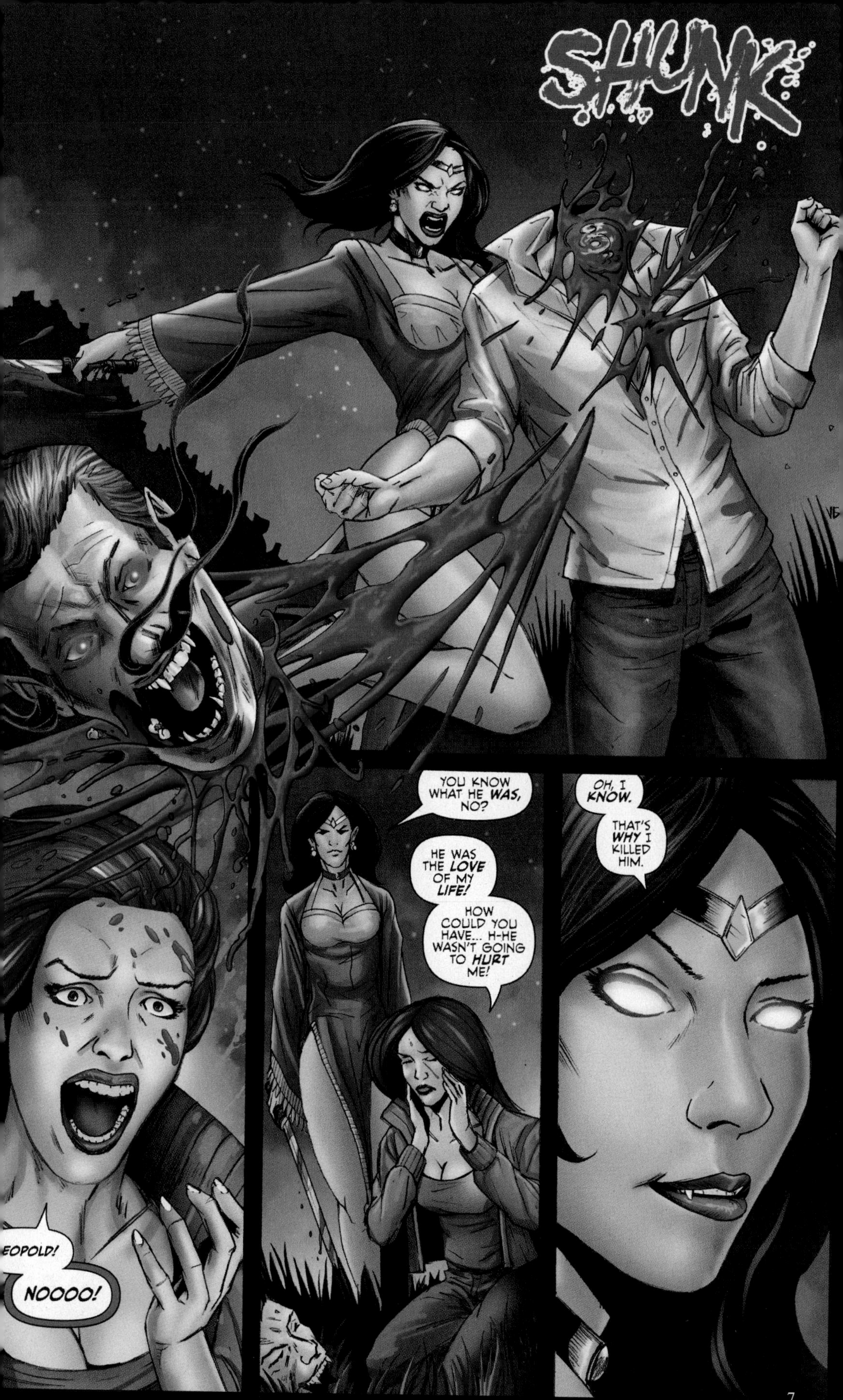
SHUNK
EOPOLD!
NOOOO!
YOU KNOW WHAT HE WAS, NO?
HE WAS THE LOVE OF MY LIFE!
HOW COULD YOU HAVE... H-HE WASN'T GOING TO HURT ME!
OH, I KNOW.
THAT'S WHY I KILLED HIM.

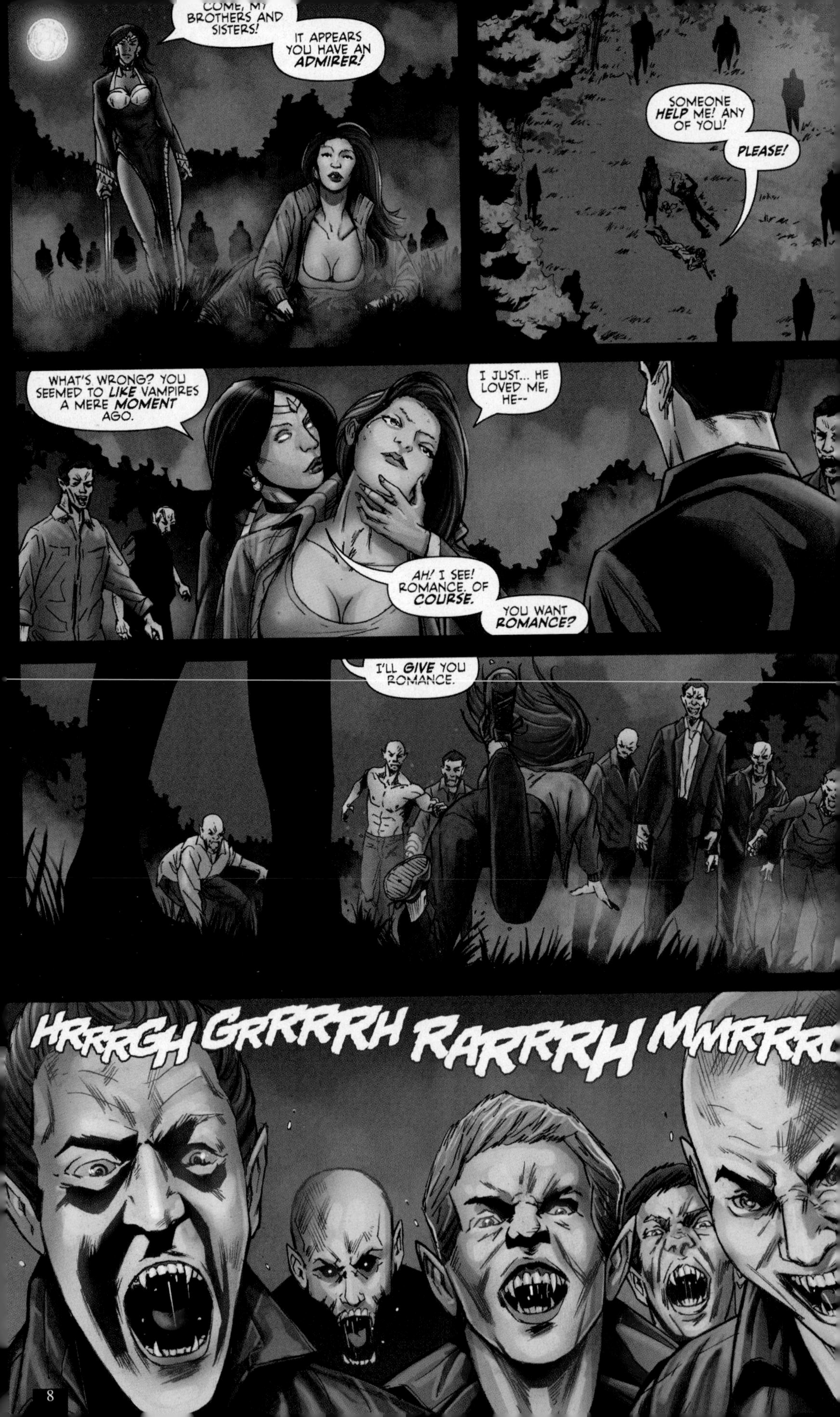
COME, MY BROTHERS AND SISTERS!
IT APPEARS YOU HAVE AN ADMIRER!
SOMEONE HELP ME! ANY OF YOU!
PLEASE!
WHAT'S WRONG? YOU SEEMED TO LIKE VAMPIRES A MERE MOMENT AGO.
I JUST... HE LOVED ME, HE--
AH! I SEE! ROMANCE. OF COURSE.
YOU WANT ROMANCE?
I'LL GIVE YOU ROMANCE.
HRRRGH GRRRRRH RARRRRH MMRRR

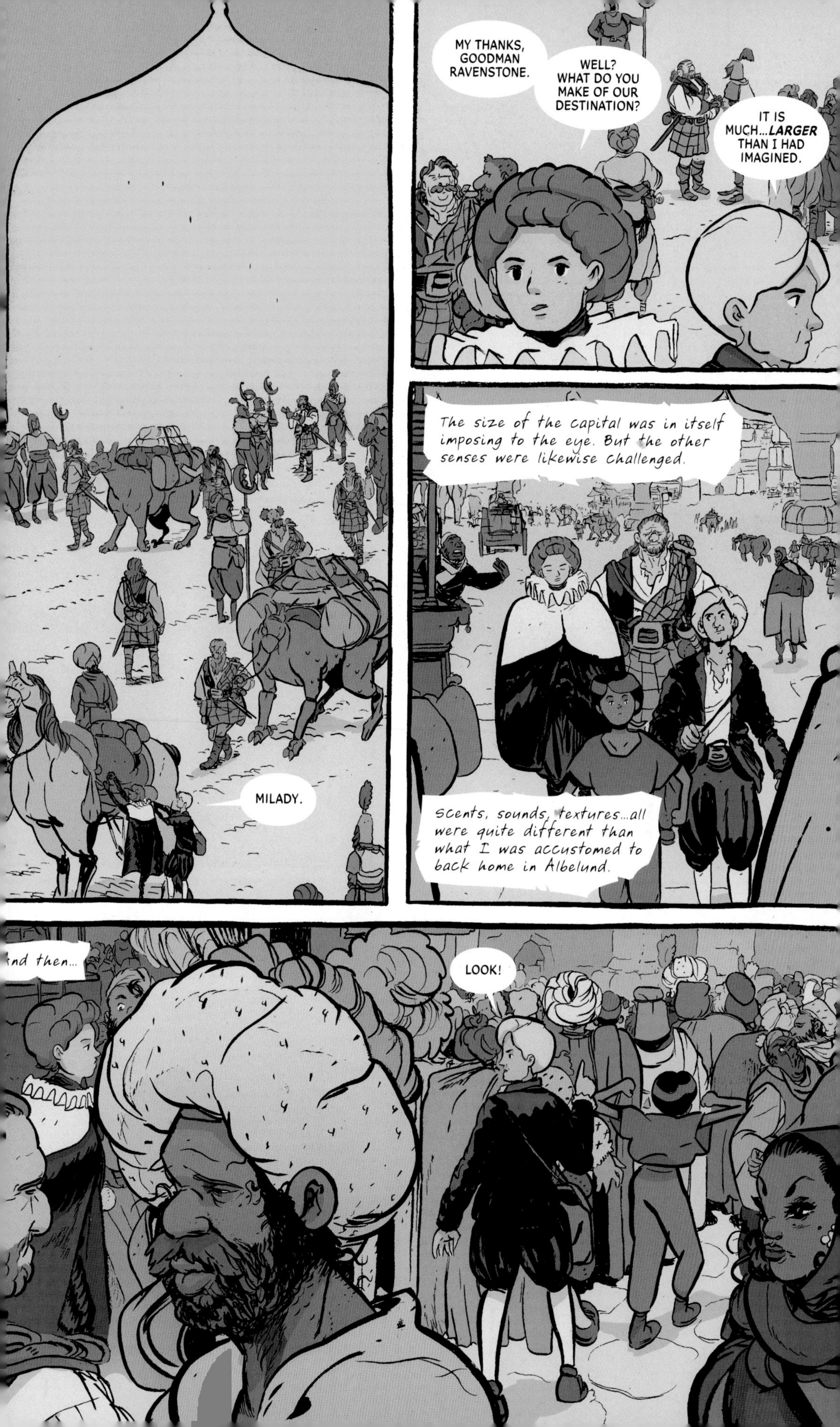
MILADY.
MY THANKS, GOODMAN RAVENSTONE.
WELL? WHAT DO YOU MAKE OF OUR DESTINATION?
IT IS MUCH...**LARGER** THAN I HAD IMAGINED.
The size of the capital was in itself imposing to the eye. But the other senses were likewise challenged.
Scents, sounds, textures...all were quite different than what I was accustomed to back home in Albelund.
and then...
LOOK!

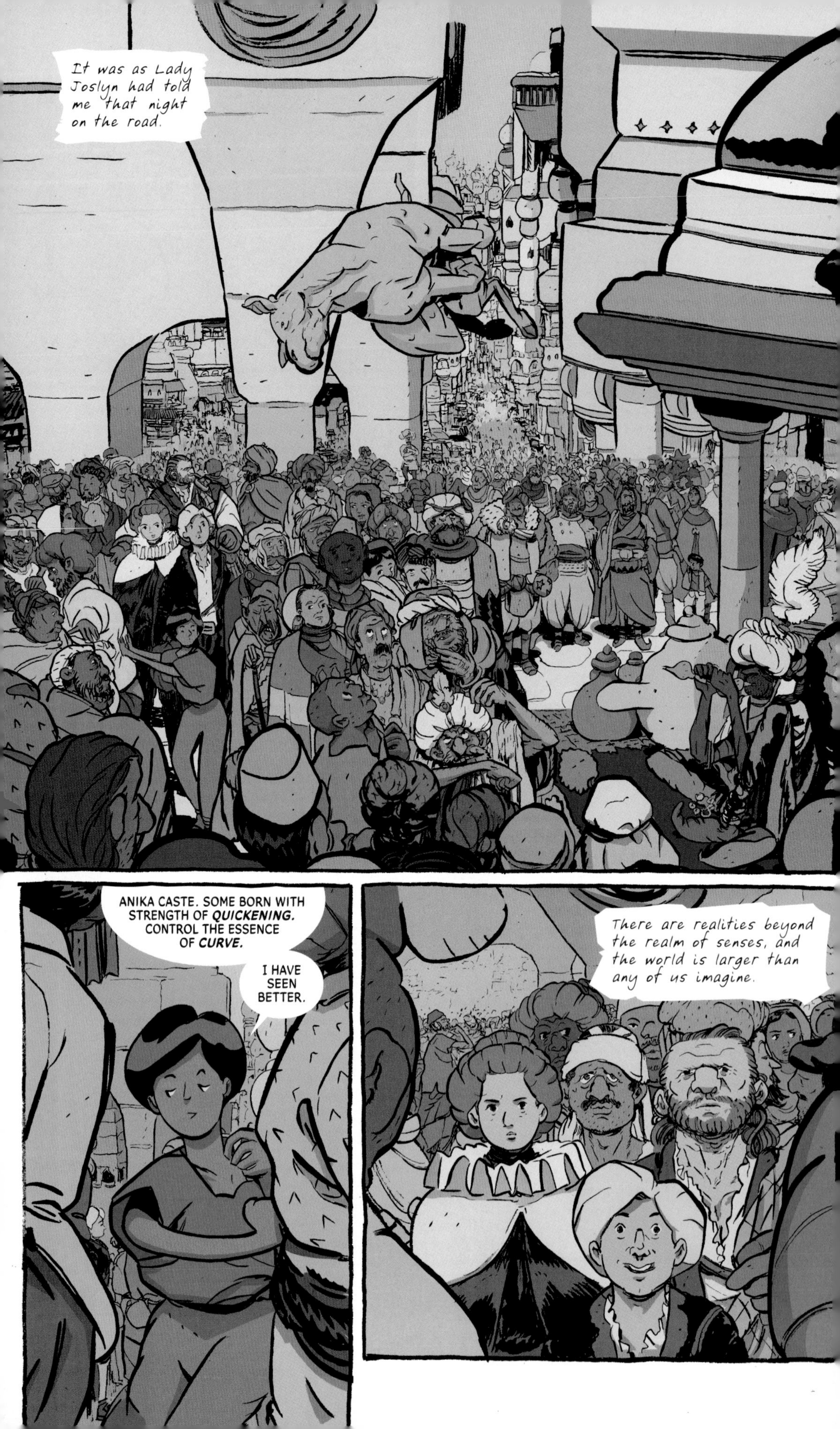
It was as Lady Joslyn had told me that night on the road.
ANIKA CASTE. SOME BORN WITH STRENGTH OF QUICKENING. CONTROL THE ESSENCE OF CURVE.
I HAVE SEEN BETTER.
There are realities beyond the realm of senses, and the world is larger than any of us imagine.

COME and SEE

Reality exists independent of our beliefs about it. If one does not believe in something, it does not mean that thing is not true.

—Pol Ravenstone's
private journal

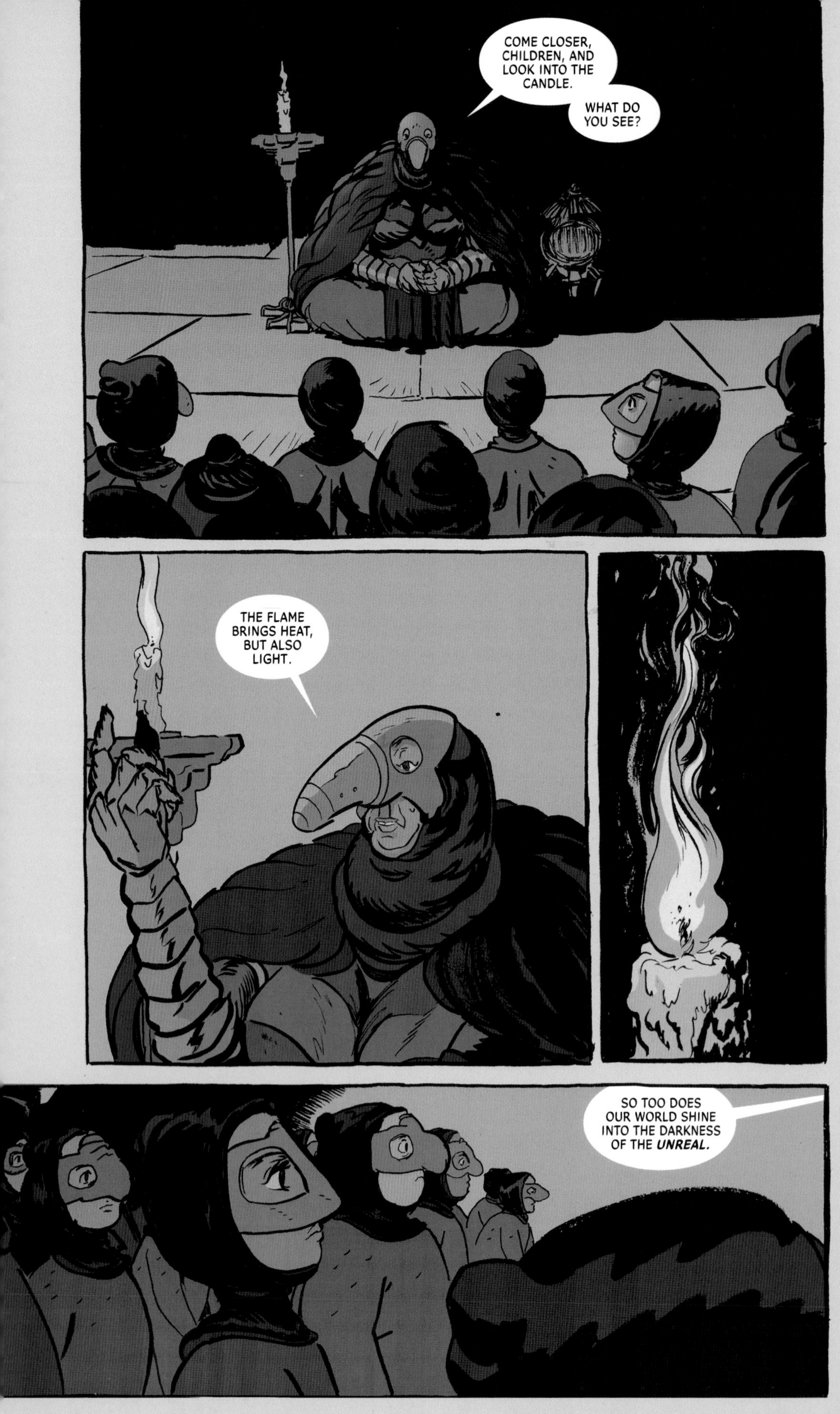
COME CLOSER, CHILDREN, AND LOOK INTO THE CANDLE.
WHAT DO YOU SEE?
THE FLAME BRINGS HEAT, BUT ALSO LIGHT.
SO TOO DOES OUR WORLD SHINE INTO THE DARKNESS OF THE *UNREAL.*

YOU'VE BEEN SO *FAMISHED*, I KNOW.

YOUR THIRST WILL BE *QUENCHED* -- THIS I *PROMISE*.

BUT WE ARE NO [...] CREATURES DRIV[...] *SURVIVAL*, ARE WE? [...] RETURNED TO OUR [...] AND IT HAS *RIPENED* [...] A FRUIT, WAITING FOR [...] TO SUCK ITS SWEET *JUICES*.

WITH *ETERNITY* OPENING UP BEFORE US ONCE MORE, A SPLENDID DREAM WEIGHS ON OUR SHOULDERS.

SOME OF US WERE LEFT ON EARTH WHEN THE WAR ENDED, WHILE WE, THE *TRUE* VAMPIRES, GREW *STRONGER* IN THE *SHADOWLANDS*.*

WE MUST FIND OUR *KIN* AND RECRUIT THEM FOR THE COMING *WAR*...

*See *Unleashed #1*.

...AND *EXTERMINATE* THOSE THAT HAVE BEEN POLLUTED BY THE PLAGUE CALLED *HUMANITY*.

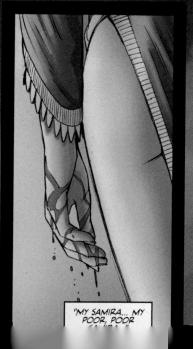

"MY SAMIRA... MY POOR, POOR

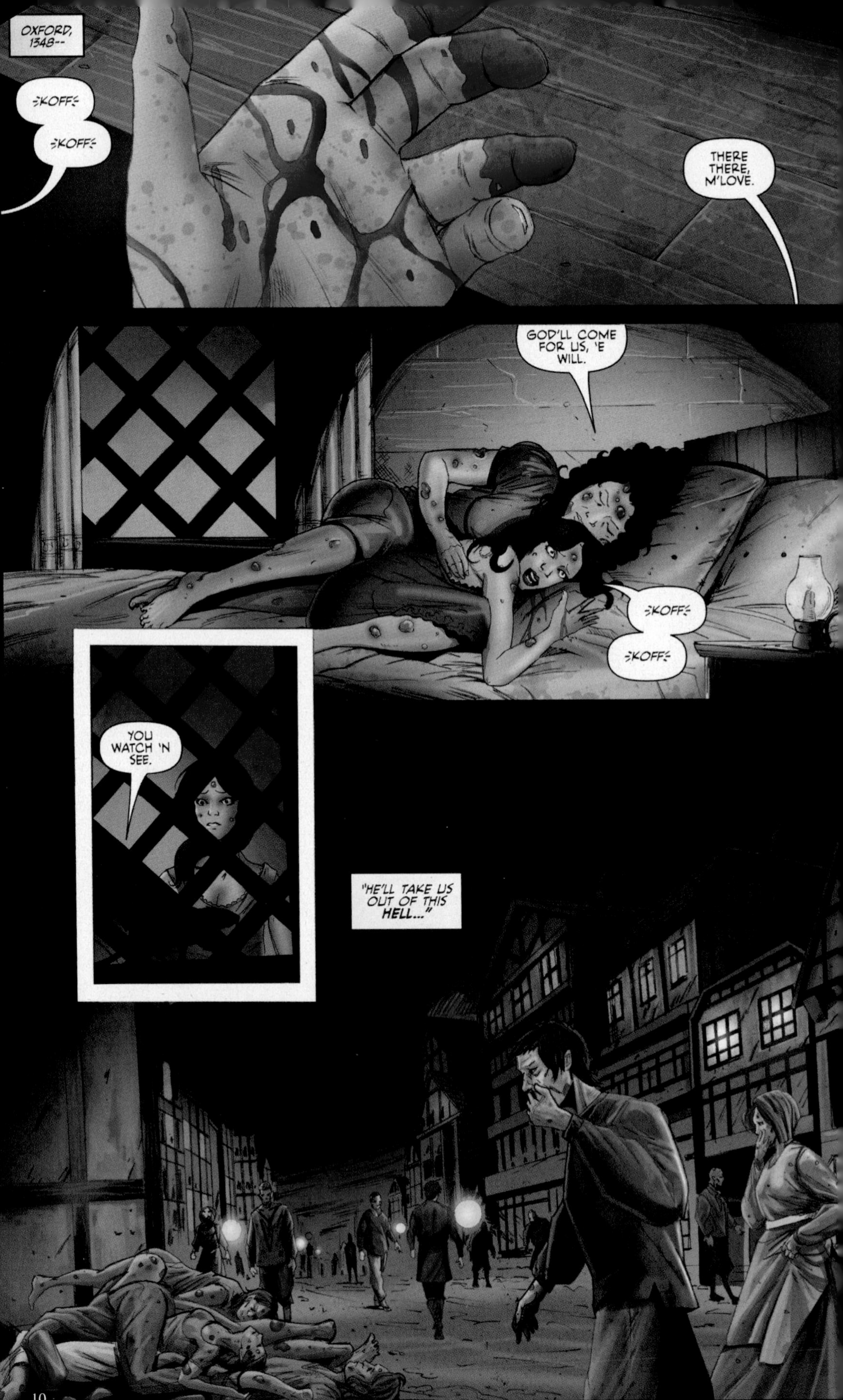
OXFORD, 1348--
-KOFF-
-KOFF-
THERE THERE, M'LOVE.
GOD'LL COME FOR US, 'E WILL.
-KOFF-
-KOFF-
YOU WATCH 'N SEE.
"HE'LL TAKE US OUT OF THIS **HELL**..."

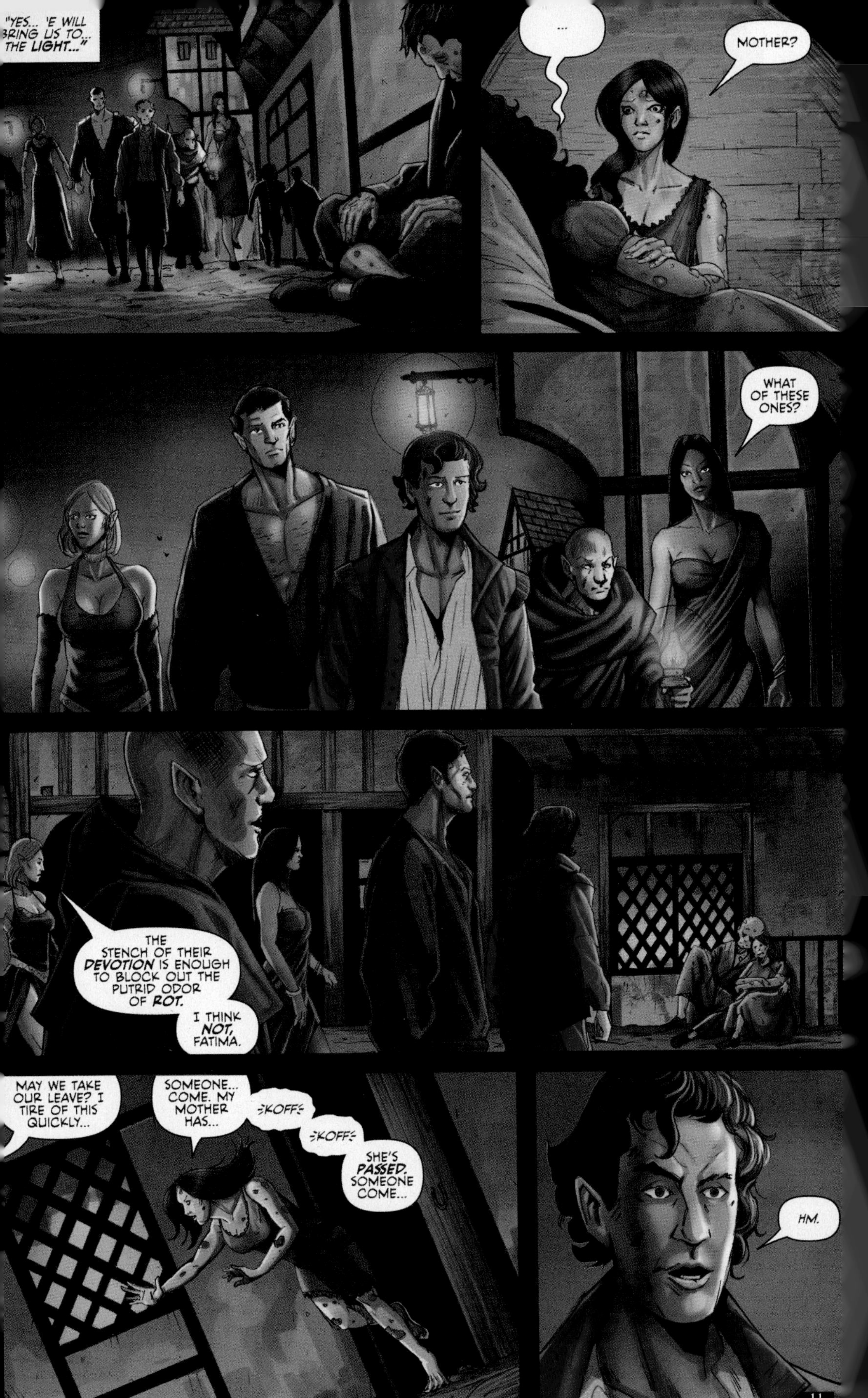
"YES... 'E WILL BRING US TO... THE LIGHT..."
...
MOTHER?
WHAT OF THESE ONES?
THE STENCH OF THEIR DEVOTION IS ENOUGH TO BLOCK OUT THE PUTRID ODOR OF ROT.
I THINK NOT, FATIMA.
MAY WE TAKE OUR LEAVE? I TIRE OF THIS QUICKLY...
SOMEONE... COME. MY MOTHER HAS...
KOFF
KOFF
SHE'S PASSED. SOMEONE COME...
HM.

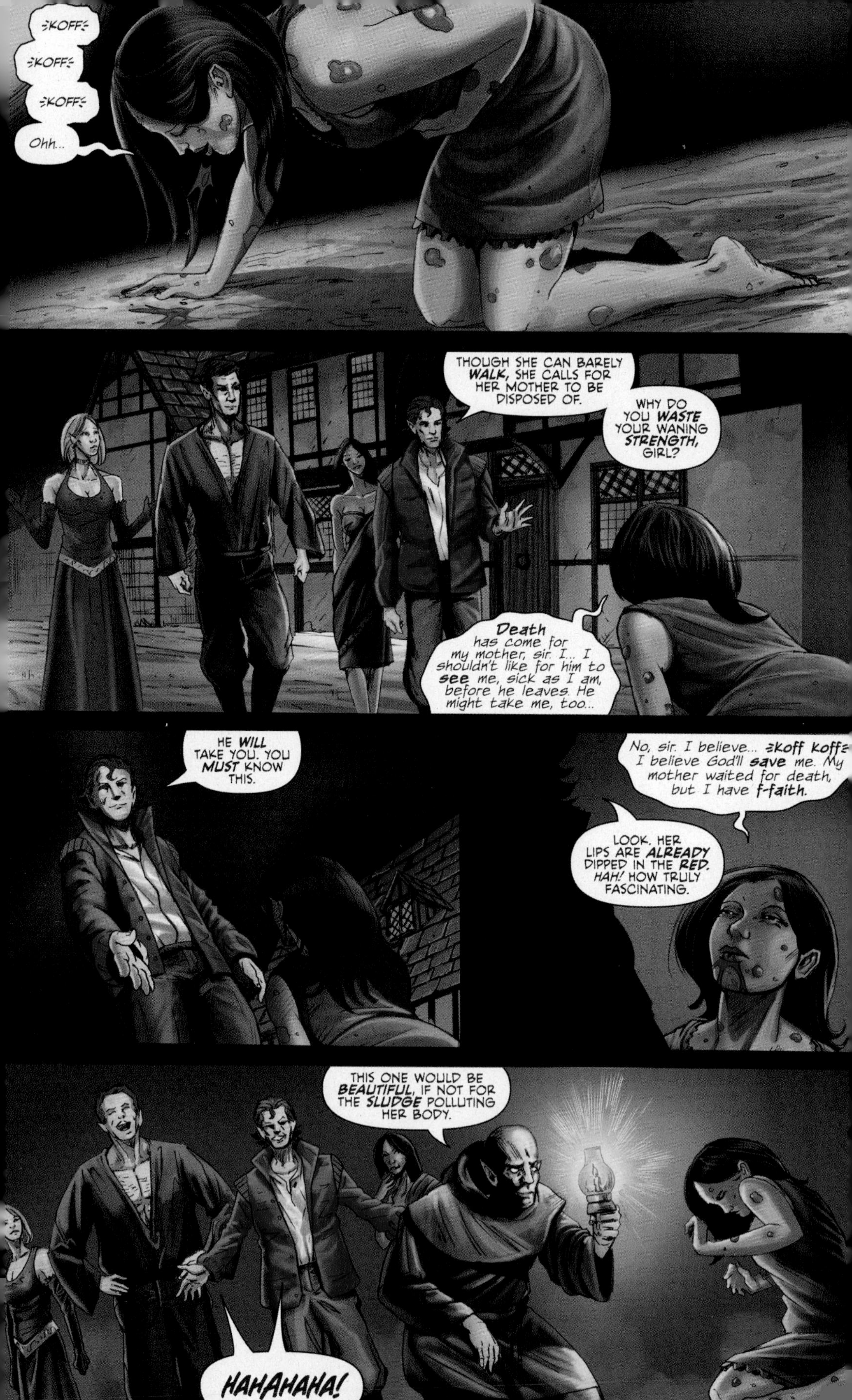

=KOFF=
=KOFF=
=KOFF=
Ohh...
THOUGH SHE CAN BARELY WALK, SHE CALLS FOR HER MOTHER TO BE DISPOSED OF.
WHY DO YOU WASTE YOUR WANING STRENGTH, GIRL?
Death has come for my mother, sir. I... I shouldn't like for him to see me, sick as I am, before he leaves. He might take me, too...
HE WILL TAKE YOU. YOU MUST KNOW THIS.
No, sir. I believe... =koff koff= I believe God'll save me. My mother waited for death, but I have f-faith.
LOOK. HER LIPS ARE ALREADY DIPPED IN THE RED. HAH! HOW TRULY FASCINATING.
THIS ONE WOULD BE BEAUTIFUL, IF NOT FOR THE SLUDGE POLLUTING HER BODY.
HAHAHAHA!

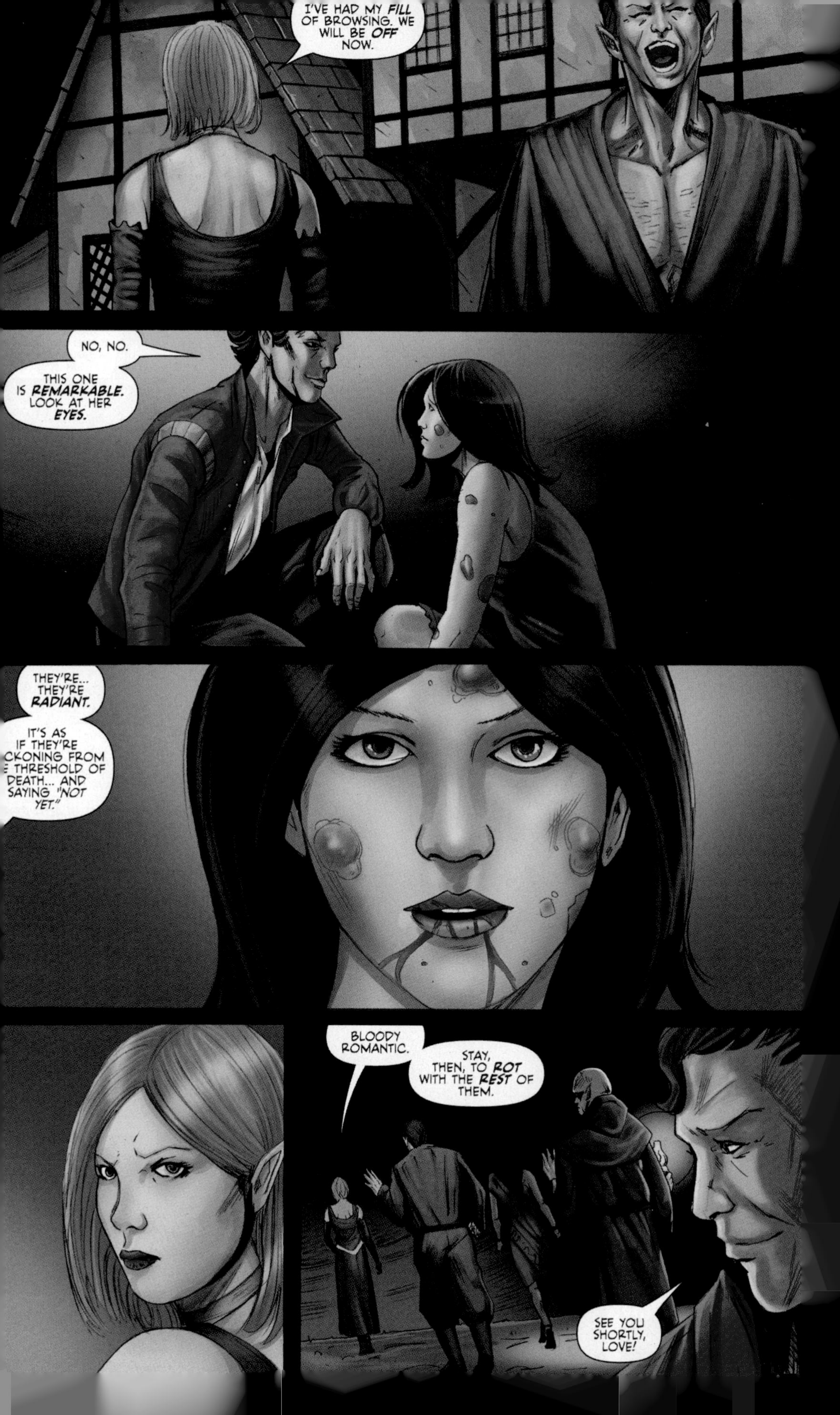

I'VE HAD MY *FILL* OF BROWSING. WE WILL BE *OFF* NOW.
NO, NO.
THIS ONE IS ***REMARKABLE.*** LOOK AT HER ***EYES.***
THEY'RE... THEY'RE ***RADIANT.***
IT'S AS IF THEY'RE CKONING FROM THRESHOLD OF DEATH... AND SAYING *"NOT YET."*
BLOODY ROMANTIC.
STAY, THEN, TO *ROT* WITH THE *REST* OF THEM.
SEE YOU SHORTLY, LOVE!

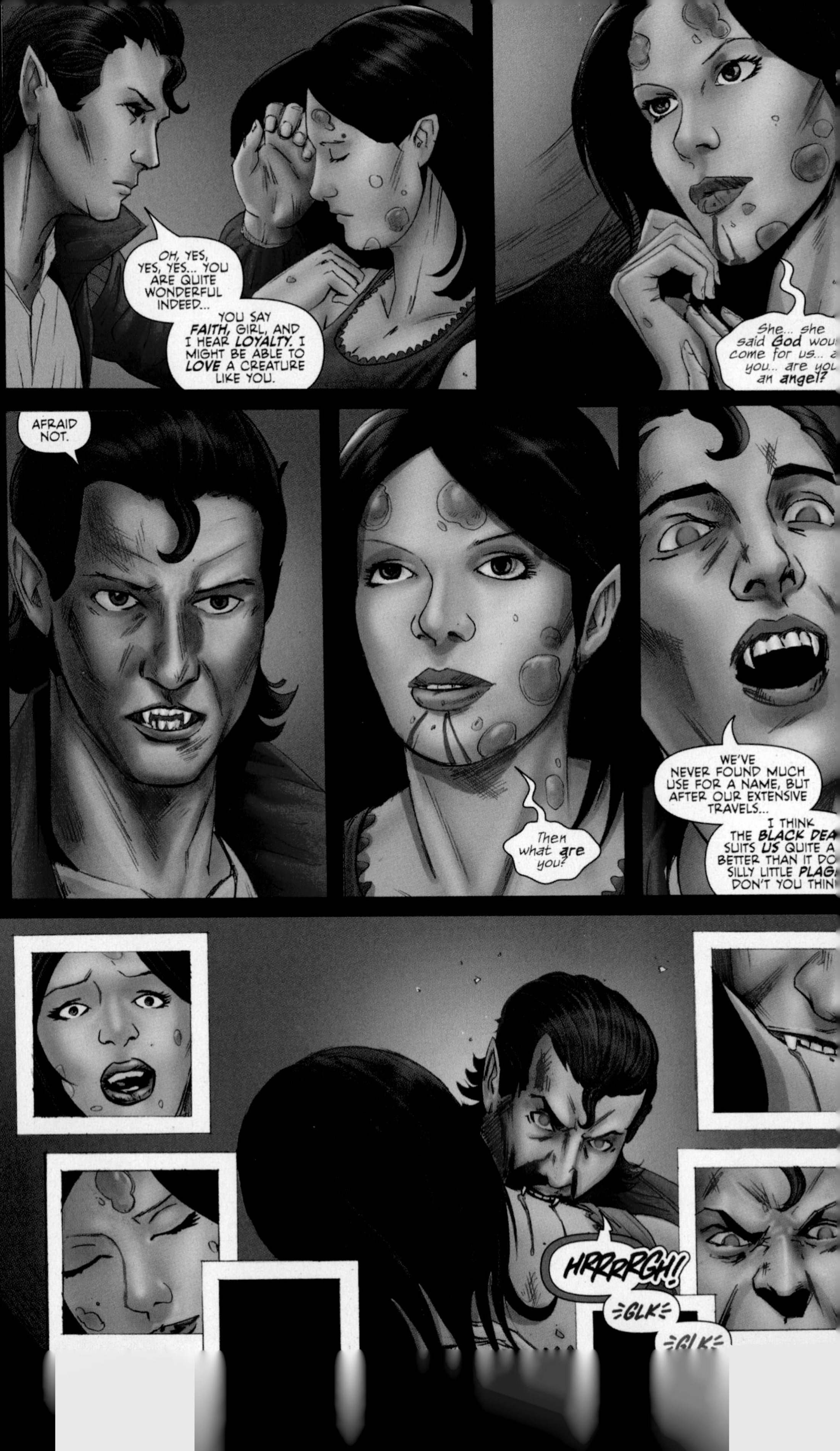

OH, YES, YES, YES... YOU ARE QUITE WONDERFUL INDEED...
YOU SAY FAITH, GIRL, AND I HEAR LOYALTY. I MIGHT BE ABLE TO LOVE A CREATURE LIKE YOU.
She... she said God wou come for us... a you... are you an angel?
AFRAID NOT.
Then what are you?
WE'VE NEVER FOUND MUCH USE FOR A NAME, BUT AFTER OUR EXTENSIVE TRAVELS...
I THINK THE BLACK DEA SUITS US QUITE A BETTER THAN IT DO SILLY LITTLE PLAG DON'T YOU THIN
HRRRRGH!!
GLK
GLK

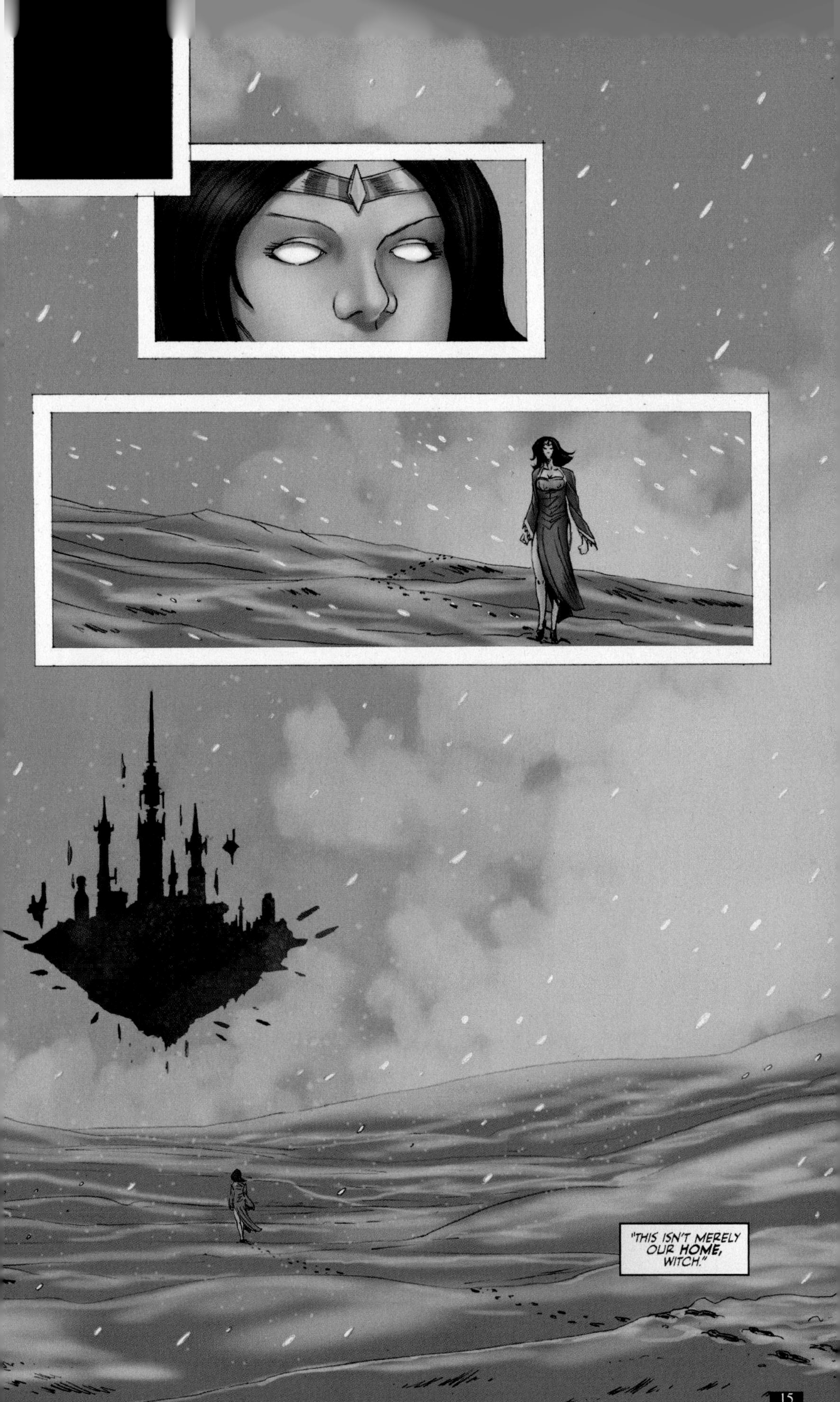
"THIS ISN'T MERELY OUR **HOME,** WITCH."

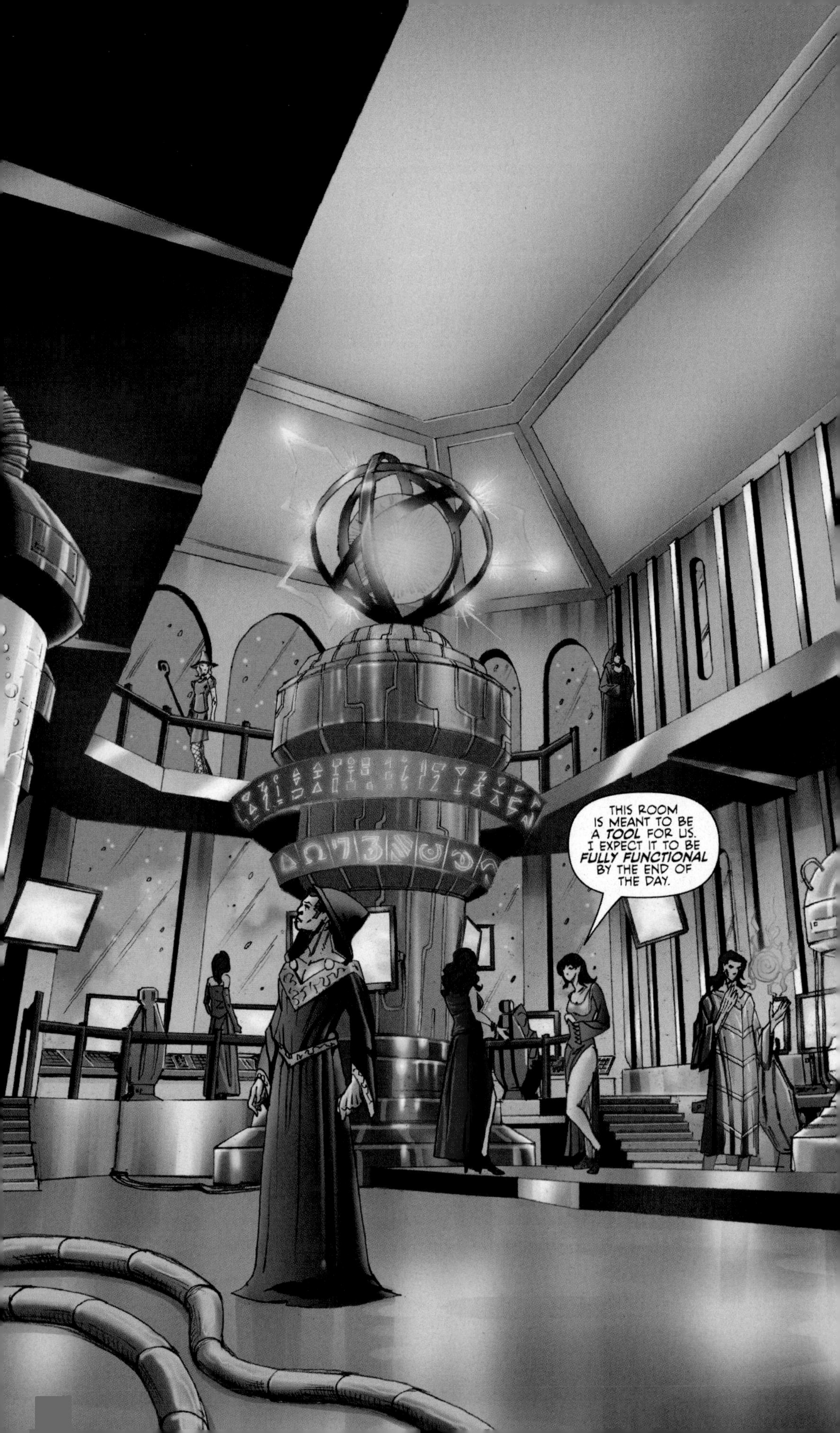
THIS ROOM IS MEANT TO BE A TOOL FOR US. I EXPECT IT TO BE FULLY FUNCTIONAL BY THE END OF THE DAY.

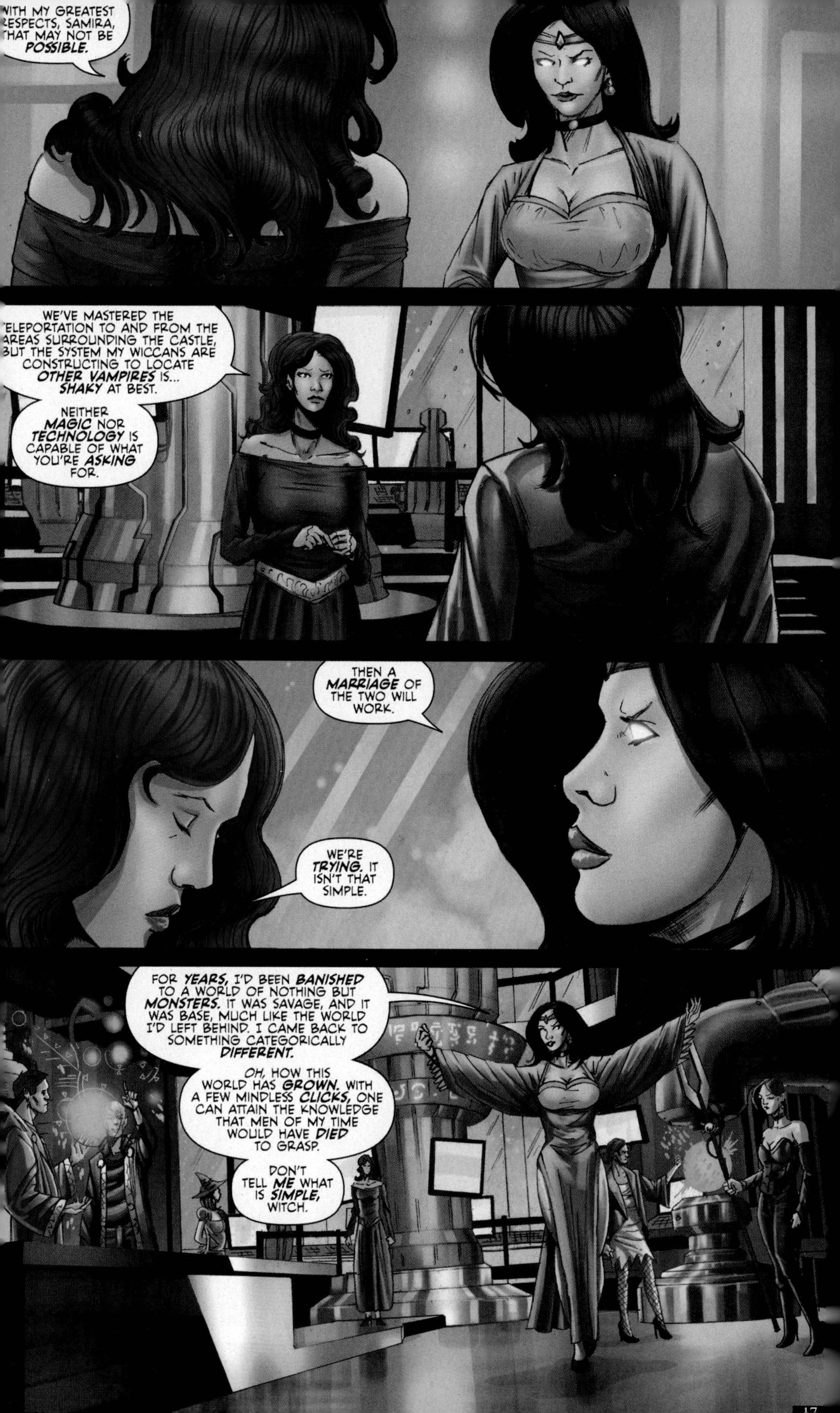
WITH MY GREATEST RESPECTS, SAMIRA, THAT MAY NOT BE POSSIBLE.
WE'VE MASTERED THE TELEPORTATION TO AND FROM THE AREAS SURROUNDING THE CASTLE, BUT THE SYSTEM MY WICCANS ARE CONSTRUCTING TO LOCATE OTHER VAMPIRES IS... SHAKY AT BEST.
NEITHER MAGIC NOR TECHNOLOGY IS CAPABLE OF WHAT YOU'RE ASKING FOR.
THEN A MARRIAGE OF THE TWO WILL WORK.
WE'RE TRYING. IT ISN'T THAT SIMPLE.
FOR YEARS, I'D BEEN BANISHED TO A WORLD OF NOTHING BUT MONSTERS. IT WAS SAVAGE, AND IT WAS BASE, MUCH LIKE THE WORLD I'D LEFT BEHIND. I CAME BACK TO SOMETHING CATEGORICALLY DIFFERENT.
OH, HOW THIS WORLD HAS GROWN. WITH A FEW MINDLESS CLICKS, ONE CAN ATTAIN THE KNOWLEDGE THAT MEN OF MY TIME WOULD HAVE DIED TO GRASP.
DON'T TELL ME WHAT IS SIMPLE, WITCH.

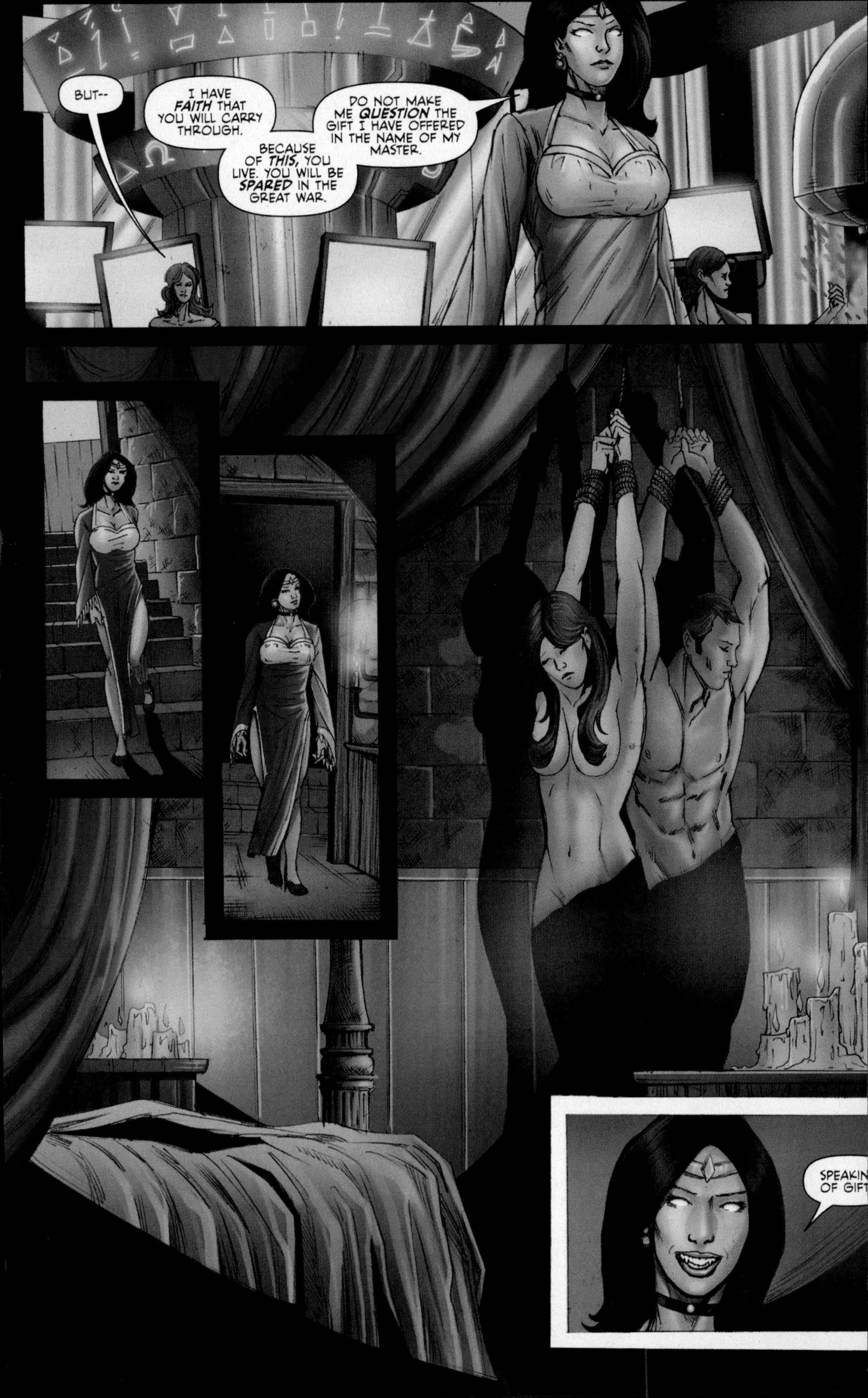
BUT--
DO NOT MAKE ME QUESTION THE GIFT I HAVE OFFERED IN THE NAME OF MY MASTER.
I HAVE FAITH THAT YOU WILL CARRY THROUGH.
BECAUSE OF THIS, YOU LIVE. YOU WILL BE SPARED IN THE GREAT WAR.
SPEAKIN OF GIFT

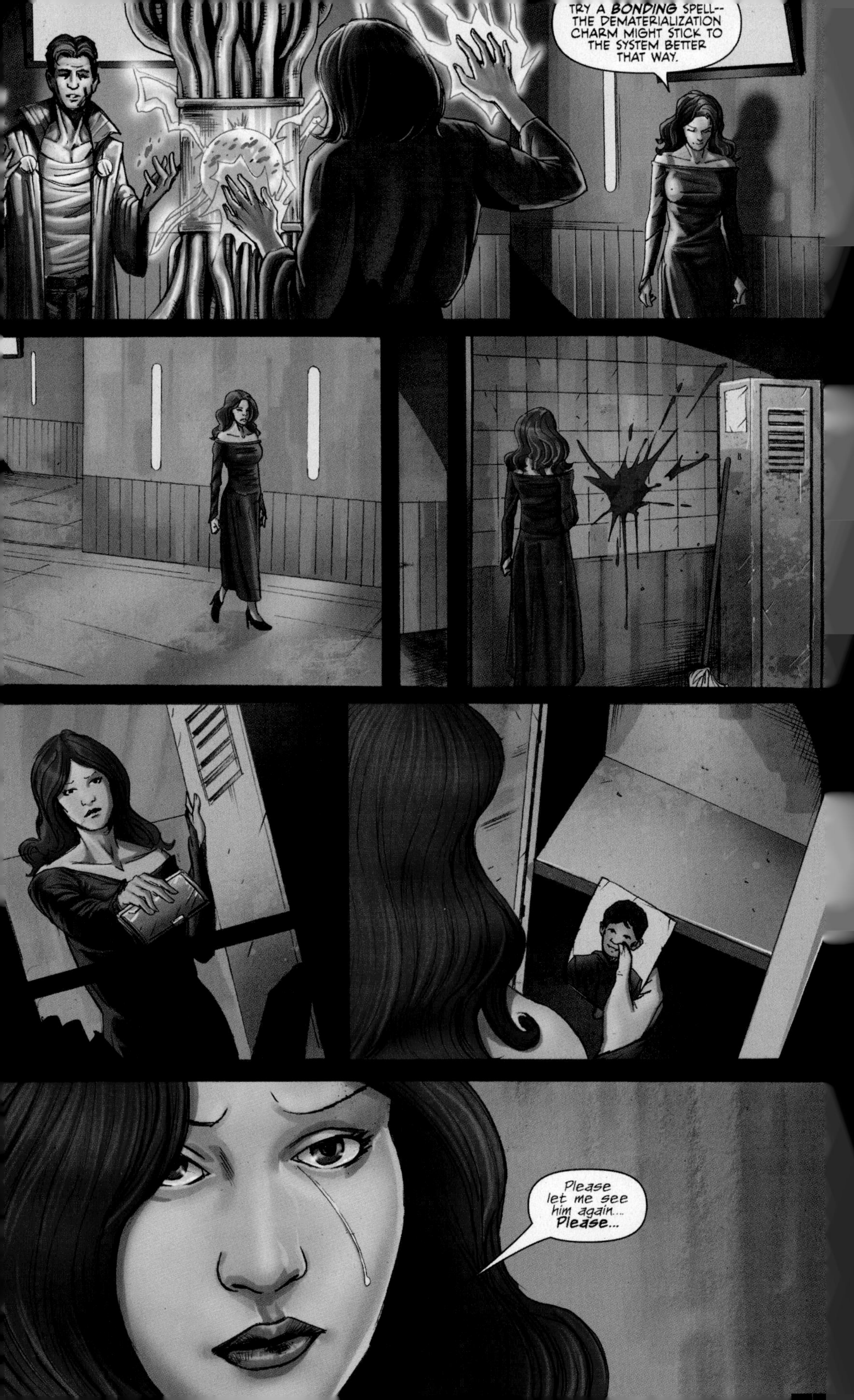
TRY A BONDING SPELL--
THE DEMATERIALIZATION
CHARM MIGHT STICK TO
THE SYSTEM BETTER
THAT WAY.
Please
let me see
him again...
Please...

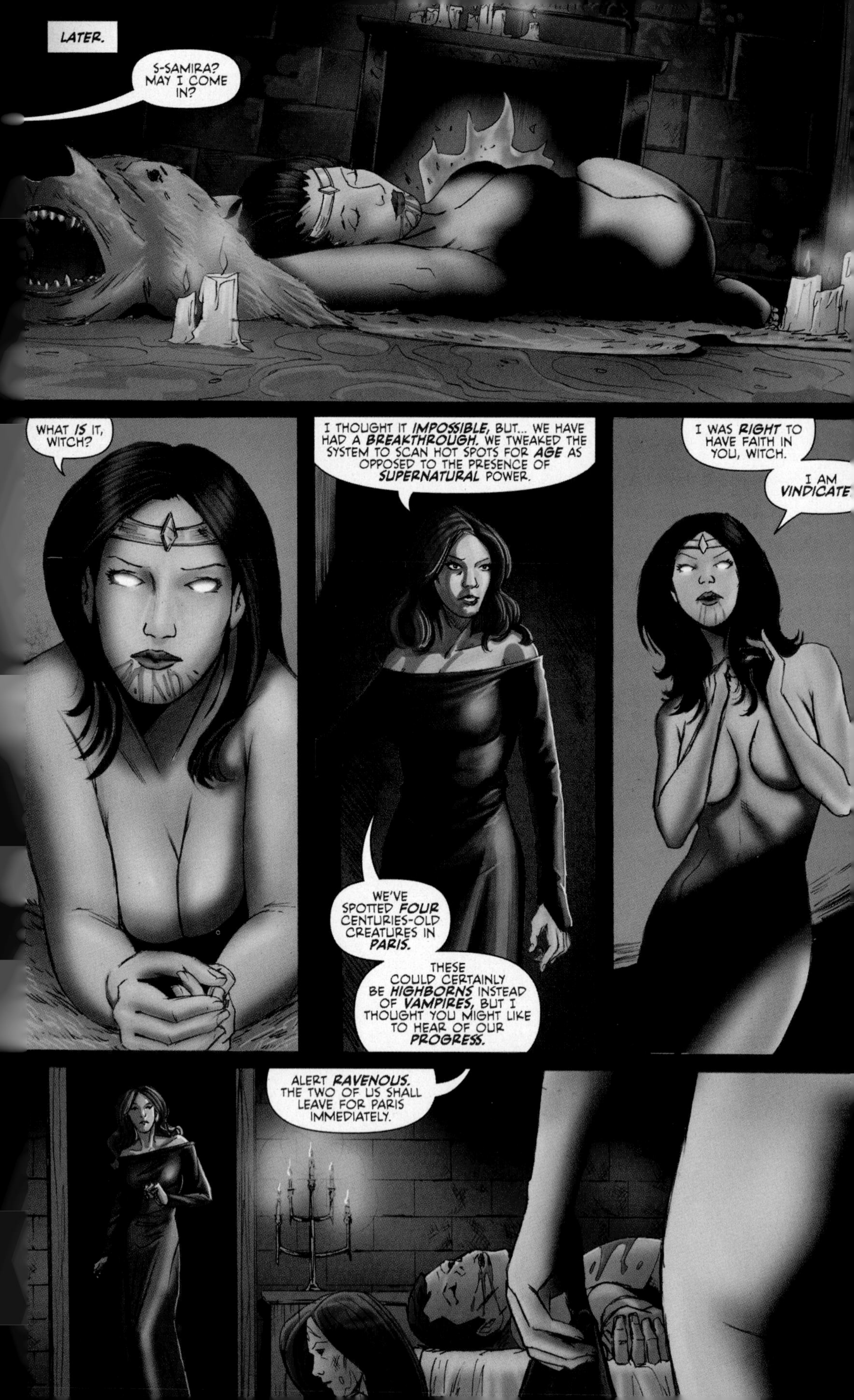
LATER.
S-SAMIRA? MAY I COME IN?
WHAT IS IT, WITCH?
I THOUGHT IT IMPOSSIBLE, BUT... WE HAVE HAD A BREAKTHROUGH. WE TWEAKED THE SYSTEM TO SCAN HOT SPOTS FOR AGE AS OPPOSED TO THE PRESENCE OF SUPERNATURAL POWER.
WE'VE SPOTTED FOUR CENTURIES-OLD CREATURES IN PARIS.
THESE COULD CERTAINLY BE HIGHBORNS INSTEAD OF VAMPIRES, BUT I THOUGHT YOU MIGHT LIKE TO HEAR OF OUR PROGRESS.
I WAS RIGHT TO HAVE FAITH IN YOU, WITCH.
I AM VINDICATE
ALERT RAVENOUS. THE TWO OF US SHALL LEAVE FOR PARIS IMMEDIATELY.

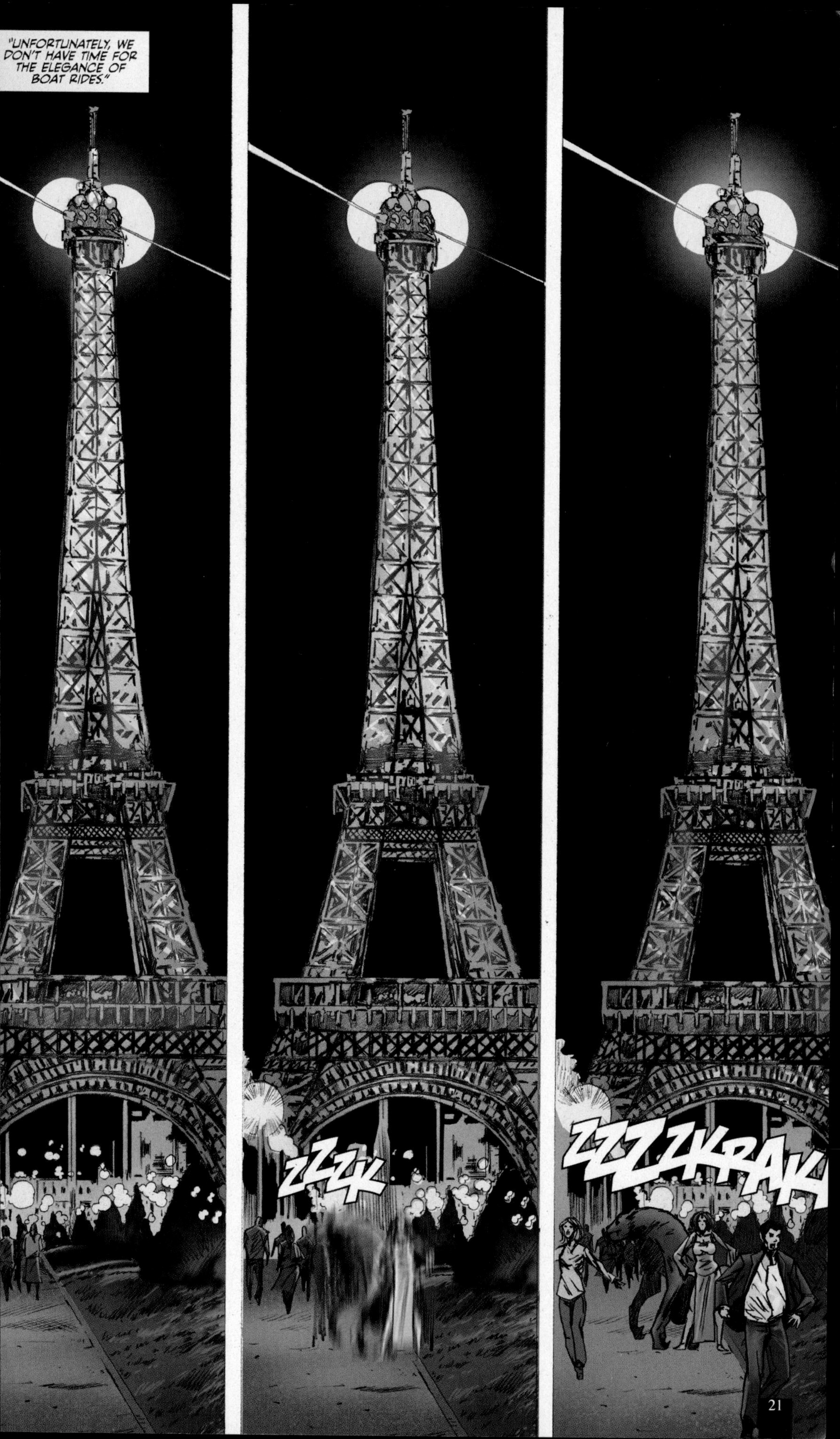
"UNFORTUNATELY, WE DON'T HAVE TIME FOR THE ELEGANCE OF BOAT RIDES."
ZZZK
ZZZZKRAK

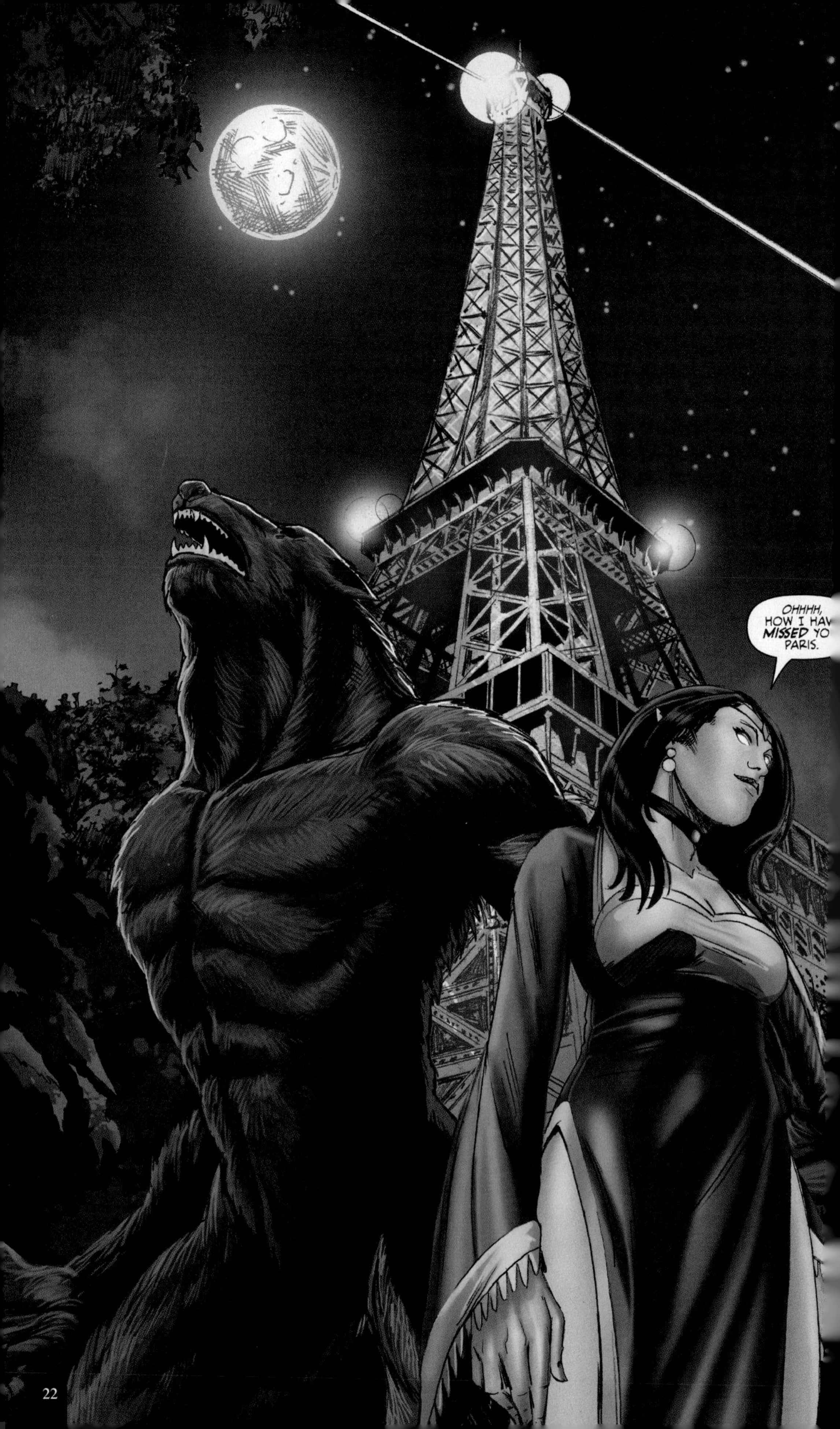
OHHHH, HOW I HAV MISSED YO PARIS.

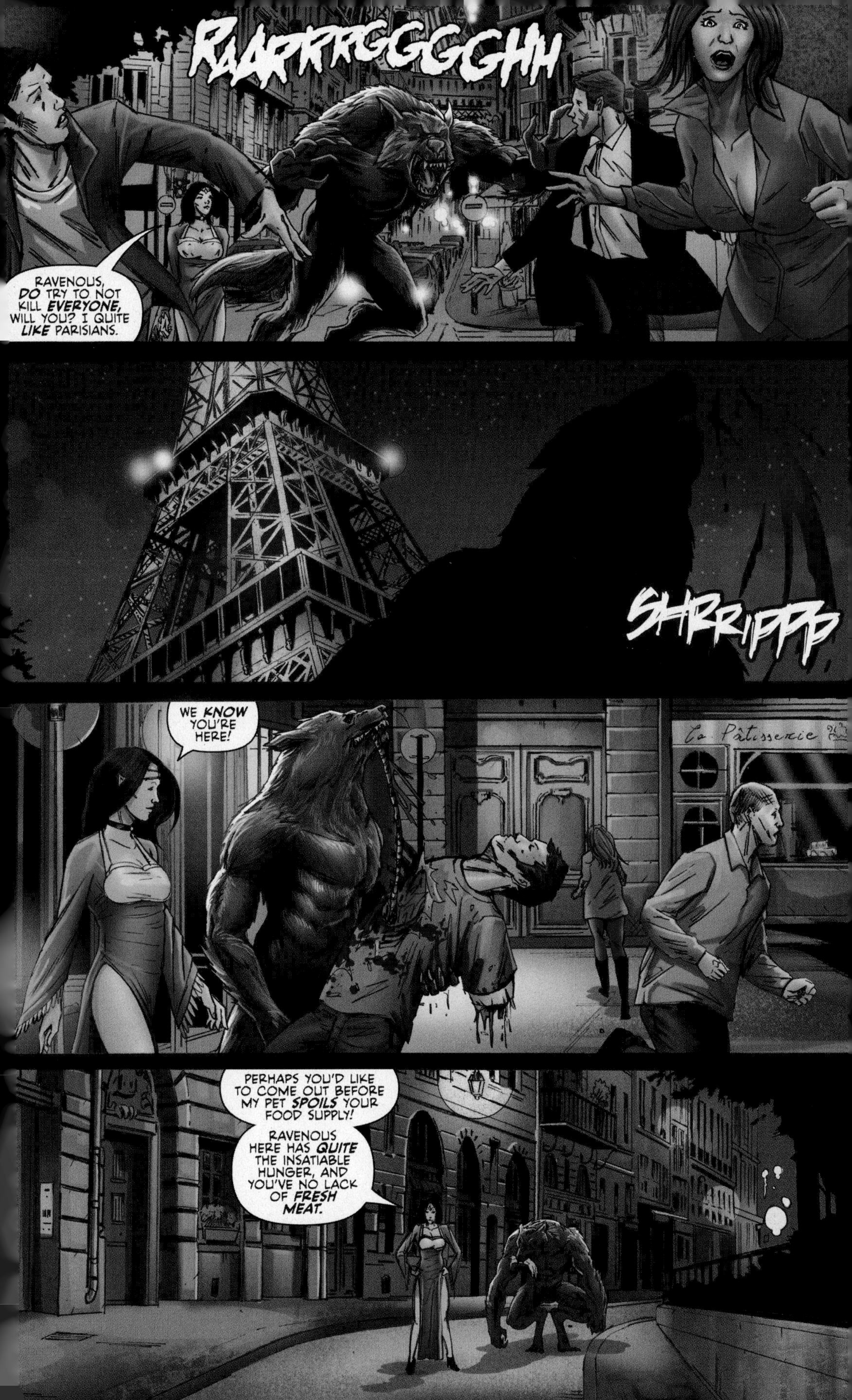
RAARRRGGGGHH
RAVENOUS, DO TRY TO NOT KILL EVERYONE, WILL YOU? I QUITE LIKE PARISIANS.
SHRRIPPP
WE KNOW YOU'RE HERE!
La Pâtisserie
PERHAPS YOU'D LIKE TO COME OUT BEFORE MY PET SPOILS YOUR FOOD SUPPLY!
RAVENOUS HERE HAS QUITE THE INSATIABLE HUNGER, AND YOU'VE NO LACK OF FRESH MEAT.

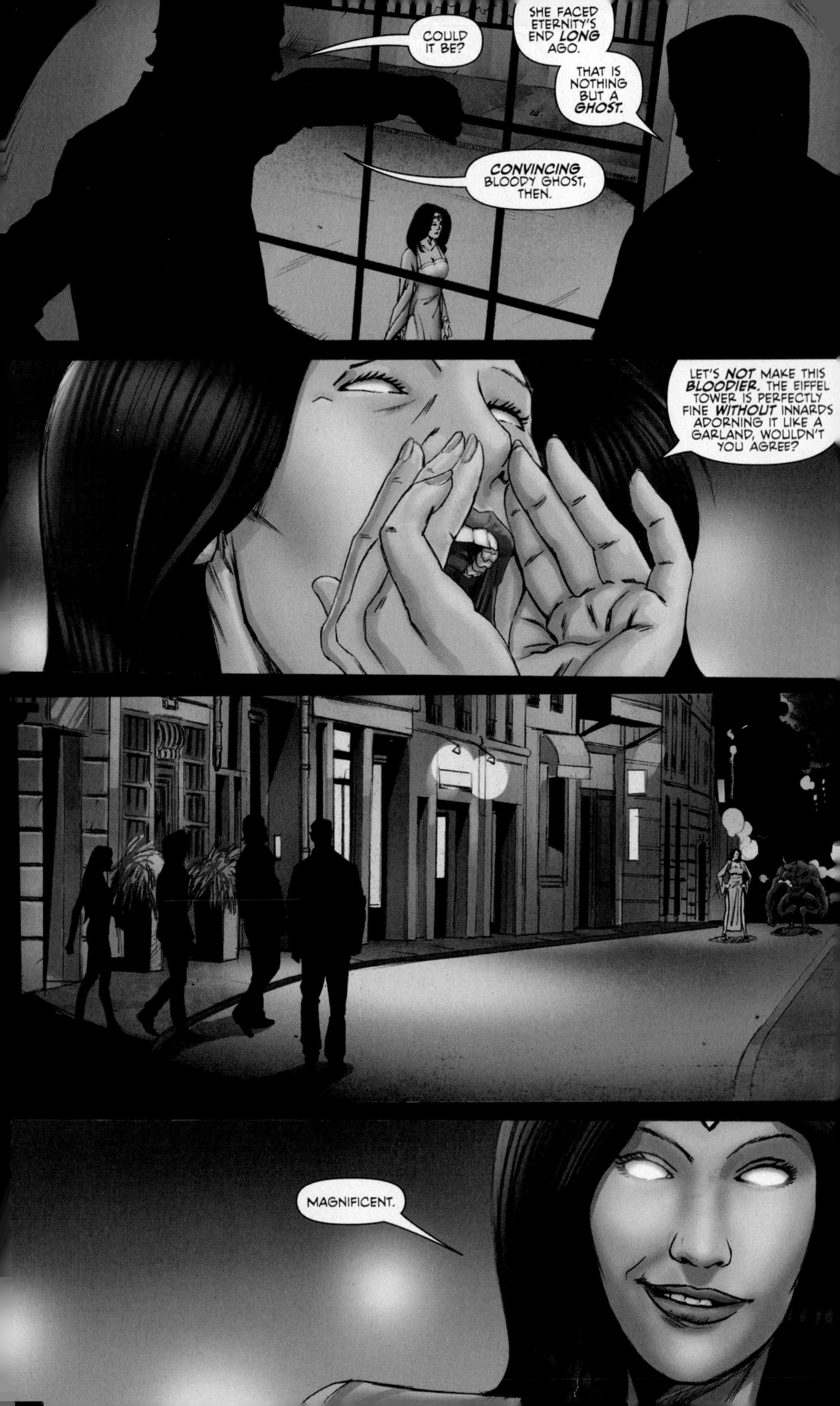
COULD IT BE?
SHE FACED ETERNITY'S END LONG AGO.
THAT IS NOTHING BUT A GHOST.
CONVINCING BLOODY GHOST, THEN.
LET'S NOT MAKE THIS BLOODIER. THE EIFFEL TOWER IS PERFECTLY FINE WITHOUT INNARDS ADORNING IT LIKE A GARLAND, WOULDN'T YOU AGREE?
MAGNIFICENT.

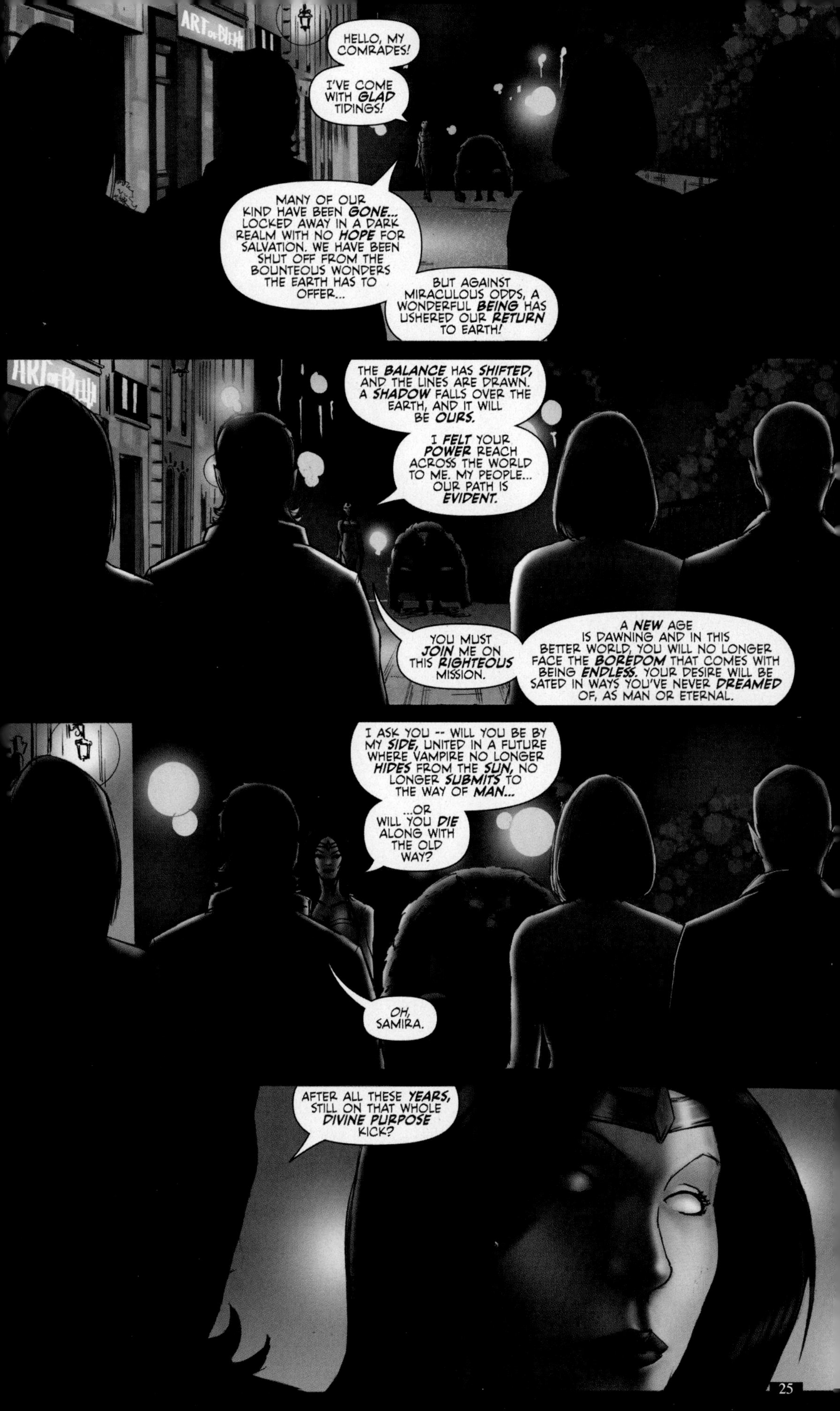

HELLO, MY COMRADES!
I'VE COME WITH GLAD TIDINGS!
MANY OF OUR KIND HAVE BEEN GONE... LOCKED AWAY IN A DARK REALM WITH NO HOPE FOR SALVATION. WE HAVE BEEN SHUT OFF FROM THE BOUNTEOUS WONDERS THE EARTH HAS TO OFFER...
BUT AGAINST MIRACULOUS ODDS, A WONDERFUL BEING HAS USHERED OUR RETURN TO EARTH!
THE BALANCE HAS SHIFTED, AND THE LINES ARE DRAWN. A SHADOW FALLS OVER THE EARTH, AND IT WILL BE OURS.
I FELT YOUR POWER REACH ACROSS THE WORLD TO ME. MY PEOPLE... OUR PATH IS EVIDENT.
YOU MUST JOIN ME ON THIS RIGHTEOUS MISSION.
A NEW AGE IS DAWNING AND IN THIS BETTER WORLD, YOU WILL NO LONGER FACE THE BOREDOM THAT COMES WITH BEING ENDLESS. YOUR DESIRE WILL BE SATED IN WAYS YOU'VE NEVER DREAMED OF, AS MAN OR ETERNAL.
I ASK YOU -- WILL YOU BE BY MY SIDE, UNITED IN A FUTURE WHERE VAMPIRE NO LONGER HIDES FROM THE SUN, NO LONGER SUBMITS TO THE WAY OF MAN...
...OR WILL YOU DIE ALONG WITH THE OLD WAY?
OH, SAMIRA.
AFTER ALL THESE YEARS, STILL ON THAT WHOLE DIVINE PURPOSE KICK?

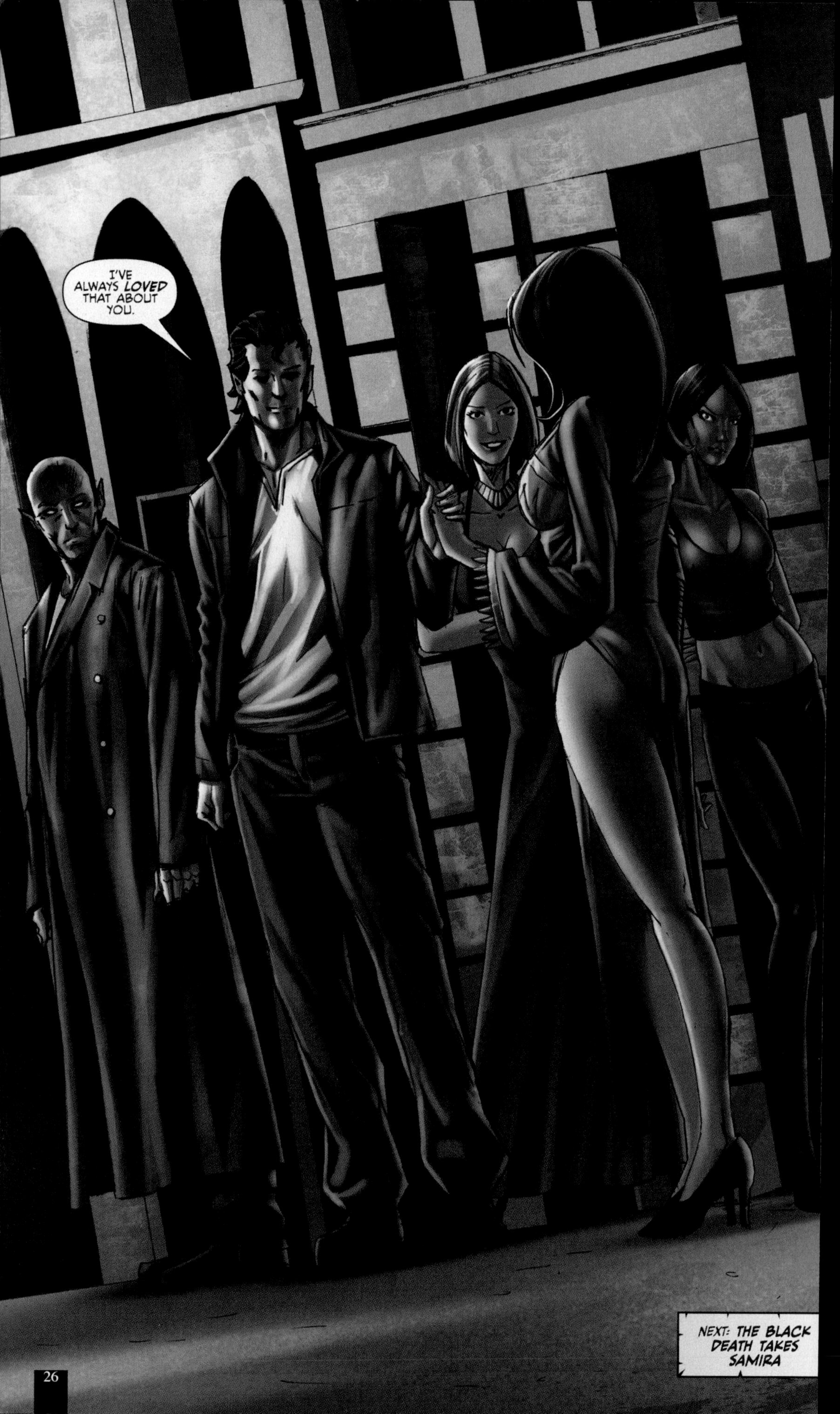
I'VE ALWAYS LOVED THAT ABOUT YOU.
NEXT: THE BLACK DEATH TAKES SAMIRA

Grimm Fairy Tales
presents:

Vampires
&
Werewolves

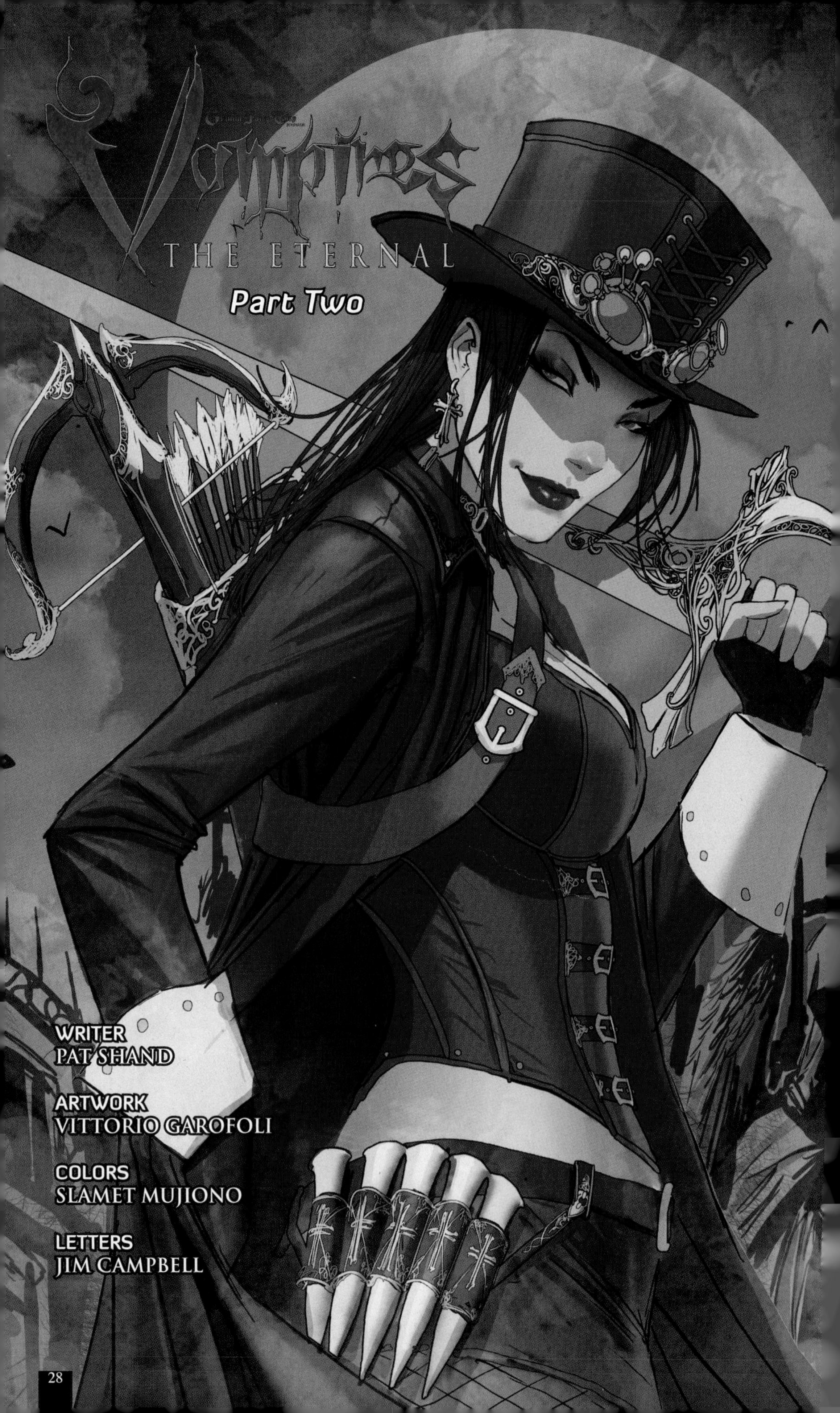
Vampires
THE ETERNAL
Part Two
WRITER
PAT SHAND
ARTWORK
VITTORIO GAROFOLI
COLORS
SLAMET MUJIONO
LETTERS
JIM CAMPBELL

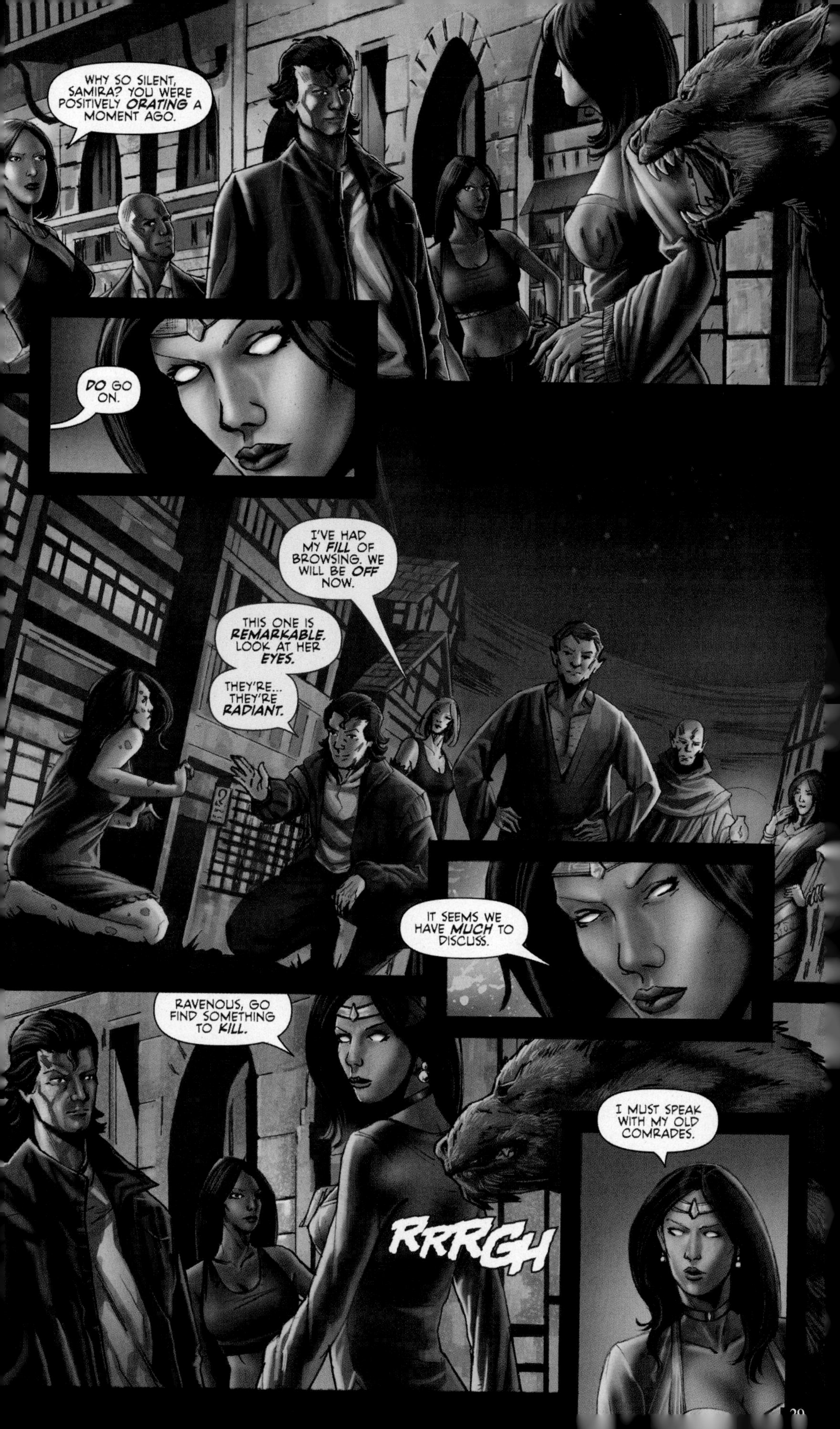

WHY SO SILENT, SAMIRA? YOU WERE POSITIVELY ORATING A MOMENT AGO.
DO GO ON.
I'VE HAD MY FILL OF BROWSING. WE WILL BE OFF NOW.
THIS ONE IS REMARKABLE. LOOK AT HER EYES.
THEY'RE... THEY'RE RADIANT.
IT SEEMS WE HAVE MUCH TO DISCUSS.
RAVENOUS, GO FIND SOMETHING TO KILL.
RRRGH
I MUST SPEAK WITH MY OLD COMRADES.

I BELIEVED YOU DEAD.

DEATH HAS HUNTED ME SINCE MY HEART STILL BEAT, AND YET SHE *STILL* SEARCHES.

FATIMA. MUND.

VANESSA.

I'M STILL *WAITING* FOR YOU TO DELIVER THESE *GLAD TIDINGS*.

WHERE IS *BRECA*?

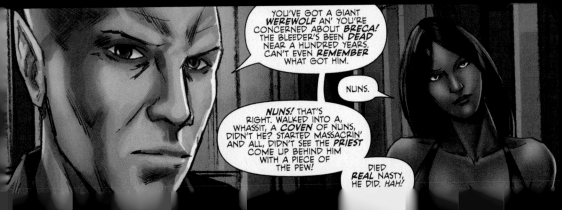

YOU'VE GOT A GIANT *WEREWOLF* AN' YOU'RE CONCERNED ABOUT *BRECA!* THE BLEEDER'S BEEN *DEAD* NEAR A HUNDRED YEARS. CAN'T EVEN *REMEMBER* WHAT GOT HIM.

NUNS.

NUNS! THAT'S RIGHT. WALKED INTO A, WHASSIT, A *COVEN* OF NUNS, DIDN'T HE? STARTED MASSACRIN' AND ALL, DIDN'T SEE THE *PRIEST* COME UP BEHIND HIM WITH A PIECE OF THE PEW!

DIED *REAL* NASTY, HE DID. *HAH!*

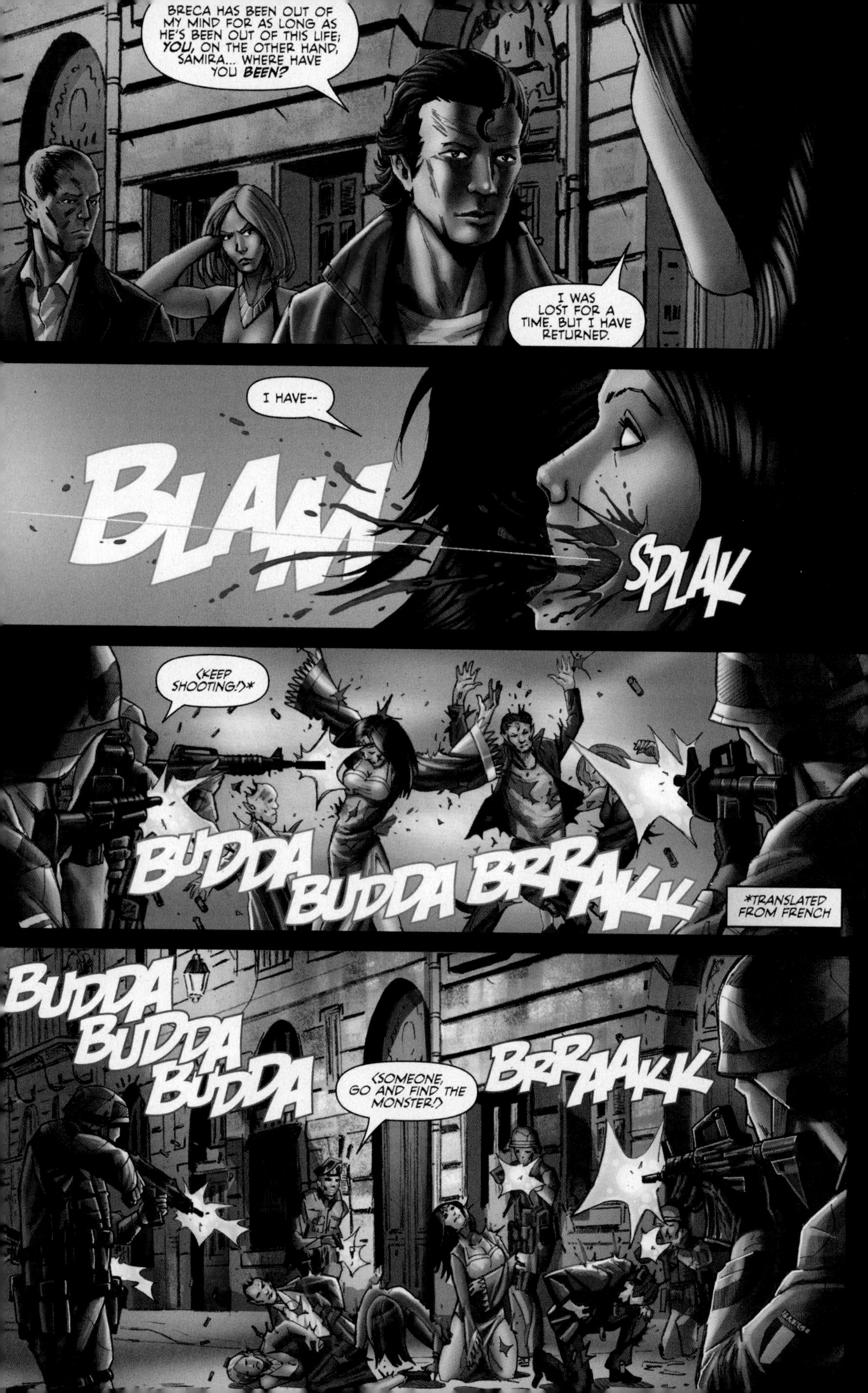
BRECA HAS BEEN OUT OF MY MIND FOR AS LONG AS HE'S BEEN OUT OF THIS LIFE; *YOU*, ON THE OTHER HAND, SAMIRA... WHERE HAVE YOU *BEEN?*
I WAS LOST FOR A TIME. BUT I HAVE RETURNED.
I HAVE--
BLAM
SPLAK
<KEEP SHOOTING!>*
BUDDA BUDDA BRRAKK
*TRANSLATED FROM FRENCH
BUDDA BUDDA BUDDA
<SOMEONE, GO AND FIND THE MONSTER!>
BRRAAKK

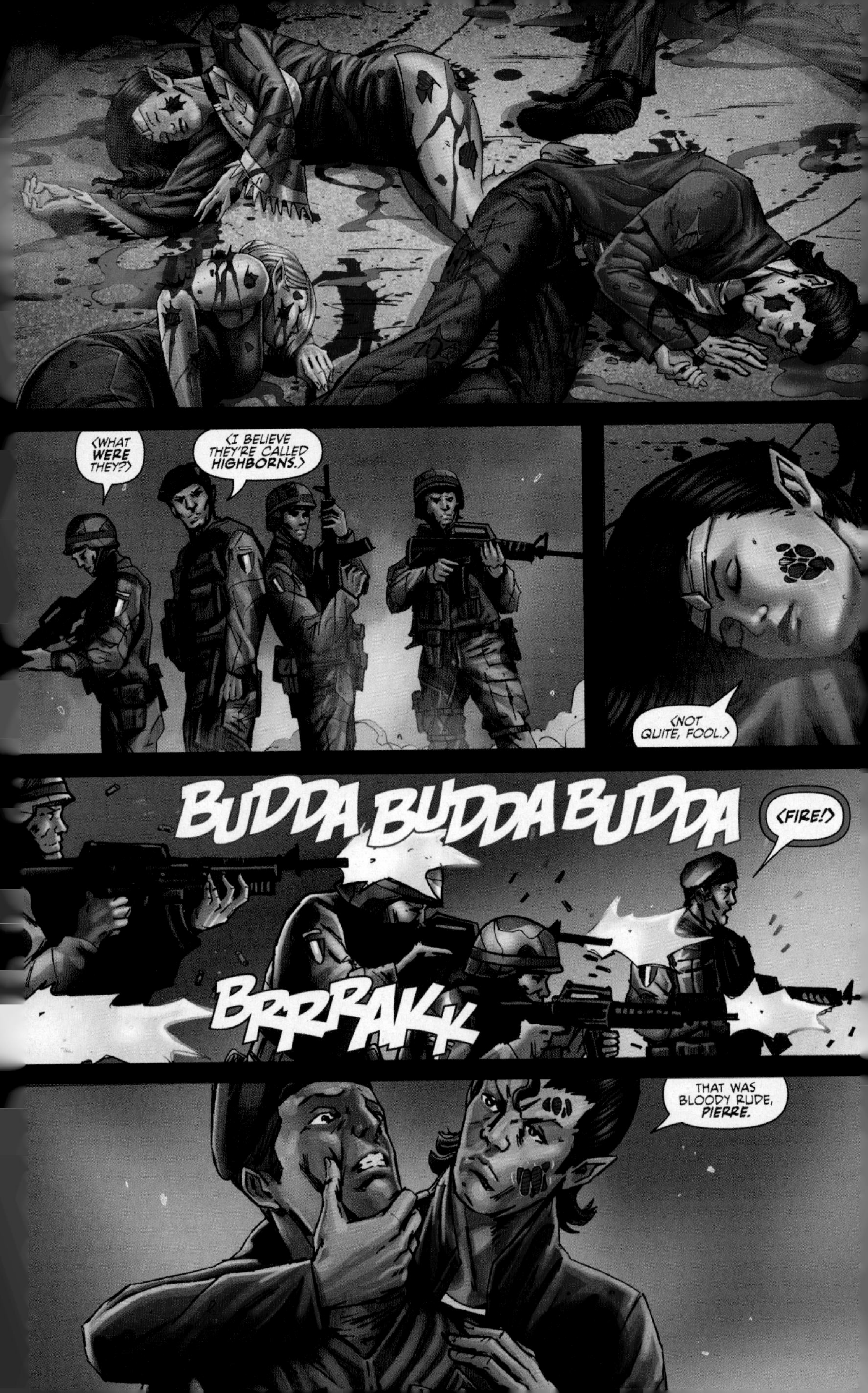

<WHAT WERE THEY?>
<I BELIEVE THEY'RE CALLED HIGHBORNS.>
<NOT QUITE, FOOL.>
BUDDA BUDDA BUDDA
<FIRE!>
BRRRAKK
THAT WAS BLOODY RUDE, PIERRE.

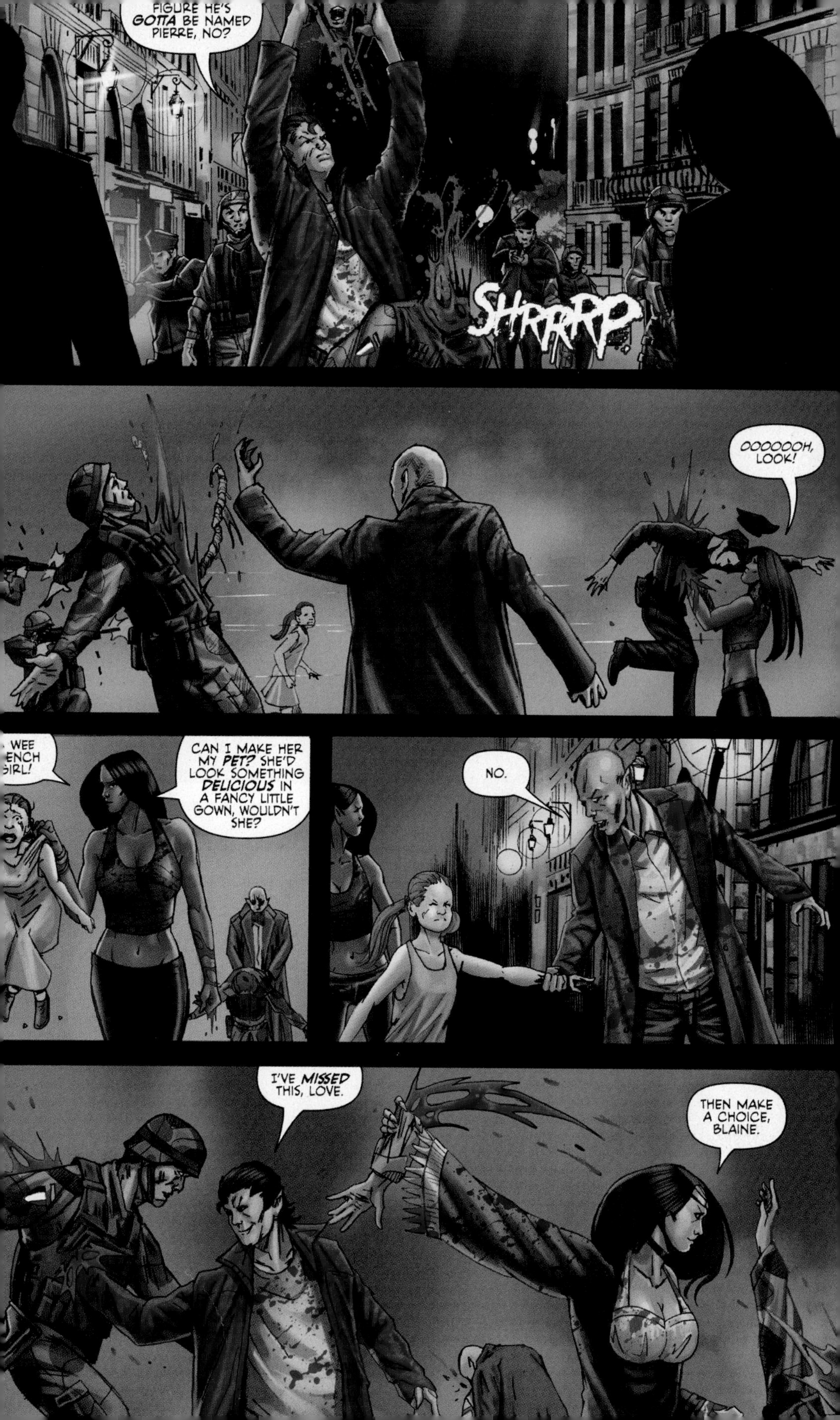
FIGURE HE'S GOTTA BE NAMED PIERRE, NO?
SHRRRP
OOOOOOH, LOOK!
WEE ENCH GIRL!
CAN I MAKE HER MY PET? SHE'D LOOK SOMETHING DELICIOUS IN A FANCY LITTLE GOWN, WOULDN'T SHE?
NO.
I'VE MISSED THIS, LOVE.
THEN MAKE A CHOICE, BLAINE.

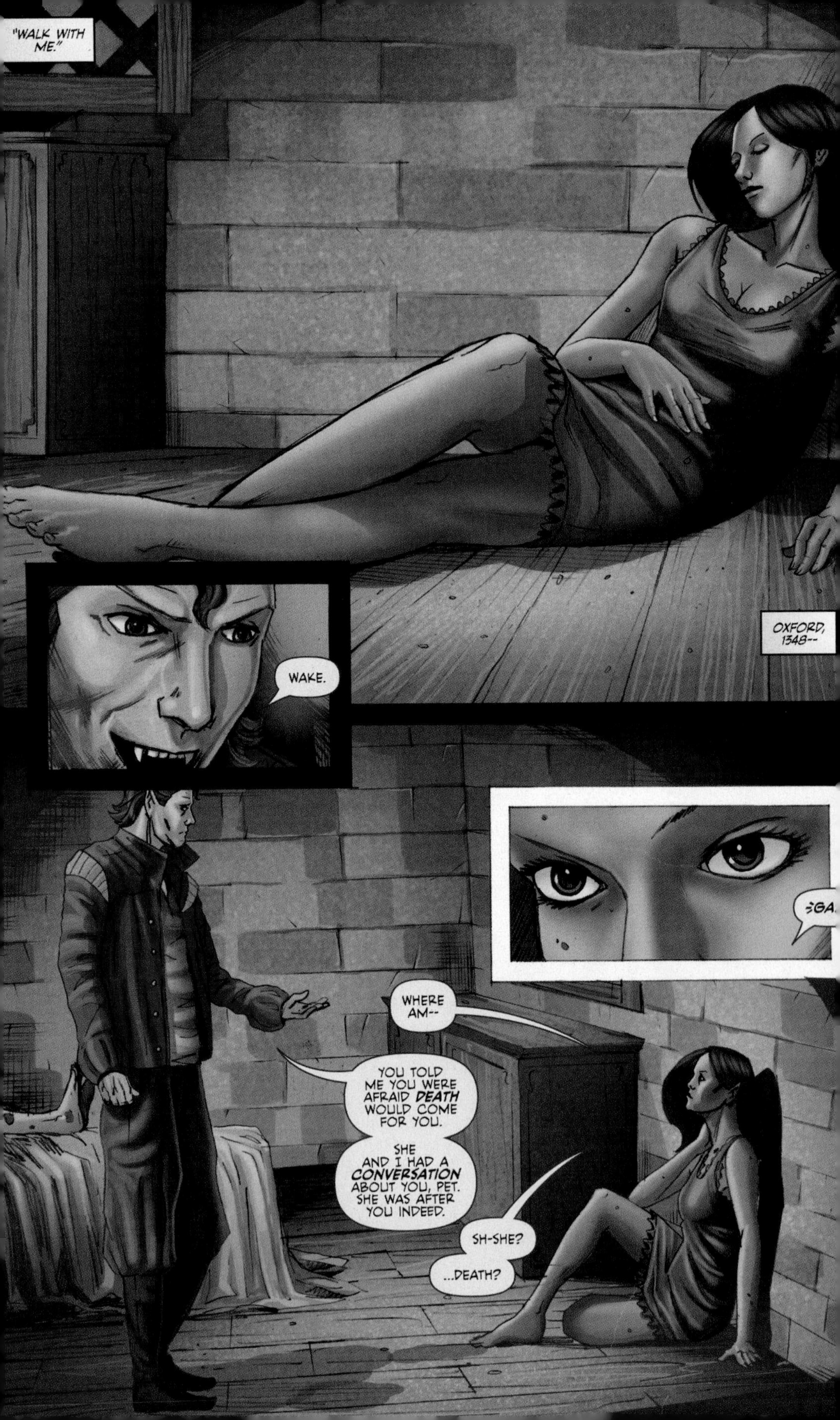
"WALK WITH ME."
WAKE.
OXFORD, 1348--
GA
WHERE AM--
YOU TOLD ME YOU WERE AFRAID DEATH WOULD COME FOR YOU.
SHE AND I HAD A CONVERSATION ABOUT YOU, PET. SHE WAS AFTER YOU INDEED.
SH-SHE?
...DEATH?

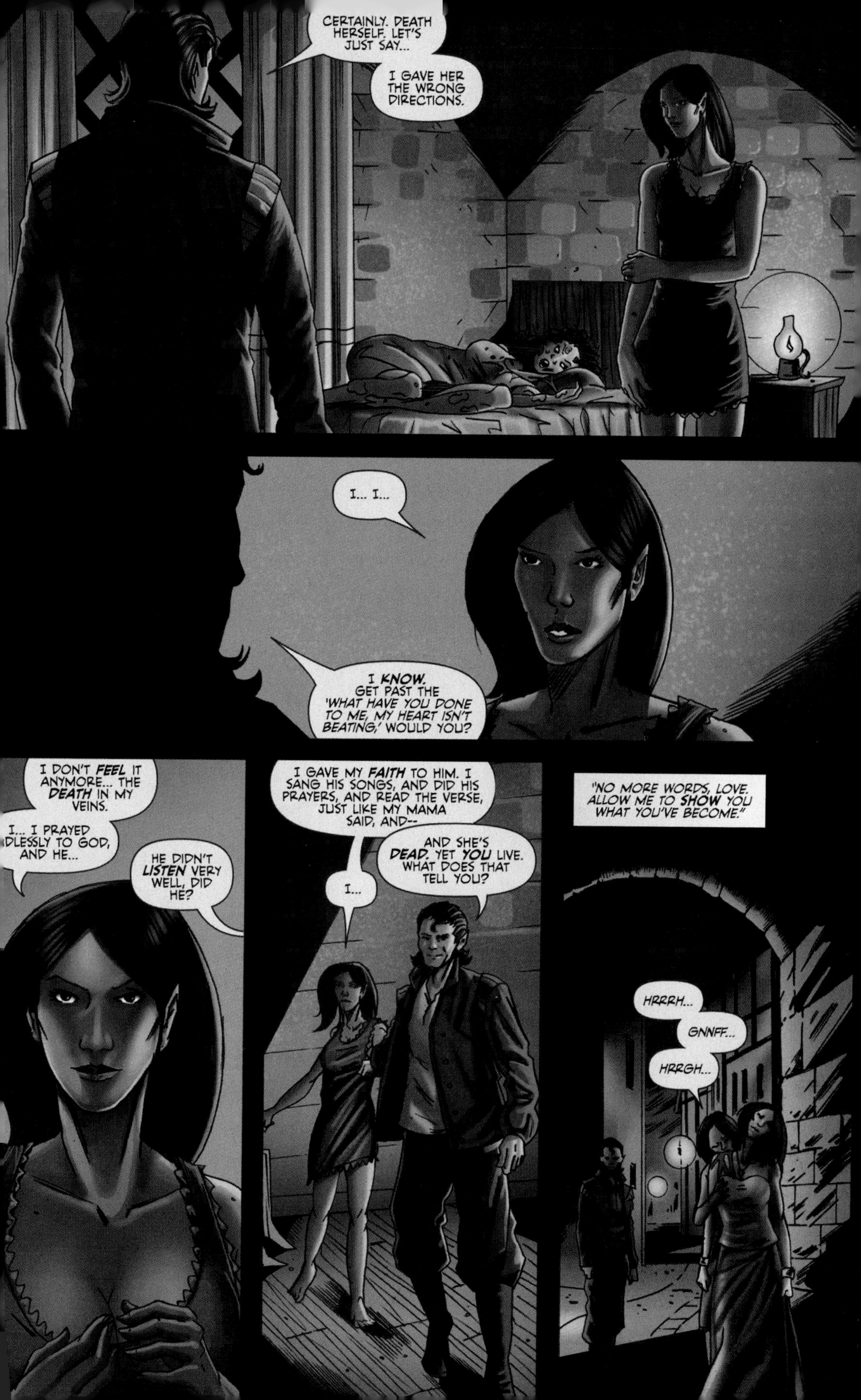
CERTAINLY. DEATH HERSELF. LET'S JUST SAY...
I GAVE HER THE WRONG DIRECTIONS.
I... I...
I KNOW. GET PAST THE 'WHAT HAVE YOU DONE TO ME, MY HEART ISN'T BEATING,' WOULD YOU?
I DON'T FEEL IT ANYMORE... THE DEATH IN MY VEINS.
I... I PRAYED DLESSLY TO GOD, AND HE...
HE DIDN'T LISTEN VERY WELL, DID HE?
I GAVE MY FAITH TO HIM. I SANG HIS SONGS, AND DID HIS PRAYERS, AND READ THE VERSE, JUST LIKE MY MAMA SAID, AND--
AND SHE'S DEAD. YET YOU LIVE. WHAT DOES THAT TELL YOU?
I...
"NO MORE WORDS, LOVE. ALLOW ME TO SHOW YOU WHAT YOU'VE BECOME."
HRRRH...
GNNFF...
HRRGH...

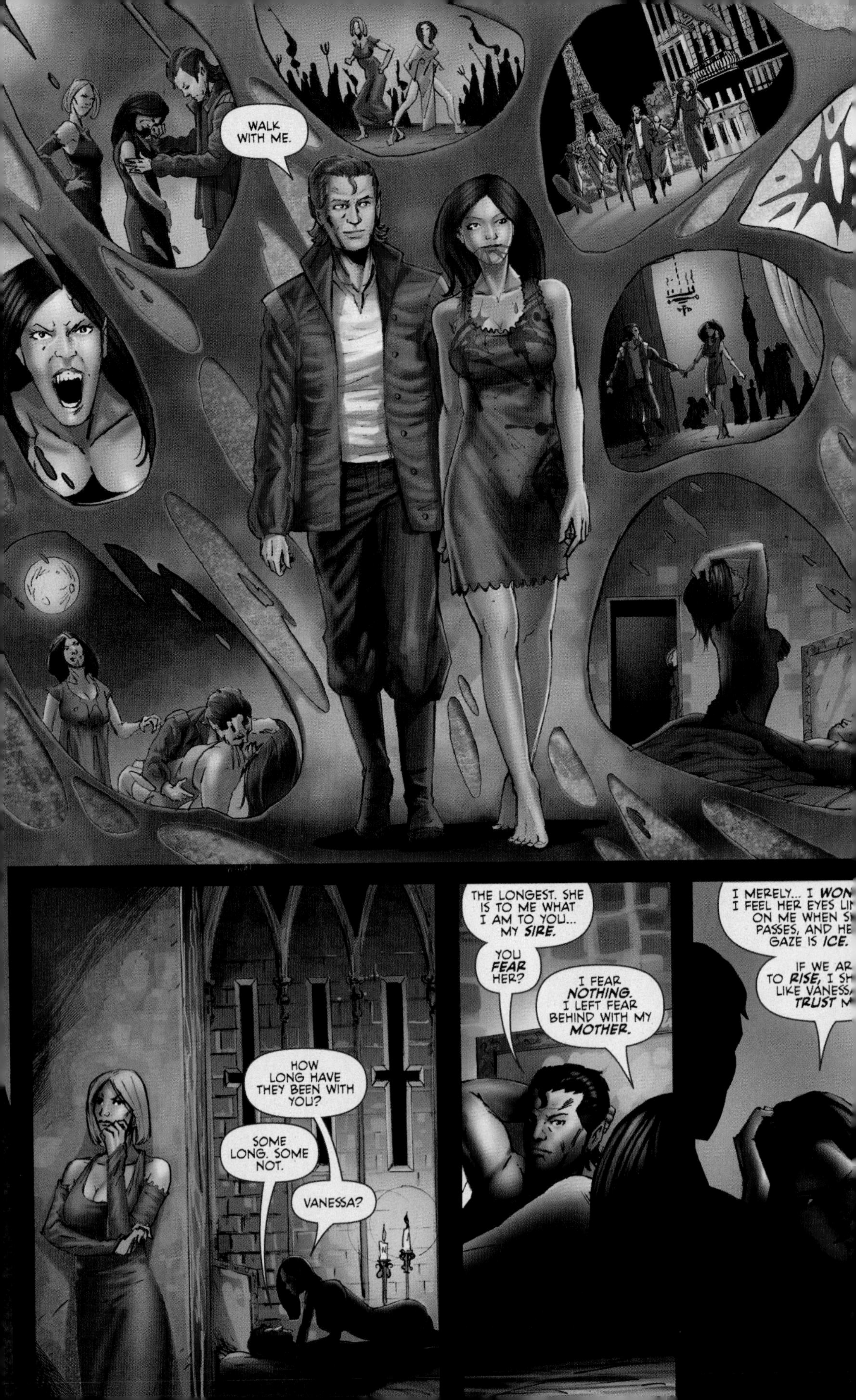
WALK WITH ME.
HOW LONG HAVE THEY BEEN WITH YOU?
SOME LONG. SOME NOT.
VANESSA?
THE LONGEST. SHE IS TO ME WHAT I AM TO YOU... MY SIRE.
YOU FEAR HER?
I FEAR NOTHING. I LEFT FEAR BEHIND WITH MY MOTHER.
I MERELY... I WON
I FEEL HER EYES LI
ON ME WHEN S
PASSES, AND HE
GAZE IS ICE.
IF WE AR
TO RISE, I SH
LIKE VANESS
TRUST M

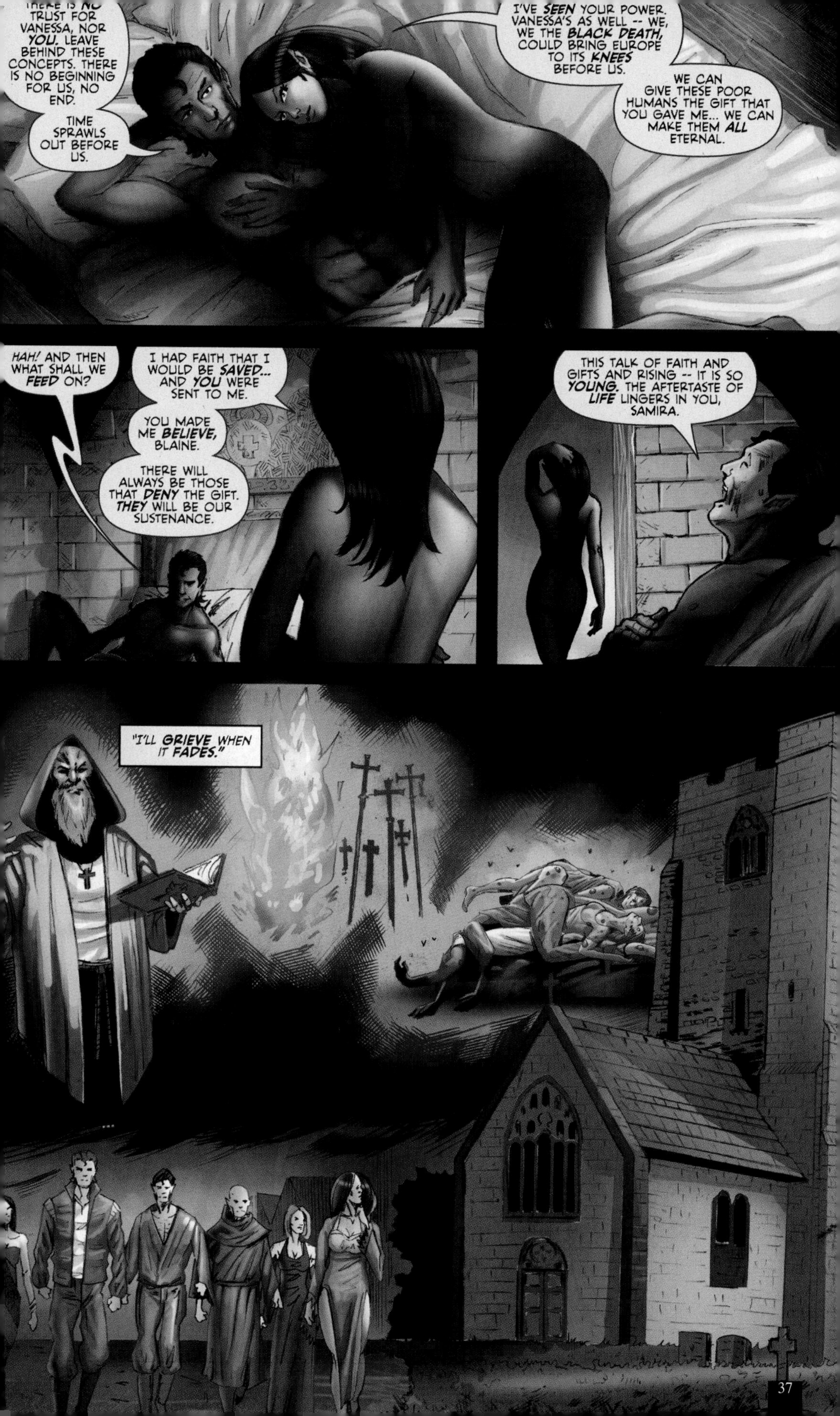
THERE IS NO TRUST FOR VANESSA, NOR YOU. LEAVE BEHIND THESE CONCEPTS. THERE IS NO BEGINNING FOR US, NO END.
TIME SPRAWLS OUT BEFORE US.
I'VE SEEN YOUR POWER. VANESSA'S AS WELL -- WE, WE THE BLACK DEATH, COULD BRING EUROPE TO ITS KNEES BEFORE US.
WE CAN GIVE THESE POOR HUMANS THE GIFT THAT YOU GAVE ME... WE CAN MAKE THEM ALL ETERNAL.
HAH! AND THEN WHAT SHALL WE FEED ON?
I HAD FAITH THAT I WOULD BE SAVED... AND YOU WERE SENT TO ME.
YOU MADE ME BELIEVE, BLAINE.
THERE WILL ALWAYS BE THOSE THAT DENY THE GIFT. THEY WILL BE OUR SUSTENANCE.
THIS TALK OF FAITH AND GIFTS AND RISING -- IT IS SO YOUNG. THE AFTERTASTE OF LIFE LINGERS IN YOU, SAMIRA.
"I'LL GRIEVE WHEN IT FADES."

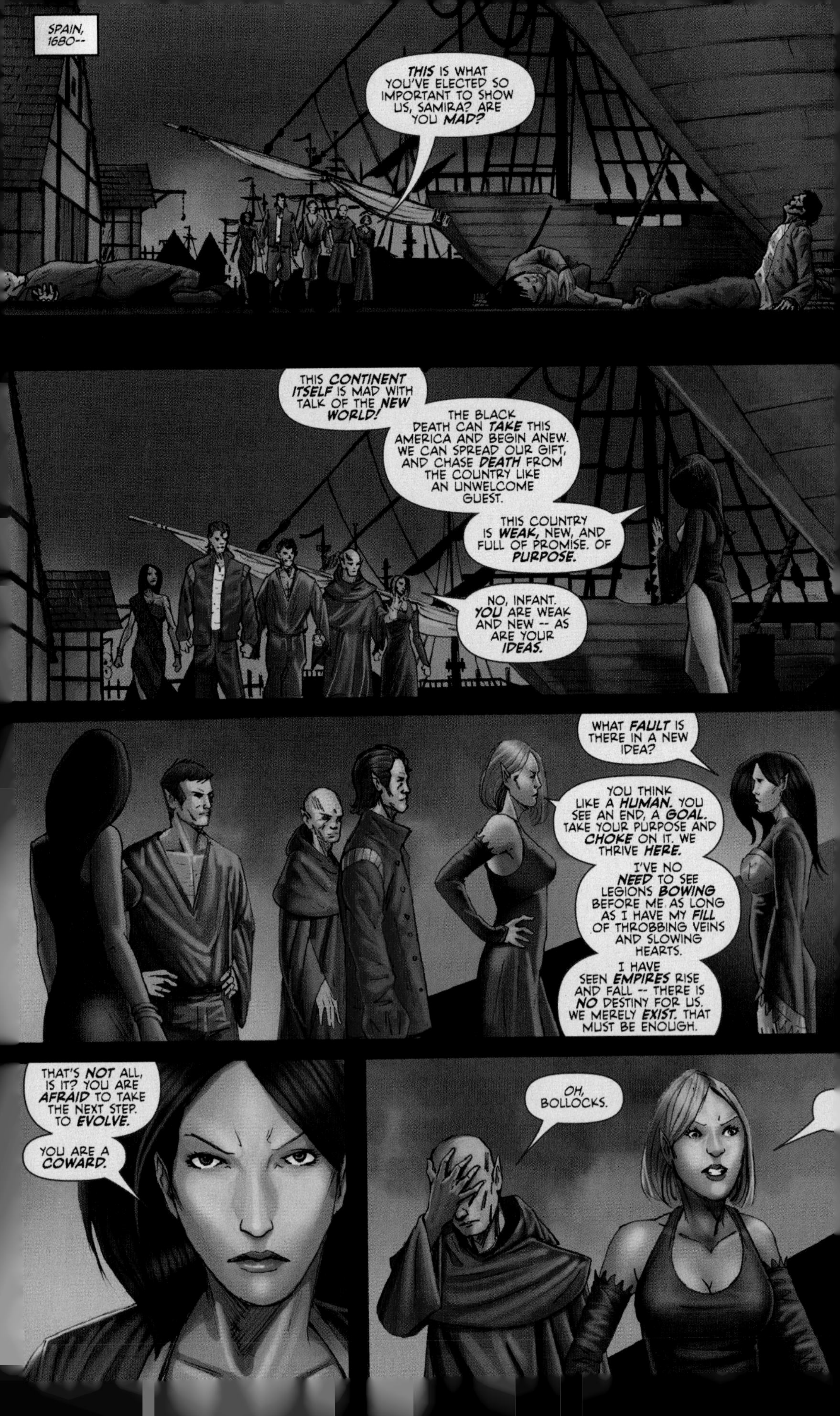
SPAIN, 1680--
THIS IS WHAT YOU'VE ELECTED SO IMPORTANT TO SHOW US, SAMIRA? ARE YOU MAD?
THIS CONTINENT ITSELF IS MAD WITH TALK OF THE NEW WORLD!
THE BLACK DEATH CAN TAKE THIS AMERICA AND BEGIN ANEW. WE CAN SPREAD OUR GIFT, AND CHASE DEATH FROM THE COUNTRY LIKE AN UNWELCOME GUEST.
THIS COUNTRY IS WEAK, NEW, AND FULL OF PROMISE. OF PURPOSE.
NO, INFANT. YOU ARE WEAK AND NEW -- AS ARE YOUR IDEAS.
WHAT FAULT IS THERE IN A NEW IDEA?
YOU THINK LIKE A HUMAN. YOU SEE AN END, A GOAL. TAKE YOUR PURPOSE AND CHOKE ON IT. WE THRIVE HERE.
I'VE NO NEED TO SEE LEGIONS BOWING BEFORE ME AS LONG AS I HAVE MY FILL OF THROBBING VEINS AND SLOWING HEARTS.
I HAVE SEEN EMPIRES RISE AND FALL -- THERE IS NO DESTINY FOR US. WE MERELY EXIST. THAT MUST BE ENOUGH.
THAT'S NOT ALL, IS IT? YOU ARE AFRAID TO TAKE THE NEXT STEP. TO EVOLVE.
YOU ARE A COWARD.
OH, BOLLOCKS.

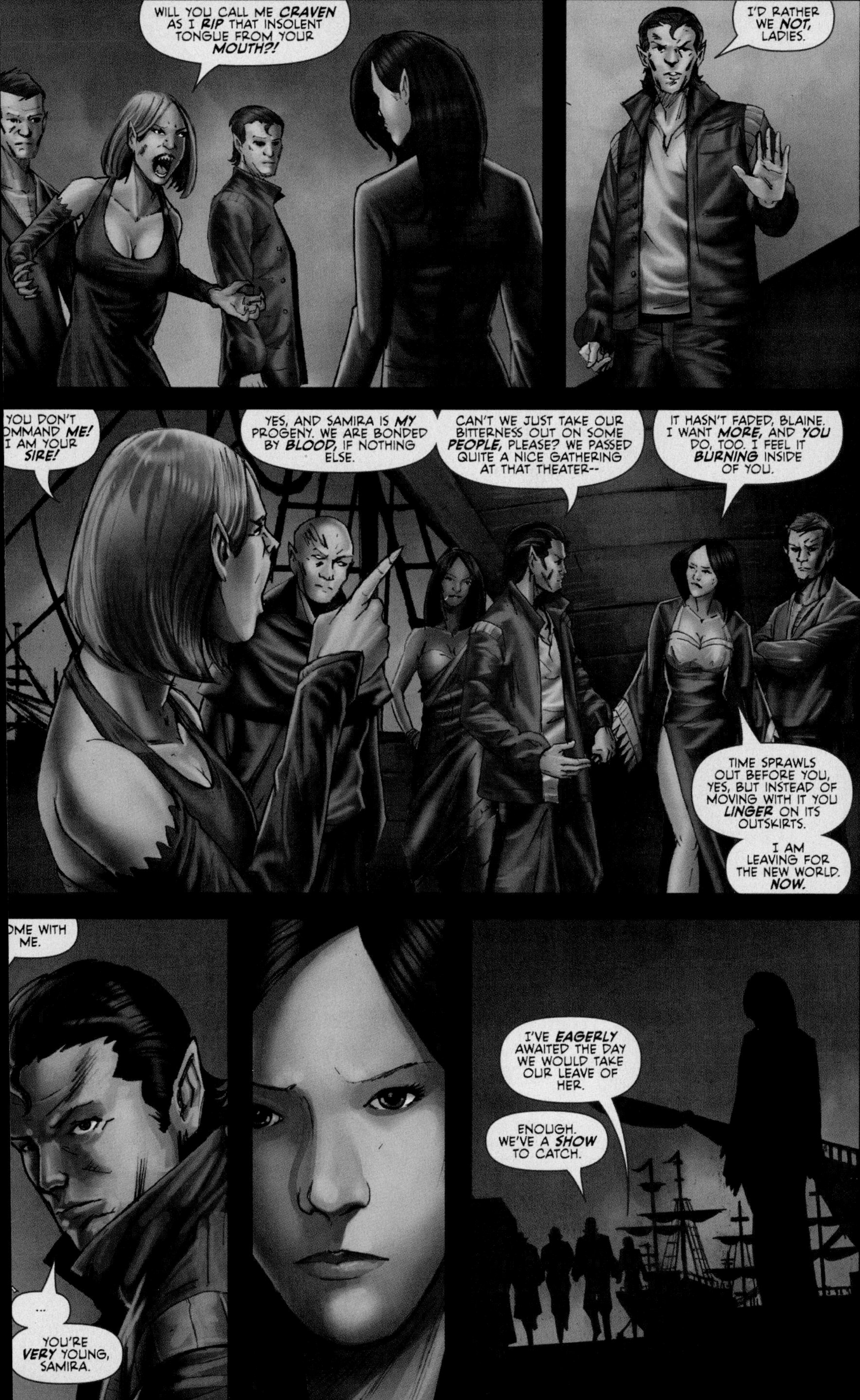
WILL YOU CALL ME CRAVEN AS I RIP THAT INSOLENT TONGUE FROM YOUR MOUTH?!
I'D RATHER WE NOT, LADIES.
YOU DON'T OMMAND ME! I AM YOUR SIRE!
YES, AND SAMIRA IS MY PROGENY. WE ARE BONDED BY BLOOD, IF NOTHING ELSE.
CAN'T WE JUST TAKE OUR BITTERNESS OUT ON SOME PEOPLE, PLEASE? WE PASSED QUITE A NICE GATHERING AT THAT THEATER--
IT HASN'T FADED, BLAINE. I WANT MORE, AND YOU DO, TOO. I FEEL IT BURNING INSIDE OF YOU.
TIME SPRAWLS OUT BEFORE YOU, YES, BUT INSTEAD OF MOVING WITH IT YOU LINGER ON ITS OUTSKIRTS.
I AM LEAVING FOR THE NEW WORLD. NOW.
OME WITH ME.
...
YOU'RE VERY YOUNG, SAMIRA.
I'VE EAGERLY AWAITED THE DAY WE WOULD TAKE OUR LEAVE OF HER.
ENOUGH. WE'VE A SHOW TO CATCH.

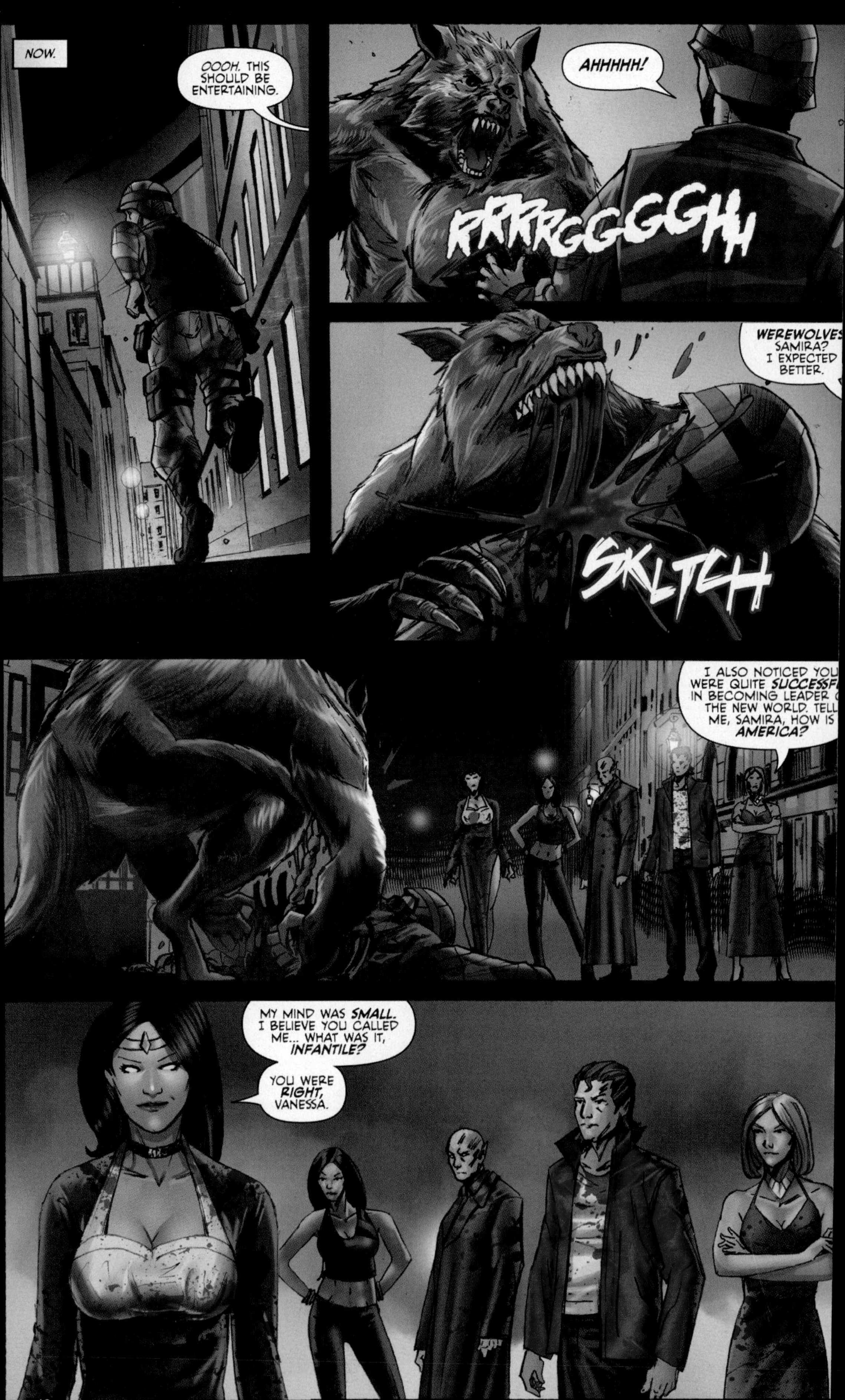
NOW.
OOOH. THIS SHOULD BE ENTERTAINING.
AHHHHH!
RRRRGGGGHH
WEREWOLVES SAMIRA? I EXPECTED BETTER.
SKLTCH
I ALSO NOTICED YOU WERE QUITE SUCCESSF IN BECOMING LEADER THE NEW WORLD. TELL ME, SAMIRA, HOW IS AMERICA?
MY MIND WAS SMALL. I BELIEVE YOU CALLED ME... WHAT WAS IT, INFANTILE?
YOU WERE RIGHT, VANESSA.

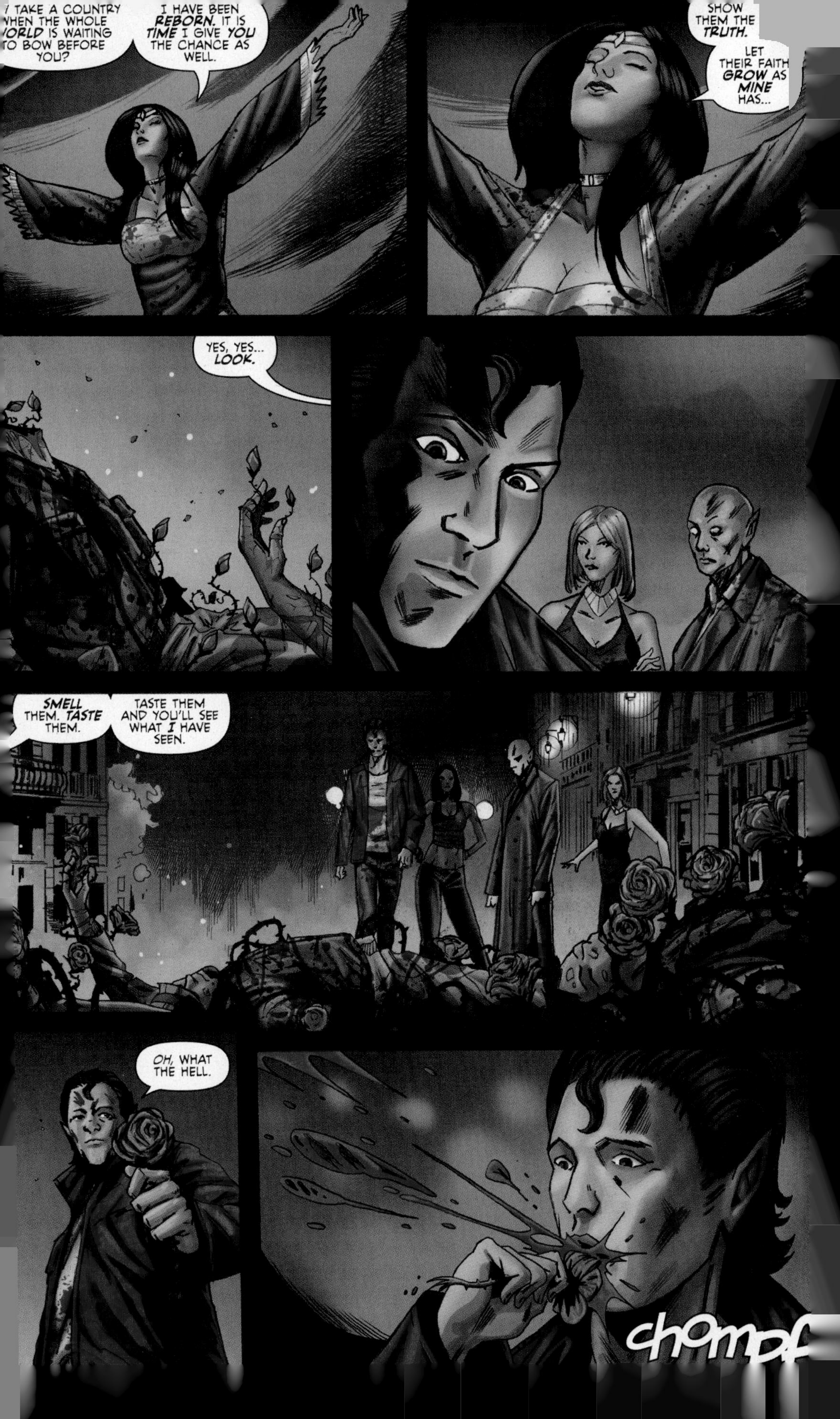

/ TAKE A COUNTRY WHEN THE WHOLE WORLD IS WAITING TO BOW BEFORE YOU?
I HAVE BEEN REBORN. IT IS TIME I GIVE YOU THE CHANCE AS WELL.
SHOW THEM THE TRUTH.
LET THEIR FAITH GROW AS MINE HAS...
YES, YES... LOOK.
SMELL THEM. TASTE THEM.
TASTE THEM AND YOU'LL SEE WHAT I HAVE SEEN.
OH, WHAT THE HELL.
chomp

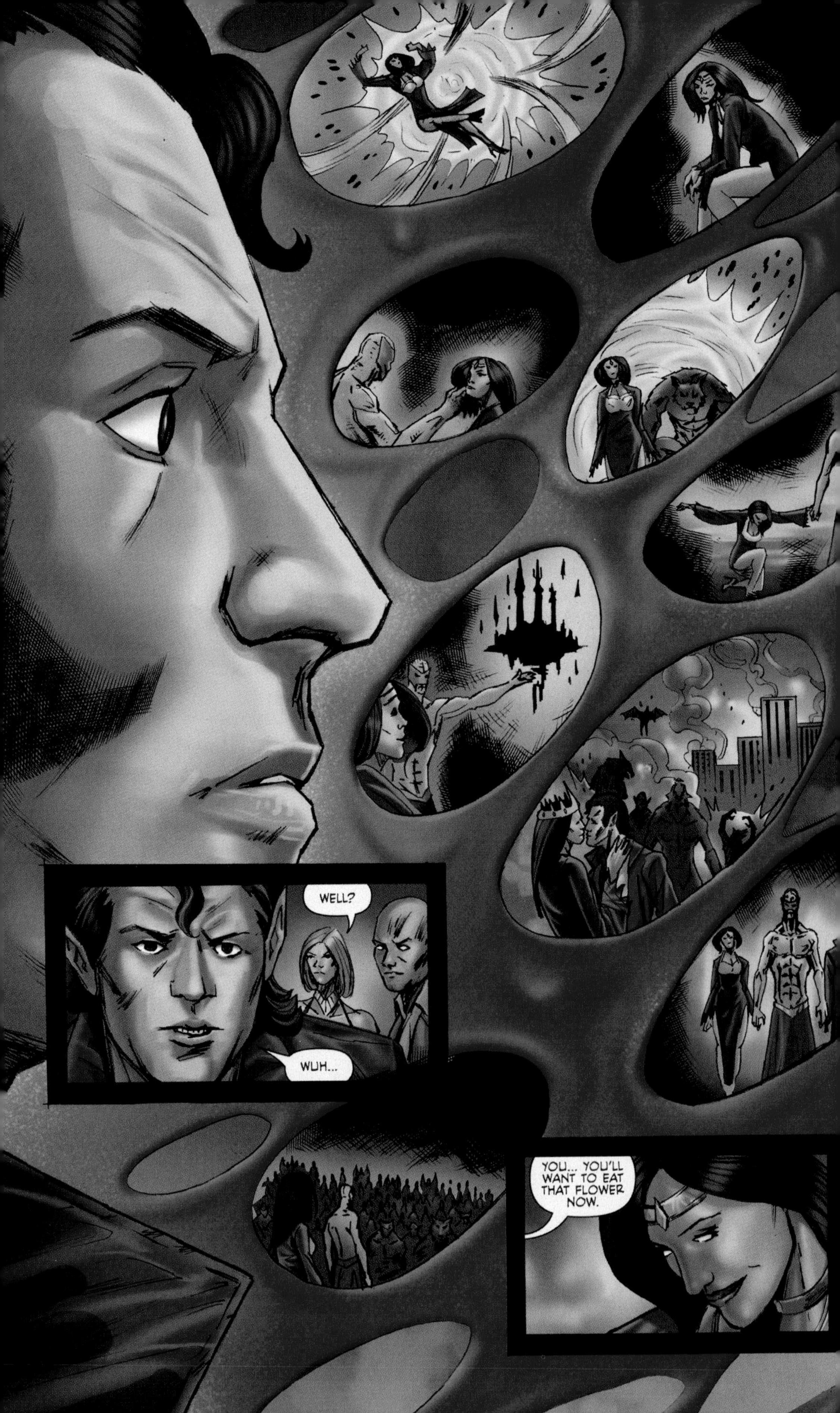
WELL?
WUH...
YOU... YOU'LL WANT TO EAT THAT FLOWER NOW.

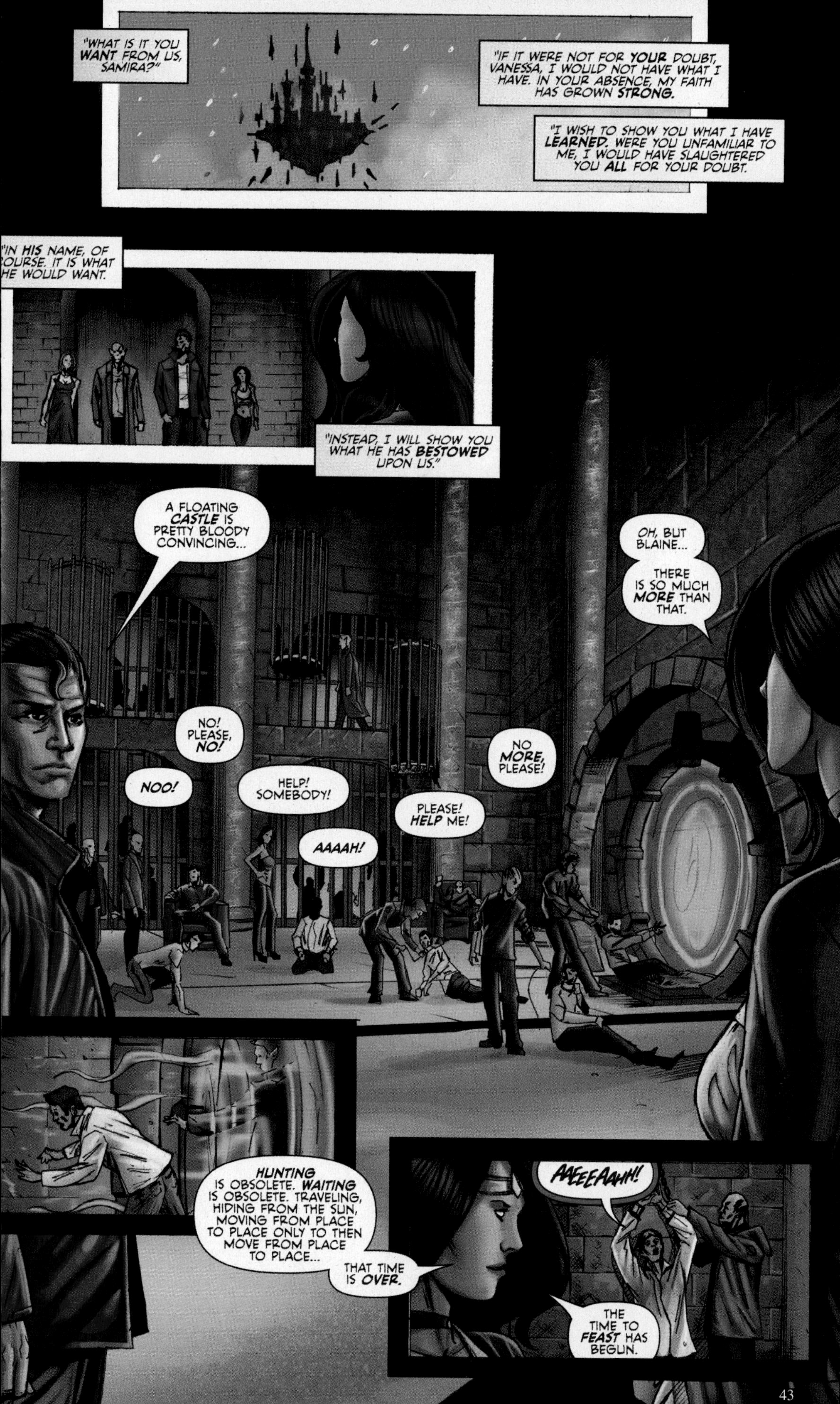
"WHAT IS IT YOU WANT FROM US, SAMIRA?"
"IF IT WERE NOT FOR YOUR DOUBT, VANESSA, I WOULD NOT HAVE WHAT I HAVE. IN YOUR ABSENCE, MY FAITH HAS GROWN STRONG.
"I WISH TO SHOW YOU WHAT I HAVE LEARNED. WERE YOU UNFAMILIAR TO ME, I WOULD HAVE SLAUGHTERED YOU ALL FOR YOUR DOUBT.
"IN HIS NAME, OF COURSE. IT IS WHAT HE WOULD WANT.
"INSTEAD, I WILL SHOW YOU WHAT HE HAS BESTOWED UPON US."
A FLOATING CASTLE IS PRETTY BLOODY CONVINCING...
OH, BUT BLAINE...
THERE IS SO MUCH MORE THAN THAT.
NO! PLEASE, NO!
NOO!
HELP! SOMEBODY!
NO MORE, PLEASE!
PLEASE! HELP ME!
AAAAH!
HUNTING IS OBSOLETE. WAITING IS OBSOLETE. TRAVELING, HIDING FROM THE SUN, MOVING FROM PLACE TO PLACE ONLY TO THEN MOVE FROM PLACE TO PLACE...
THAT TIME IS OVER.
AAEEEAAHH!
THE TIME TO FEAST HAS BEGUN.

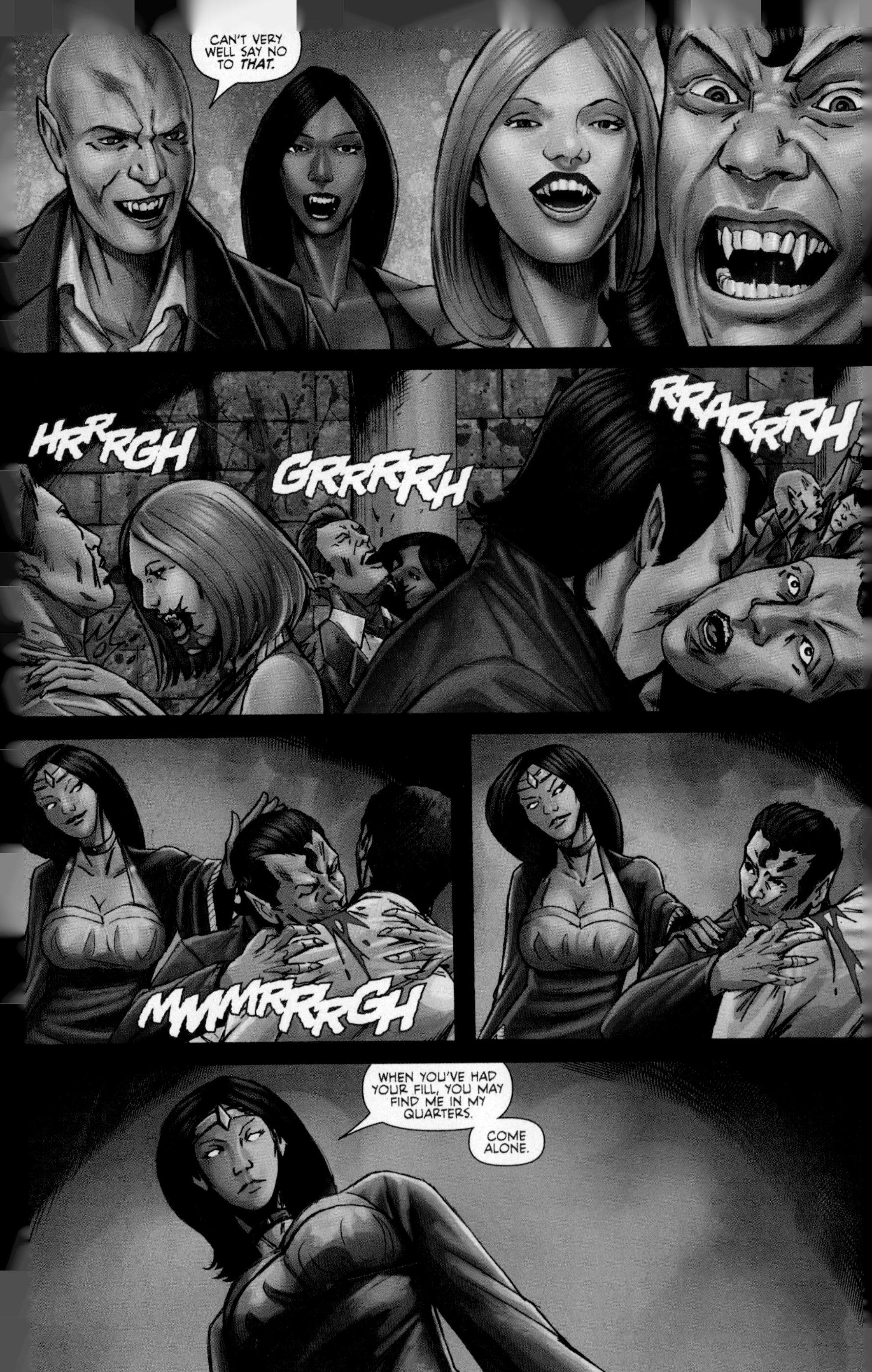
CAN'T VERY WELL SAY NO TO *THAT.*
HRRRGH
GRRRRRH
RRARRRRH
MMMRRRRGH
WHEN YOU'VE HAD YOUR FILL, YOU MAY FIND ME IN MY QUARTERS.
COME ALONE.

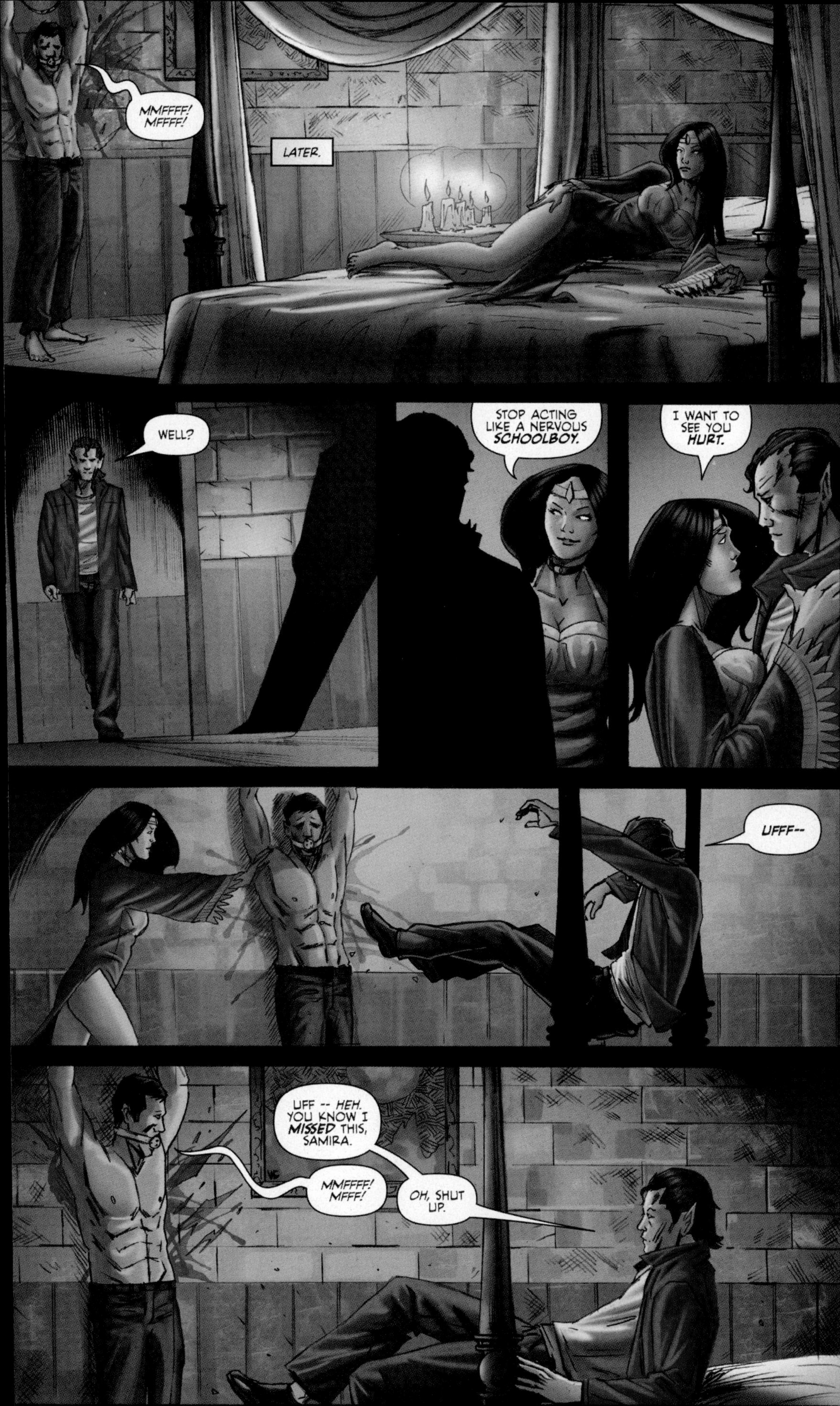

MMFFFF! MFFFF!
LATER.
WELL?
STOP ACTING LIKE A NERVOUS SCHOOLBOY.
I WANT TO SEE YOU HURT.
UFFF--
UFF -- HEH. YOU KNOW I MISSED THIS, SAMIRA.
MMFFFF! MFFF!
OH, SHUT UP.

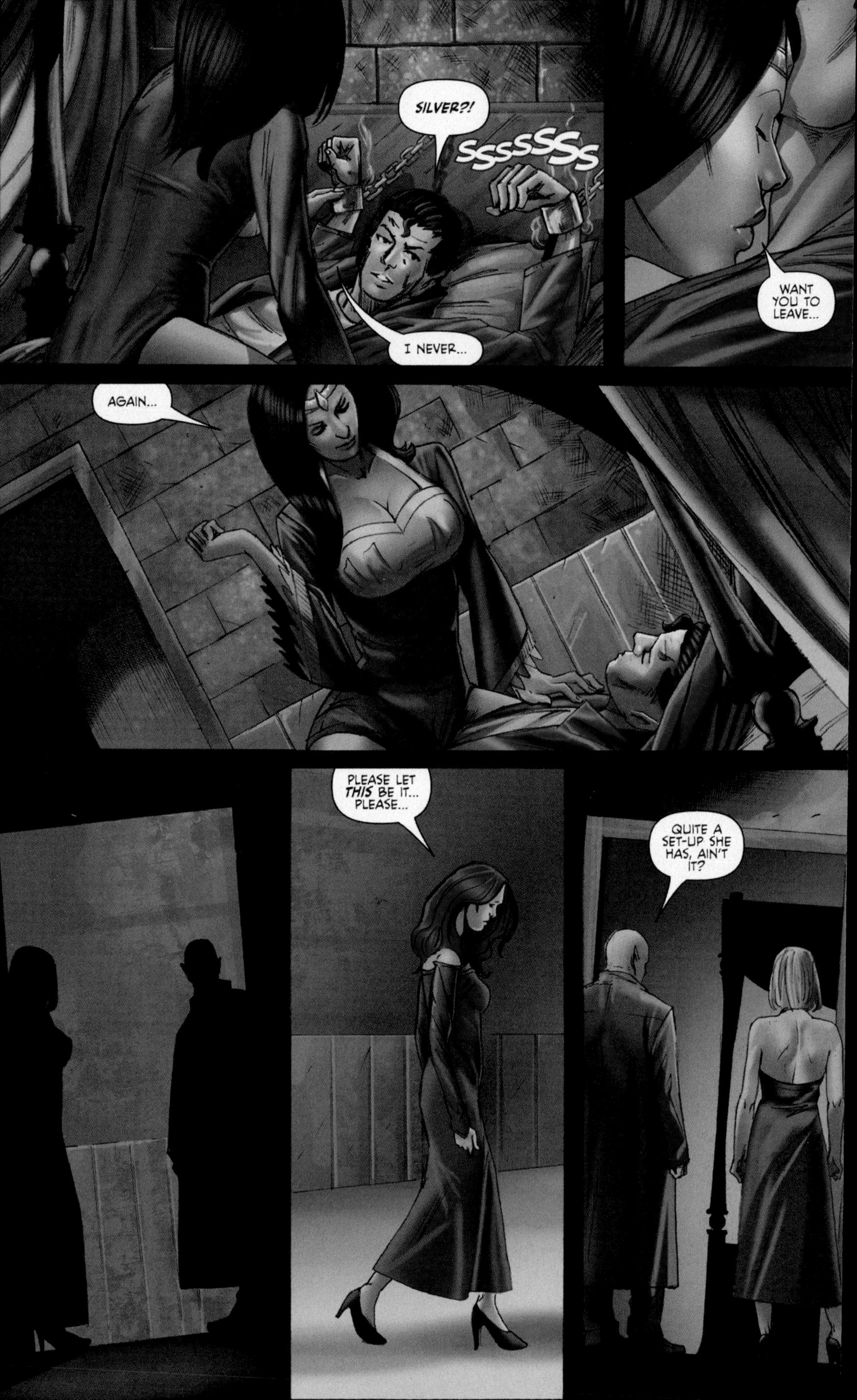
SILVER?!
SSSSSSS
I NEVER...
WANT YOU TO LEAVE...
AGAIN...
PLEASE LET THIS BE IT... PLEASE...
QUITE A SET-UP SHE HAS, AIN'T IT?

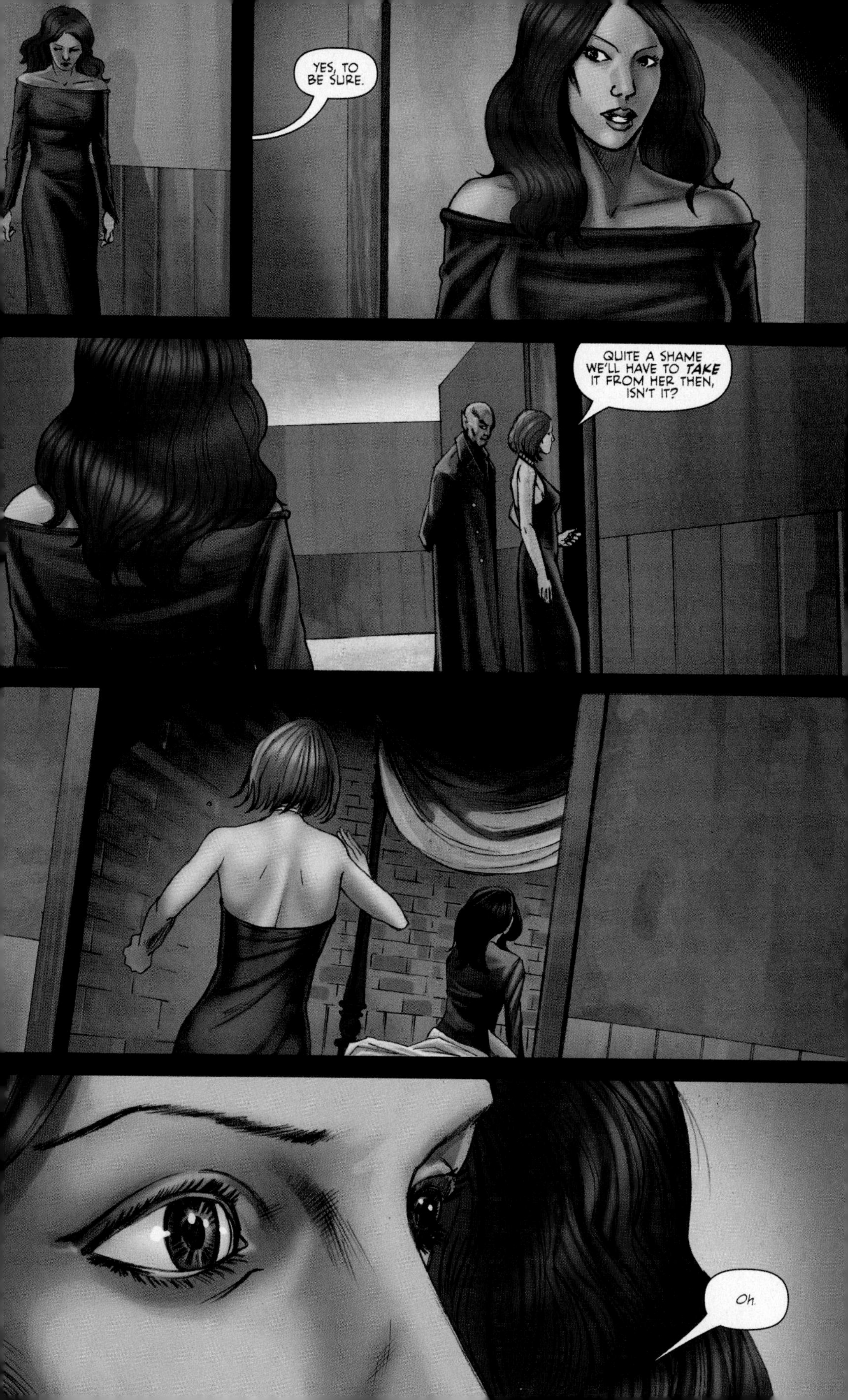
YES, TO BE SURE.
QUITE A SHAME WE'LL HAVE TO TAKE IT FROM HER THEN, ISN'T IT?
Oh.

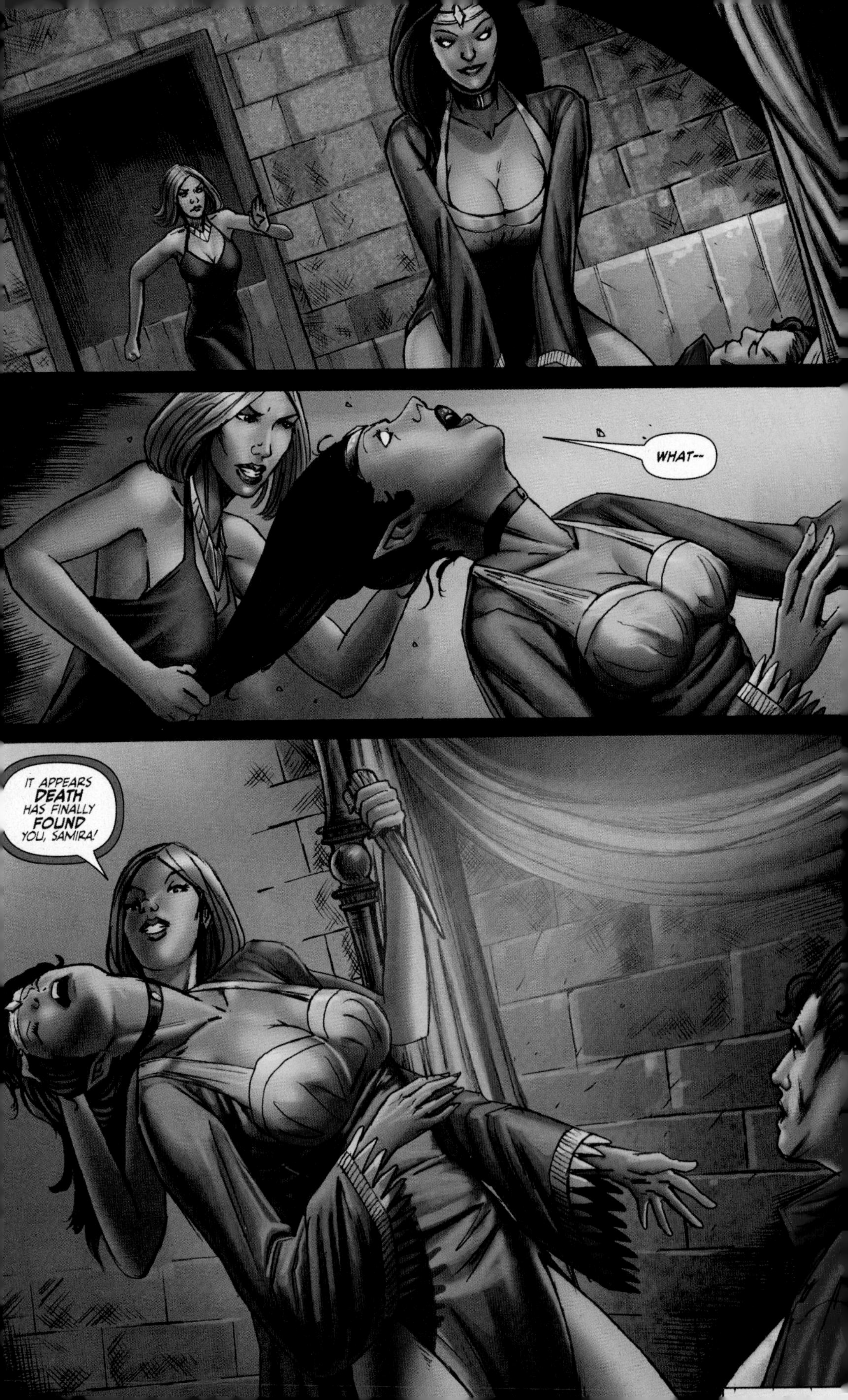
WHAT--
IT APPEARS DEATH HAS FINALLY FOUND YOU, SAMIRA!

Grimm Fairy Tales
presents:

Vampires
&
Werewolves

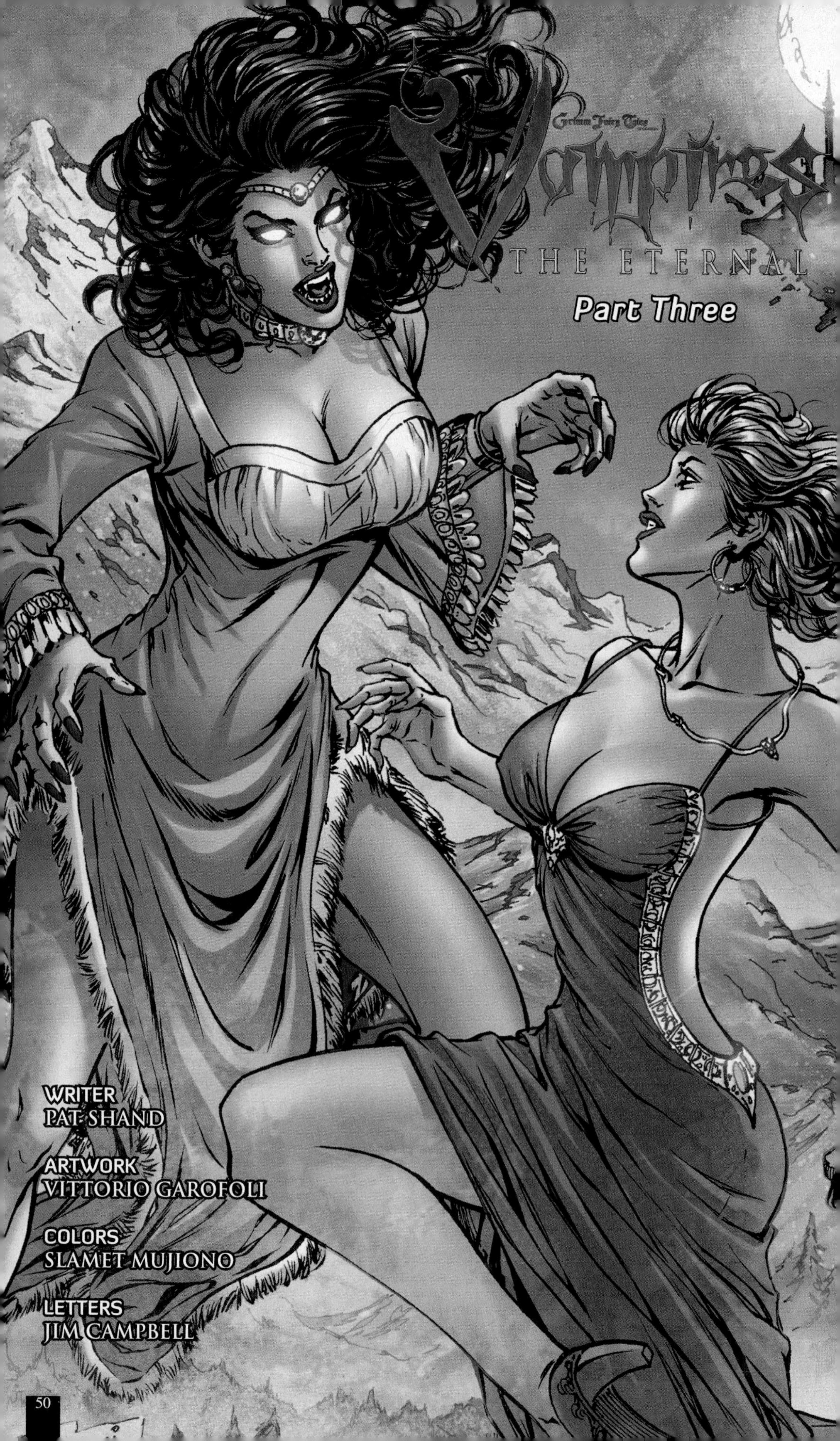
Grimm Fairy Tales
Vampires
THE ETERNAL
Part Three
WRITER
PAT SHAND
ARTWORK
VITTORIO GAROFOLI
COLORS
SLAMET MUJIONO
LETTERS
JIM CAMPBELL

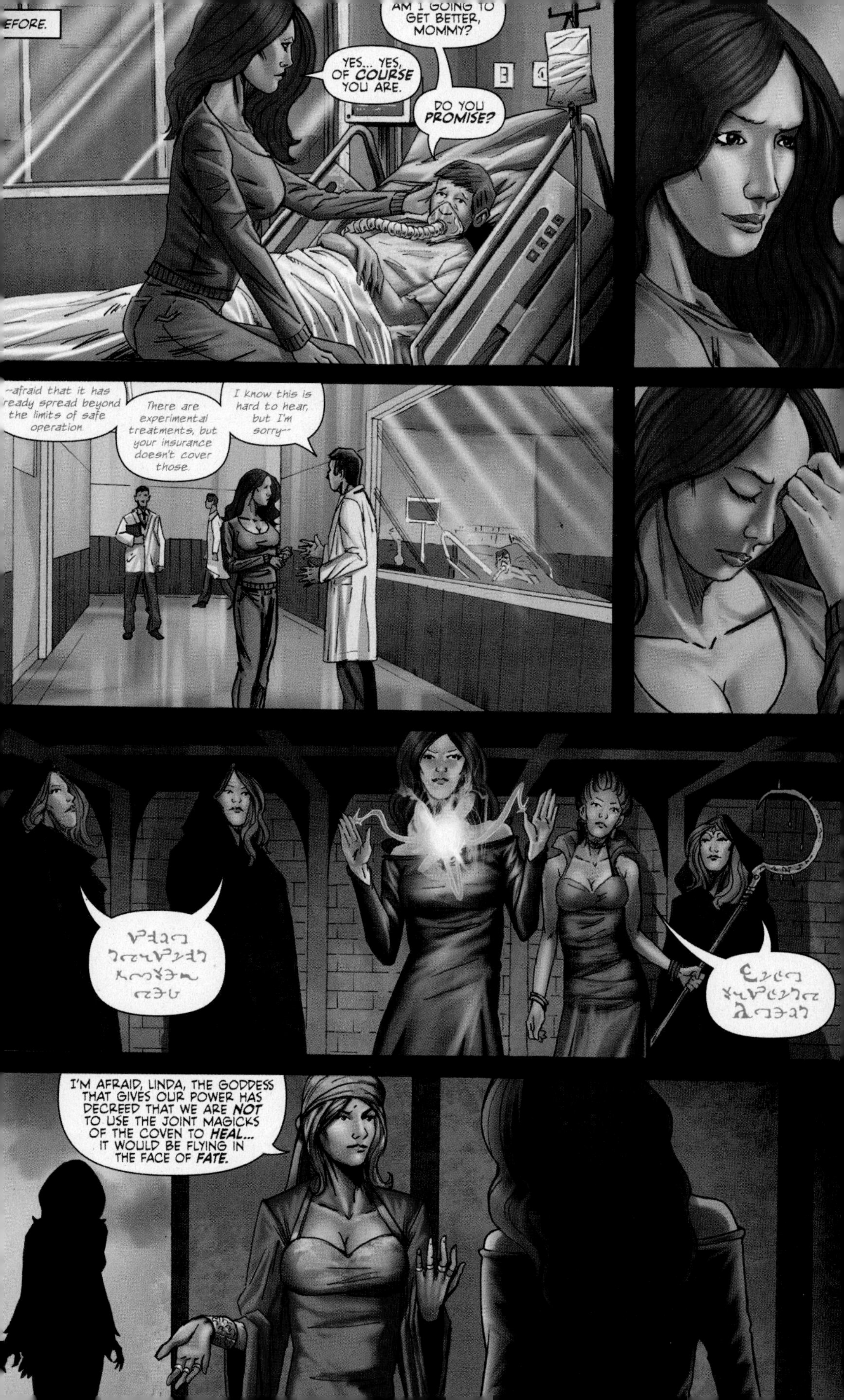
EFORE.
AM I GOING TO GET BETTER, MOMMY?
YES... YES, OF COURSE YOU ARE.
DO YOU PROMISE?
--afraid that it has ready spread beyond the limits of safe operation.
There are experimental treatments, but your insurance doesn't cover those.
I know this is hard to hear, but I'm sorry--
I'M AFRAID, LINDA, THE GODDESS THAT GIVES OUR POWER HAS DECREED THAT WE ARE NOT TO USE THE JOINT MAGICKS OF THE COVEN TO HEAL... IT WOULD BE FLYING IN THE FACE OF FATE.

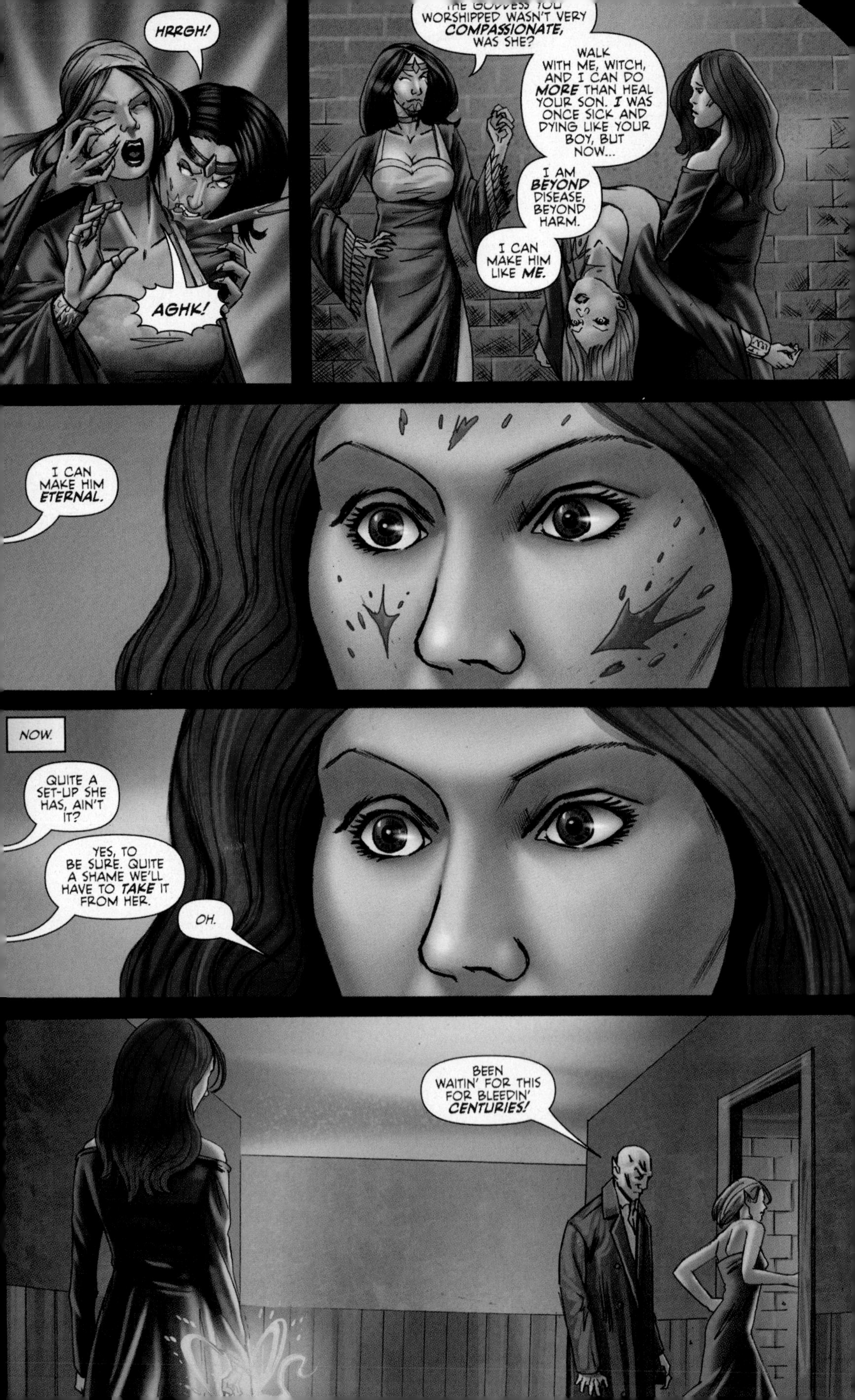
HRRGH!
AGHK!
THE GODDESS YOU WORSHIPPED WASN'T VERY COMPASSIONATE, WAS SHE?
WALK WITH ME, WITCH, AND I CAN DO MORE THAN HEAL YOUR SON. I WAS ONCE SICK AND DYING LIKE YOUR BOY, BUT NOW...
I AM BEYOND DISEASE, BEYOND HARM.
I CAN MAKE HIM LIKE ME.
I CAN MAKE HIM ETERNAL.
NOW.
QUITE A SET-UP SHE HAS, AIN'T IT?
YES, TO BE SURE. QUITE A SHAME WE'LL HAVE TO TAKE IT FROM HER.
OH.
BEEN WAITIN' FOR THIS FOR BLEEDIN' CENTURIES!

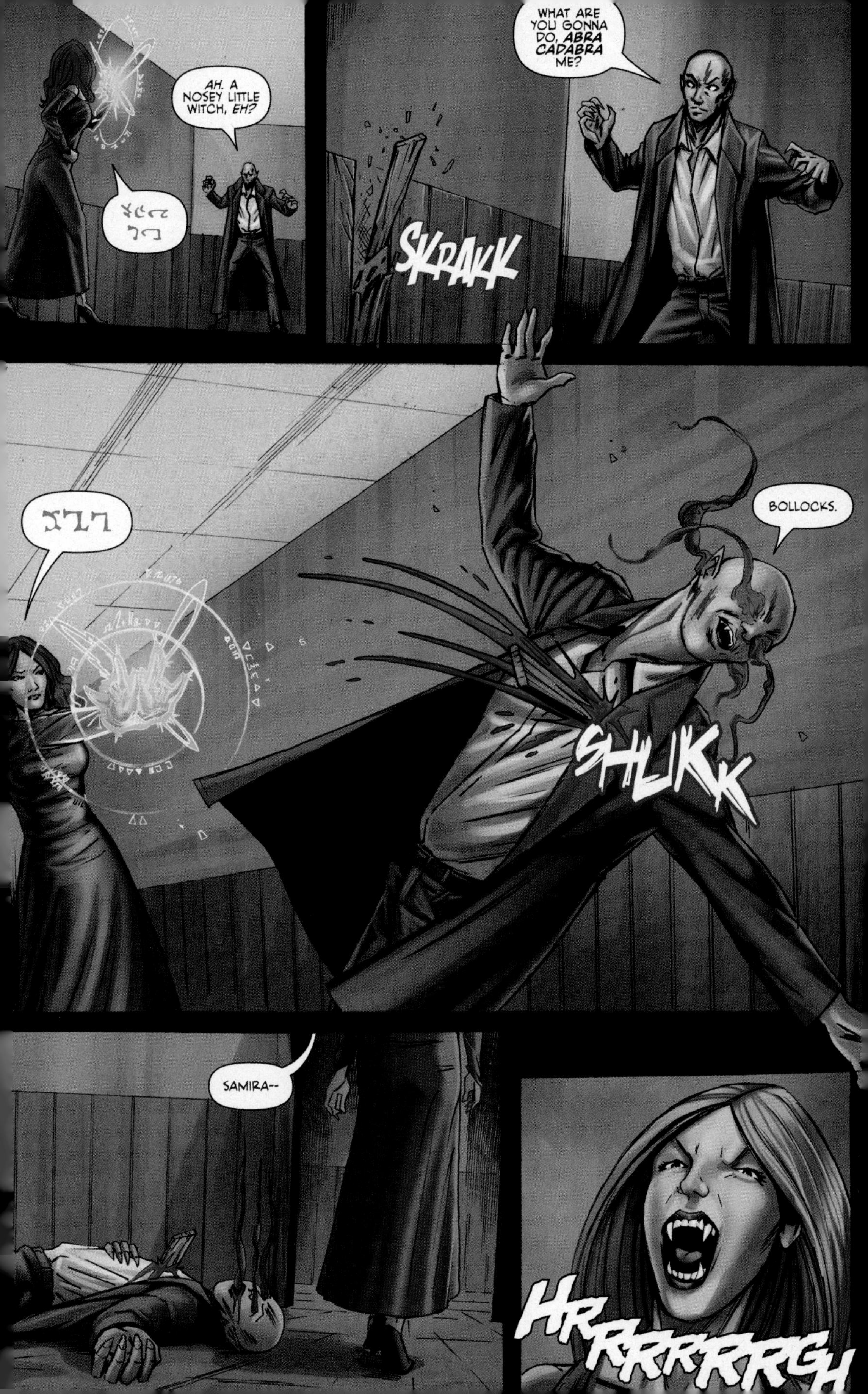
AH. A NOSEY LITTLE WITCH, EH?
WHAT ARE YOU GONNA DO, ABRA CADABRA ME?
SKRAKK
BOLLOCKS.
SHLIKK
SAMIRA--
HRRRRRRGH

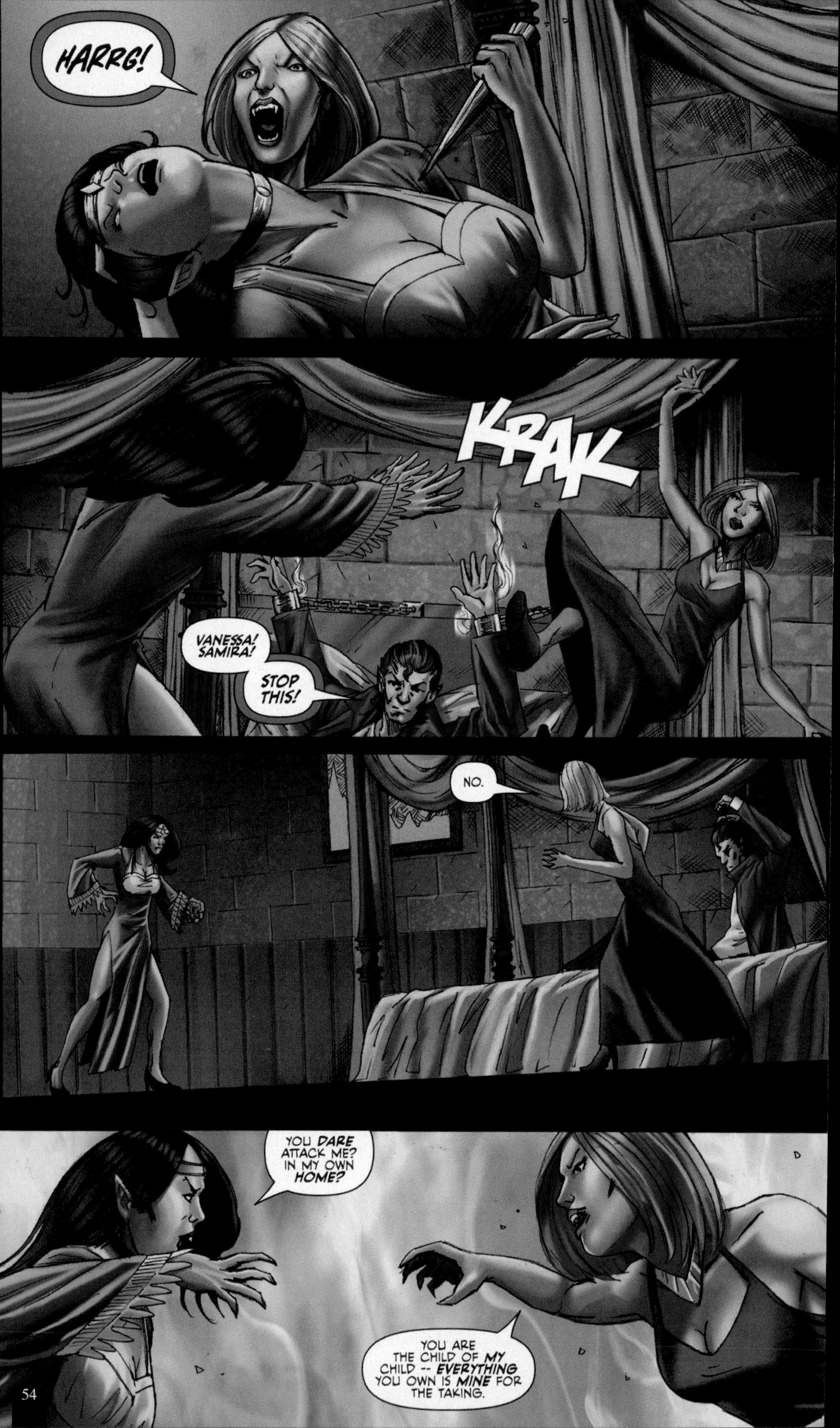
HARRG!
KRAK
VANESSA! SAMIRA!
STOP THIS!
NO.
YOU DARE ATTACK ME? IN MY OWN HOME?
YOU ARE THE CHILD OF MY CHILD -- EVERYTHING YOU OWN IS MINE FOR THE TAKING.

TRY TO TAKE IT!

KRAKK

RAARGH!

JEALOUSY HAS *ALWAYS* BEEN YOUR SIN, VANESSA. IT--

LINDA?

GRRRRRRRR

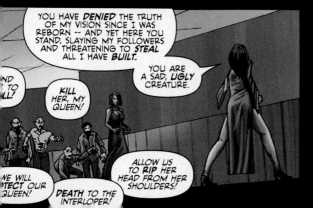

YOU HAVE *DENIED* THE TRUTH OF MY VISION SINCE I WAS REBORN -- AND YET HERE YOU STAND, SLAYING MY FOLLOWERS AND THREATENING TO *STEAL* ALL I HAVE *BUILT*.

YOU ARE A *SAD*, *UGLY* CREATURE.

...ND TO ...LL!

KILL HER, MY QUEEN!

...WE WILL ...TECT OUR QUEEN!

DEATH TO THE INTERLOPER!

ALLOW US TO *RIP* HER HEAD FROM HER SHOULDERS!

NO!

SHE IS *MINE*.

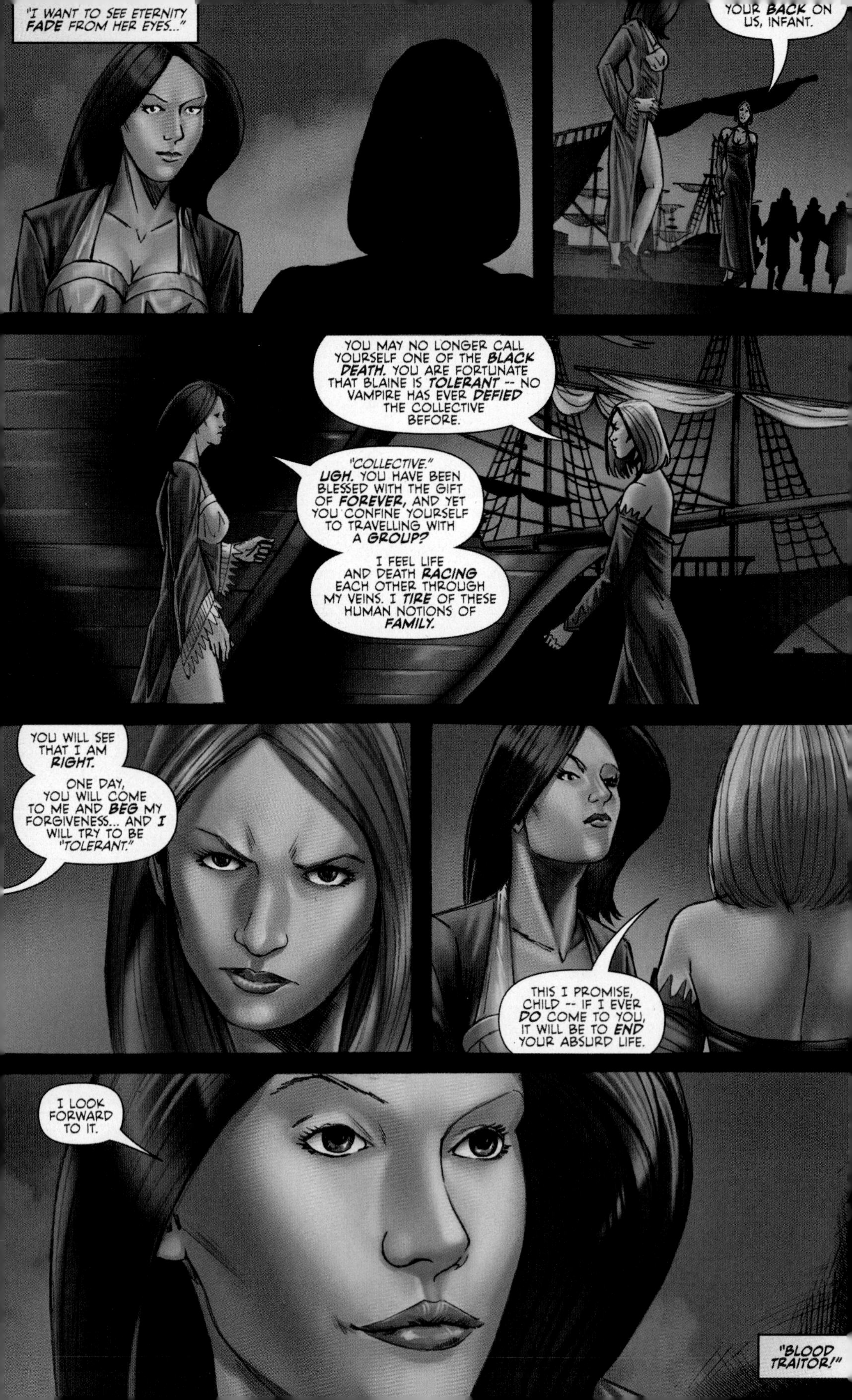
"I WANT TO SEE ETERNITY FADE FROM HER EYES..."
YOUR BACK ON US, INFANT.
YOU MAY NO LONGER CALL YOURSELF ONE OF THE BLACK DEATH. YOU ARE FORTUNATE THAT BLAINE IS TOLERANT -- NO VAMPIRE HAS EVER DEFIED THE COLLECTIVE BEFORE.
"COLLECTIVE." UGH. YOU HAVE BEEN BLESSED WITH THE GIFT OF FOREVER, AND YET YOU CONFINE YOURSELF TO TRAVELLING WITH A GROUP?
I FEEL LIFE AND DEATH RACING EACH OTHER THROUGH MY VEINS. I TIRE OF THESE HUMAN NOTIONS OF FAMILY.
YOU WILL SEE THAT I AM RIGHT.
ONE DAY, YOU WILL COME TO ME AND BEG MY FORGIVENESS... AND I WILL TRY TO BE "TOLERANT."
THIS I PROMISE, CHILD -- IF I EVER DO COME TO YOU, IT WILL BE TO END YOUR ABSURD LIFE.
I LOOK FORWARD TO IT.
"BLOOD TRAITOR!"

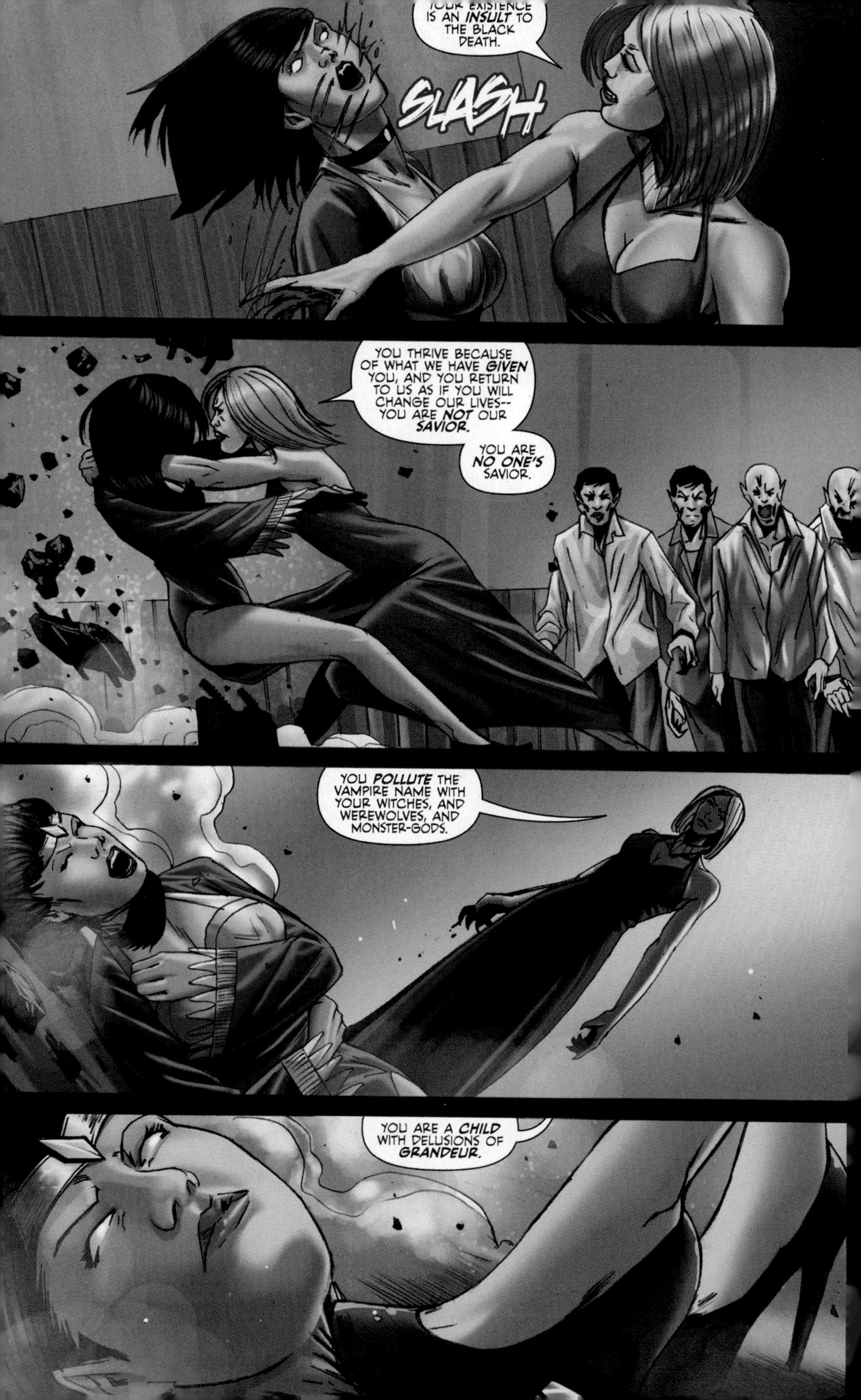
YOUR EXISTENCE IS AN INSULT TO THE BLACK DEATH.
SLASH
YOU THRIVE BECAUSE OF WHAT WE HAVE GIVEN YOU, AND YOU RETURN TO US AS IF YOU WILL CHANGE OUR LIVES-- YOU ARE NOT OUR SAVIOR.
YOU ARE NO ONE'S SAVIOR.
YOU POLLUTE THE VAMPIRE NAME WITH YOUR WITCHES, AND WEREWOLVES, AND MONSTER-GODS.
YOU ARE A CHILD WITH DELUSIONS OF GRANDEUR.

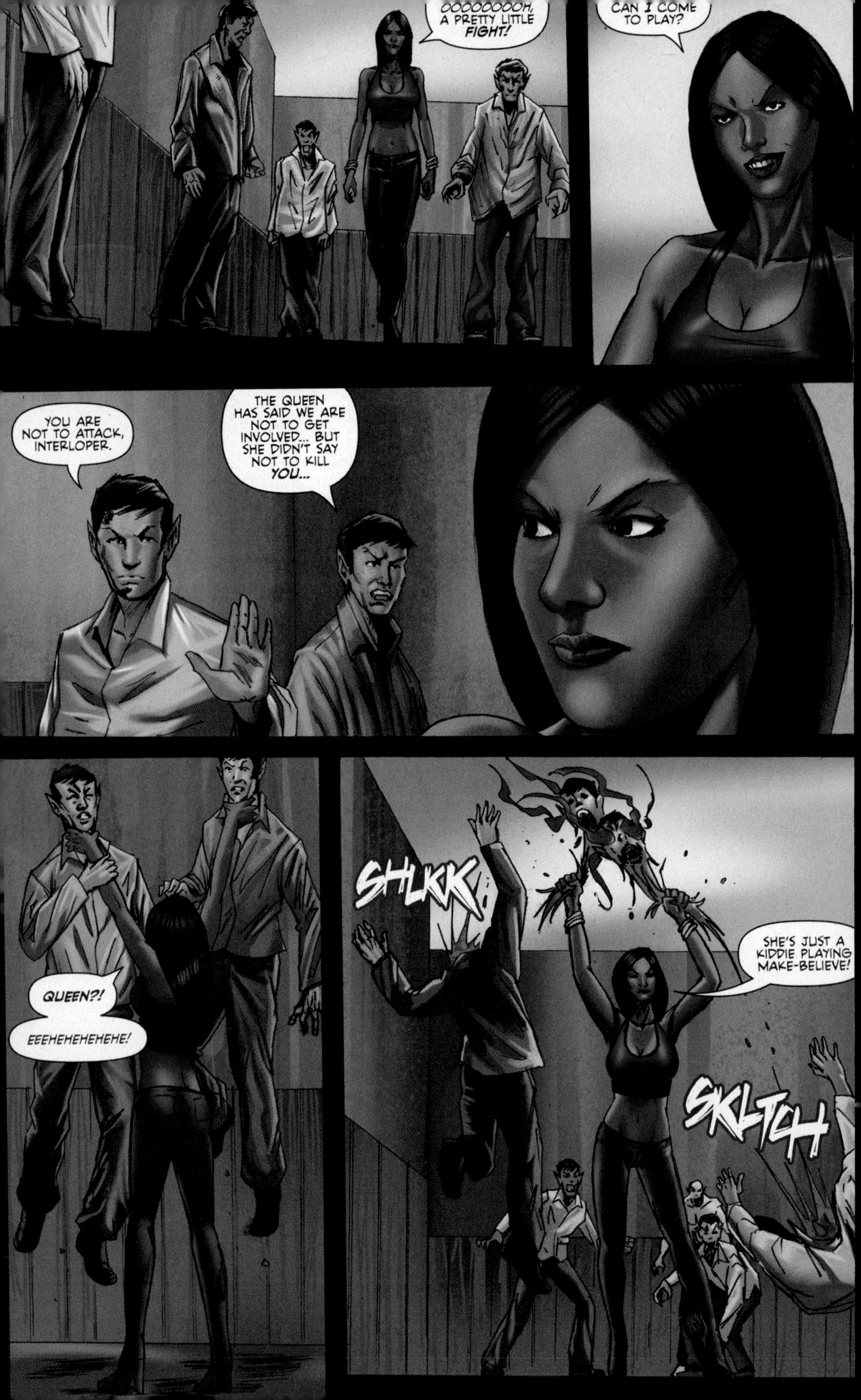
OOOOOOOOOH, A PRETTY LITTLE FIGHT!
CAN I COME TO PLAY?
YOU ARE NOT TO ATTACK, INTERLOPER.
THE QUEEN HAS SAID WE ARE NOT TO GET INVOLVED... BUT SHE DIDN'T SAY NOT TO KILL YOU...
QUEEN?!
EEEHEHEHEHEHE!
SHLKK
SHE'S JUST A KIDDIE PLAYING MAKE-BELIEVE!
SKLTCH

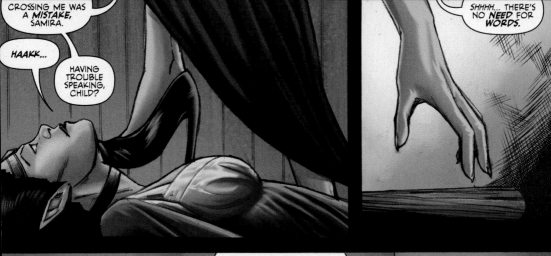

CROSSING ME WAS A *MISTAKE*, SAMIRA.

HAAKK...

HAVING TROUBLE SPEAKING, CHILD?

SHHHH... THERE'S NO *NEED* FOR *WORDS*.

YOU'VE HAD QUITE A LOT TO SAY, AND I *TIRE* OF IT ALL. I AM GOING TO *TAKE* YOUR GAUDY CASTLE AND MAKE YOUR MINIONS BOW TO *ME*.

I WILL *DRAIN* YOUR HUMANS, MAKE YOUR PUP MY PET, AND MOVE ON... BECAUSE THAT IS *OUR* WAY. I ASK YOU NOW, SAMIRA, *WHO IS THE FOOL?*

ME... OR THE CHILD WHO CHOSE TO CROSS SOMEONE *TEN TIMES* HER AGE?

SMAK

YOU ARE, VANESSA. YOU SHOULD KNOW *BETTER*.

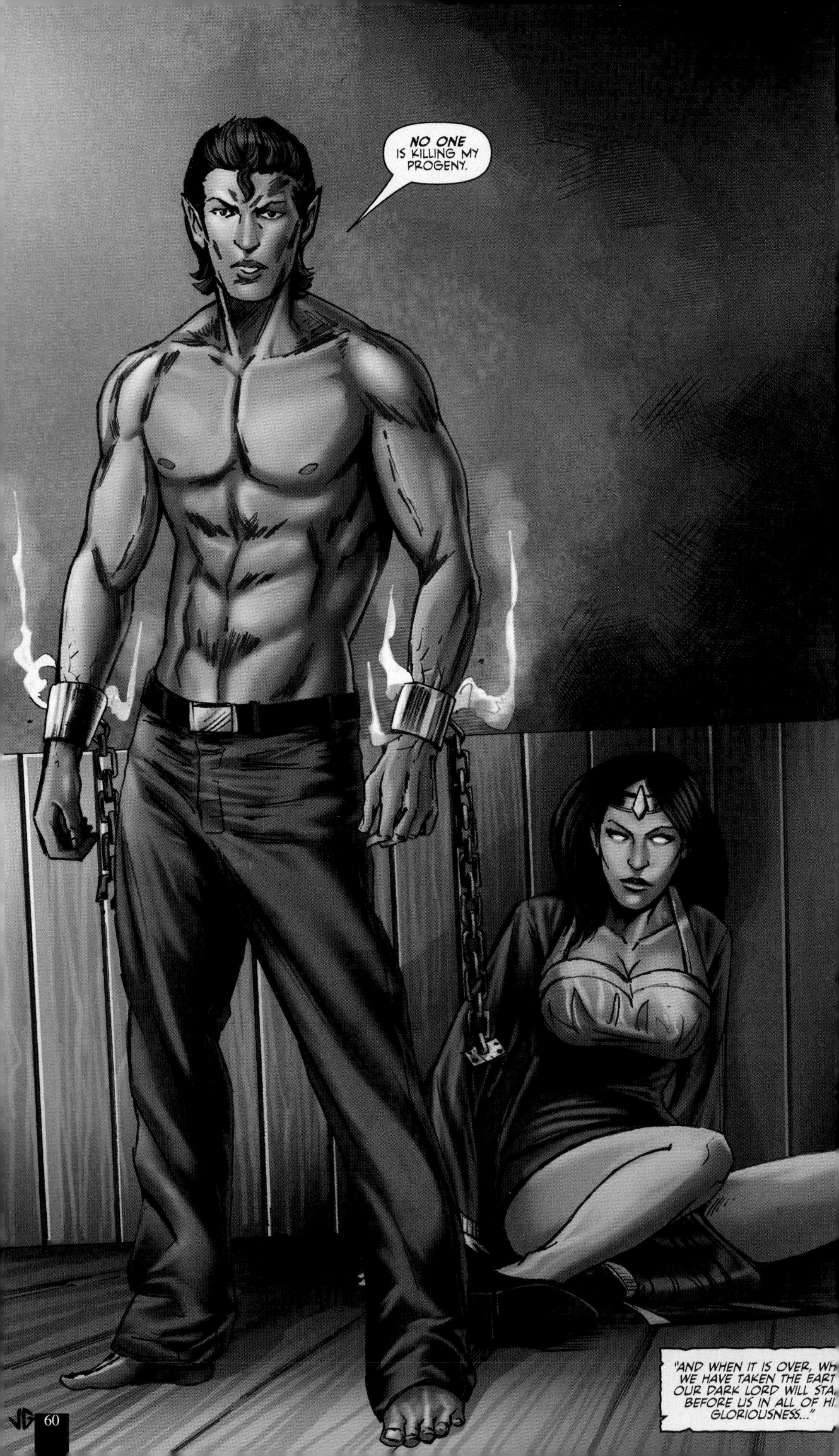
NO ONE IS KILLING MY PROGENY.
"AND WHEN IT IS OVER, WH WE HAVE TAKEN THE EART OUR DARK LORD WILL STA BEFORE US IN ALL OF HI GLORIOUSNESS..."

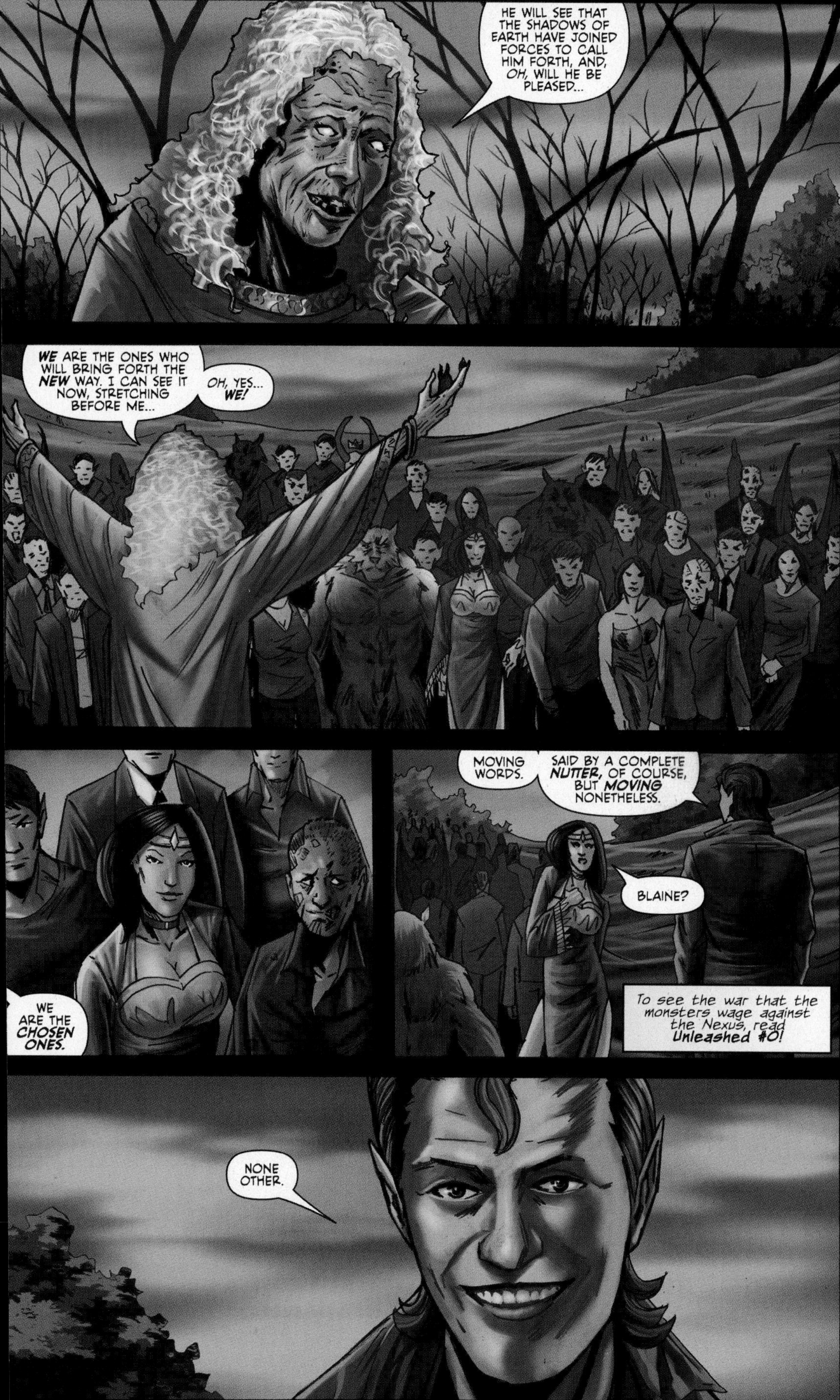

HE WILL SEE THAT THE SHADOWS OF EARTH HAVE JOINED FORCES TO CALL HIM FORTH, AND, *OH,* WILL HE BE PLEASED...
WE ARE THE ONES WHO WILL BRING FORTH THE ***NEW*** WAY. I CAN SEE IT NOW, STRETCHING BEFORE ME...
OH, YES... ***WE!***
WE ARE THE ***CHOSEN ONES.***
MOVING WORDS.
SAID BY A COMPLETE ***NUTTER,*** OF COURSE, BUT ***MOVING*** NONETHELESS.
BLAINE?
To see the war that the monsters wage against the Nexus, read **Unleashed #0!**
NONE OTHER.

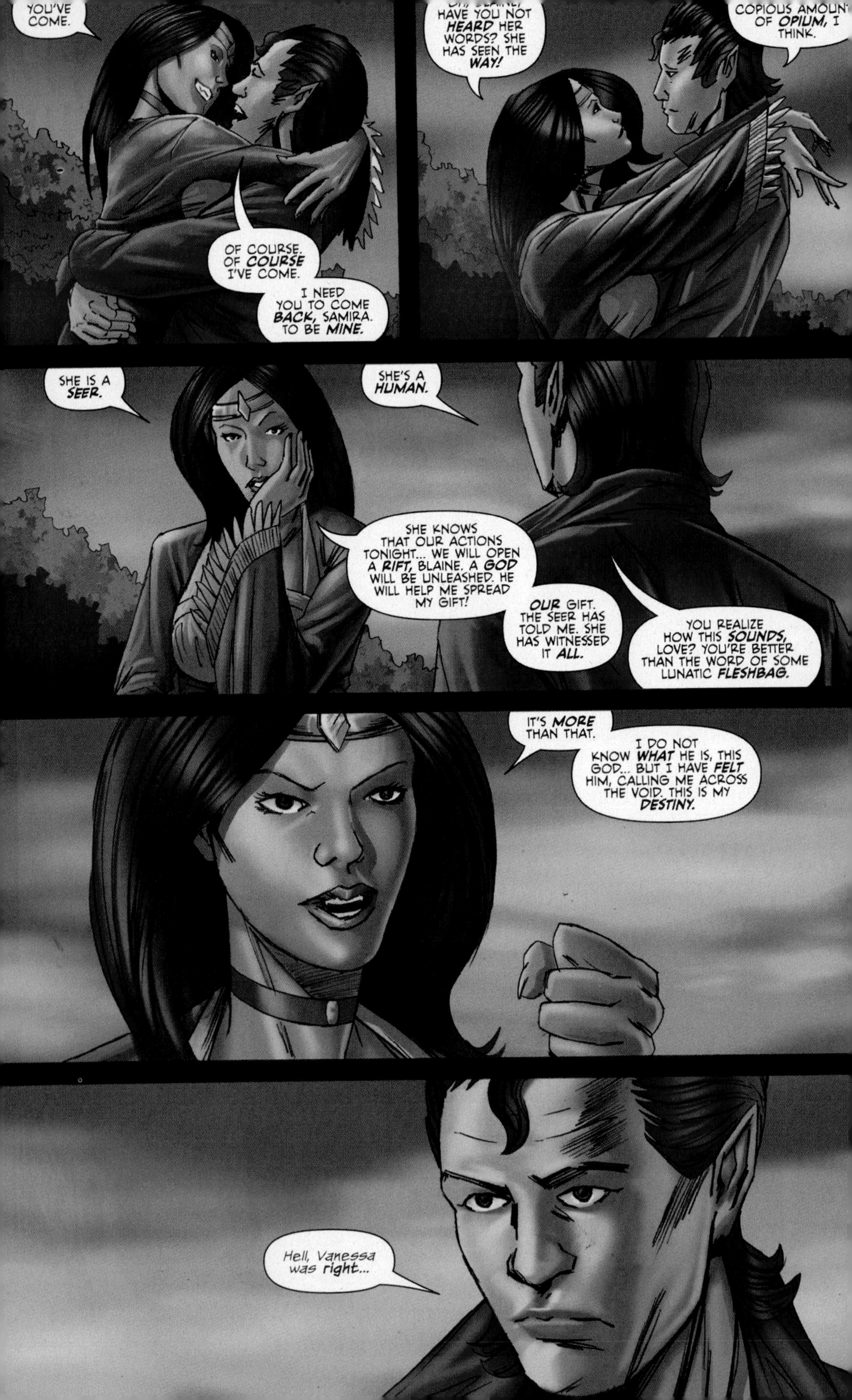

YOU'VE COME.
OF COURSE. OF COURSE I'VE COME.
I NEED YOU TO COME BACK, SAMIRA. TO BE MINE.
HAVE YOU NOT HEARD HER WORDS? SHE HAS SEEN THE WAY!
COPIOUS AMOUN OF OPIUM, I THINK.
SHE IS A SEER.
SHE'S A HUMAN.
SHE KNOWS THAT OUR ACTIONS TONIGHT... WE WILL OPEN A RIFT, BLAINE. A GOD WILL BE UNLEASHED. HE WILL HELP ME SPREAD MY GIFT!
OUR GIFT. THE SEER HAS TOLD ME. SHE HAS WITNESSED IT ALL.
YOU REALIZE HOW THIS SOUNDS, LOVE? YOU'RE BETTER THAN THE WORD OF SOME LUNATIC FLESHBAG.
IT'S MORE THAN THAT.
I DO NOT KNOW WHAT HE IS, THIS GOD... BUT I HAVE FELT HIM, CALLING ME ACROSS THE VOID. THIS IS MY DESTINY.
Hell, Vanessa was right...

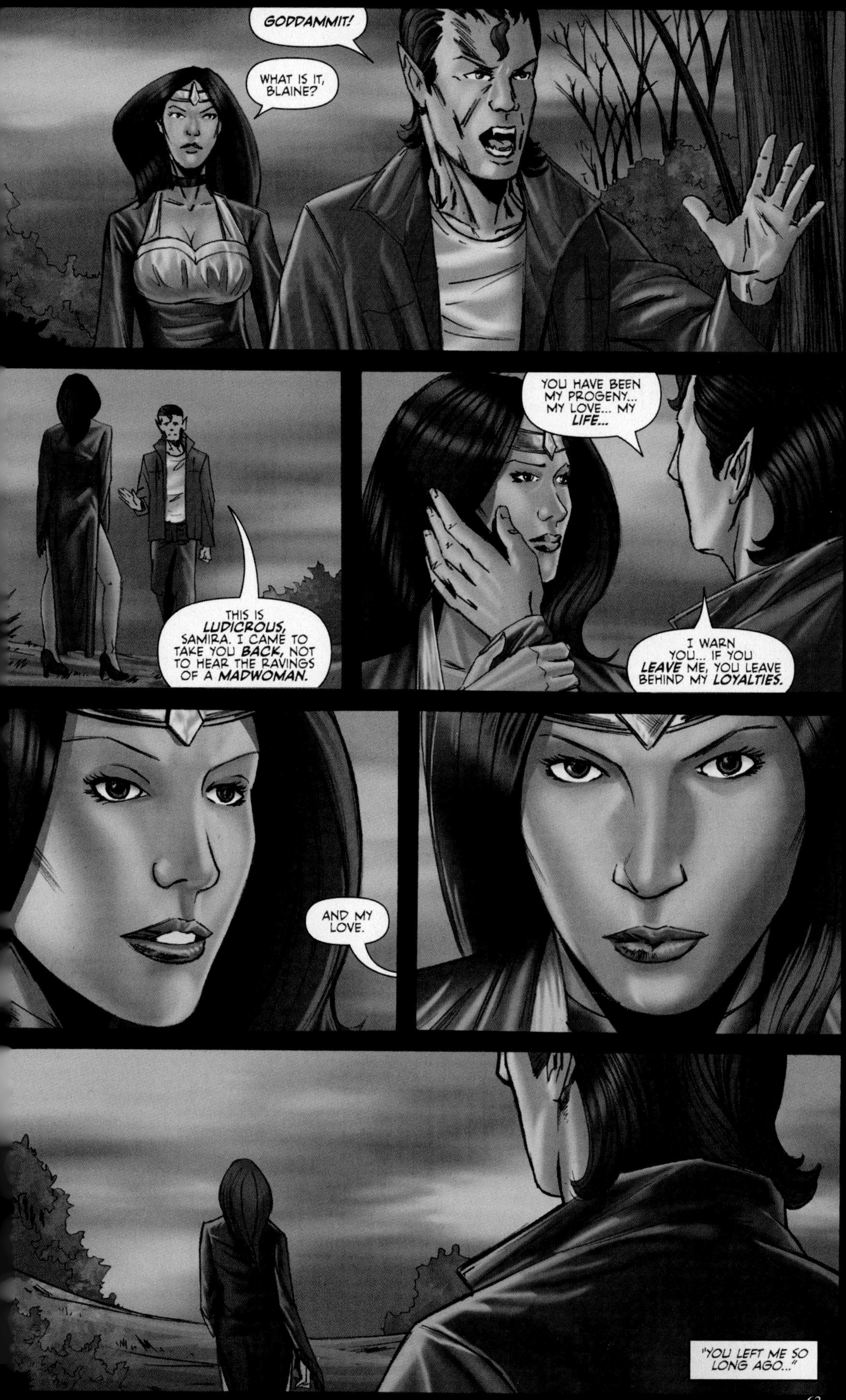
GODDAMMIT!
WHAT IS IT, BLAINE?
THIS IS LUDICROUS, SAMIRA. I CAME TO TAKE YOU BACK, NOT TO HEAR THE RAVINGS OF A MADWOMAN.
YOU HAVE BEEN MY PROGENY... MY LOVE... MY LIFE...
I WARN YOU... IF YOU LEAVE ME, YOU LEAVE BEHIND MY LOYALTIES.
AND MY LOVE.
"YOU LEFT ME SO LONG AGO..."

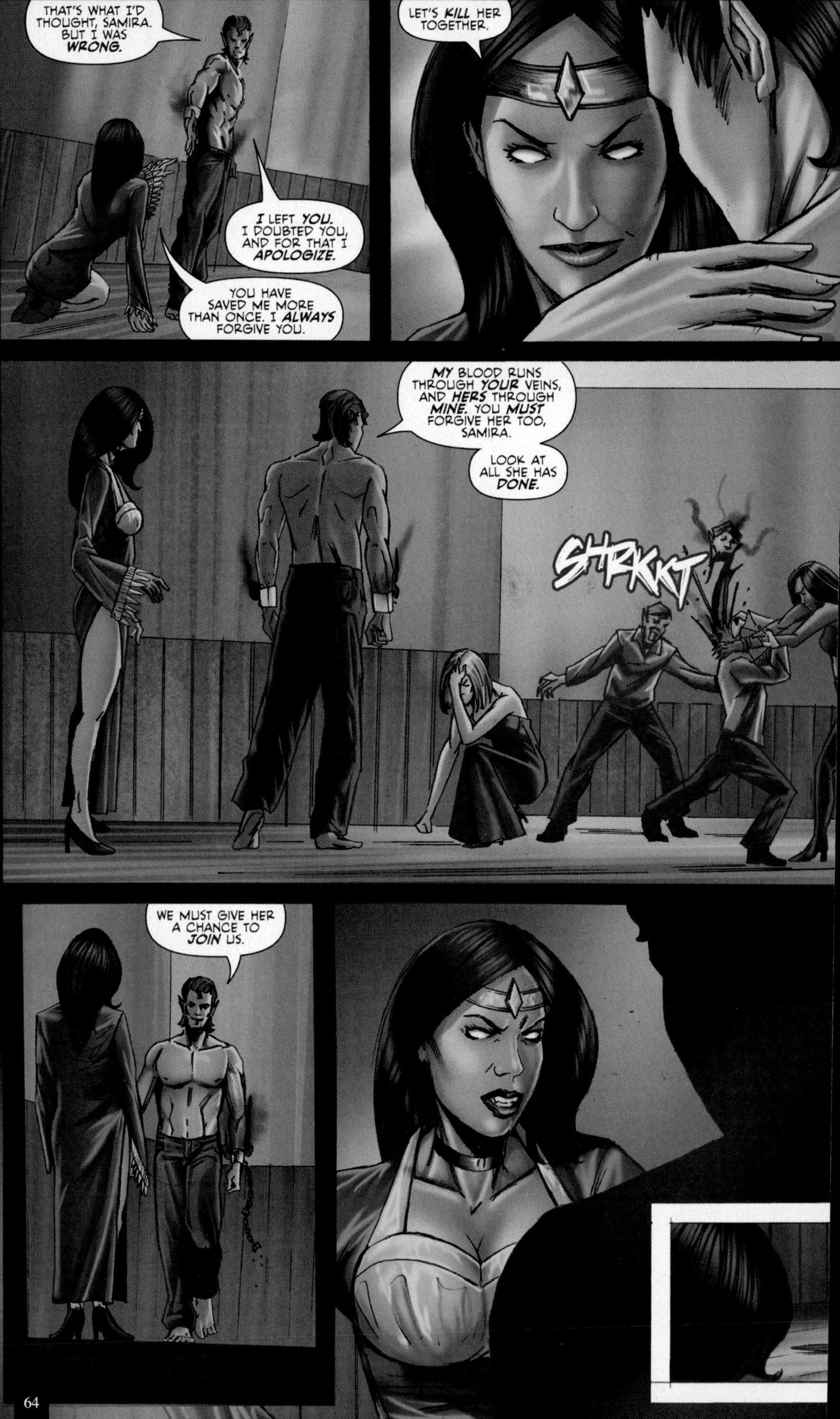
THAT'S WHAT I'D THOUGHT, SAMIRA. BUT I WAS WRONG.
I LEFT YOU. I DOUBTED YOU, AND FOR THAT I APOLOGIZE.
YOU HAVE SAVED ME MORE THAN ONCE. I ALWAYS FORGIVE YOU.
LET'S KILL HER TOGETHER.
MY BLOOD RUNS THROUGH YOUR VEINS, AND HERS THROUGH MINE. YOU MUST FORGIVE HER TOO, SAMIRA.
LOOK AT ALL SHE HAS DONE.
SHRKKT
WE MUST GIVE HER A CHANCE TO JOIN US.

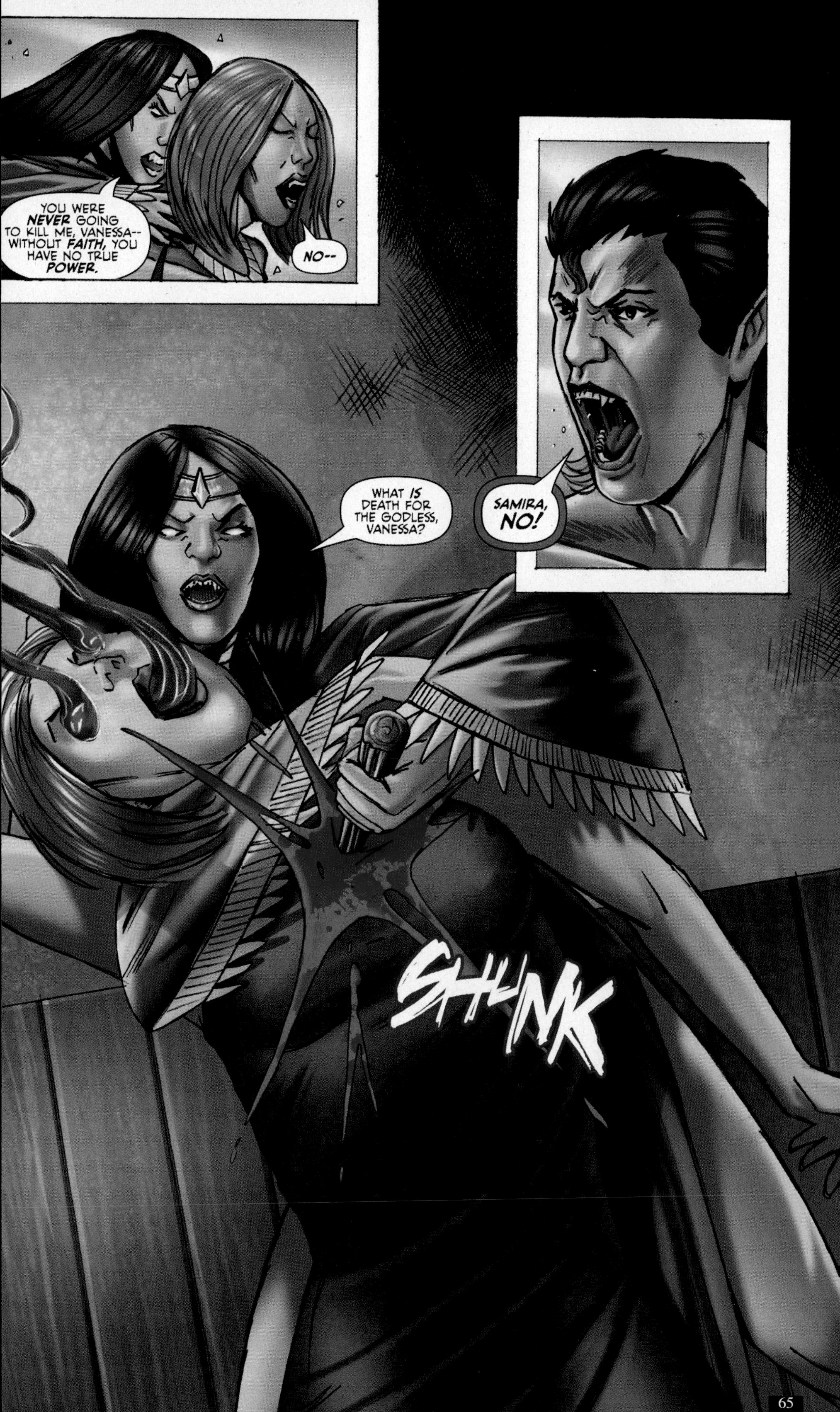

YOU WERE NEVER GOING TO KILL ME, VANESSA-- WITHOUT FAITH, YOU HAVE NO TRUE POWER.
NO--
SAMIRA, NO!
WHAT IS DEATH FOR THE GODLESS, VANESSA?
SHUNK

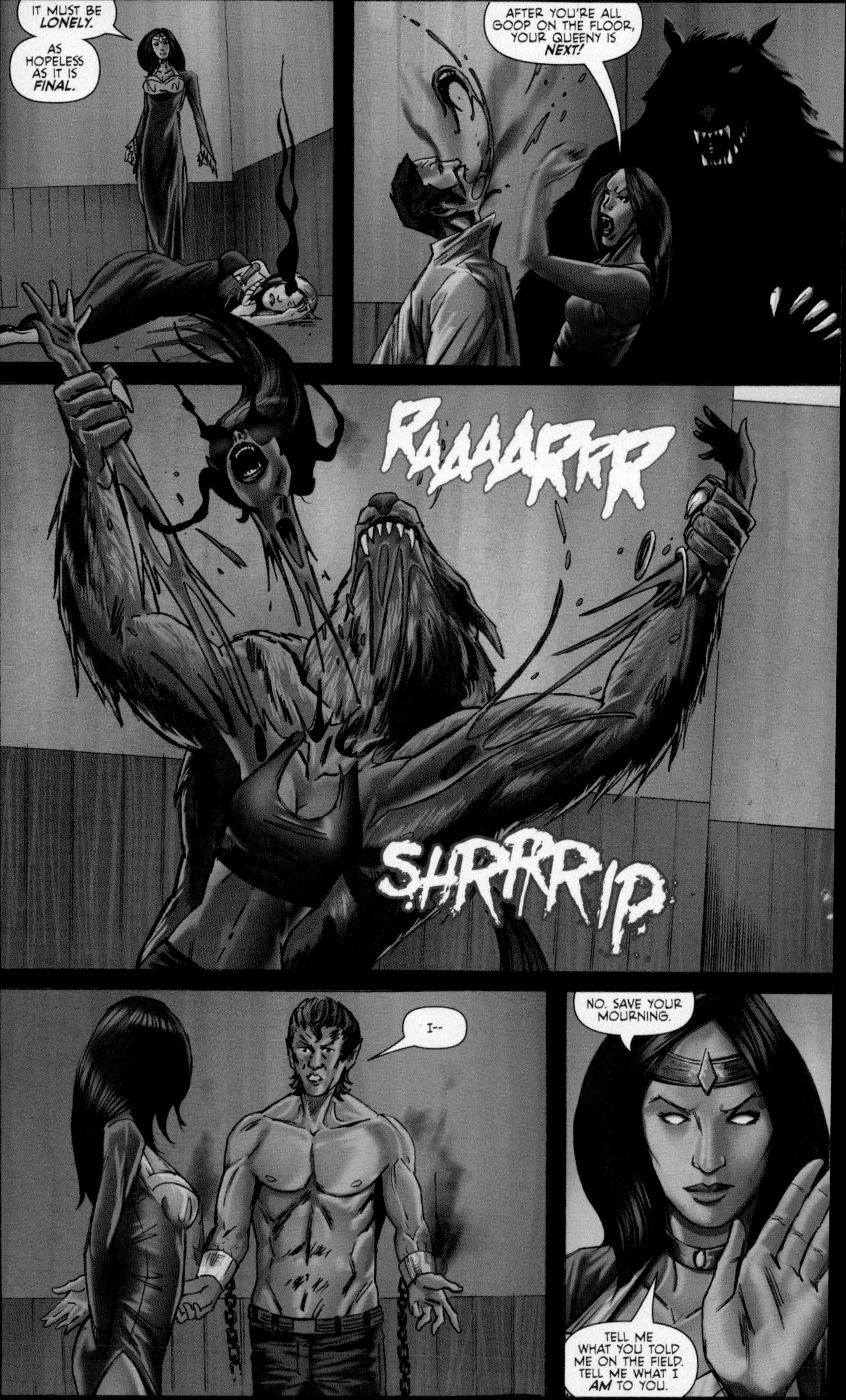
IT MUST BE LONELY.
AS HOPELESS AS IT IS FINAL.
AFTER YOU'RE ALL GOOP ON THE FLOOR, YOUR QUEENY IS NEXT!
RAAAARRR
SHRRRIP
I--
NO. SAVE YOUR MOURNING.
TELL ME WHAT YOU TOLD ME ON THE FIELD. TELL ME WHAT I AM TO YOU.

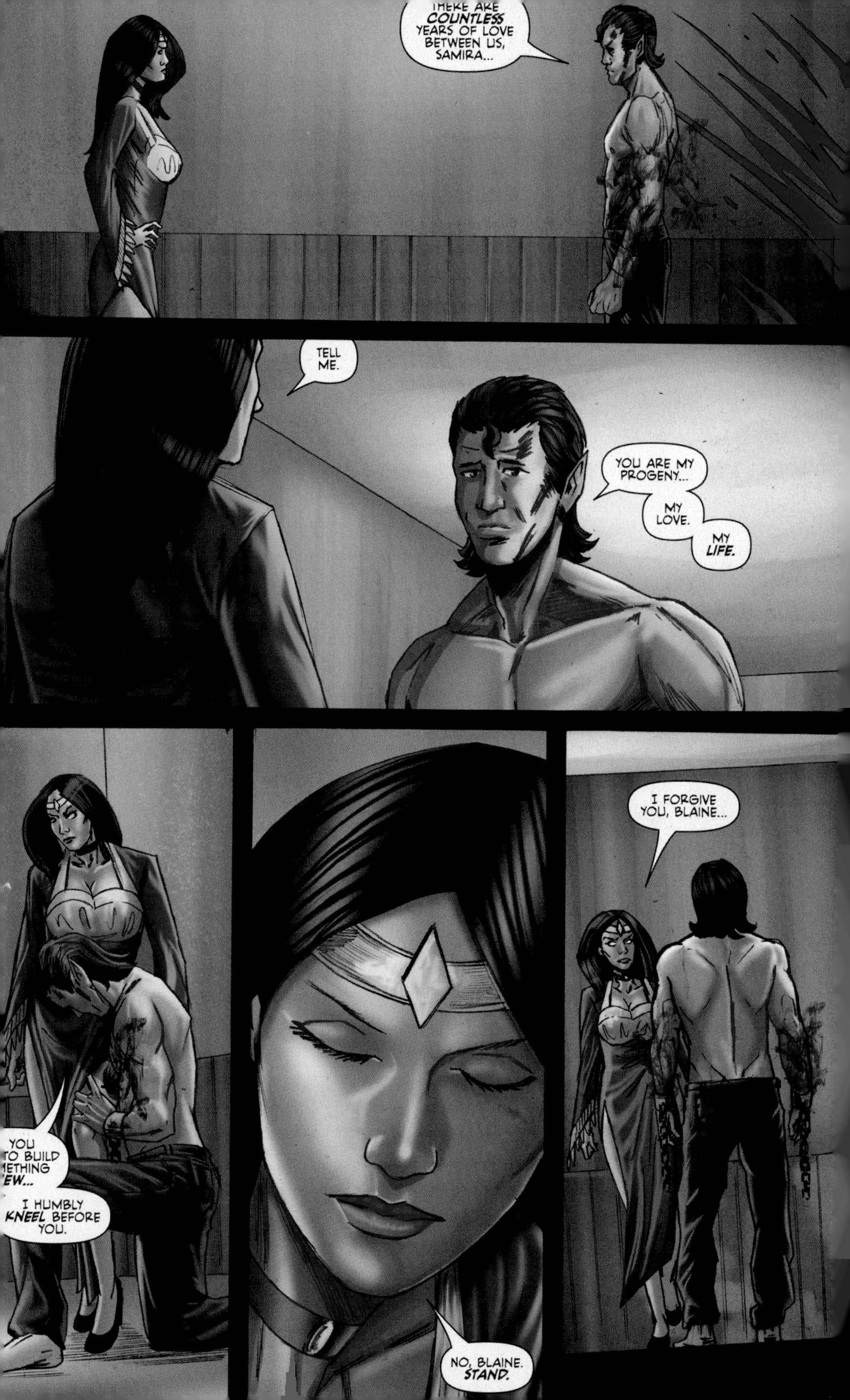
THERE ARE COUNTLESS YEARS OF LOVE BETWEEN US, SAMIRA...
TELL ME.
YOU ARE MY PROGENY...
MY LOVE.
MY LIFE.
YOU
TO BUILD
ETHING
EW...
I HUMBLY KNEEL BEFORE YOU.
NO, BLAINE. STAND.
I FORGIVE YOU, BLAINE...

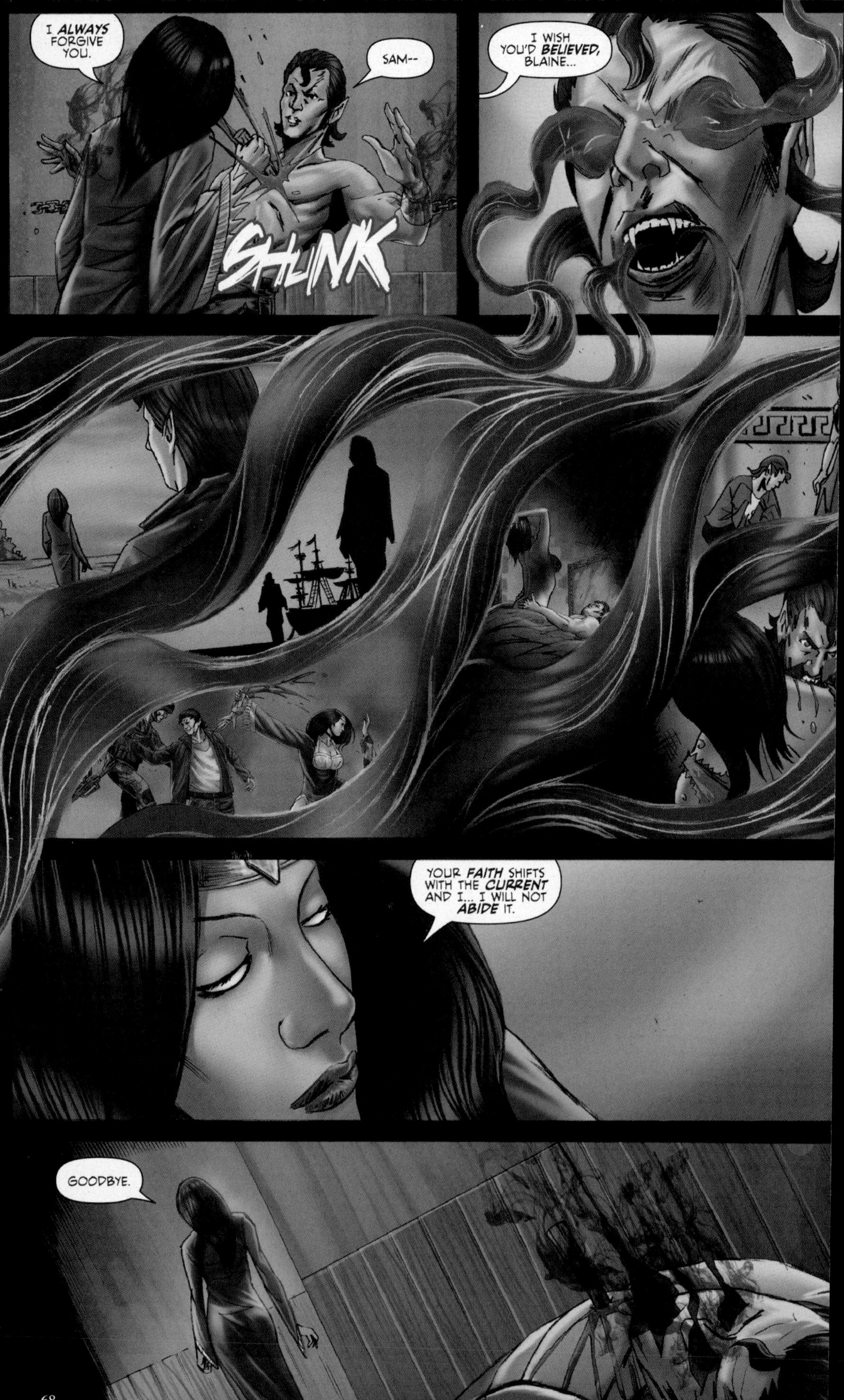
I ALWAYS FORGIVE YOU.
SAM--
SHUNK
I WISH YOU'D BELIEVED, BLAINE...
YOUR FAITH SHIFTS WITH THE CURRENT AND I... I WILL NOT ABIDE IT.
GOODBYE.

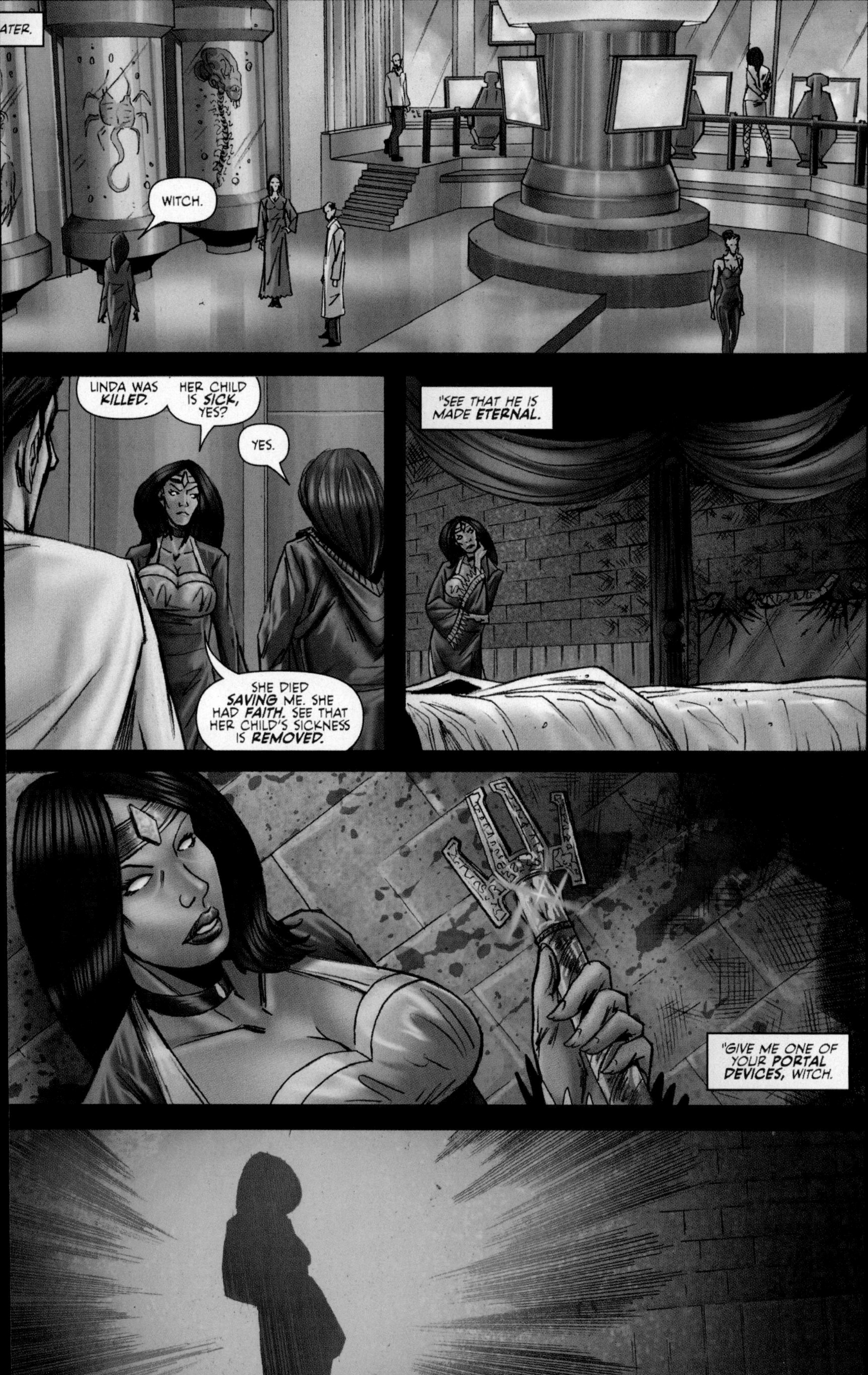

ATER.
WITCH.
LINDA WAS KILLED.
HER CHILD IS SICK, YES?
YES.
SHE DIED SAVING ME. SHE HAD FAITH. SEE THAT HER CHILD'S SICKNESS IS REMOVED.
"SEE THAT HE IS MADE ETERNAL.
"GIVE ME ONE OF YOUR PORTAL DEVICES, WITCH.
"I WISH TO TAKE A WALK."

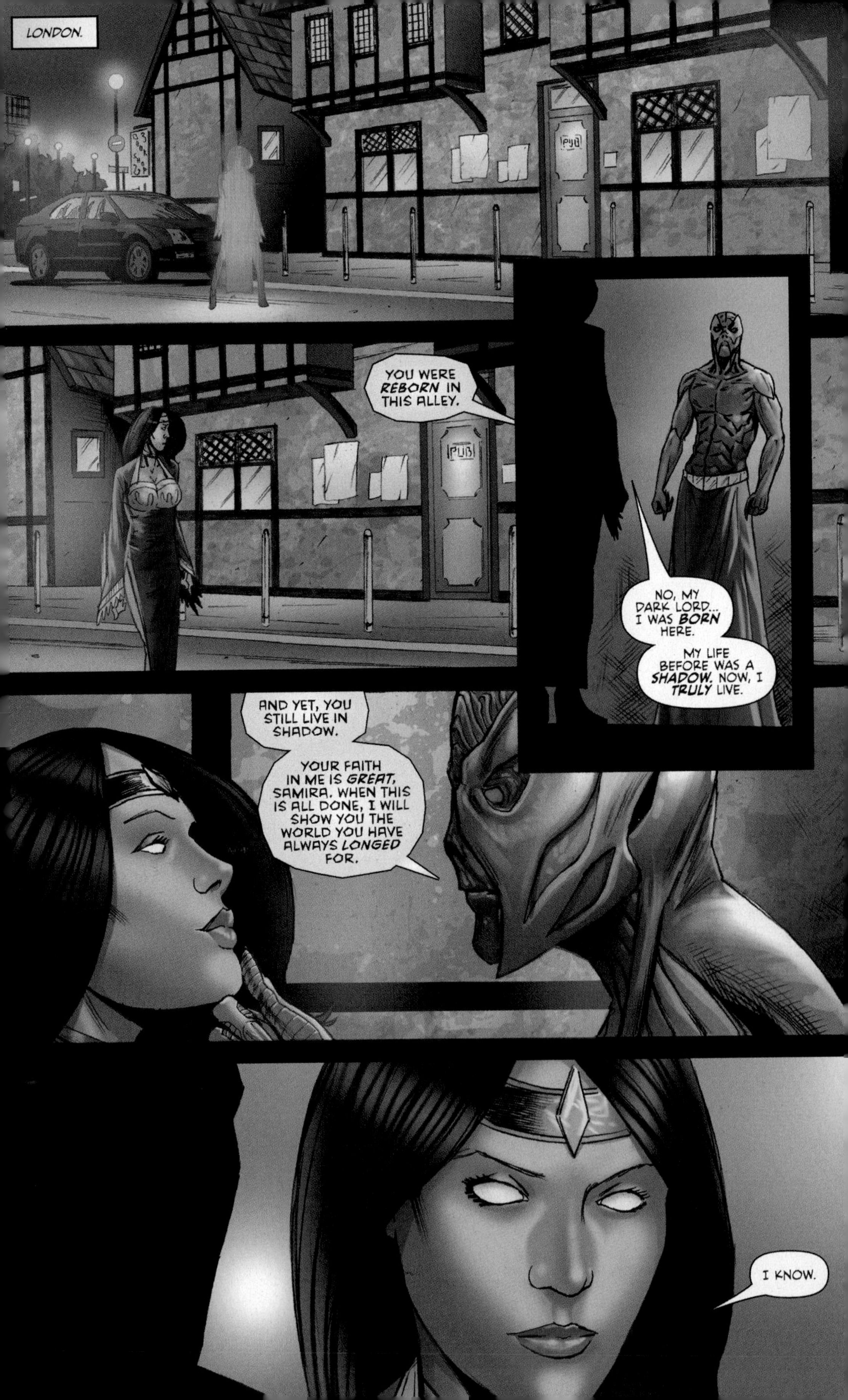
LONDON.
YOU WERE REBORN IN THIS ALLEY.
NO, MY DARK LORD... I WAS BORN HERE.
MY LIFE BEFORE WAS A SHADOW. NOW, I TRULY LIVE.
AND YET, YOU STILL LIVE IN SHADOW.
YOUR FAITH IN ME IS GREAT, SAMIRA. WHEN THIS IS ALL DONE, I WILL SHOW YOU THE WORLD YOU HAVE ALWAYS LONGED FOR.
I KNOW.

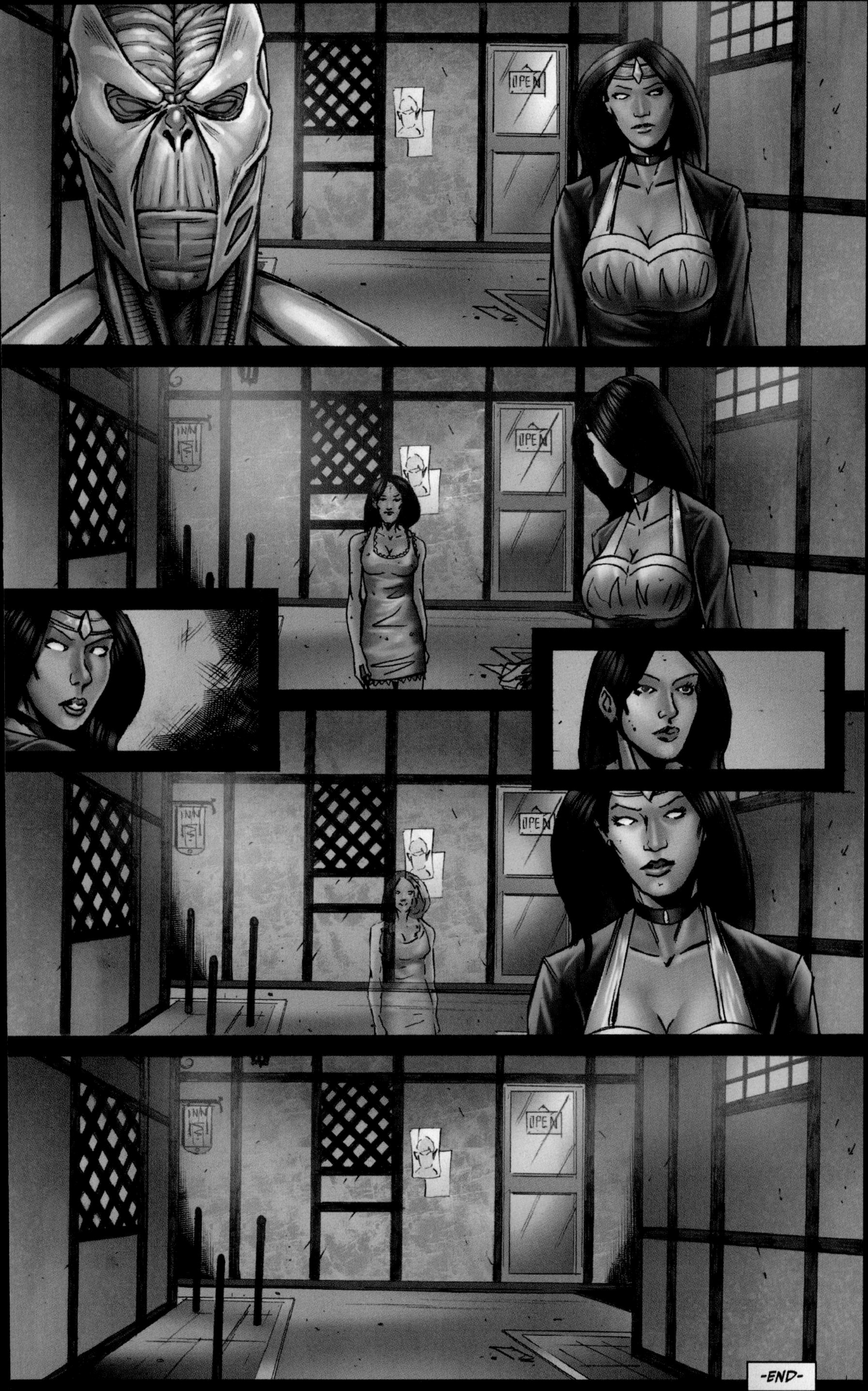
OPEN
INN
-END-

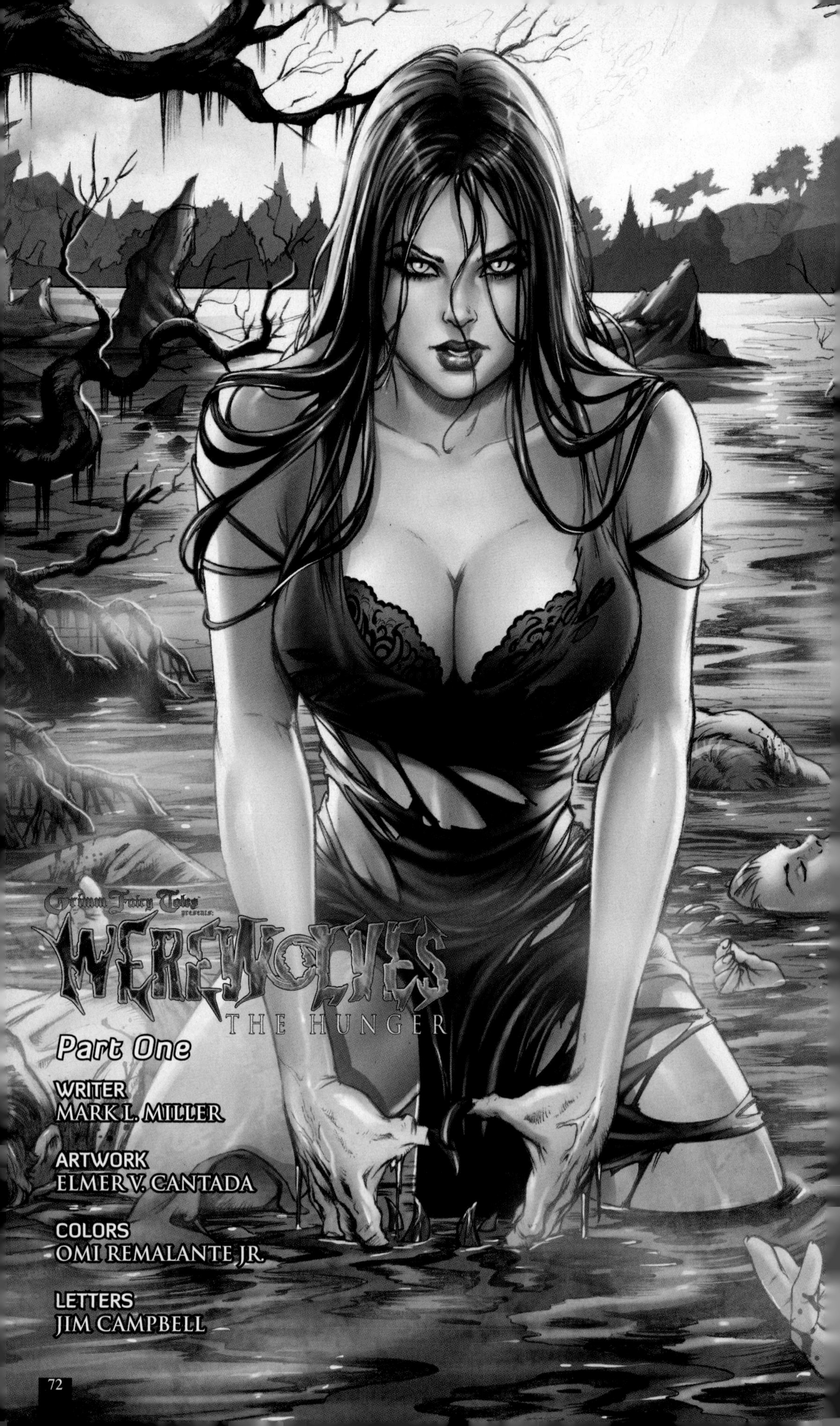
Grimm Fairy Tales presents:
WEREWOLVES
THE HUNGER
Part One
WRITER
MARK L. MILLER
ARTWORK
ELMER V. CANTADA
COLORS
OMI REMALANTE JR.
LETTERS
JIM CAMPBELL

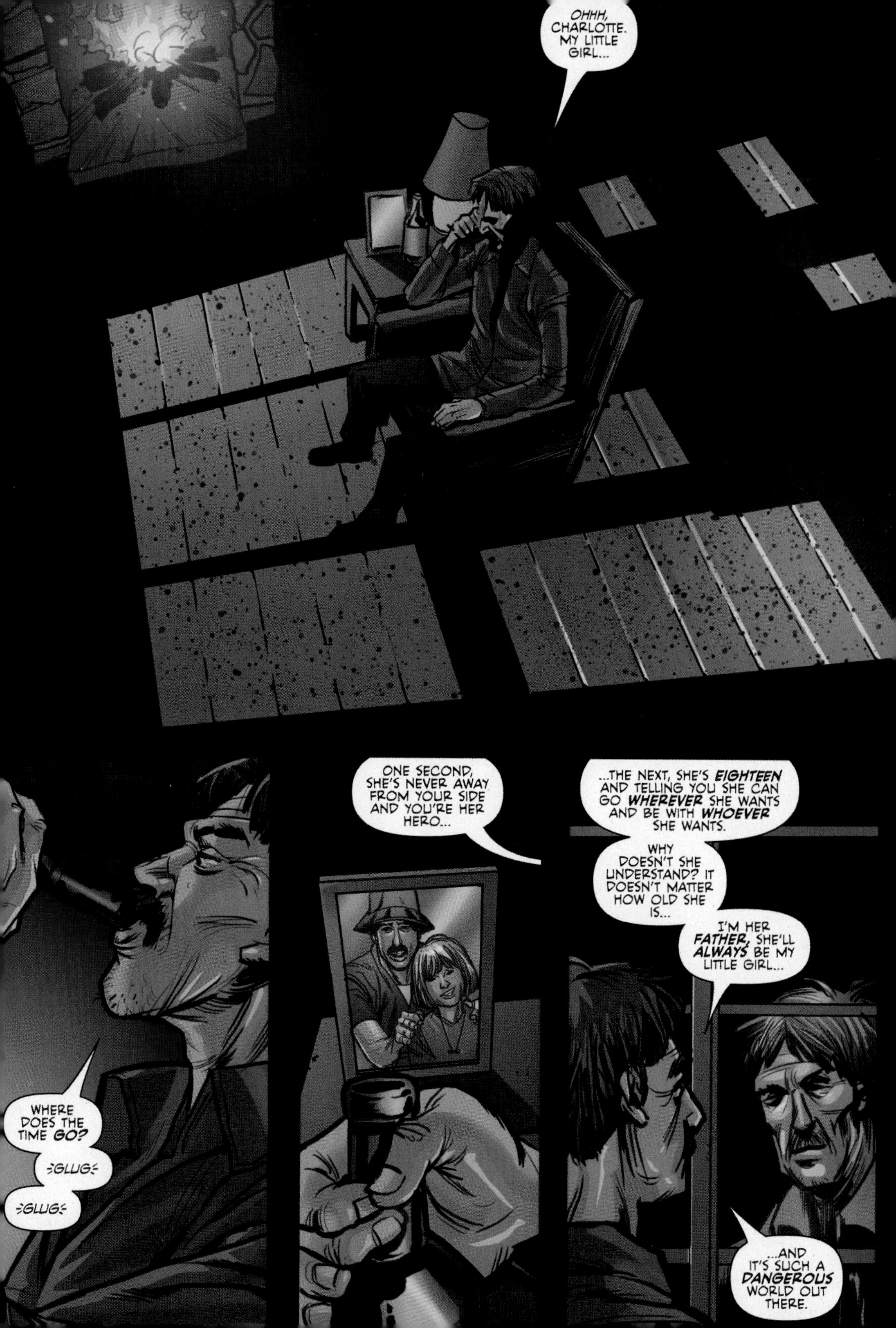
OHHH, CHARLOTTE. MY LITTLE GIRL...
WHERE DOES THE TIME GO?
GLUG
GLUG
ONE SECOND, SHE'S NEVER AWAY FROM YOUR SIDE AND YOU'RE HER HERO...
...THE NEXT, SHE'S EIGHTEEN AND TELLING YOU SHE CAN GO WHEREVER SHE WANTS AND BE WITH WHOEVER SHE WANTS.
WHY DOESN'T SHE UNDERSTAND? IT DOESN'T MATTER HOW OLD SHE IS...
I'M HER FATHER, SHE'LL ALWAYS BE MY LITTLE GIRL...
...AND IT'S SUCH A DANGEROUS WORLD OUT THERE.

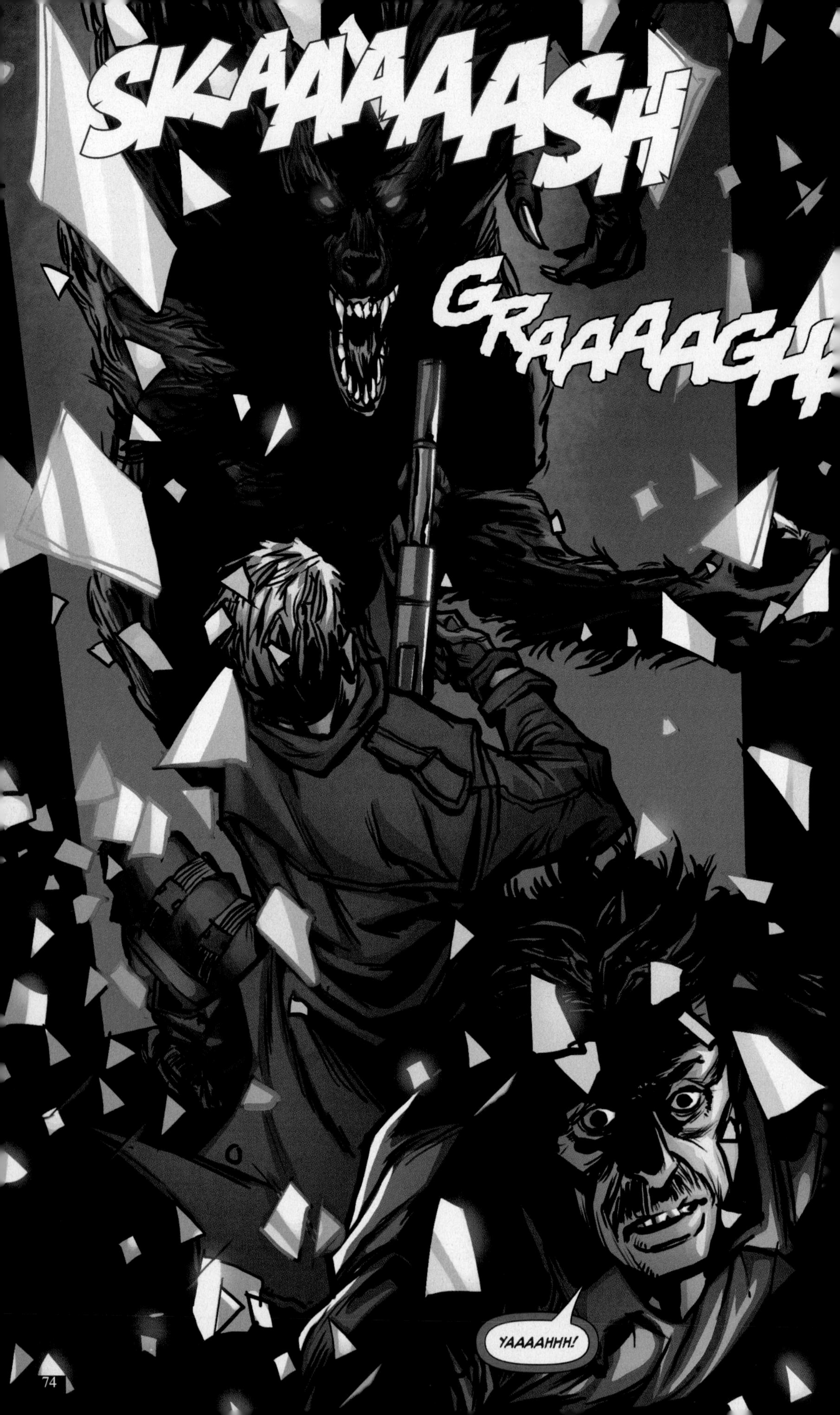
SKAAAAAASH
GRAAAAGH
YAAAAHHH!

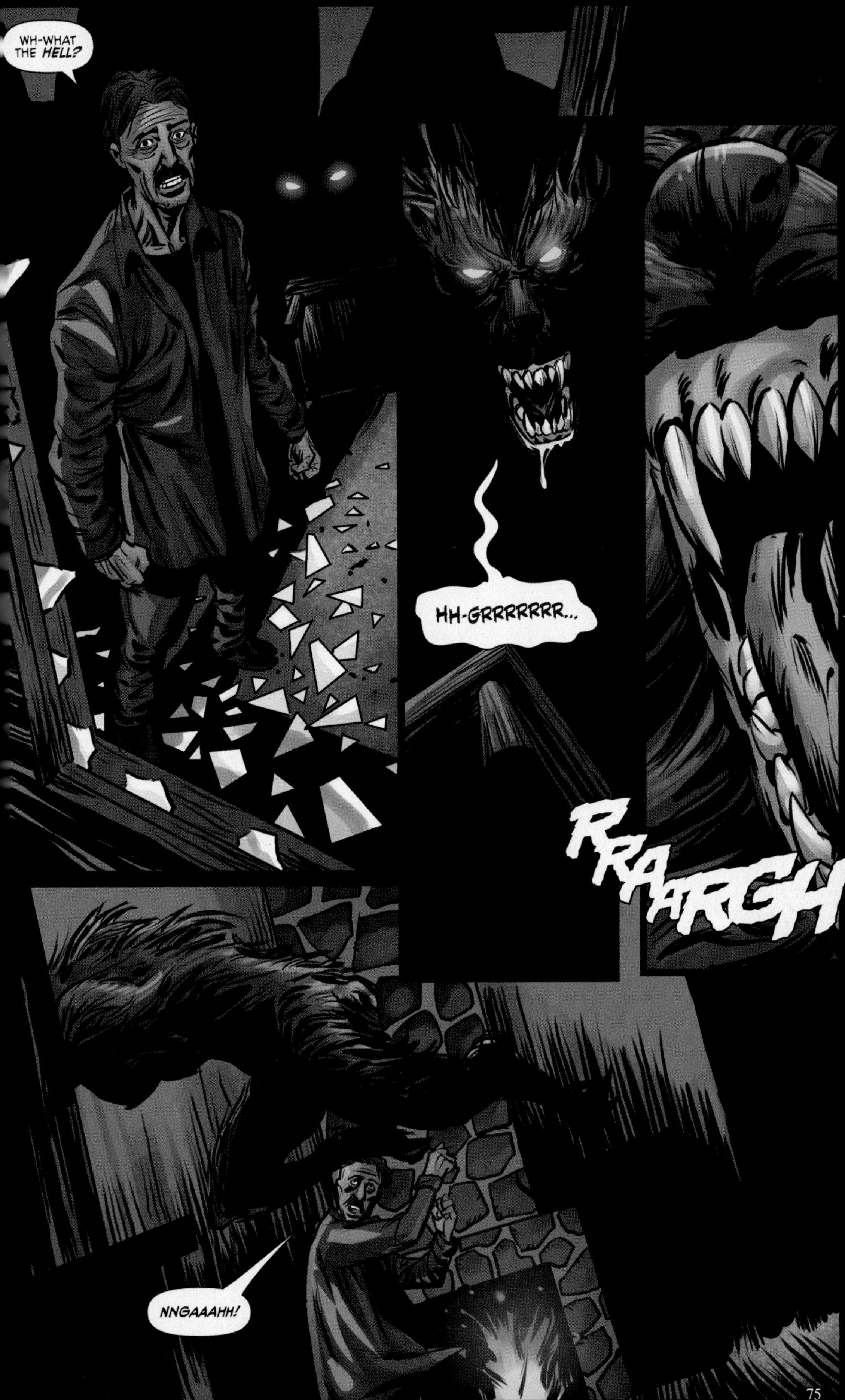
WH-WHAT THE HELL?
HH-GRRRRRRR...
RRAARGH
NNGAAAHH!

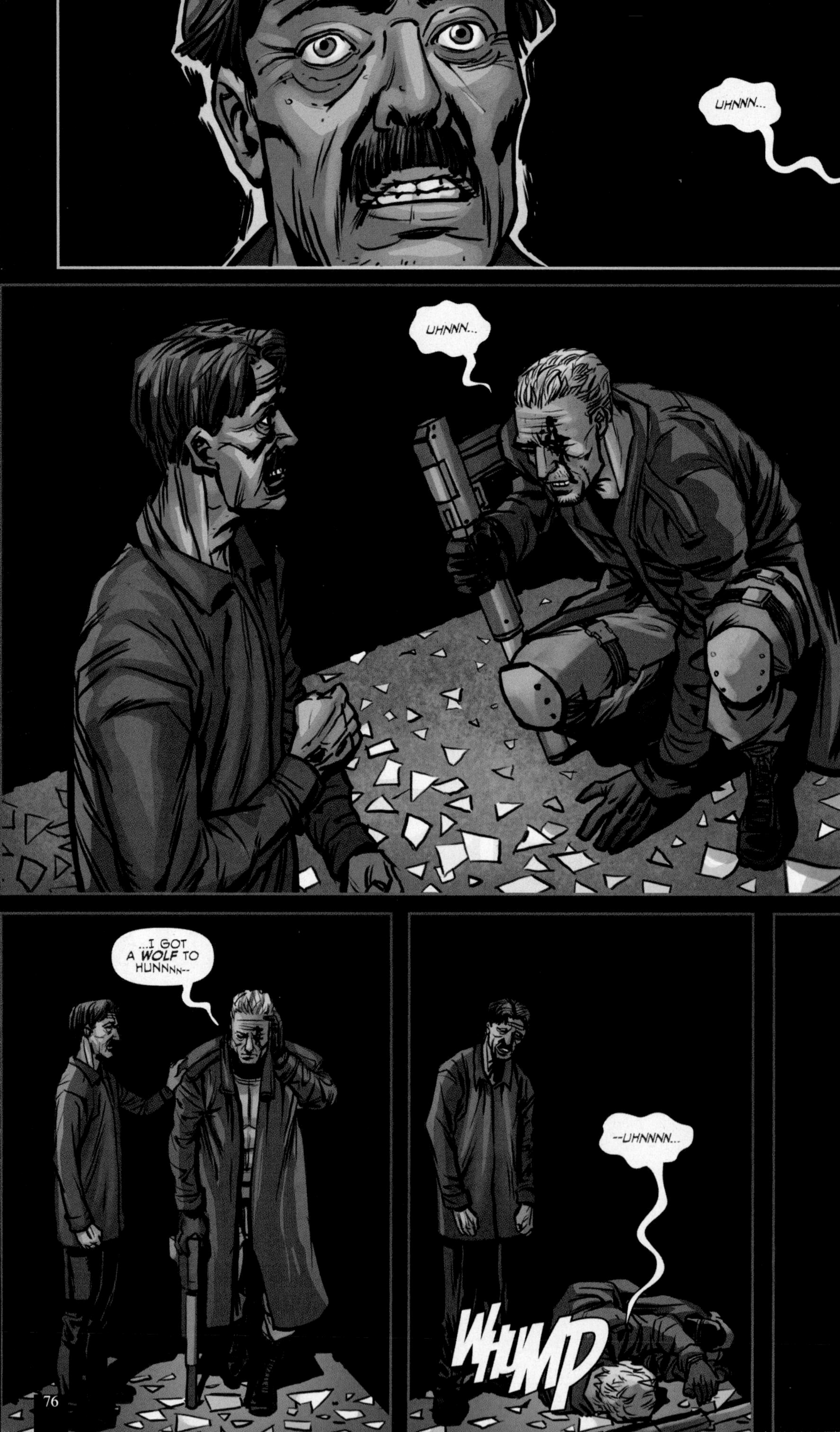

UHNNN...
UHNNN...
...I GOT A WOLF TO HUNNNNN--
--UHNNNN...
WHUMP

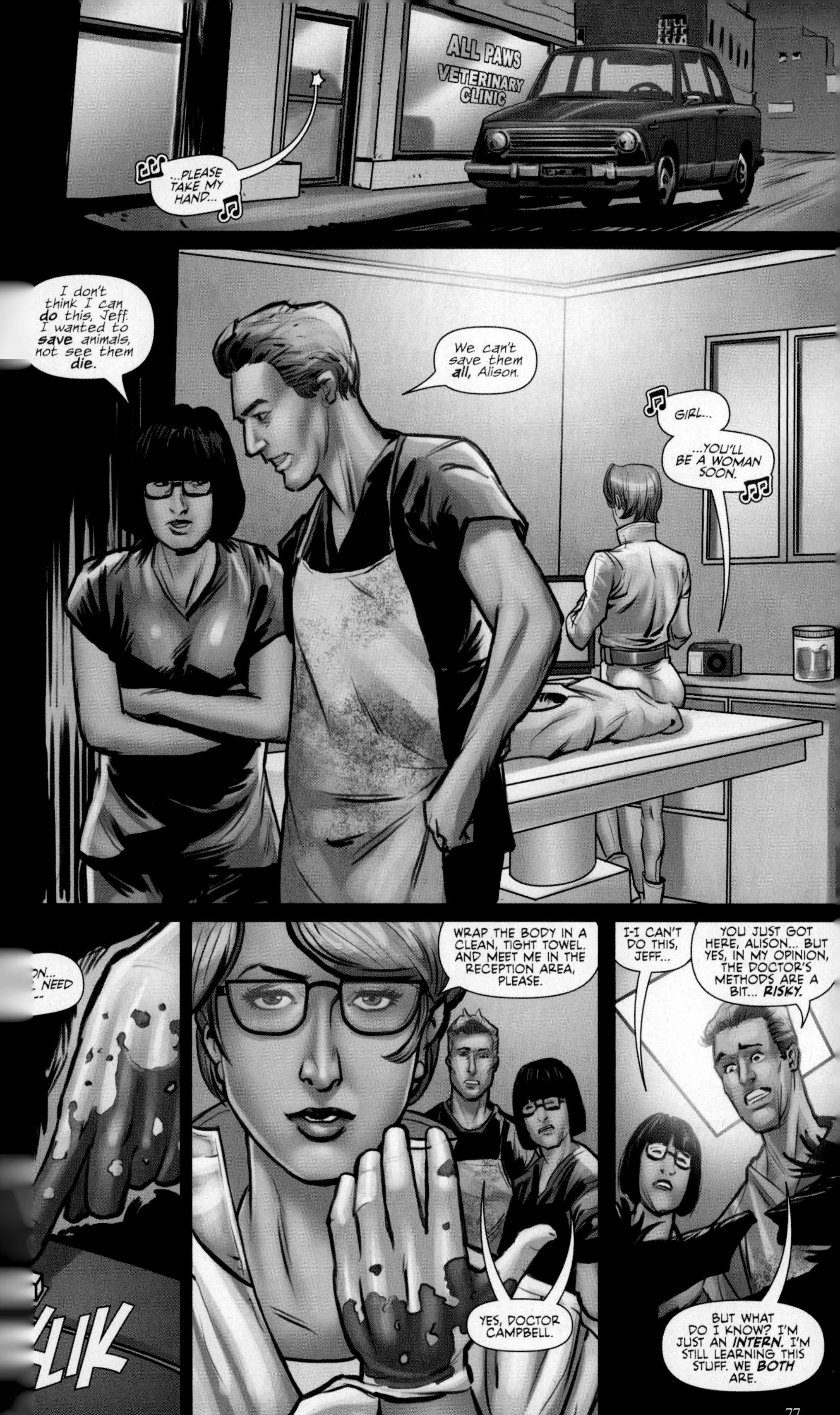
ALL PAWS
VETERINARY
CLINIC
...PLEASE TAKE MY HAND...
I don't think I can do this, Jeff. I wanted to save animals, not see them die.
We can't save them all, Alison.
GIRL...
...YOU'LL BE A WOMAN SOON.
WRAP THE BODY IN A CLEAN, TIGHT TOWEL. AND MEET ME IN THE RECEPTION AREA, PLEASE.
YES, DOCTOR CAMPBELL.
I-I CAN'T DO THIS, JEFF...
YOU JUST GOT HERE, ALISON... BUT YES, IN MY OPINION, THE DOCTOR'S METHODS ARE A BIT... RISKY.
BUT WHAT DO I KNOW? I'M JUST AN INTERN. I'M STILL LEARNING THIS STUFF. WE BOTH ARE.

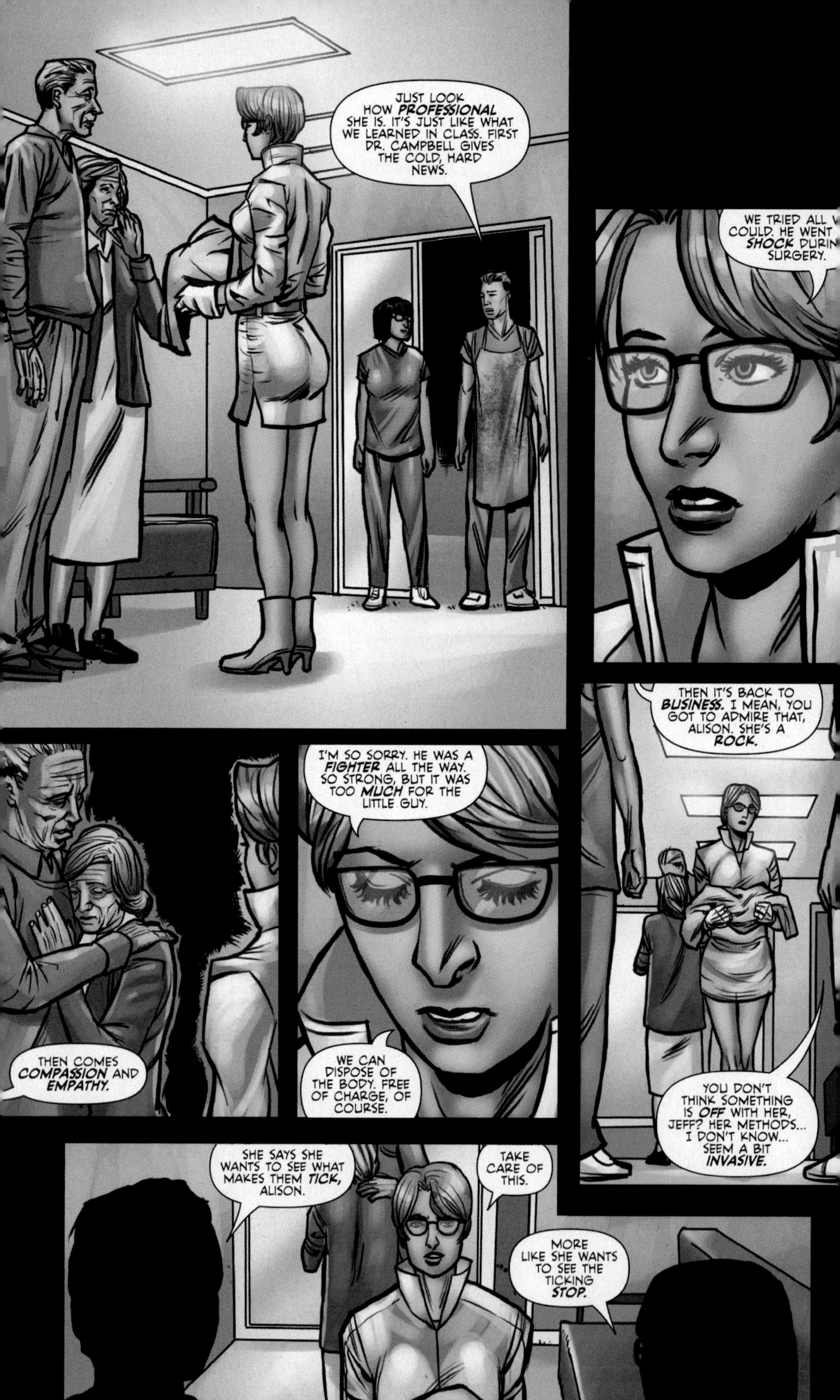
JUST LOOK HOW PROFESSIONAL SHE IS. IT'S JUST LIKE WHAT WE LEARNED IN CLASS. FIRST DR. CAMPBELL GIVES THE COLD, HARD NEWS.
WE TRIED ALL COULD. HE WENT SHOCK DURIN SURGERY.
THEN COMES COMPASSION AND EMPATHY.
I'M SO SORRY. HE WAS A FIGHTER ALL THE WAY. SO STRONG, BUT IT WAS TOO MUCH FOR THE LITTLE GUY.
WE CAN DISPOSE OF THE BODY. FREE OF CHARGE, OF COURSE.
THEN IT'S BACK TO BUSINESS. I MEAN, YOU GOT TO ADMIRE THAT, ALISON. SHE'S A ROCK.
YOU DON'T THINK SOMETHING IS OFF WITH HER, JEFF? HER METHODS... I DON'T KNOW... SEEM A BIT INVASIVE.
SHE SAYS SHE WANTS TO SEE WHAT MAKES THEM TICK, ALISON.
TAKE CARE OF THIS.
MORE LIKE SHE WANTS TO SEE THE TICKING STOP.

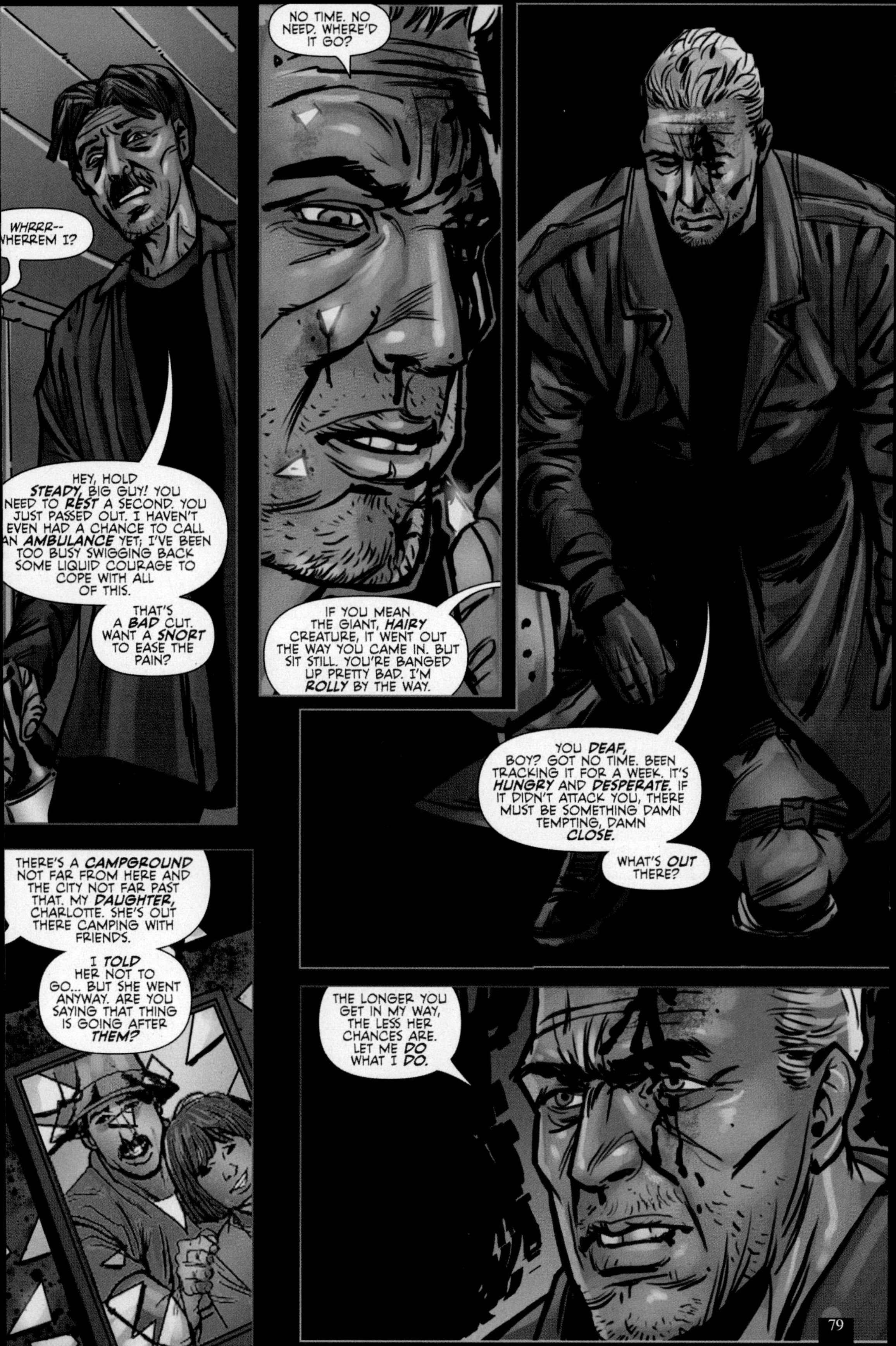

WHRRR-- WHERREM I?
NO TIME. NO NEED. WHERE'D IT GO?
HEY, HOLD STEADY, BIG GUY! YOU NEED TO REST A SECOND. YOU JUST PASSED OUT. I HAVEN'T EVEN HAD A CHANCE TO CALL AN AMBULANCE YET; I'VE BEEN TOO BUSY SWIGGING BACK SOME LIQUID COURAGE TO COPE WITH ALL OF THIS.
THAT'S A BAD CUT. WANT A SNORT TO EASE THE PAIN?
IF YOU MEAN THE GIANT, HAIRY CREATURE, IT WENT OUT THE WAY YOU CAME IN. BUT SIT STILL. YOU'RE BANGED UP PRETTY BAD. I'M ROLLY BY THE WAY.
YOU DEAF, BOY? GOT NO TIME. BEEN TRACKING IT FOR A WEEK. IT'S HUNGRY AND DESPERATE. IF IT DIDN'T ATTACK YOU, THERE MUST BE SOMETHING DAMN TEMPTING, DAMN CLOSE.
WHAT'S OUT THERE?
THERE'S A CAMPGROUND NOT FAR FROM HERE AND THE CITY NOT FAR PAST THAT. MY DAUGHTER, CHARLOTTE. SHE'S OUT THERE CAMPING WITH FRIENDS.
I TOLD HER NOT TO GO... BUT SHE WENT ANYWAY. ARE YOU SAYING THAT THING IS GOING AFTER THEM?
THE LONGER YOU GET IN MY WAY, THE LESS HER CHANCES ARE. LET ME DO WHAT I DO.

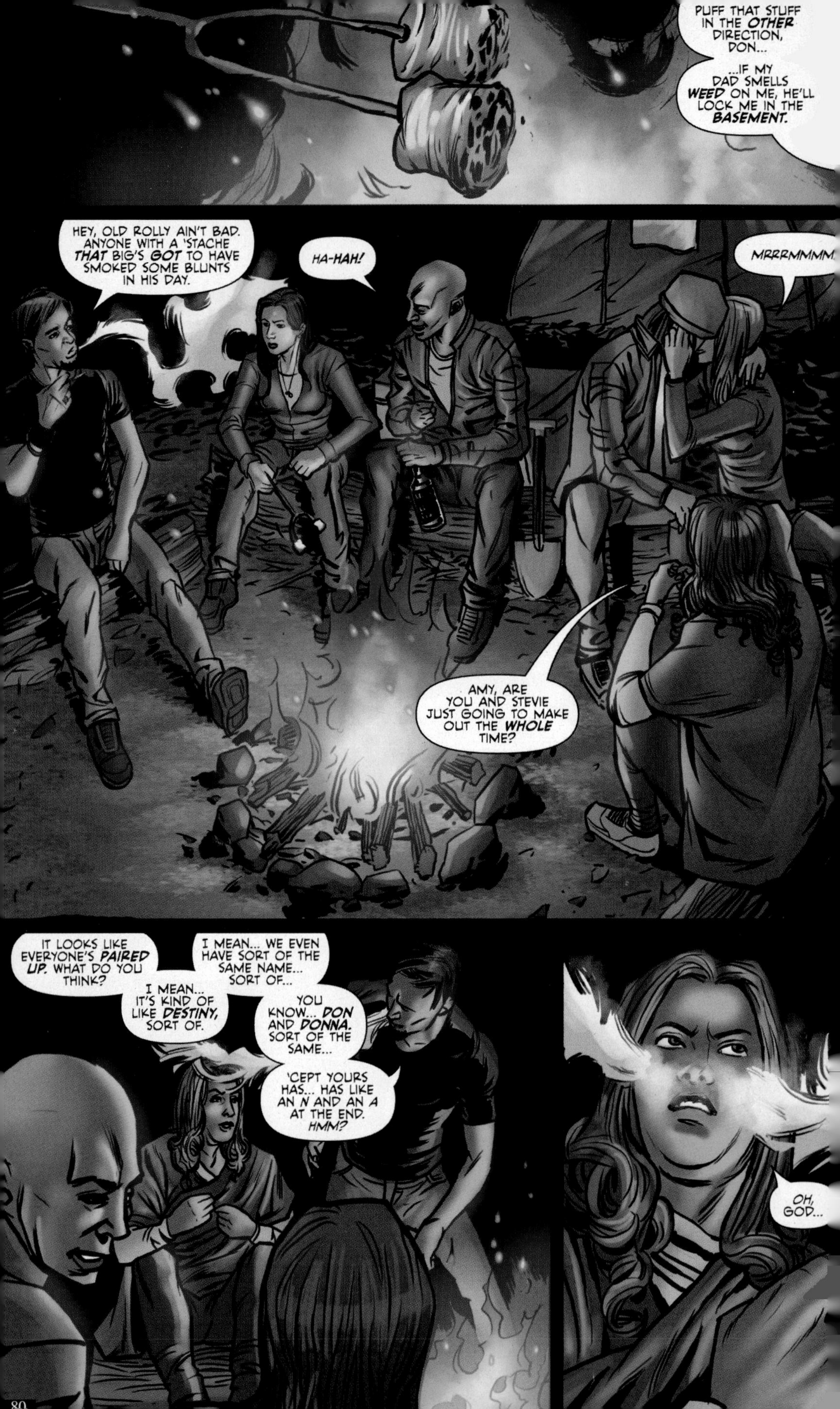
PUFF THAT STUFF IN THE OTHER DIRECTION, DON...
...IF MY DAD SMELLS WEED ON ME, HE'LL LOCK ME IN THE BASEMENT.
HEY, OLD ROLLY AIN'T BAD. ANYONE WITH A 'STACHE THAT BIG'S GOT TO HAVE SMOKED SOME BLUNTS IN HIS DAY.
HA-HAH!
MRRRMMMM.
AMY, ARE YOU AND STEVIE JUST GOING TO MAKE OUT THE WHOLE TIME?
IT LOOKS LIKE EVERYONE'S PAIRED UP. WHAT DO YOU THINK?
I MEAN... IT'S KIND OF LIKE DESTINY, SORT OF.
I MEAN... WE EVEN HAVE SORT OF THE SAME NAME... SORT OF...
YOU KNOW... DON AND DONNA. SORT OF THE SAME...
'CEPT YOURS HAS... HAS LIKE AN N AND AN A AT THE END. HMM?
OH, GOD...

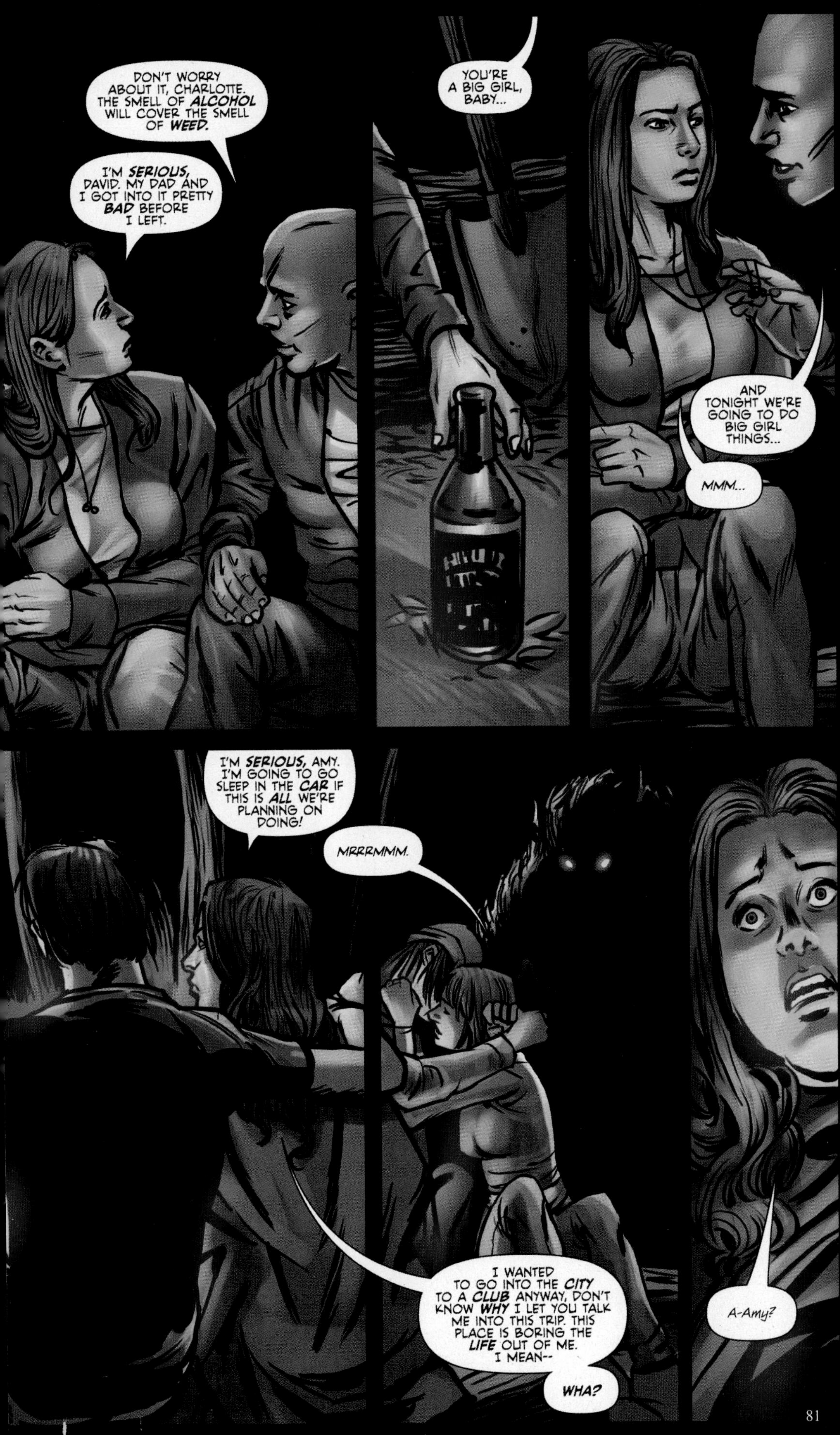

DON'T WORRY ABOUT IT, CHARLOTTE. THE SMELL OF ALCOHOL WILL COVER THE SMELL OF WEED.
I'M SERIOUS, DAVID. MY DAD AND I GOT INTO IT PRETTY BAD BEFORE I LEFT.
YOU'RE A BIG GIRL, BABY...
AND TONIGHT WE'RE GOING TO DO BIG GIRL THINGS...
MMM...
I'M SERIOUS, AMY. I'M GOING TO GO SLEEP IN THE CAR IF THIS IS ALL WE'RE PLANNING ON DOING!
MRRRMMM.
I WANTED TO GO INTO THE CITY TO A CLUB ANYWAY, DON'T KNOW WHY I LET YOU TALK ME INTO THIS TRIP. THIS PLACE IS BORING THE LIFE OUT OF ME. I MEAN--
WHA?
A-Amy?

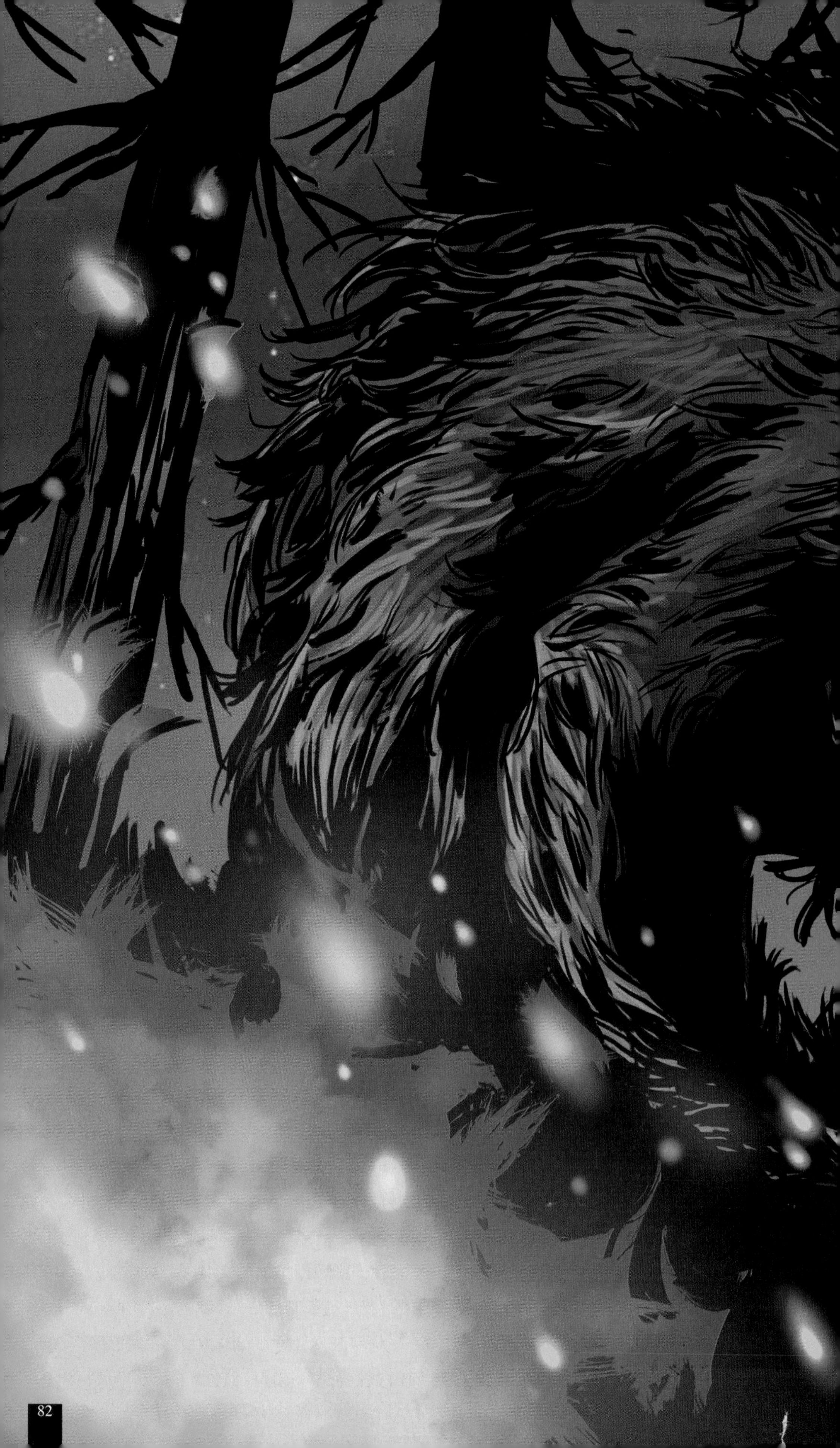

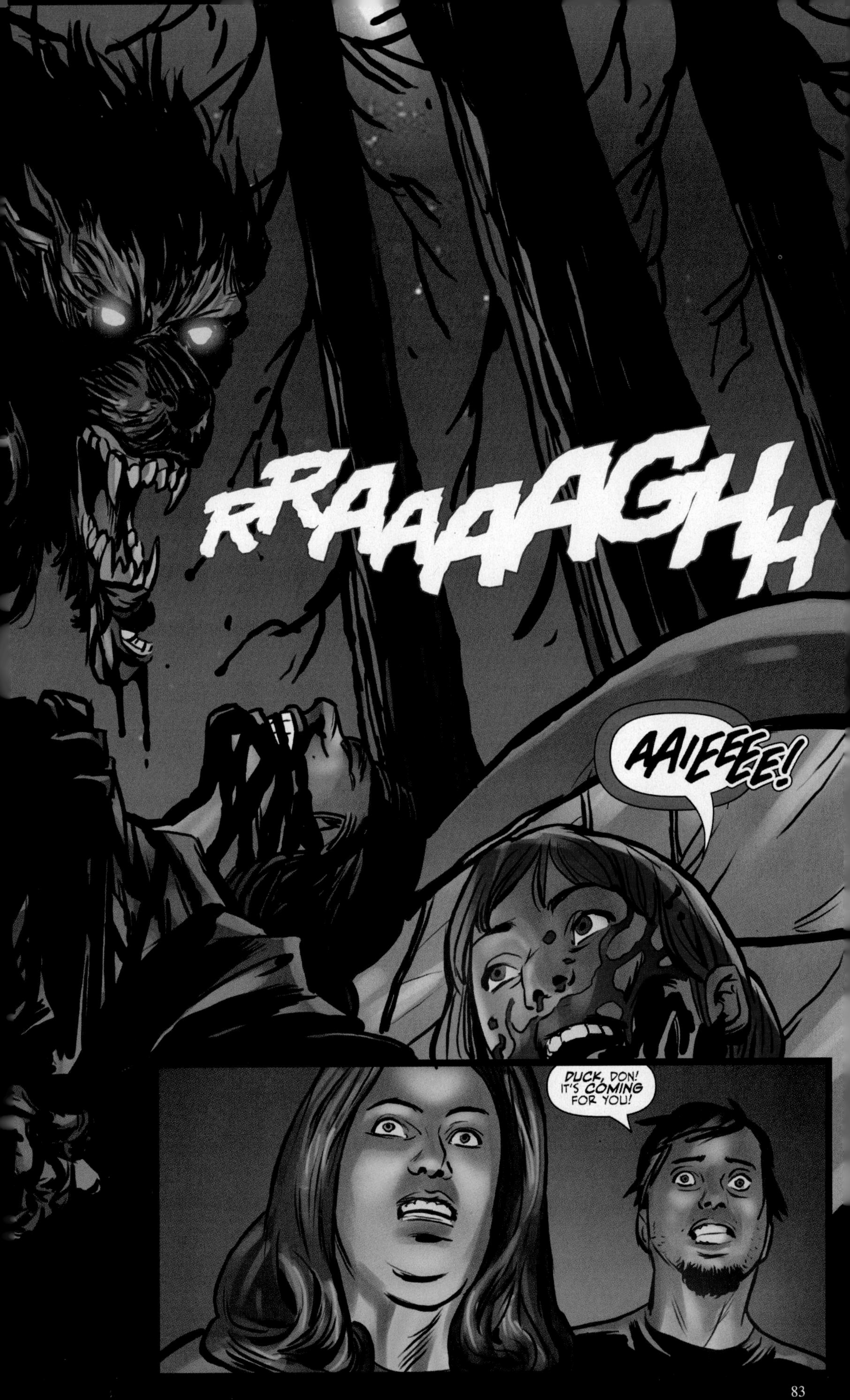
rRAAAAAGHH
AAIEEEEE!
DUCK, DON! IT'S COMING FOR YOU!

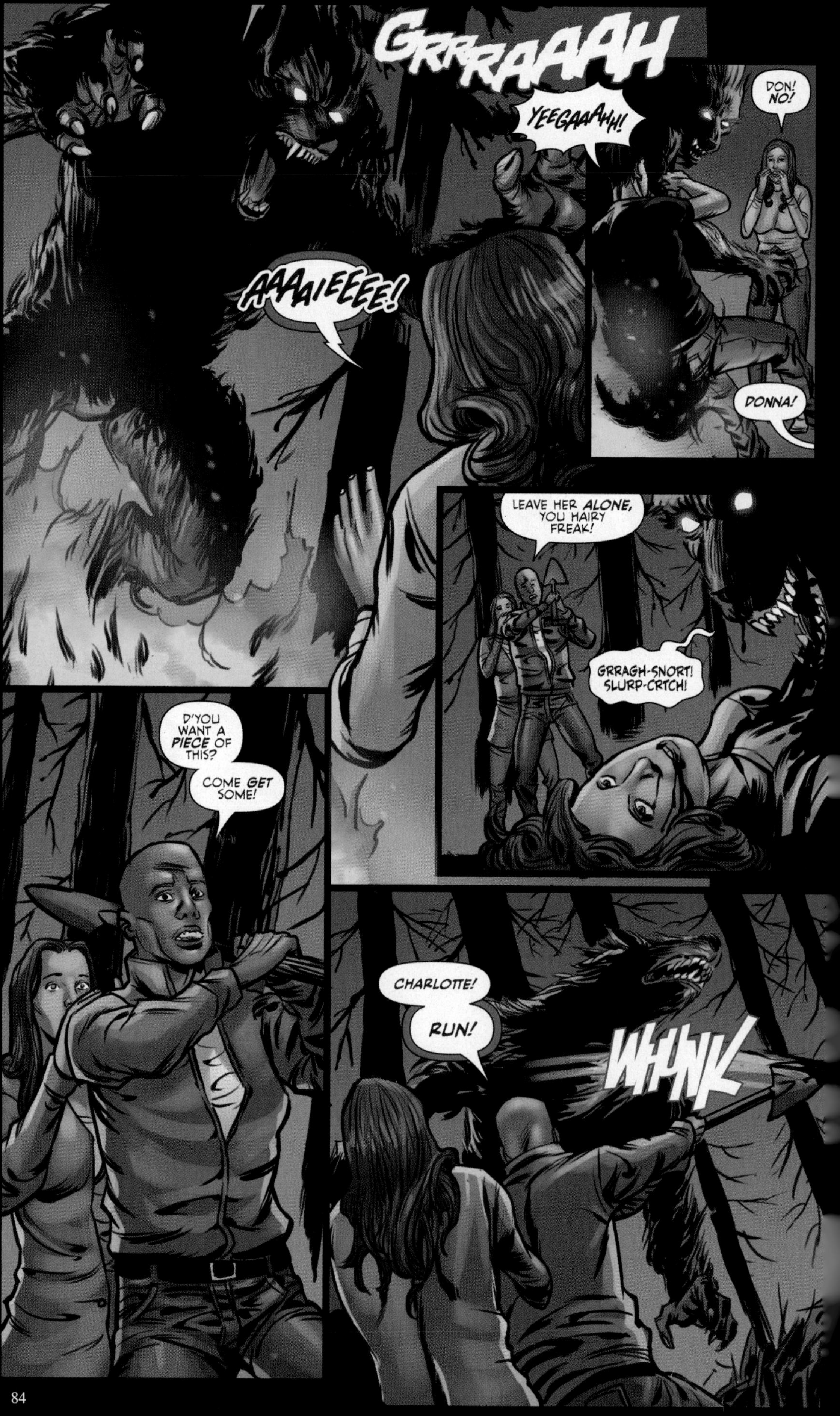
GRRRAAAAH
YEEGAAAAHH!
AAAAIEEEE!
DON! NO!
DONNA!
LEAVE HER ALONE, YOU HAIRY FREAK!
GRRAGH-SNORT! SLURP-CRTCH!
D'YOU WANT A PIECE OF THIS?
COME GET SOME!
CHARLOTTE!
RUN!
WHUNK

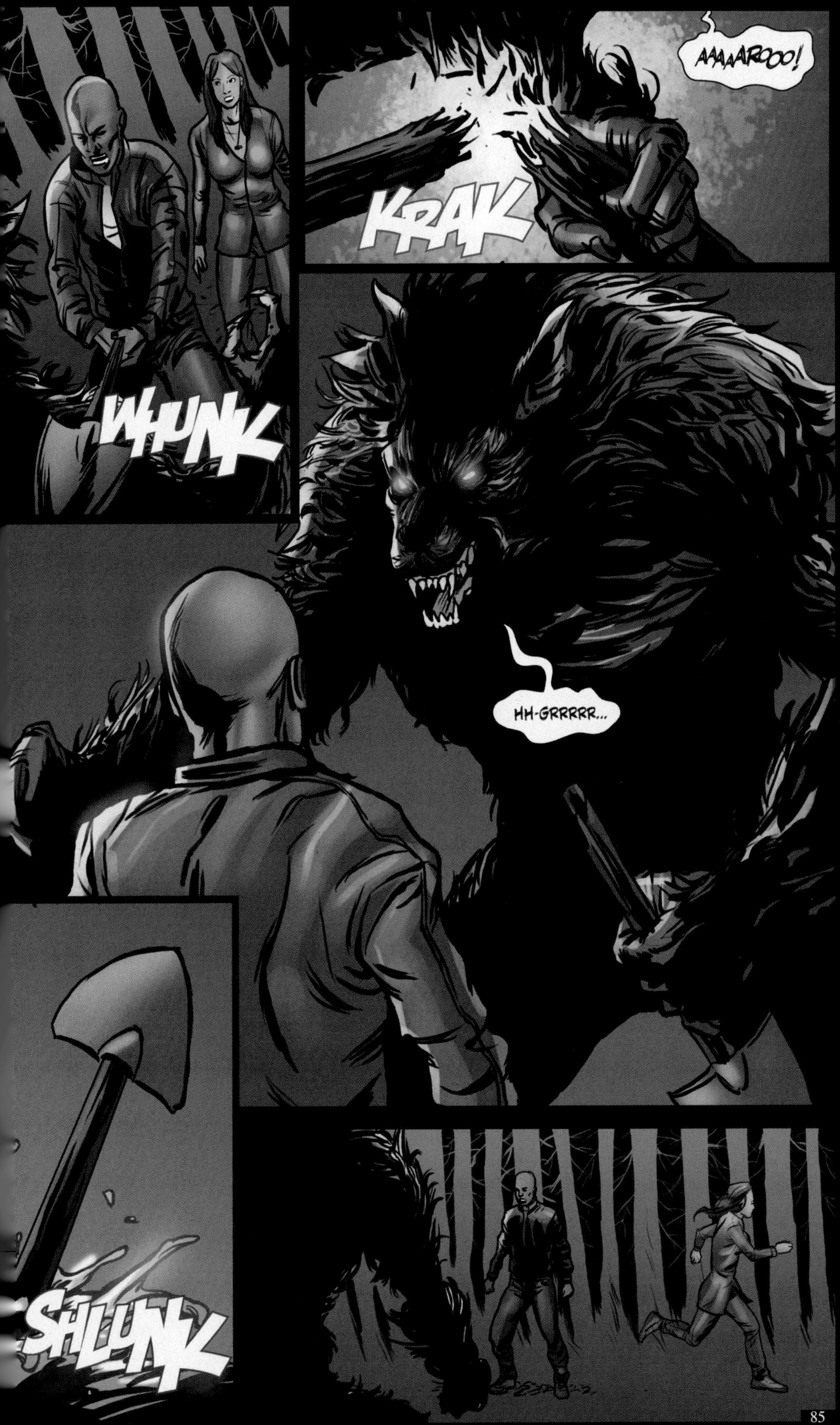
WHUNK
AAAAAROOO!
KRAK
HH-GRRRRR...
SHLUNK

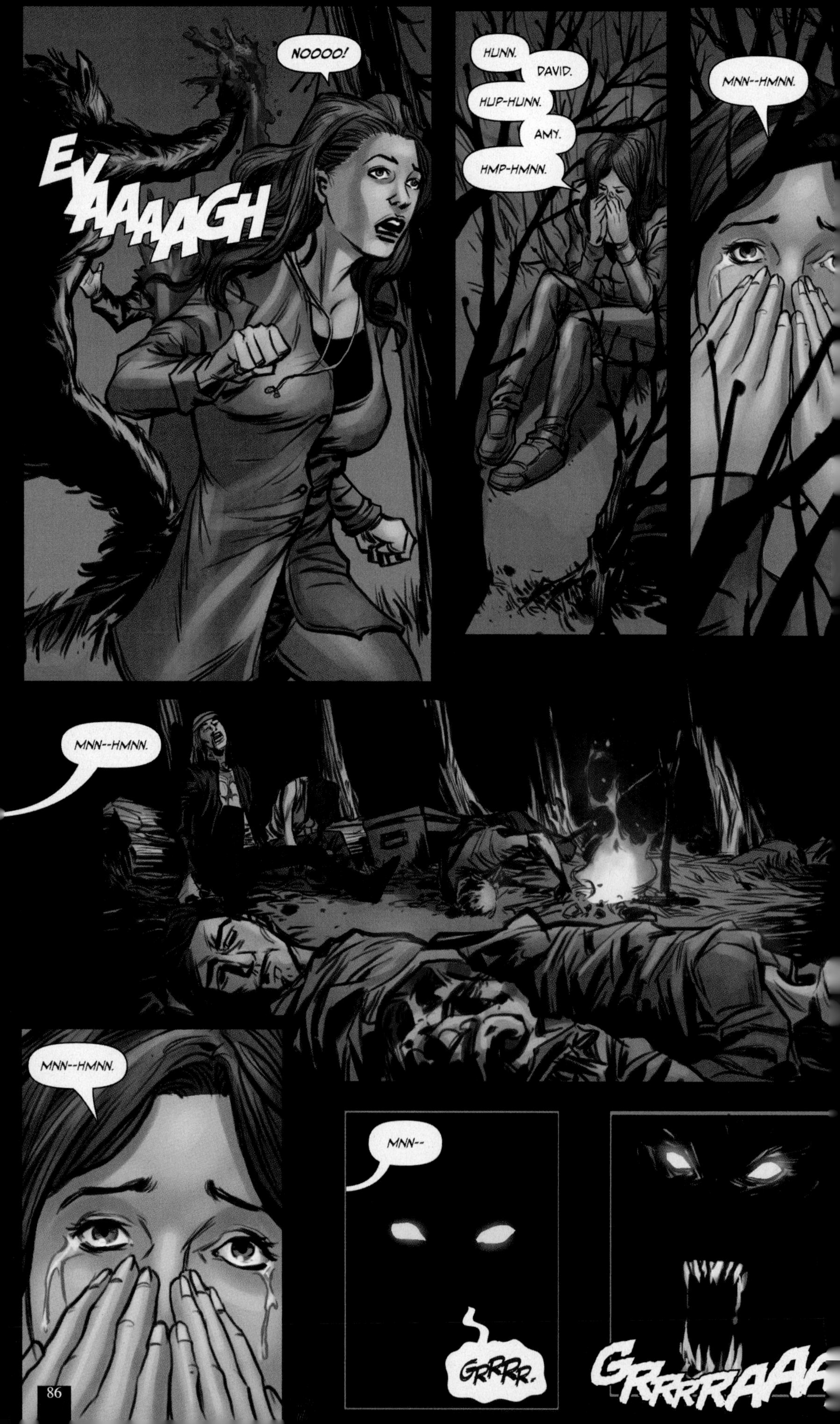
EYAAAAGH
NOOOO!
HUNN.
DAVID.
HUP-HUNN.
AMY.
HMP-HMNN.
MNN--HMNN.
MNN--HMNN.
MNN--HMNN.
MNN--
GRRRR.
GRRRRAAA

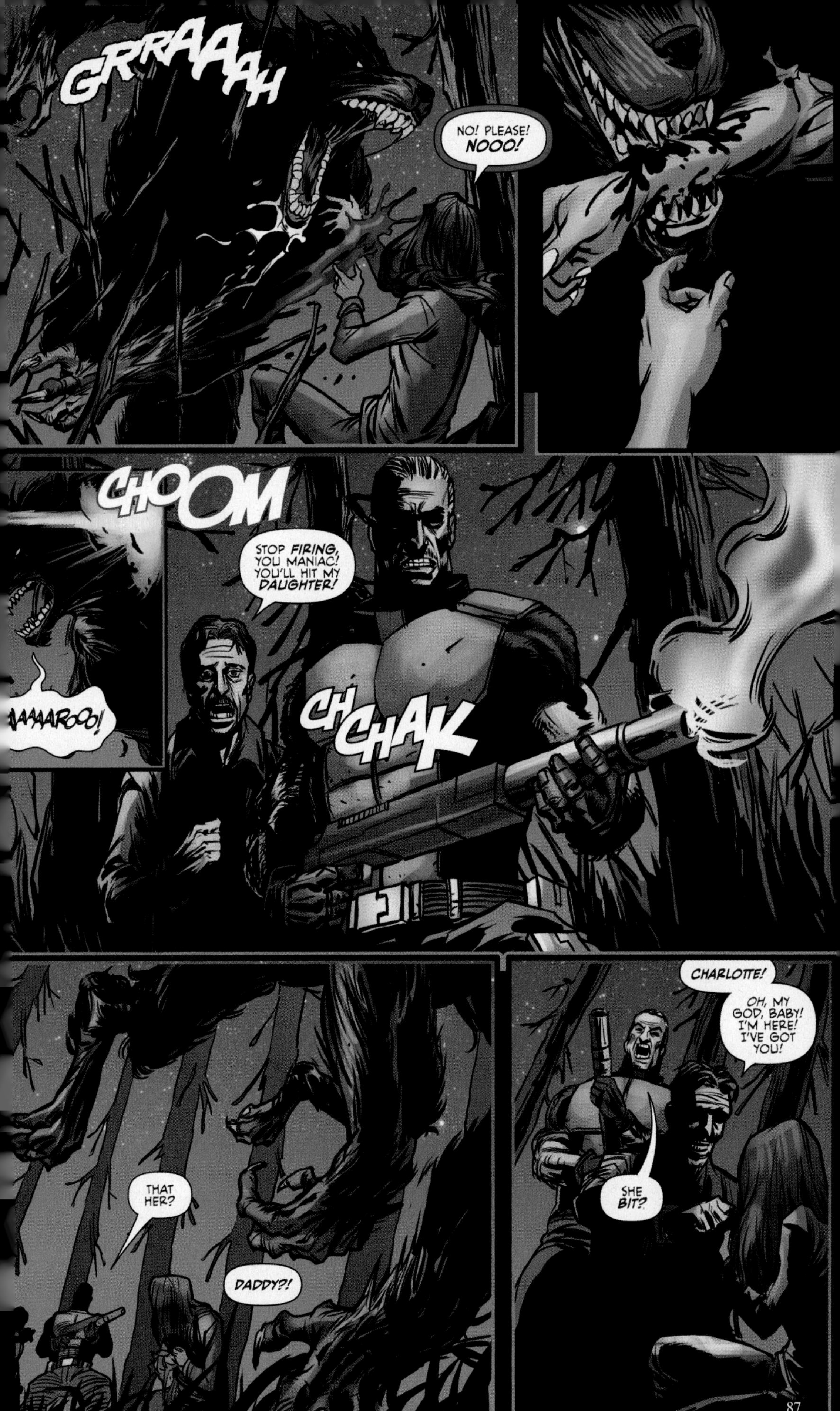
GRRAAAAH
NO! PLEASE! NOOO!
CHOOM
AAAAAROOO!
STOP FIRING, YOU MANIAC! YOU'LL HIT MY DAUGHTER!
CH CHAK
THAT HER?
DADDY?!
CHARLOTTE!
OH, MY GOD, BABY! I'M HERE! I'VE GOT YOU!
SHE BIT?

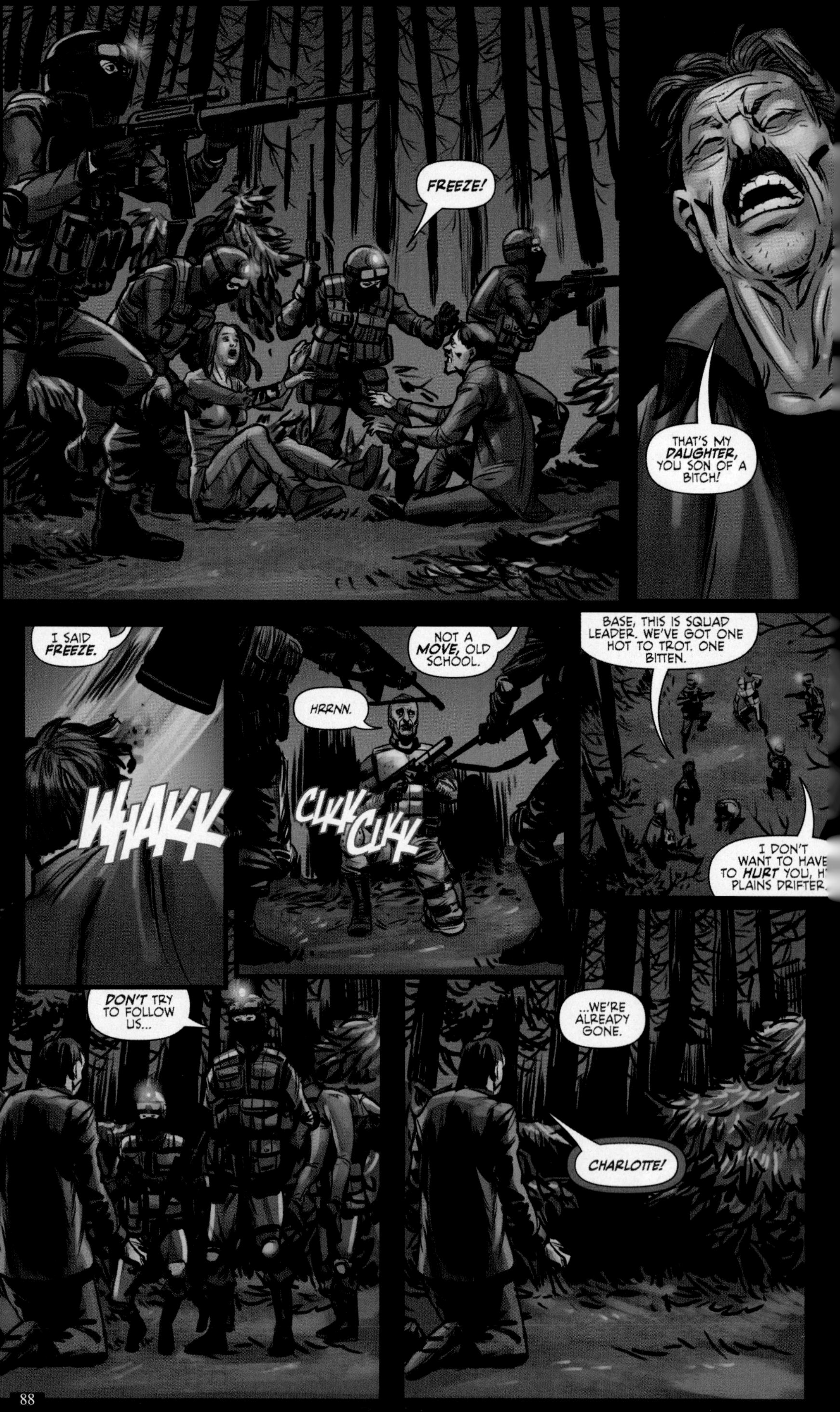
FREEZE!
THAT'S MY DAUGHTER, YOU SON OF A BITCH!
I SAID FREEZE.
WHAKK
NOT A MOVE, OLD SCHOOL.
HRRNN.
CLIKK CLIKK
BASE, THIS IS SQUAD LEADER. WE'VE GOT ONE HOT TO TROT. ONE BITTEN.
I DON'T WANT TO HAVE TO HURT YOU, H PLAINS DRIFTER.
DON'T TRY TO FOLLOW US...
...WE'RE ALREADY GONE.
CHARLOTTE!

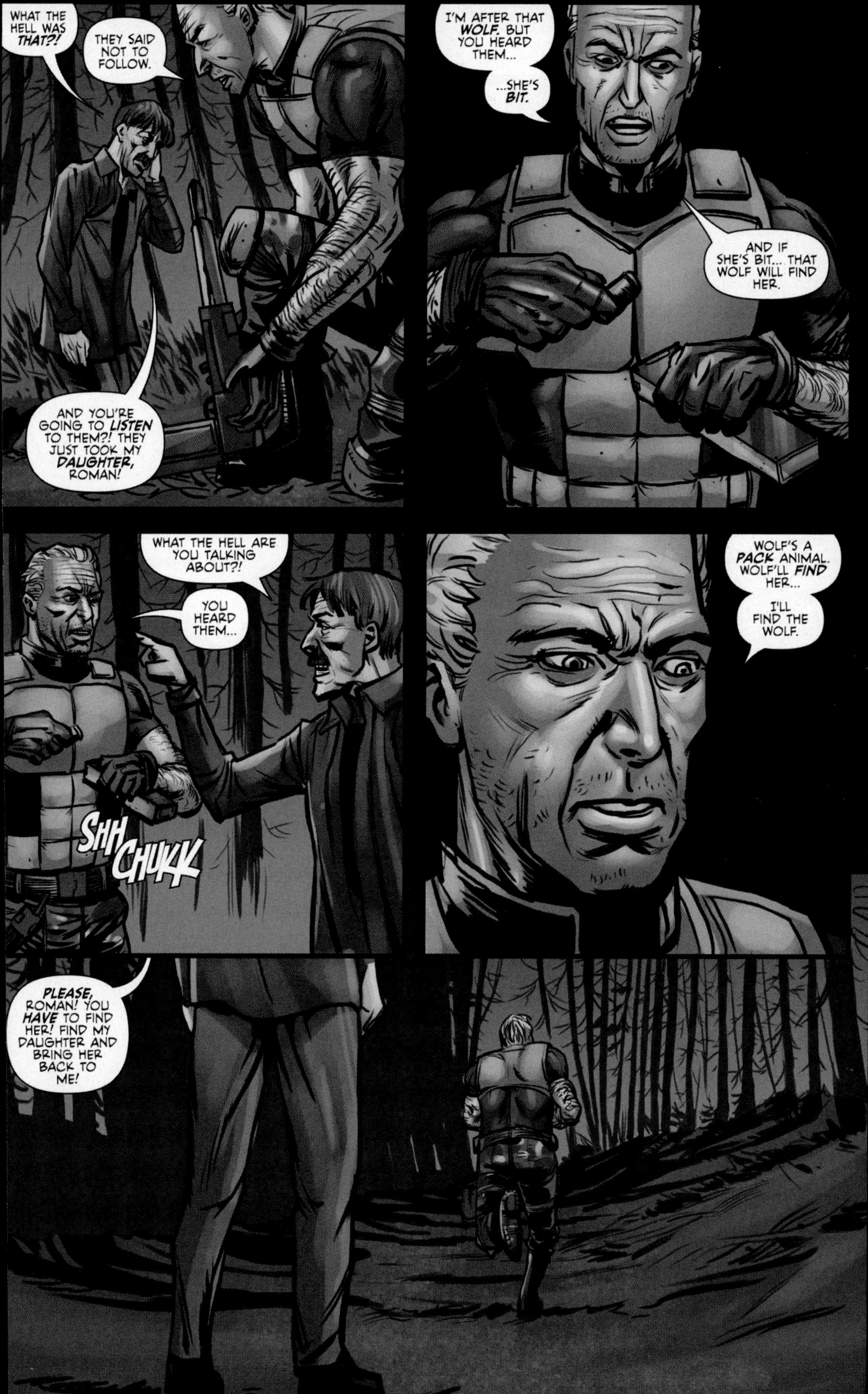
WHAT THE HELL WAS THAT?!
THEY SAID NOT TO FOLLOW.
AND YOU'RE GOING TO LISTEN TO THEM?! THEY JUST TOOK MY DAUGHTER, ROMAN!
I'M AFTER THAT WOLF. BUT YOU HEARD THEM...
...SHE'S BIT.
AND IF SHE'S BIT... THAT WOLF WILL FIND HER.
WHAT THE HELL ARE YOU TALKING ABOUT?!
YOU HEARD THEM...
SHH CHUKK
WOLF'S A PACK ANIMAL. WOLF'LL FIND HER...
I'LL FIND THE WOLF.
PLEASE, ROMAN! YOU HAVE TO FIND HER! FIND MY DAUGHTER AND BRING HER BACK TO ME!

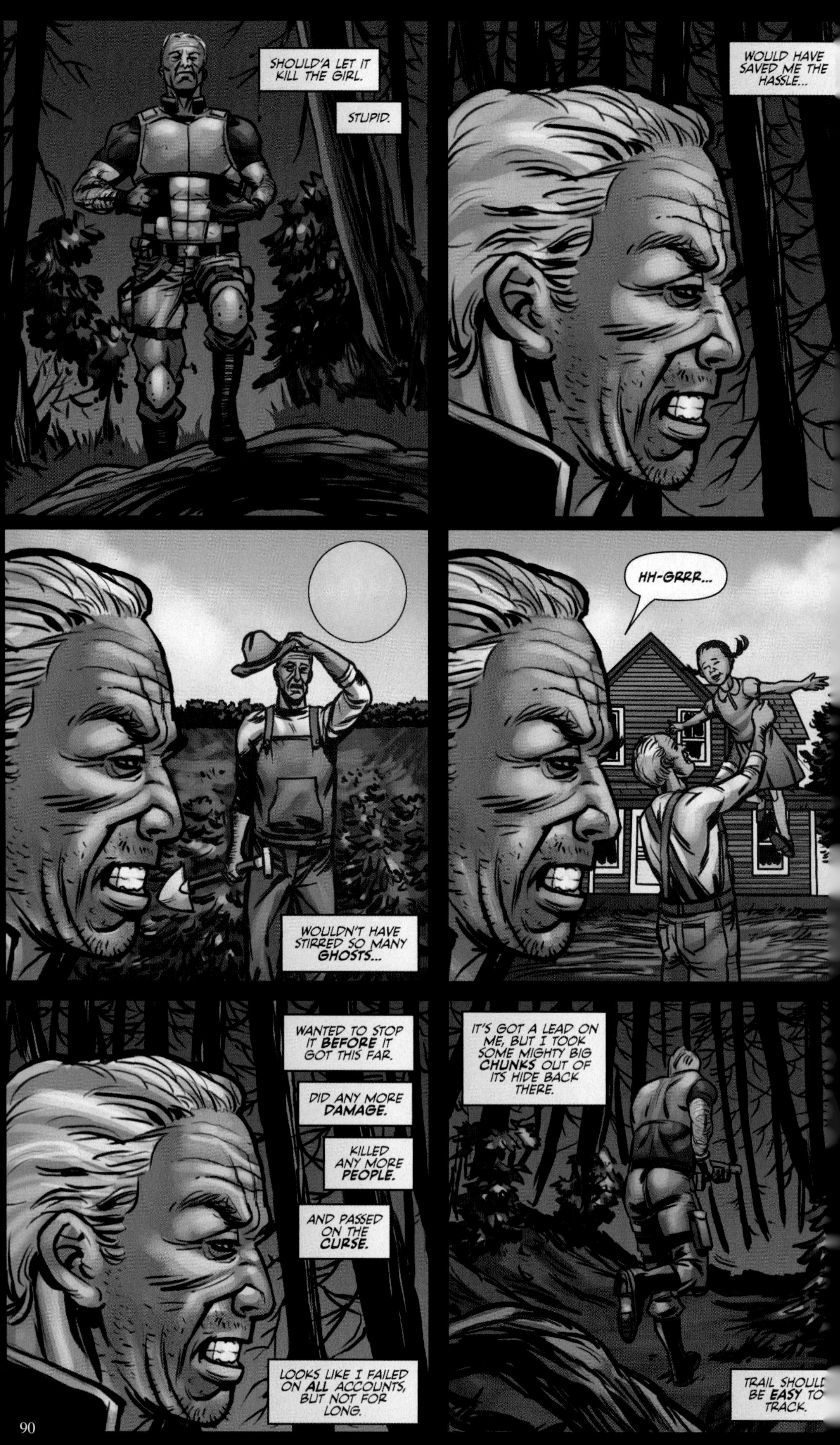
SHOULD'A LET IT KILL THE GIRL.
STUPID.
WOULD HAVE SAVED ME THE HASSLE...
WOULDN'T HAVE STIRRED SO MANY GHOSTS...
HH-GRRR...
WANTED TO STOP IT BEFORE IT GOT THIS FAR.
DID ANY MORE DAMAGE.
KILLED ANY MORE PEOPLE.
AND PASSED ON THE CURSE.
LOOKS LIKE I FAILED ON ALL ACCOUNTS, BUT NOT FOR LONG.
IT'S GOT A LEAD ON ME, BUT I TOOK SOME MIGHTY BIG CHUNKS OUT OF ITS HIDE BACK THERE.
TRAIL SHOULD BE EASY TO TRACK.

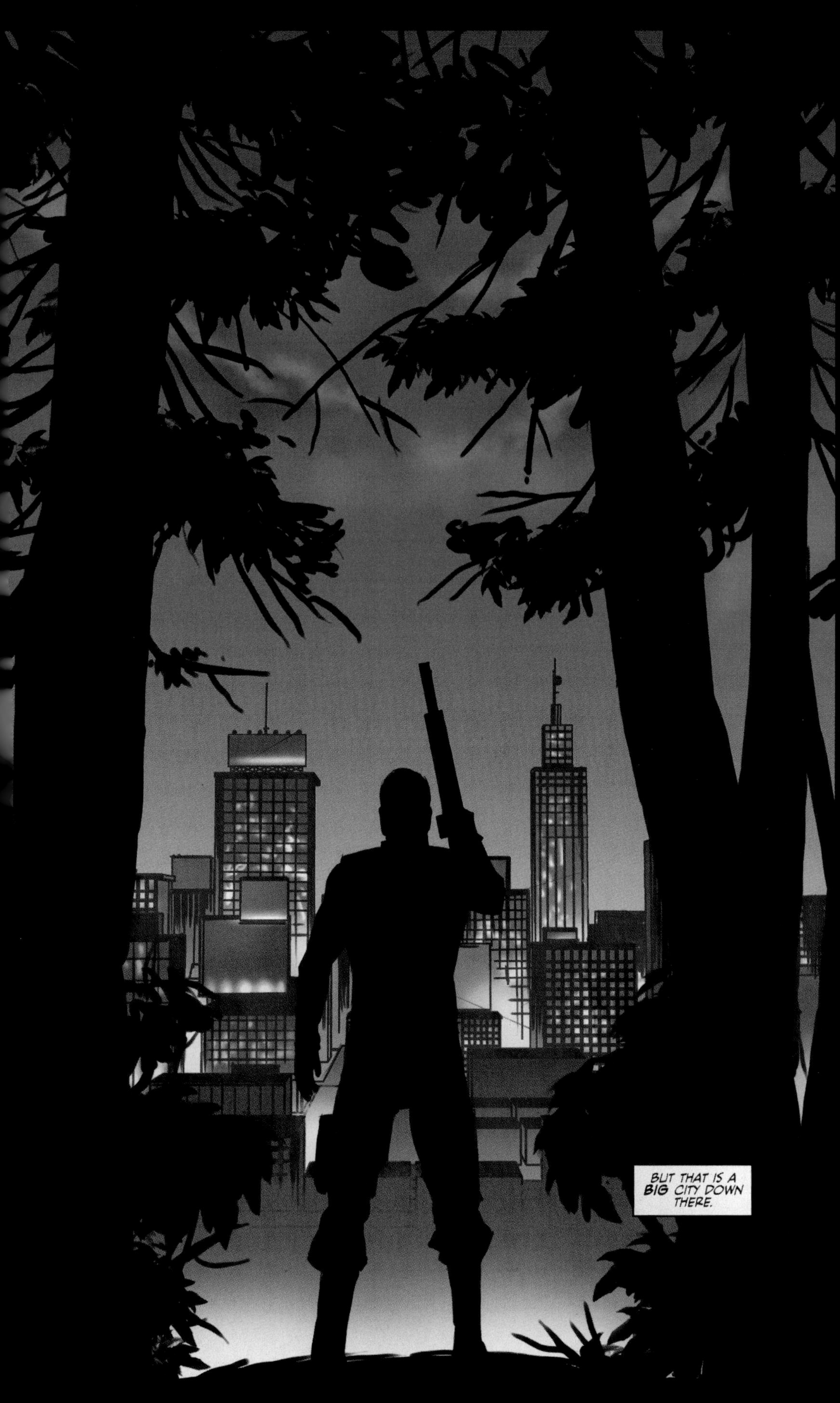
BUT THAT IS A BIG CITY DOWN THERE.

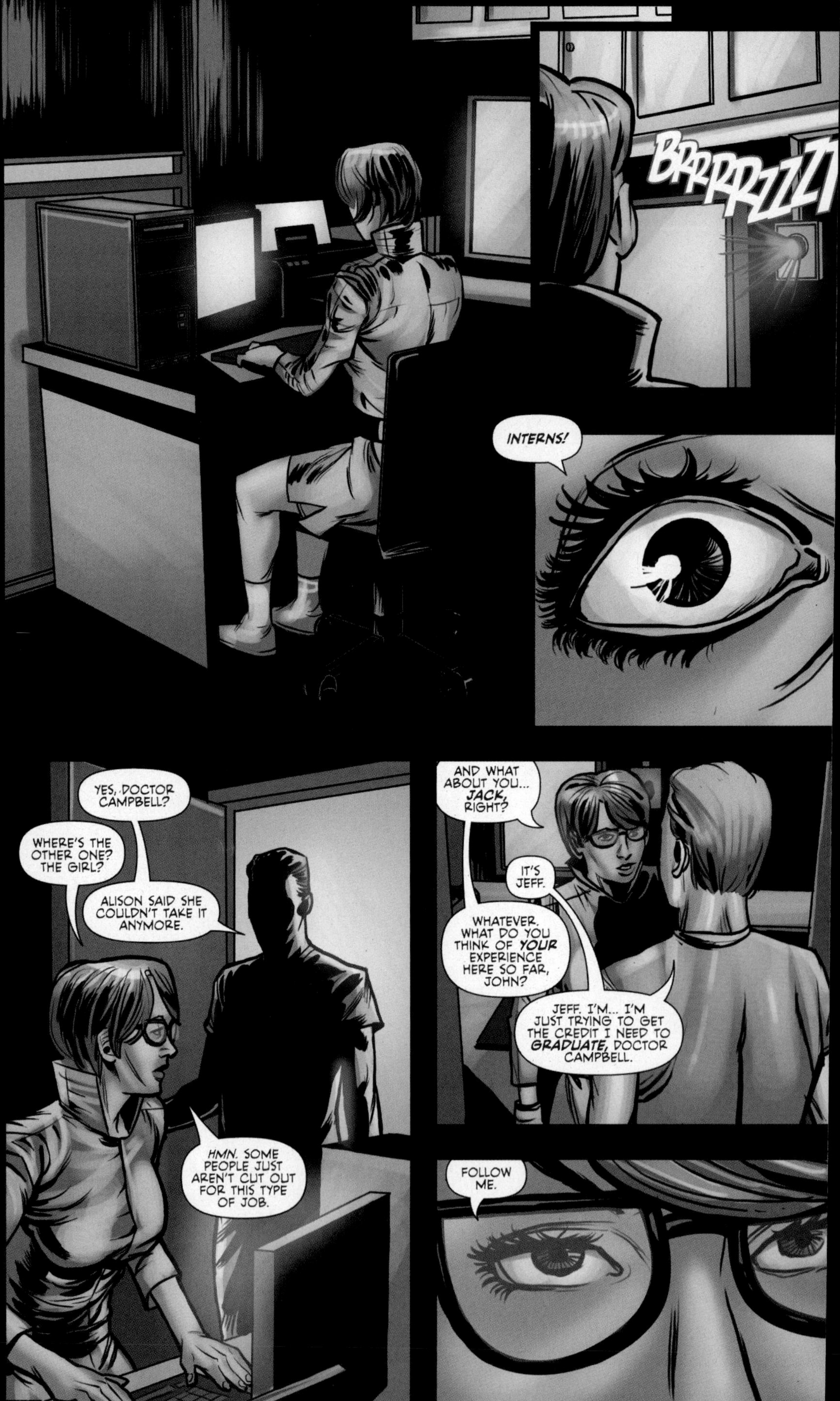
BRRRRZZZZT
INTERNS!
YES, DOCTOR CAMPBELL?
WHERE'S THE OTHER ONE? THE GIRL?
ALISON SAID SHE COULDN'T TAKE IT ANYMORE.
HMN. SOME PEOPLE JUST AREN'T CUT OUT FOR THIS TYPE OF JOB.
AND WHAT ABOUT YOU... JACK, RIGHT?
IT'S JEFF.
WHATEVER. WHAT DO YOU THINK OF YOUR EXPERIENCE HERE SO FAR, JOHN?
JEFF. I'M... I'M JUST TRYING TO GET THE CREDIT I NEED TO GRADUATE, DOCTOR CAMPBELL.
FOLLOW ME.

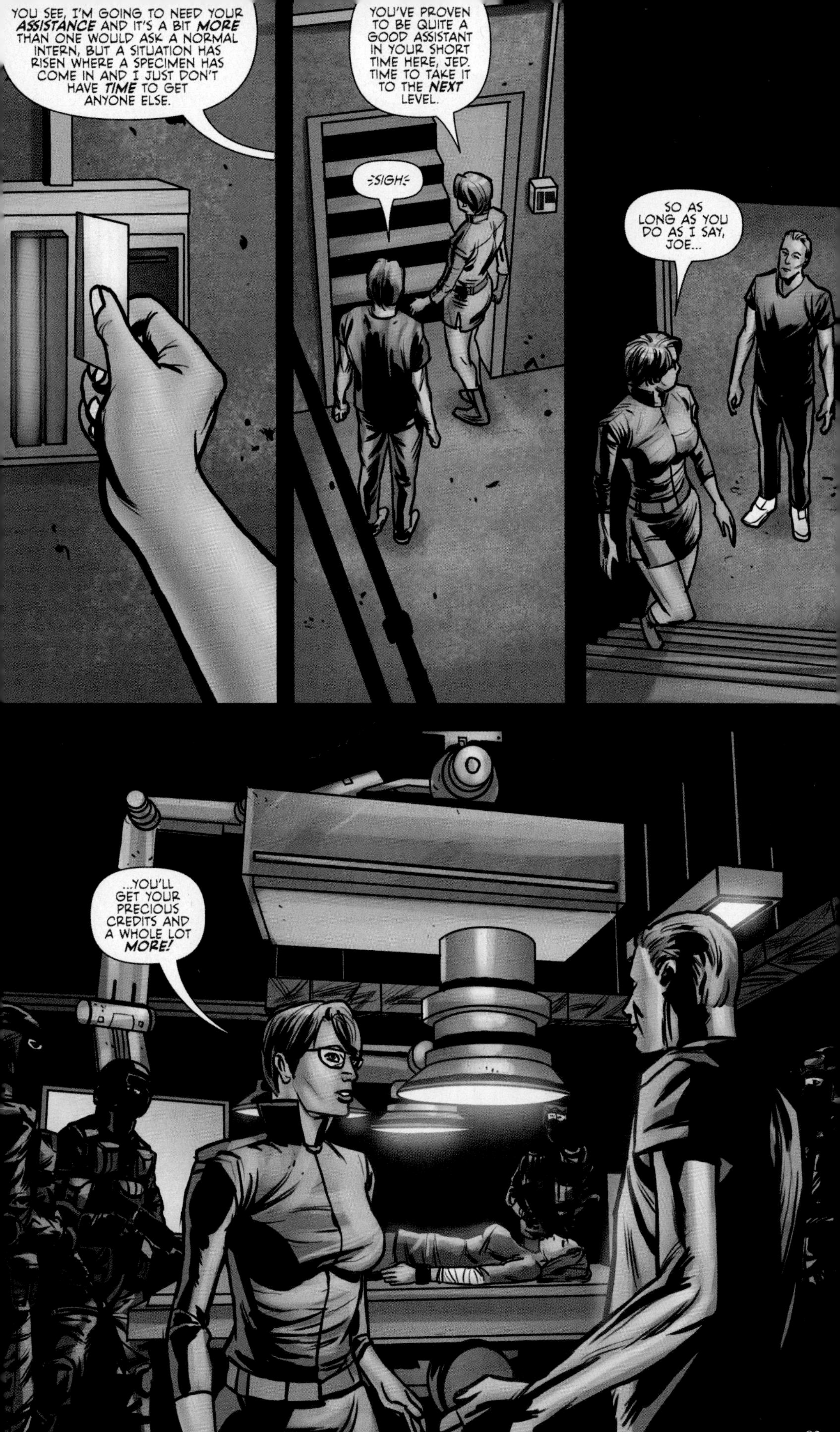
YOU SEE, I'M GOING TO NEED YOUR ASSISTANCE AND IT'S A BIT MORE THAN ONE WOULD ASK A NORMAL INTERN, BUT A SITUATION HAS RISEN WHERE A SPECIMEN HAS COME IN AND I JUST DON'T HAVE TIME TO GET ANYONE ELSE.
YOU'VE PROVEN TO BE QUITE A GOOD ASSISTANT IN YOUR SHORT TIME HERE, JED. TIME TO TAKE IT TO THE NEXT LEVEL.
SIGH
SO AS LONG AS YOU DO AS I SAY, JOE...
...YOU'LL GET YOUR PRECIOUS CREDITS AND A WHOLE LOT MORE!

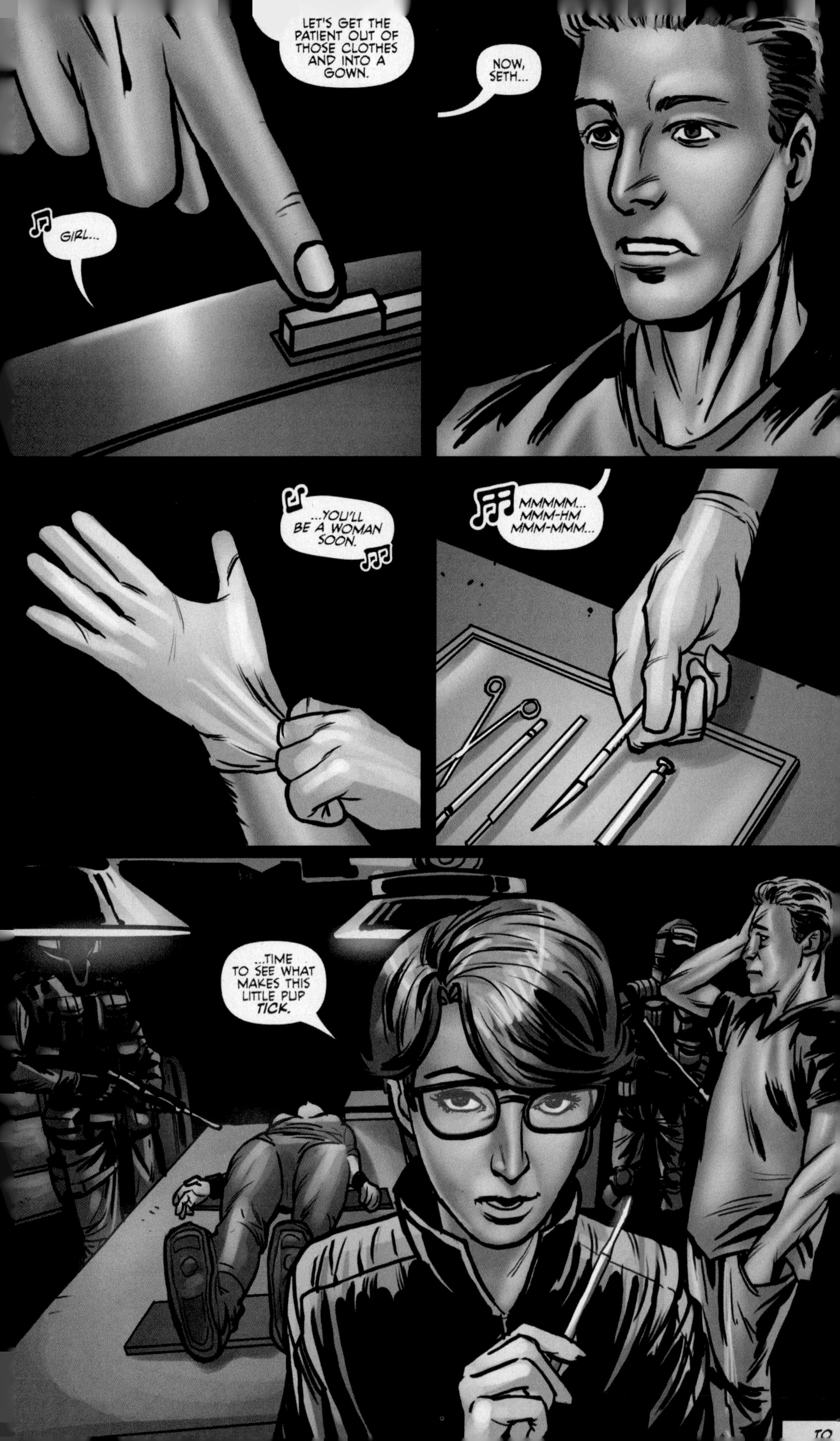

LET'S GET THE PATIENT OUT OF THOSE CLOTHES AND INTO A GOWN.
GIRL...
NOW, SETH...
...YOU'LL BE A WOMAN SOON.
MMMMM... MMM-HM MMM-MMM...
...TIME TO SEE WHAT MAKES THIS LITTLE PUP TICK.
TO

Grimm Fairy Tales
presents
Vampires
&
WEREWOLVES

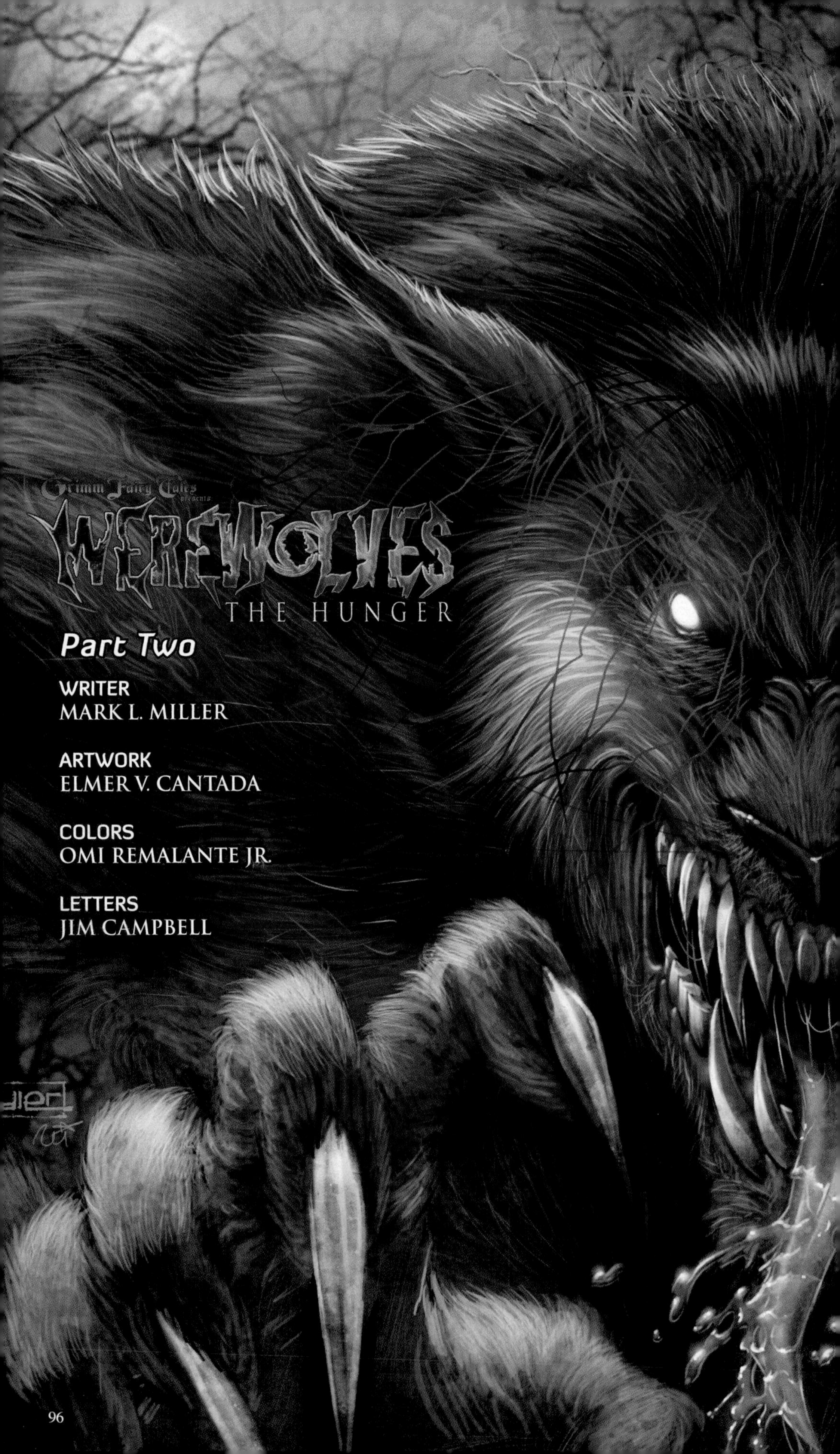
Grimm Fairy Tales presents
WEREWOLVES
THE HUNGER
Part Two
WRITER
MARK L. MILLER
ARTWORK
ELMER V. CANTADA
COLORS
OMI REMALANTE JR.
LETTERS
JIM CAMPBELL

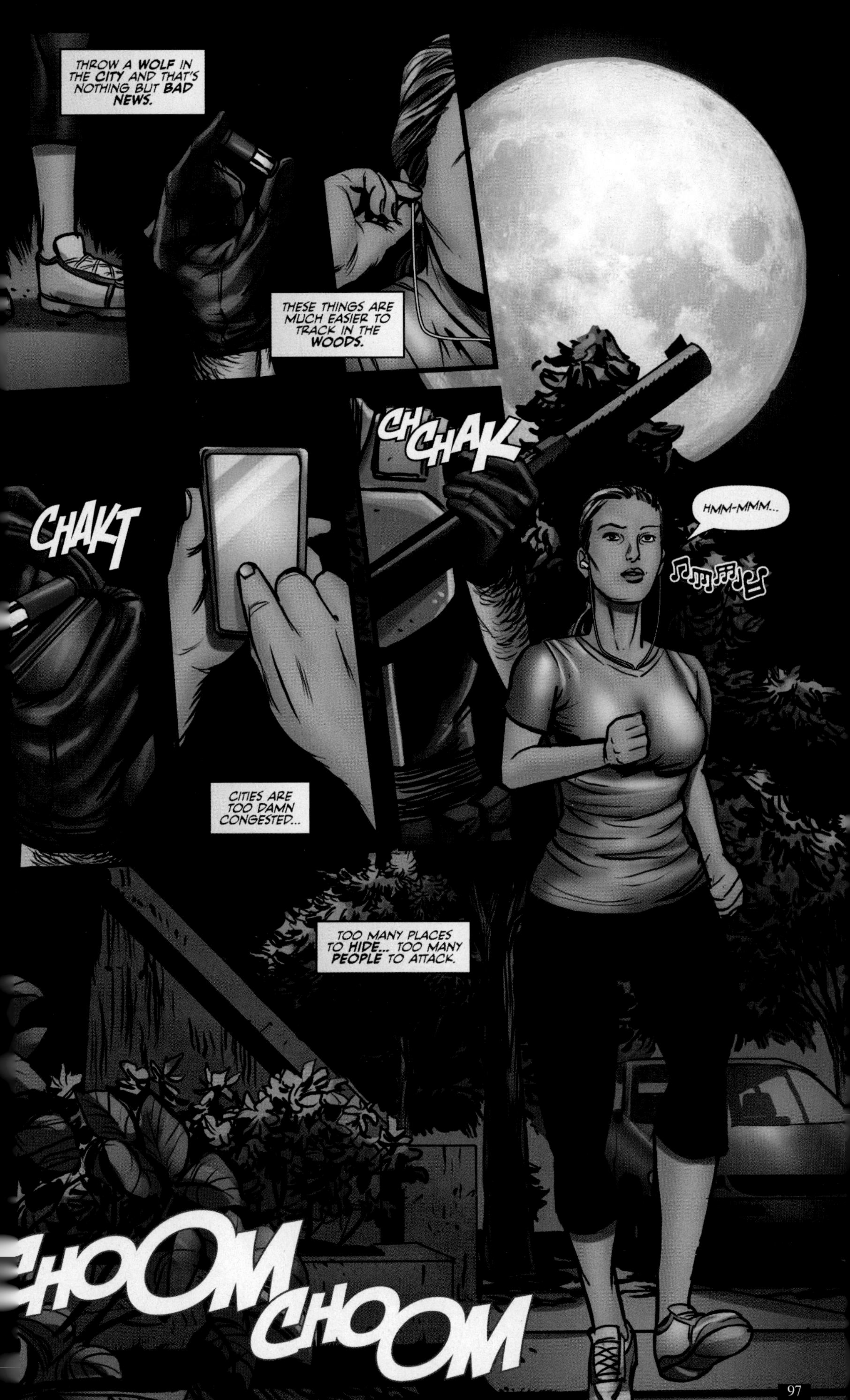
THROW A WOLF IN THE CITY AND THAT'S NOTHING BUT BAD NEWS.
THESE THINGS ARE MUCH EASIER TO TRACK IN THE WOODS.
CH CHAK
CHAKT
HMM-MMM...
CITIES ARE TOO DAMN CONGESTED...
TOO MANY PLACES TO HIDE... TOO MANY PEOPLE TO ATTACK.
CHOOM CHOOM

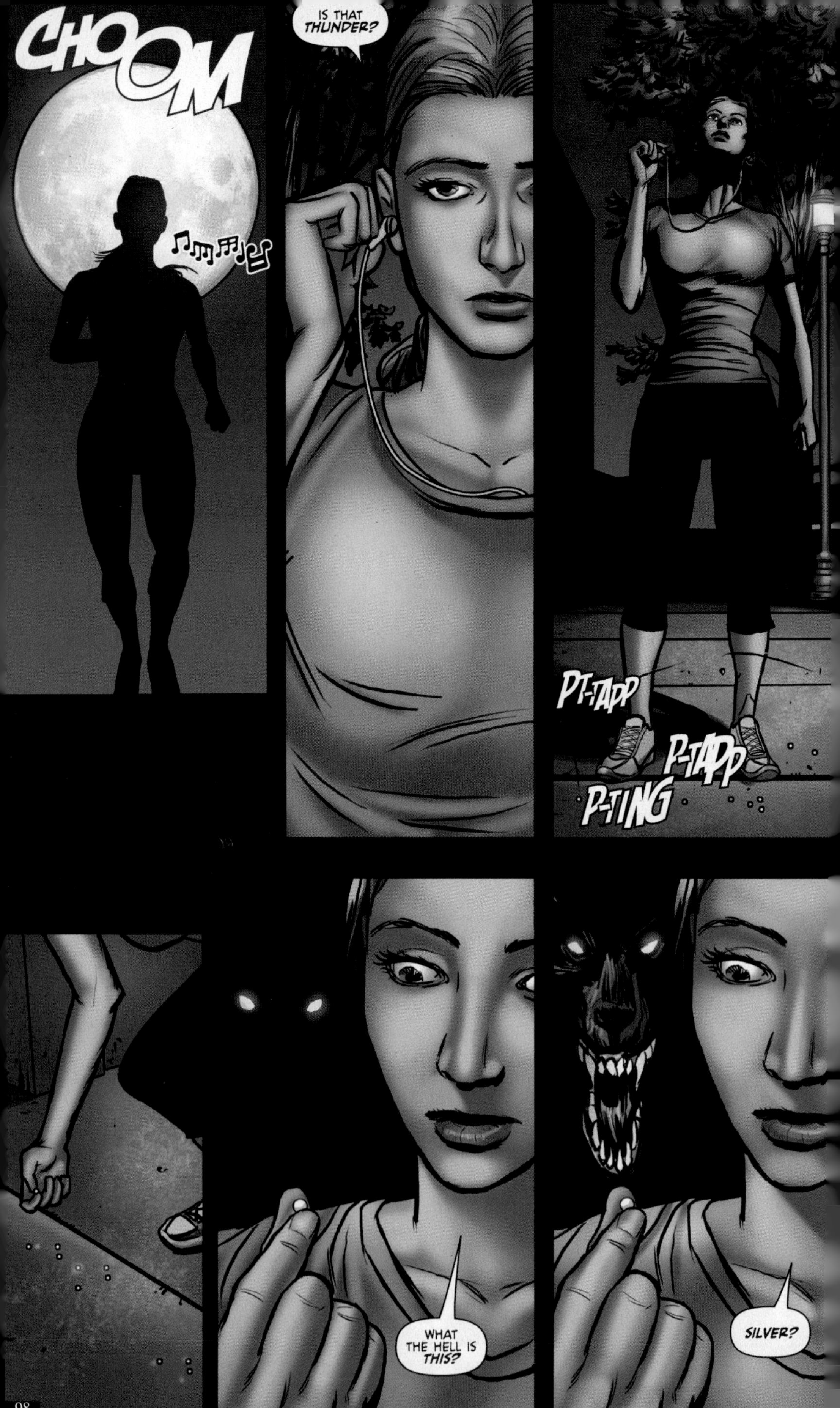
CHOOM
IS THAT THUNDER?
PT-TAPP
P-TAPP
P-TING
WHAT THE HELL IS THIS?
SILVER?

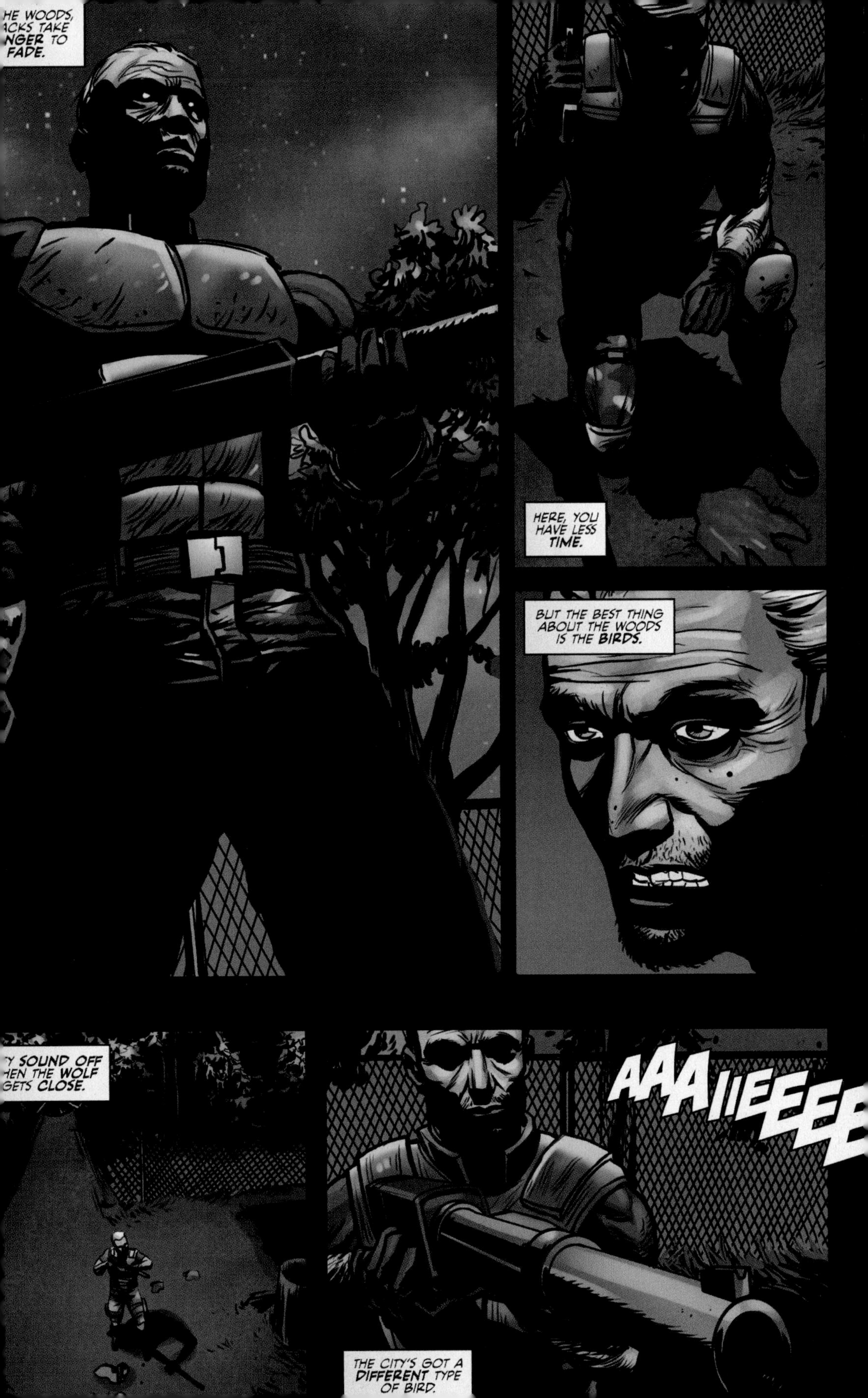
HE WOODS,
ACKS TAKE
NGER TO
FADE.
HERE, YOU
HAVE LESS
TIME.
BUT THE BEST THING
ABOUT THE WOODS
IS THE BIRDS.
Y SOUND OFF
HEN THE WOLF
GETS CLOSE.
AAAIIEEEE
THE CITY'S GOT A
DIFFERENT TYPE
OF BIRD.

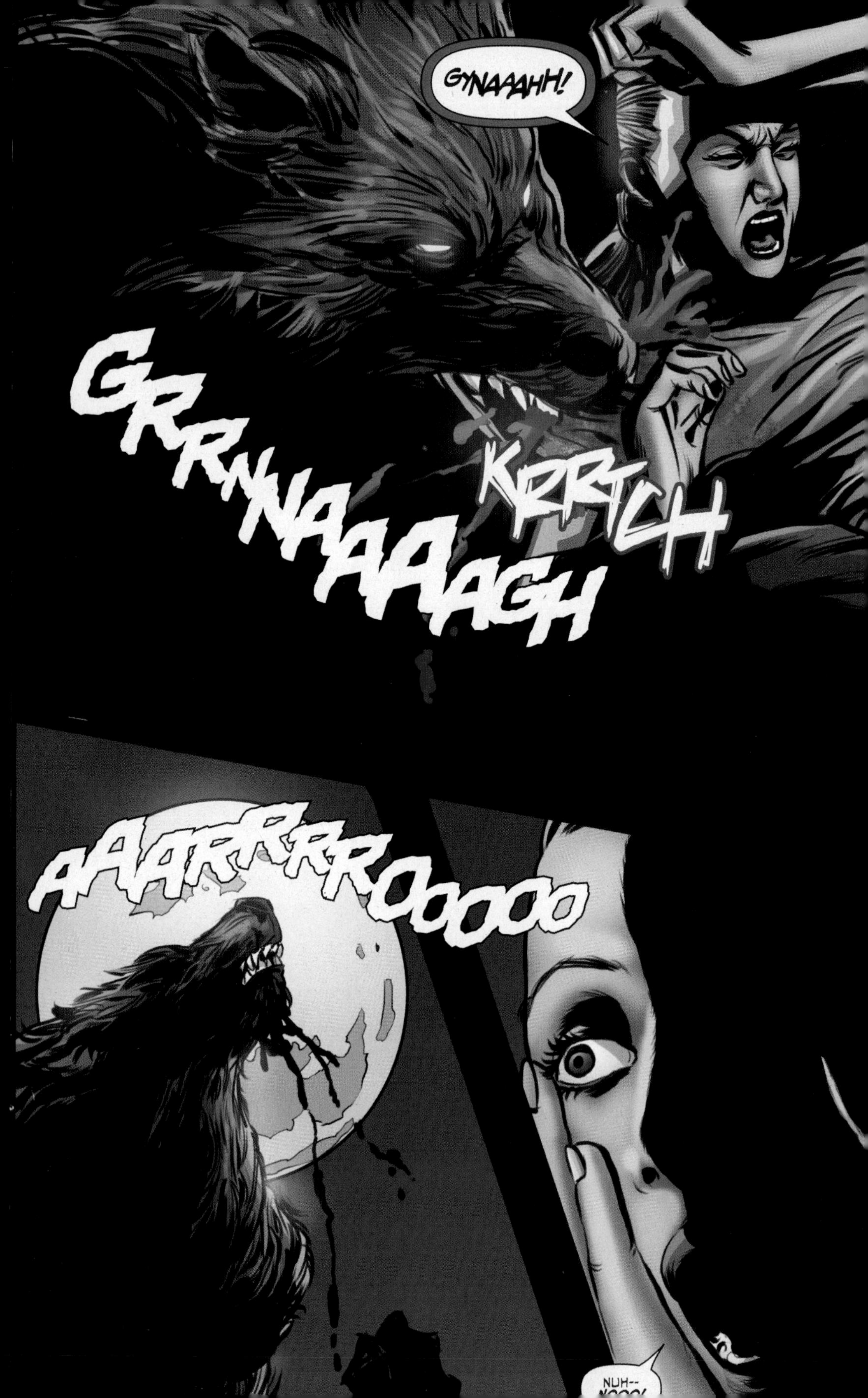
GYNAAAHH!
GRRNNAAAAGH
KRRTCH
AAARRRROOOOO
NUH--

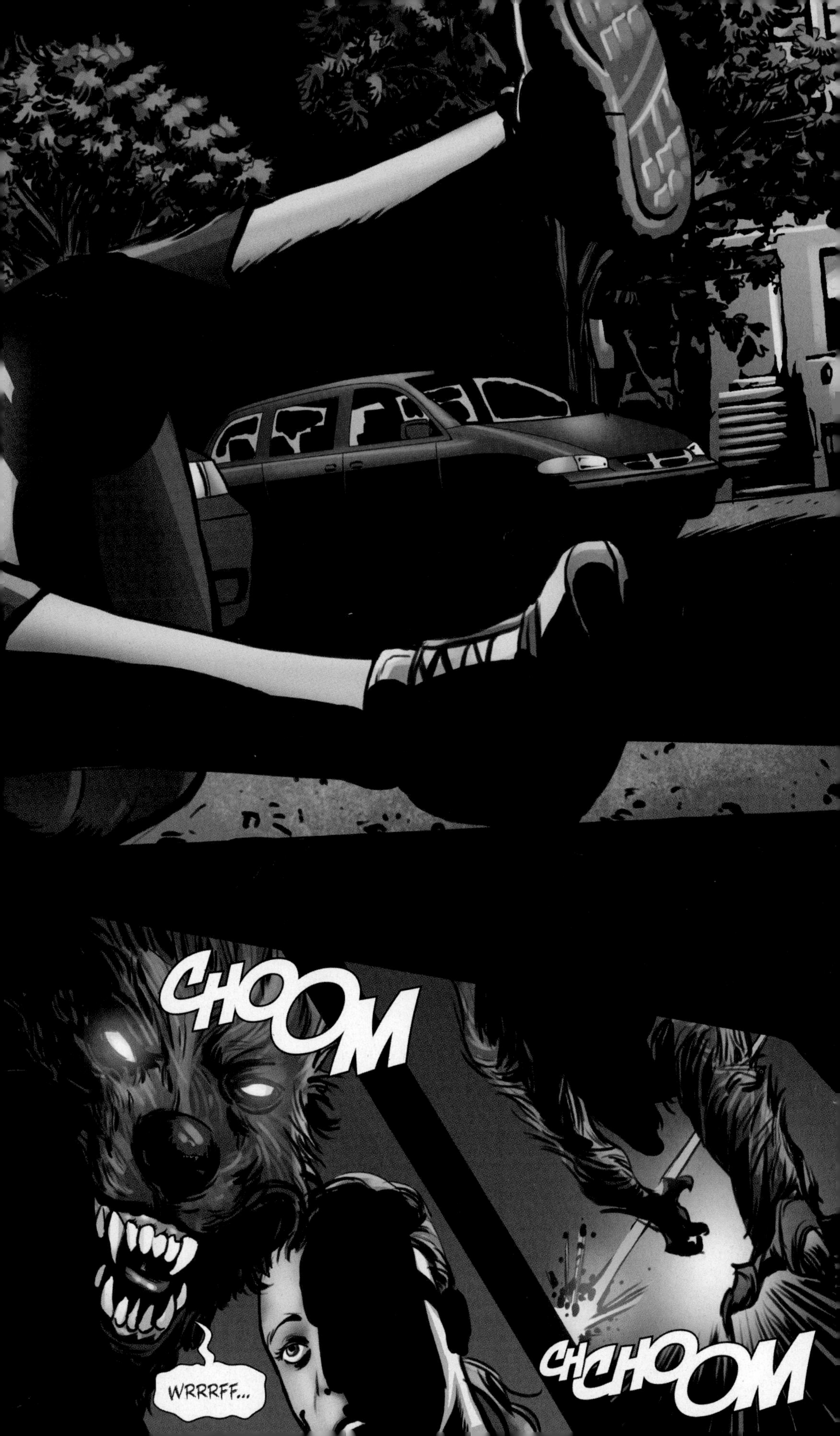
CHOOM
WRRRFF...
CHCHOOM

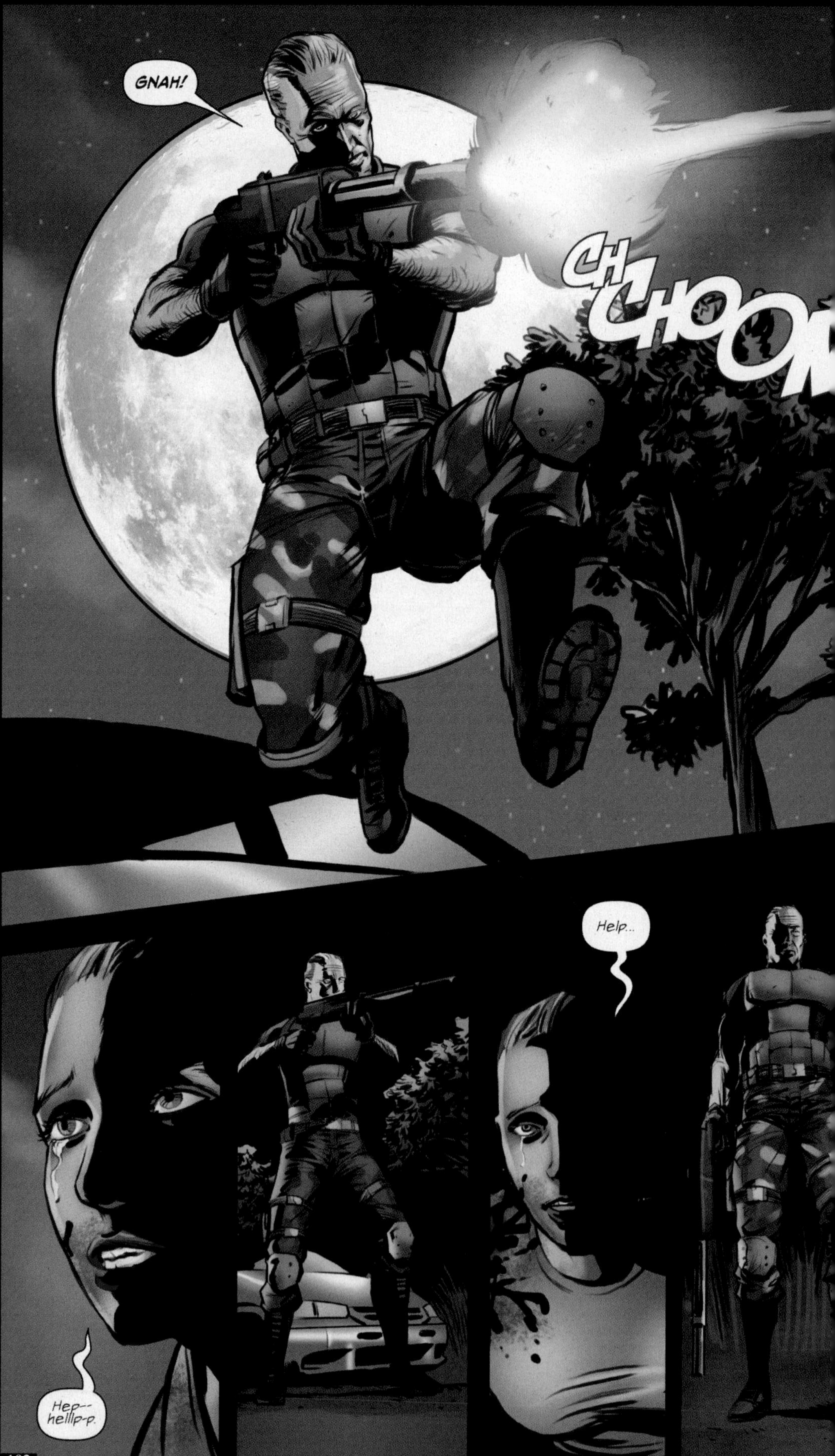
GNAH!
CH CHOO
Hep-- helllp-p.
Help...

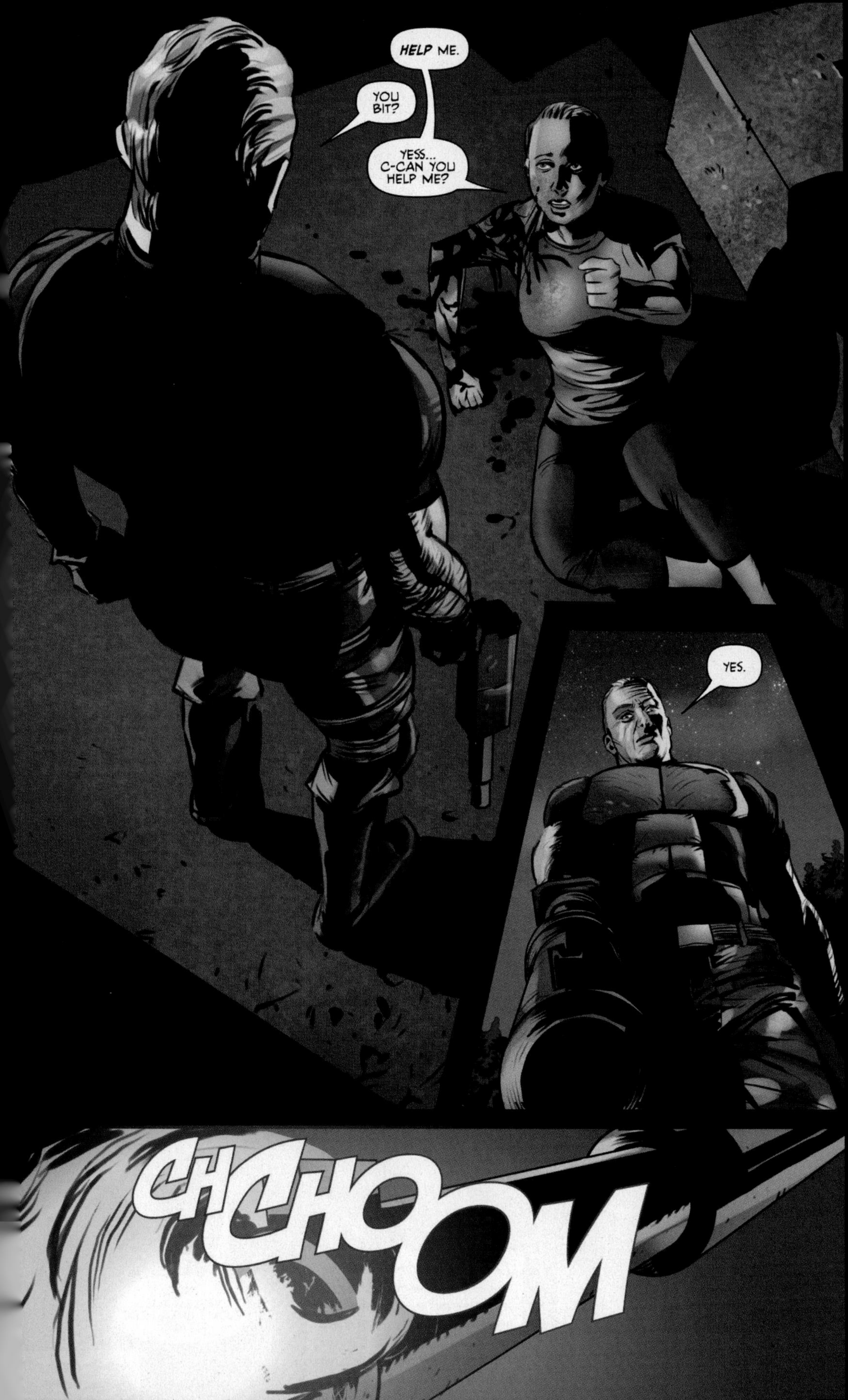
HELP ME.
YOU BIT?
YESS... C-CAN YOU HELP ME?
YES.
CHCHOOOM

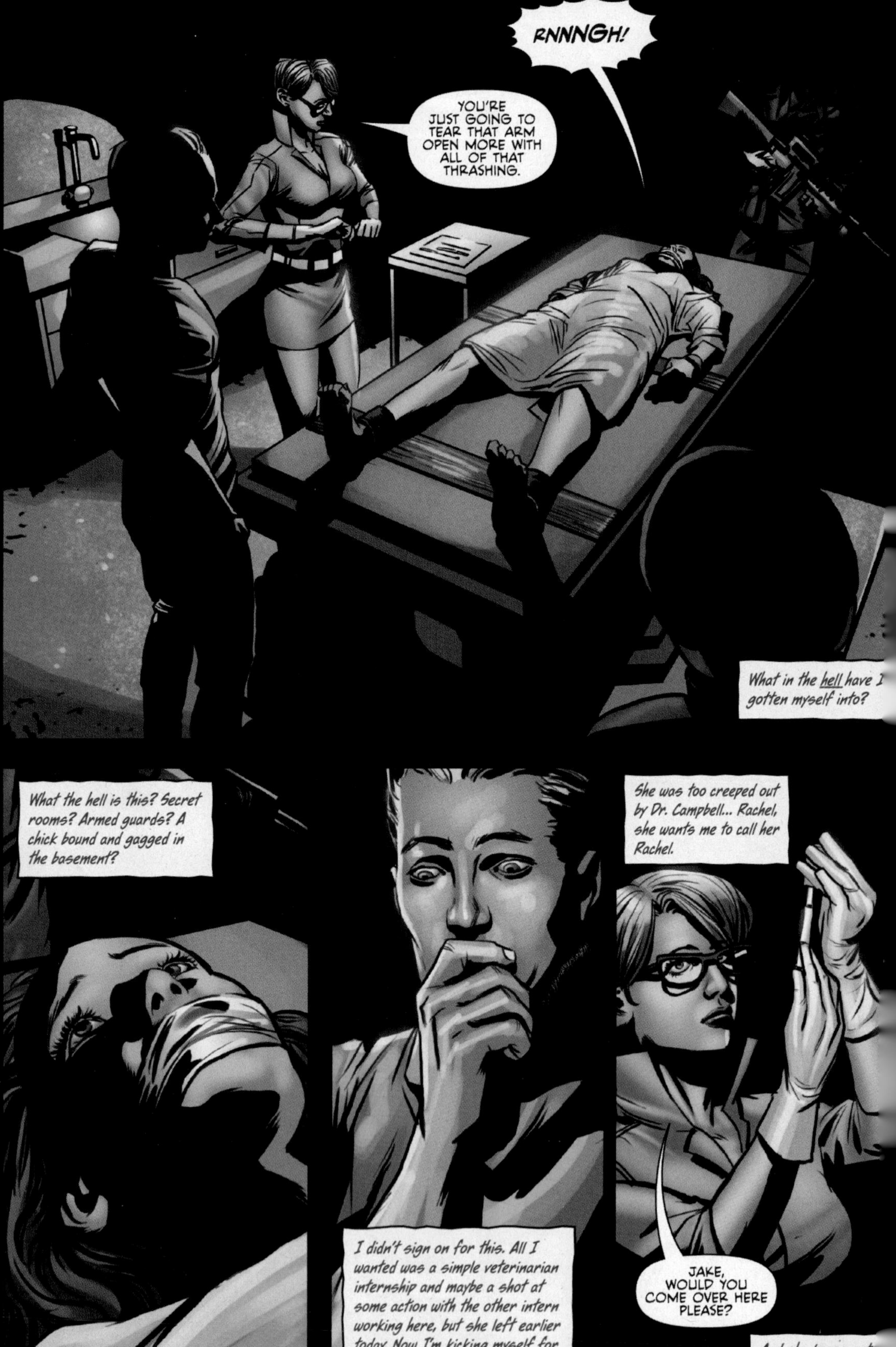
RNNNGH!
YOU'RE JUST GOING TO TEAR THAT ARM OPEN MORE WITH ALL OF THAT THRASHING.
What in the hell have I gotten myself into?
What the hell is this? Secret rooms? Armed guards? A chick bound and gagged in the basement?
I didn't sign on for this. All I wanted was a simple veterinarian internship and maybe a shot at some action with the other intern working here, but she left earlier today. Now I'm kicking myself for not following her lead.
She was too creeped out by Dr. Campbell... Rachel, she wants me to call her Rachel.
JAKE, WOULD YOU COME OVER HERE PLEASE?
And she keeps gett my name wrong.

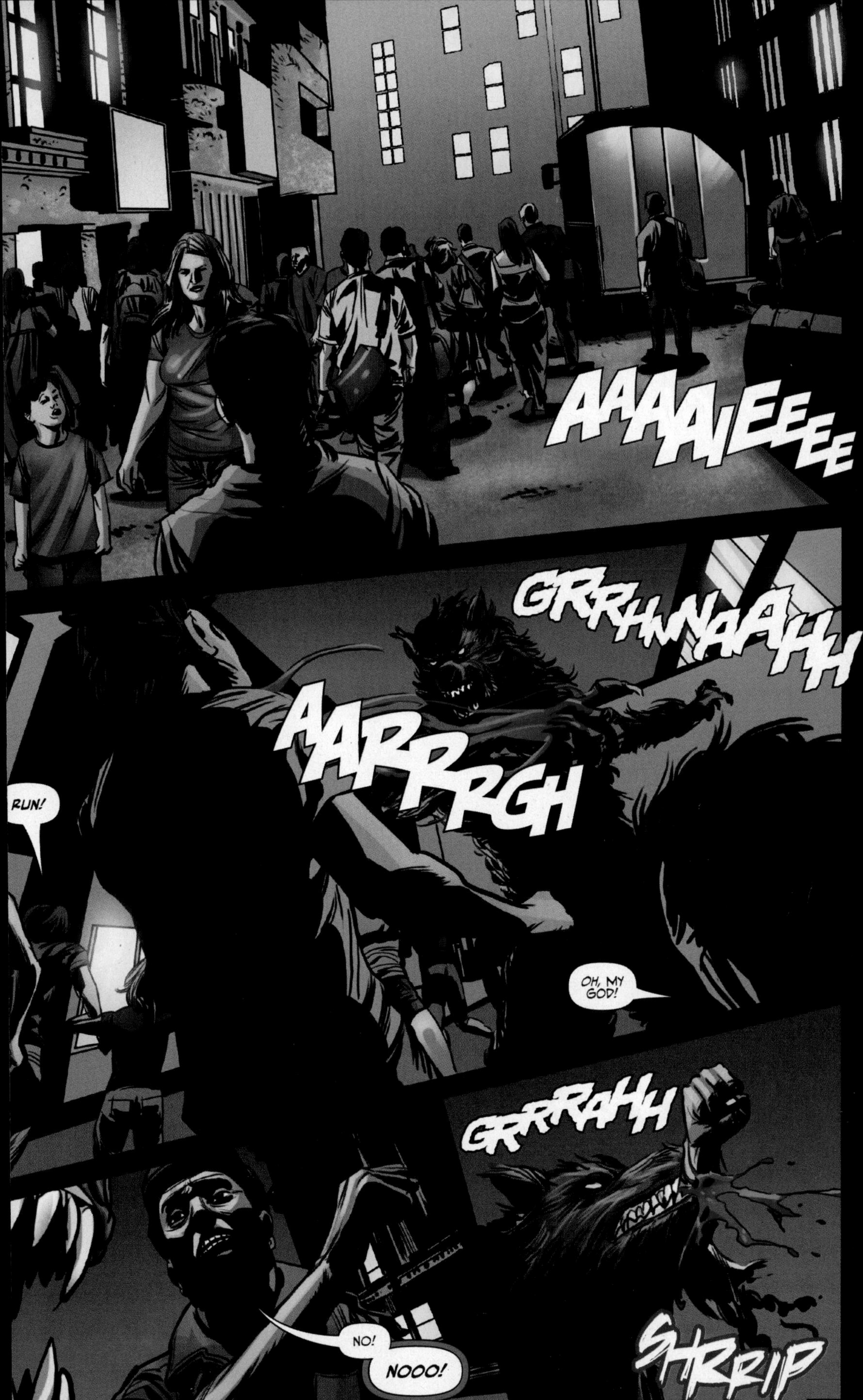
AAAAIEEEEE
GRRHNNAAHHH
AARRRGH
RUN!
OH, MY GOD!
GRRRAHH
NO!
NOOO!
SHRRIP

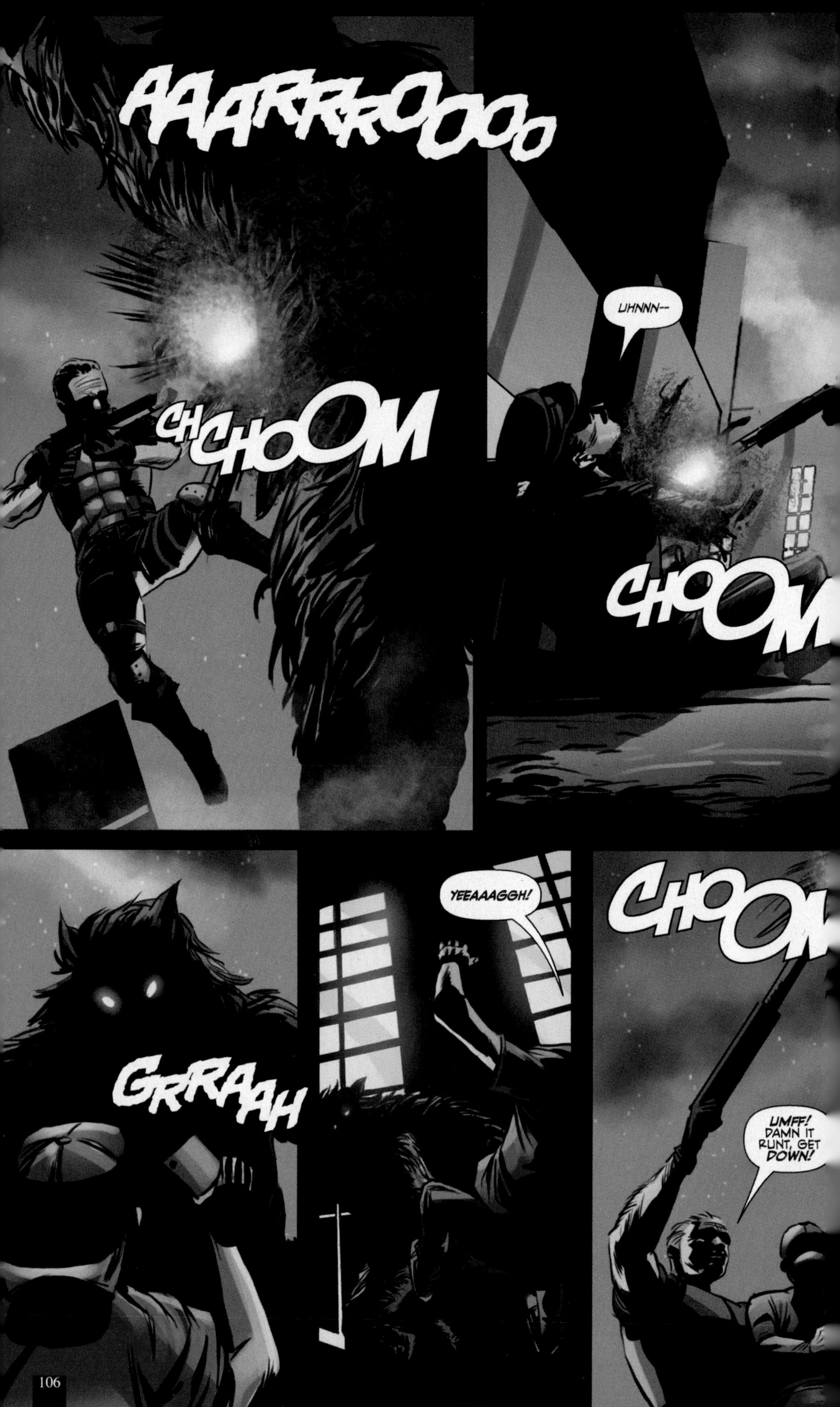
AAARRROOOOO
CHCHOOOM
UHNNN--
CHOOOM
GRRAAH
YEEAAAGGH!
CHOOOM
UMFF! DAMN IT RUNT, GET DOWN!

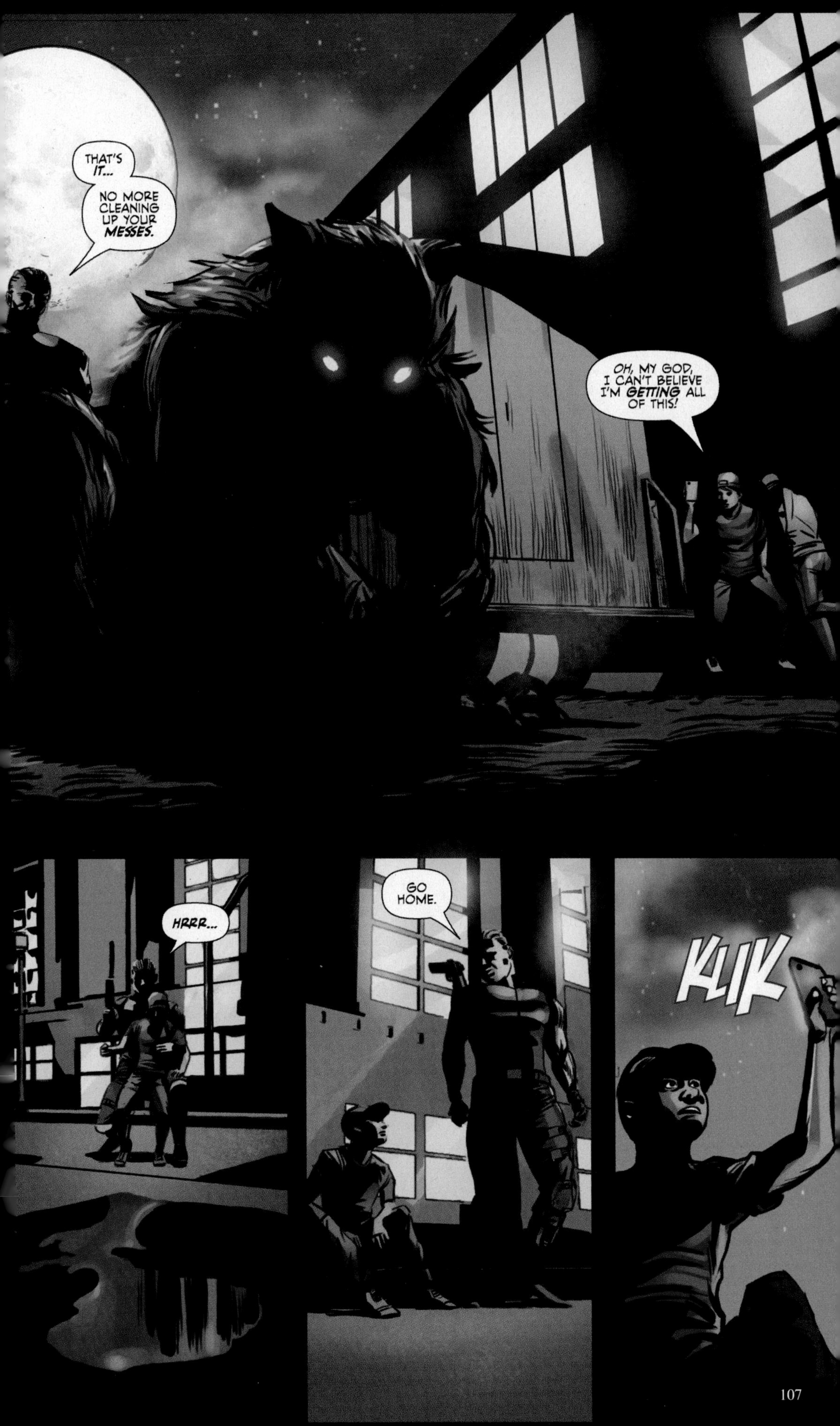

THAT'S IT...
NO MORE CLEANING UP YOUR MESSES.
OH, MY GOD, I CAN'T BELIEVE I'M GETTING ALL OF THIS!
HRRR...
GO HOME.
KLIK

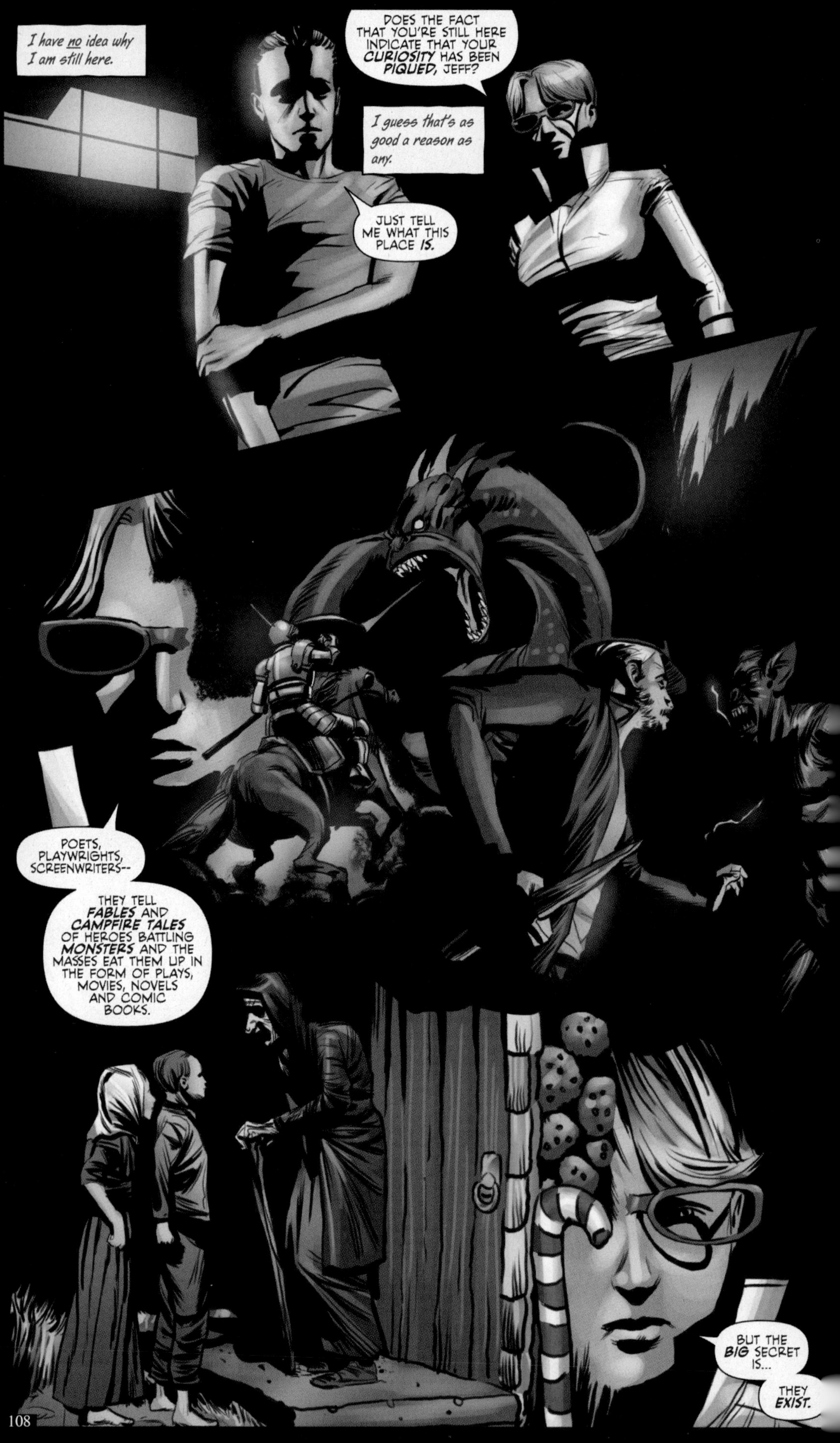

I have no idea why I am still here.
DOES THE FACT THAT YOU'RE STILL HERE INDICATE THAT YOUR CURIOSITY HAS BEEN PIQUED, JEFF?
I guess that's as good a reason as any.
JUST TELL ME WHAT THIS PLACE IS.
POETS, PLAYWRIGHTS, SCREENWRITERS--
THEY TELL FABLES AND CAMPFIRE TALES OF HEROES BATTLING MONSTERS AND THE MASSES EAT THEM UP IN THE FORM OF PLAYS, MOVIES, NOVELS AND COMIC BOOKS.
BUT THE BIG SECRET IS...
THEY EXIST.

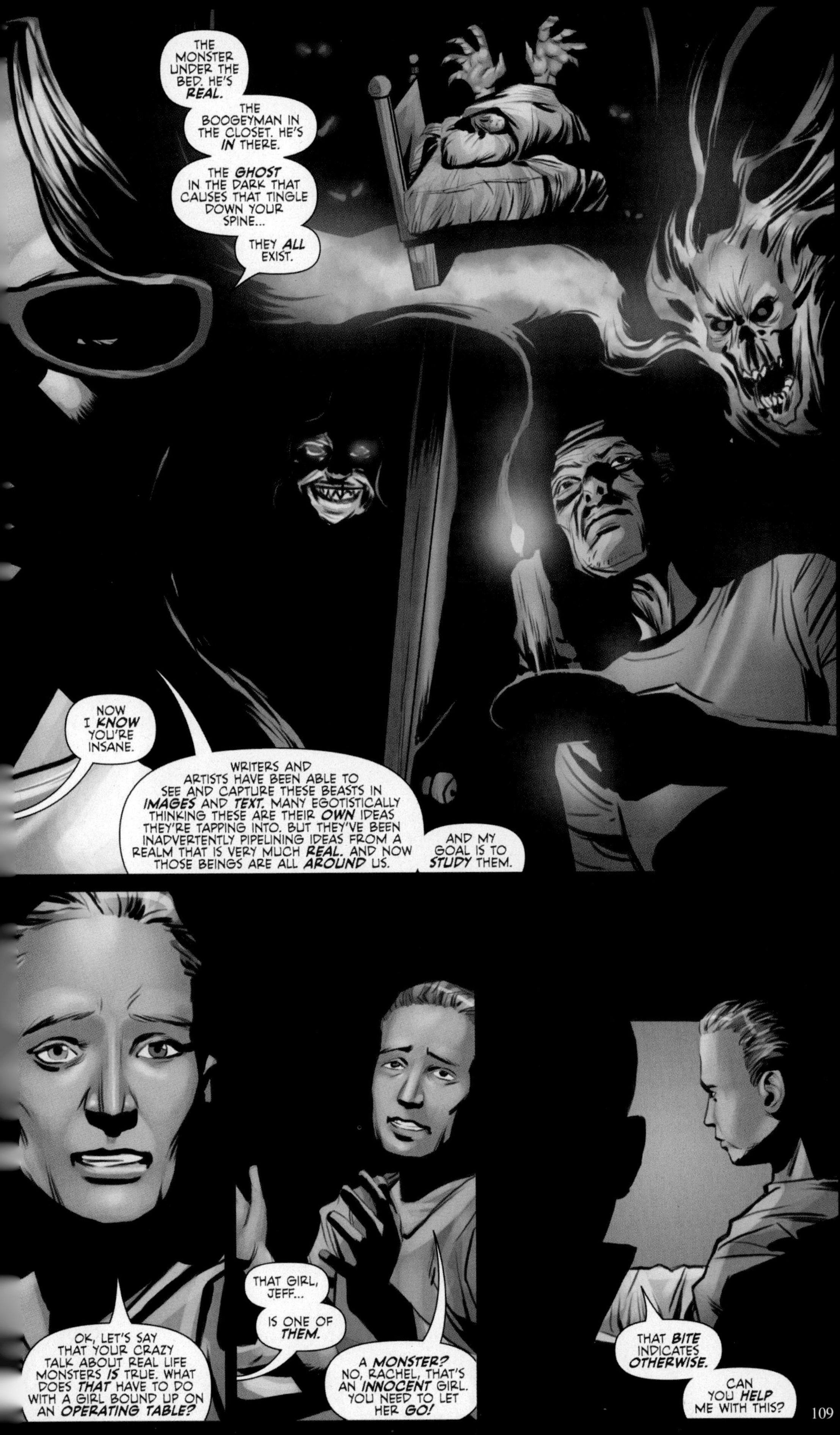
THE MONSTER UNDER THE BED. HE'S REAL.
THE BOOGEYMAN IN THE CLOSET. HE'S IN THERE.
THE GHOST IN THE DARK THAT CAUSES THAT TINGLE DOWN YOUR SPINE...
THEY ALL EXIST.
NOW I KNOW YOU'RE INSANE.
WRITERS AND ARTISTS HAVE BEEN ABLE TO SEE AND CAPTURE THESE BEASTS IN IMAGES AND TEXT. MANY EGOTISTICALLY THINKING THESE ARE THEIR OWN IDEAS THEY'RE TAPPING INTO. BUT THEY'VE BEEN INADVERTENTLY PIPELINING IDEAS FROM A REALM THAT IS VERY MUCH REAL. AND NOW THOSE BEINGS ARE ALL AROUND US.
AND MY GOAL IS TO STUDY THEM.
OK, LET'S SAY THAT YOUR CRAZY TALK ABOUT REAL LIFE MONSTERS IS TRUE. WHAT DOES THAT HAVE TO DO WITH A GIRL BOUND UP ON AN OPERATING TABLE?
THAT GIRL, JEFF...
IS ONE OF THEM.
A MONSTER? NO, RACHEL, THAT'S AN INNOCENT GIRL. YOU NEED TO LET HER GO!
THAT BITE INDICATES OTHERWISE.
CAN YOU HELP ME WITH THIS?

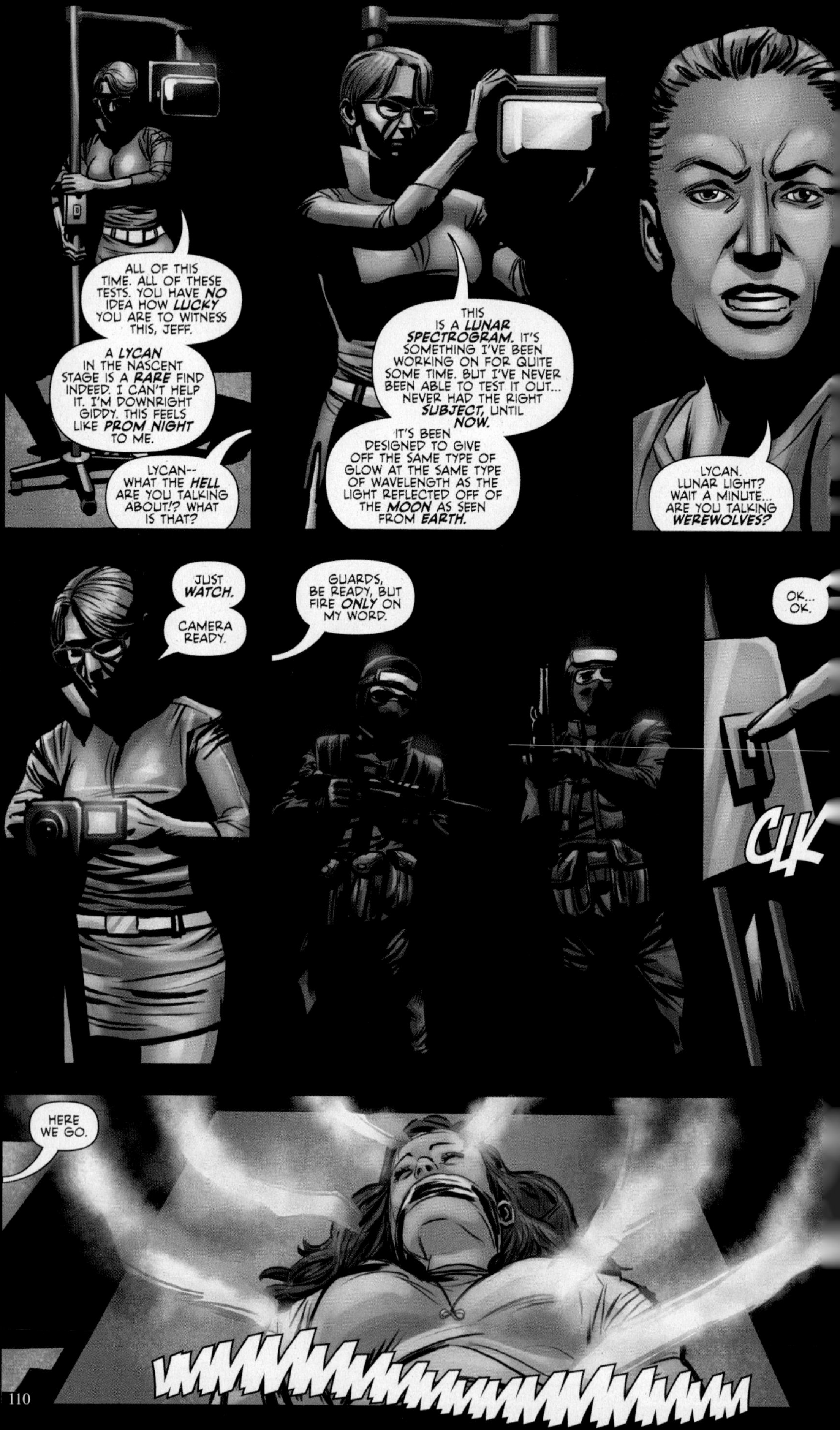
ALL OF THIS TIME. ALL OF THESE TESTS. YOU HAVE NO IDEA HOW LUCKY YOU ARE TO WITNESS THIS, JEFF.
A LYCAN IN THE NASCENT STAGE IS A RARE FIND INDEED. I CAN'T HELP IT. I'M DOWNRIGHT GIDDY. THIS FEELS LIKE PROM NIGHT TO ME.
LYCAN-- WHAT THE HELL ARE YOU TALKING ABOUT!? WHAT IS THAT?
THIS IS A LUNAR SPECTROGRAM. IT'S SOMETHING I'VE BEEN WORKING ON FOR QUITE SOME TIME. BUT I'VE NEVER BEEN ABLE TO TEST IT OUT... NEVER HAD THE RIGHT SUBJECT, UNTIL NOW.
IT'S BEEN DESIGNED TO GIVE OFF THE SAME TYPE OF GLOW AT THE SAME TYPE OF WAVELENGTH AS THE LIGHT REFLECTED OFF OF THE MOON AS SEEN FROM EARTH.
LYCAN. LUNAR LIGHT? WAIT A MINUTE... ARE YOU TALKING WEREWOLVES?
JUST WATCH.
CAMERA READY.
GUARDS, BE READY, BUT FIRE ONLY ON MY WORD.
OK... OK.
CLK
HERE WE GO.
VMMMMMMMMMMMMMMMMMMMMMMMM

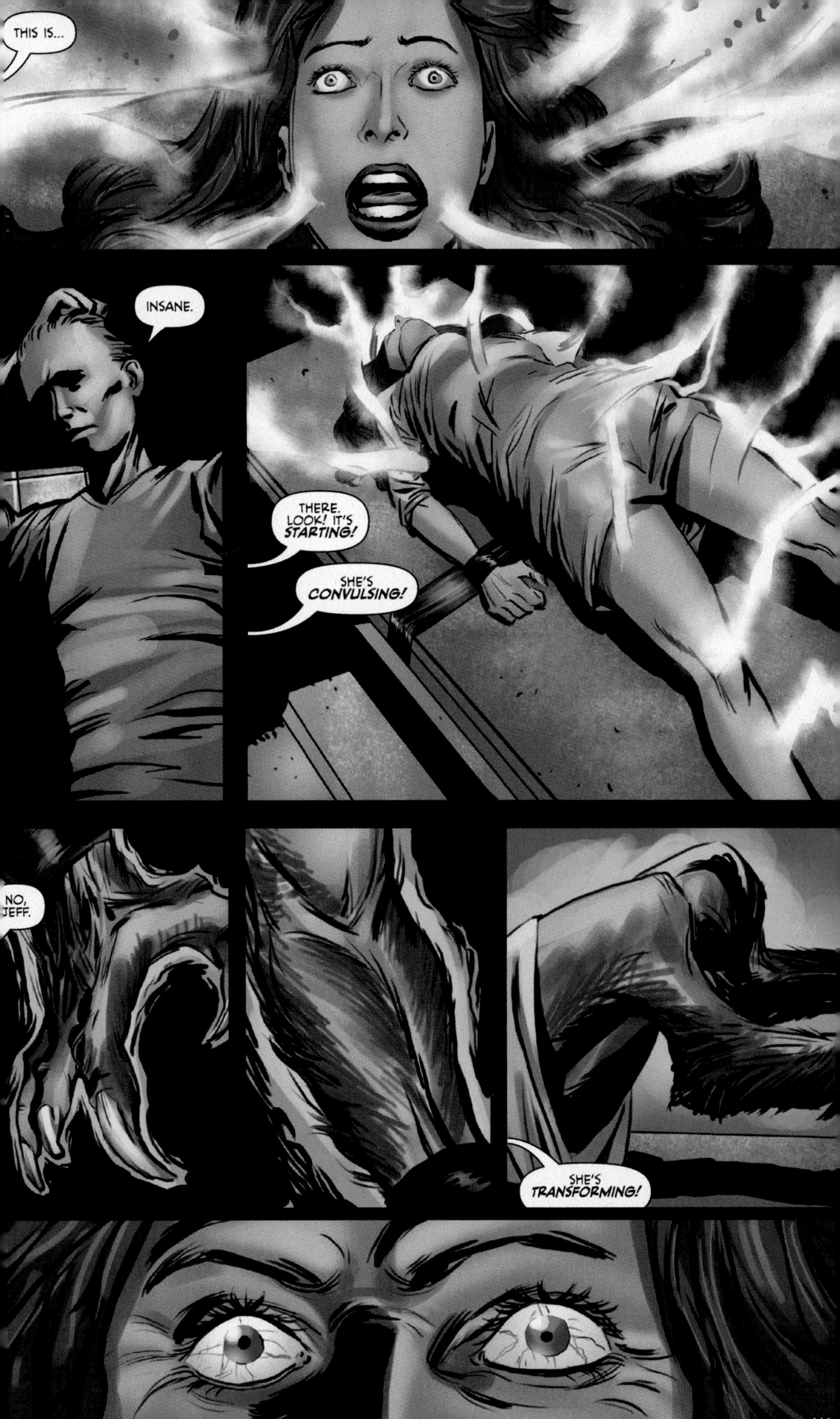
THIS IS...
INSANE.
THERE. LOOK! IT'S STARTING!
SHE'S CONVULSING!
NO, JEFF.
SHE'S TRANSFORMING!

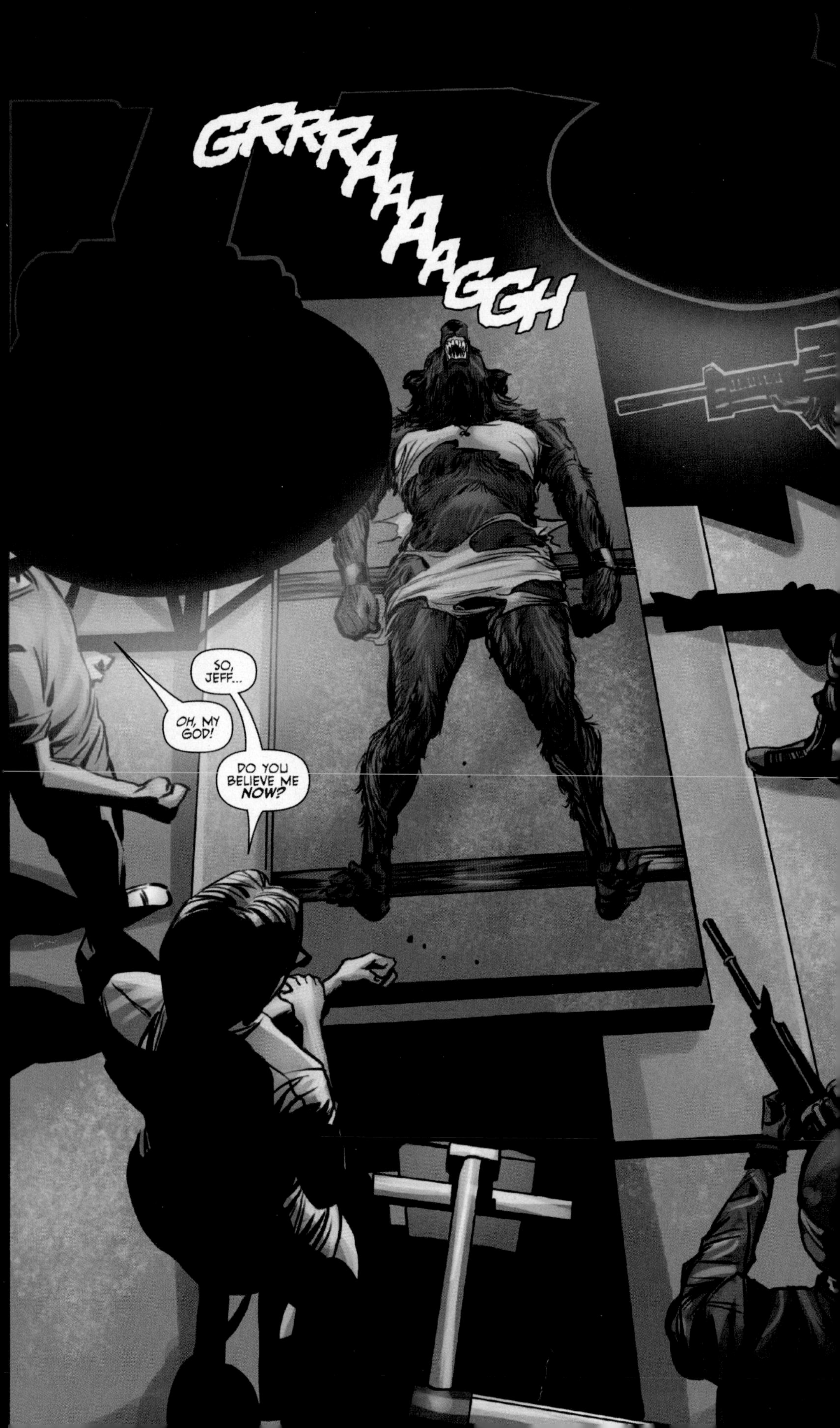
GRRRAAAAGGH
OH, MY GOD!
SO, JEFF...
DO YOU BELIEVE ME NOW?

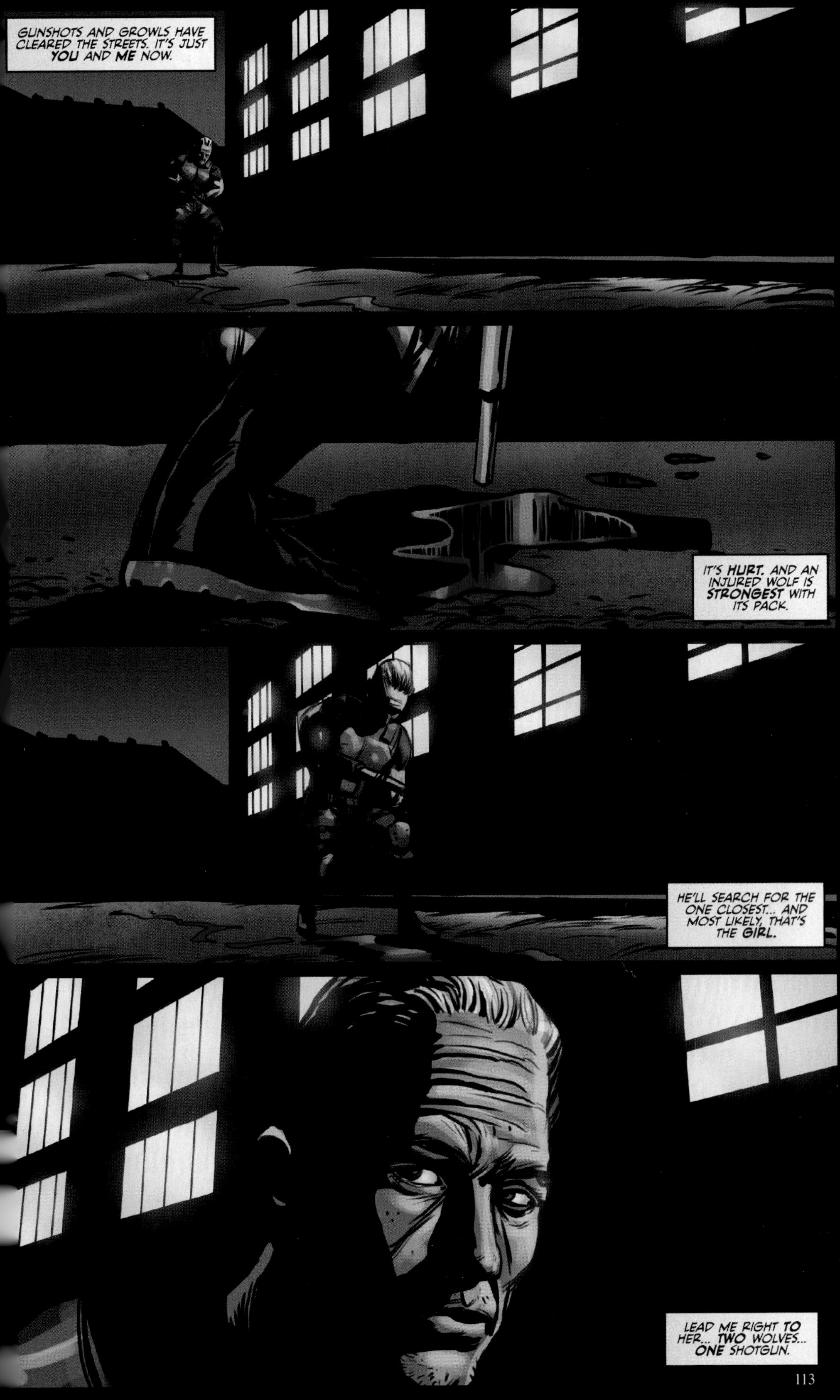
GUNSHOTS AND GROWLS HAVE CLEARED THE STREETS. IT'S JUST YOU AND ME NOW.
IT'S HURT. AND AN INJURED WOLF IS STRONGEST WITH ITS PACK.
HE'LL SEARCH FOR THE ONE CLOSEST... AND MOST LIKELY, THAT'S THE GIRL.
LEAD ME RIGHT TO HER... TWO WOLVES... ONE SHOTGUN.

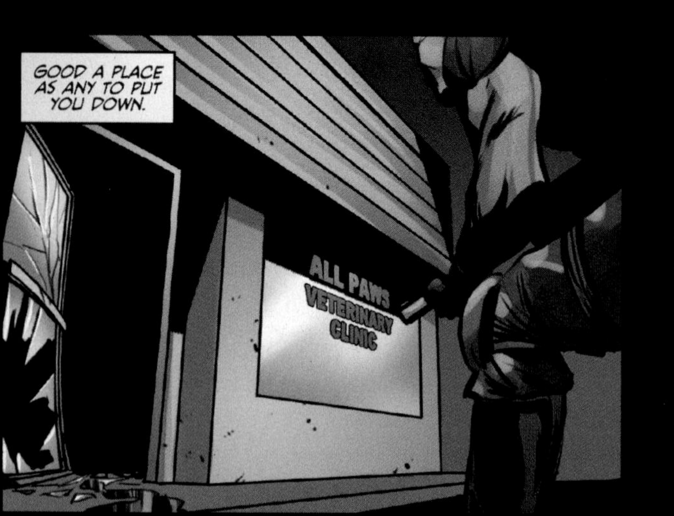
GOOD A PLACE AS ANY TO PUT YOU DOWN.
ALL PAWS VETERINARY CLINIC

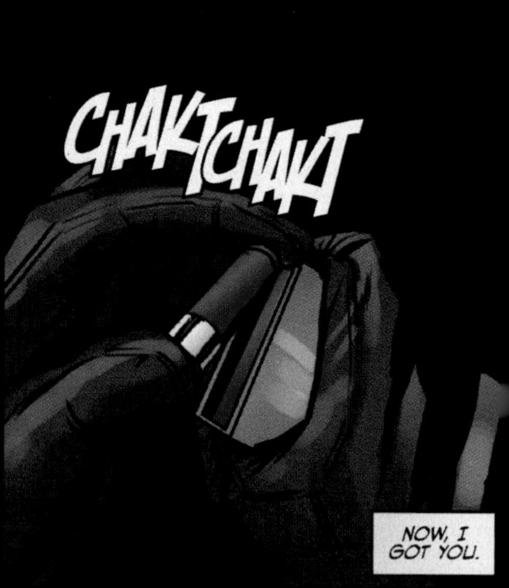
CHAKTCHAKT
NOW, I GOT YOU.

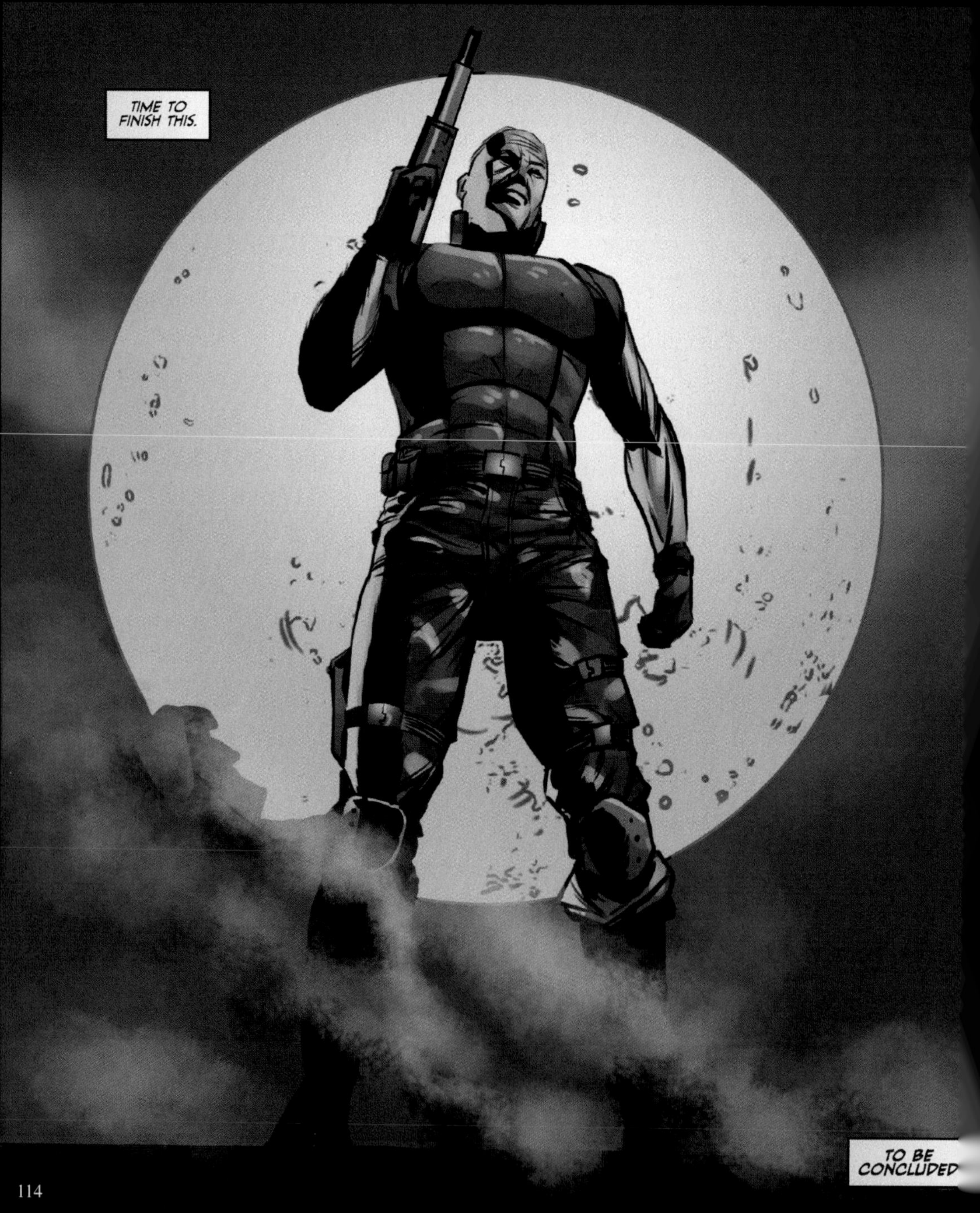
TIME TO FINISH THIS.
TO BE CONCLUDED

Grimm Fairy Tales
presents:

Vampires
&
Werewolves

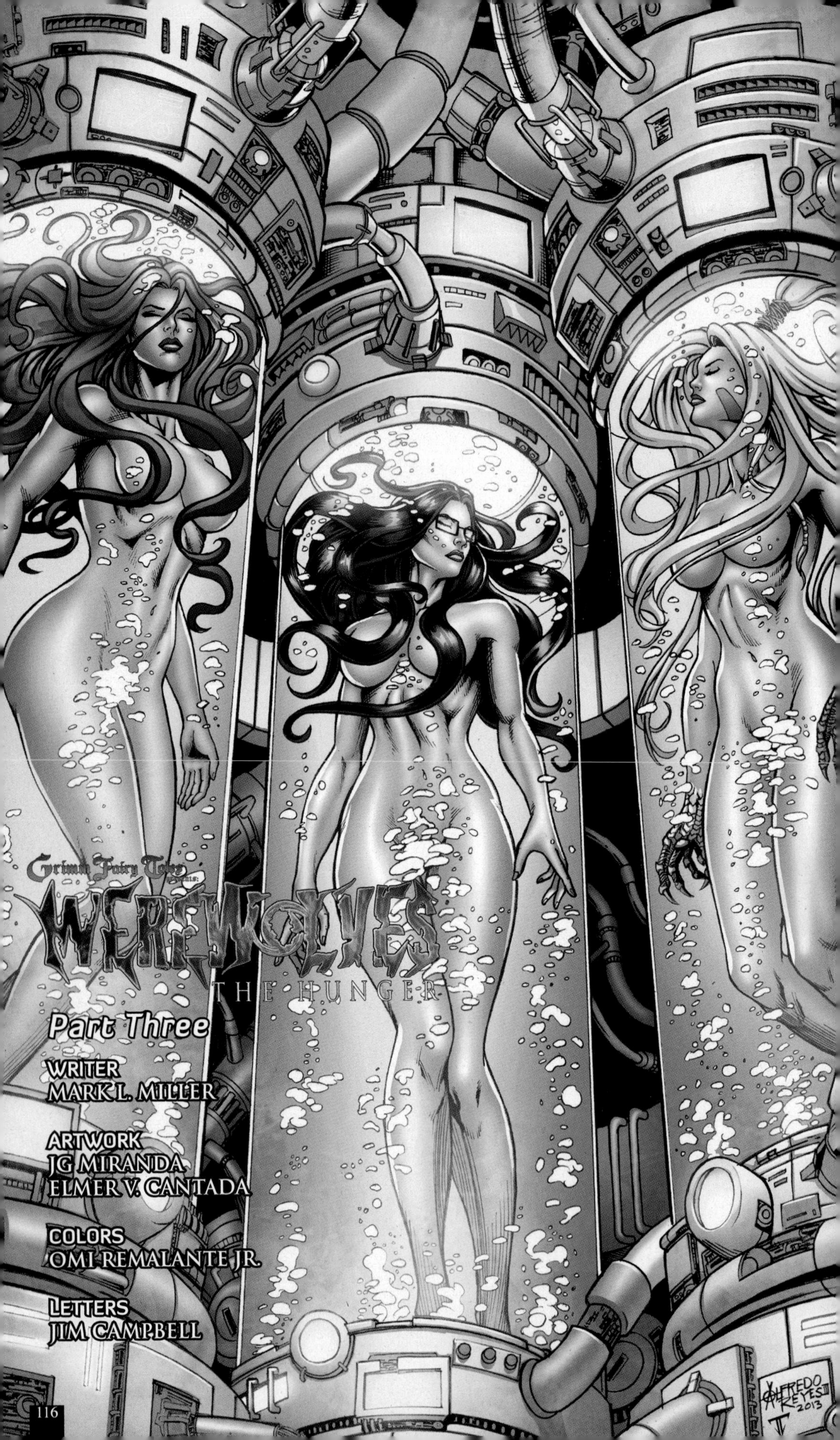
Grimm Fairy Tales presents:
WEREWOLVES
THE HUNGER
Part Three
WRITER
MARK L. MILLER
ARTWORK
JG MIRANDA
ELMER V. CANTADA
COLORS
OMI REMALANTE JR.
LETTERS
JIM CAMPBELL
ALFREDO REYES III 2013

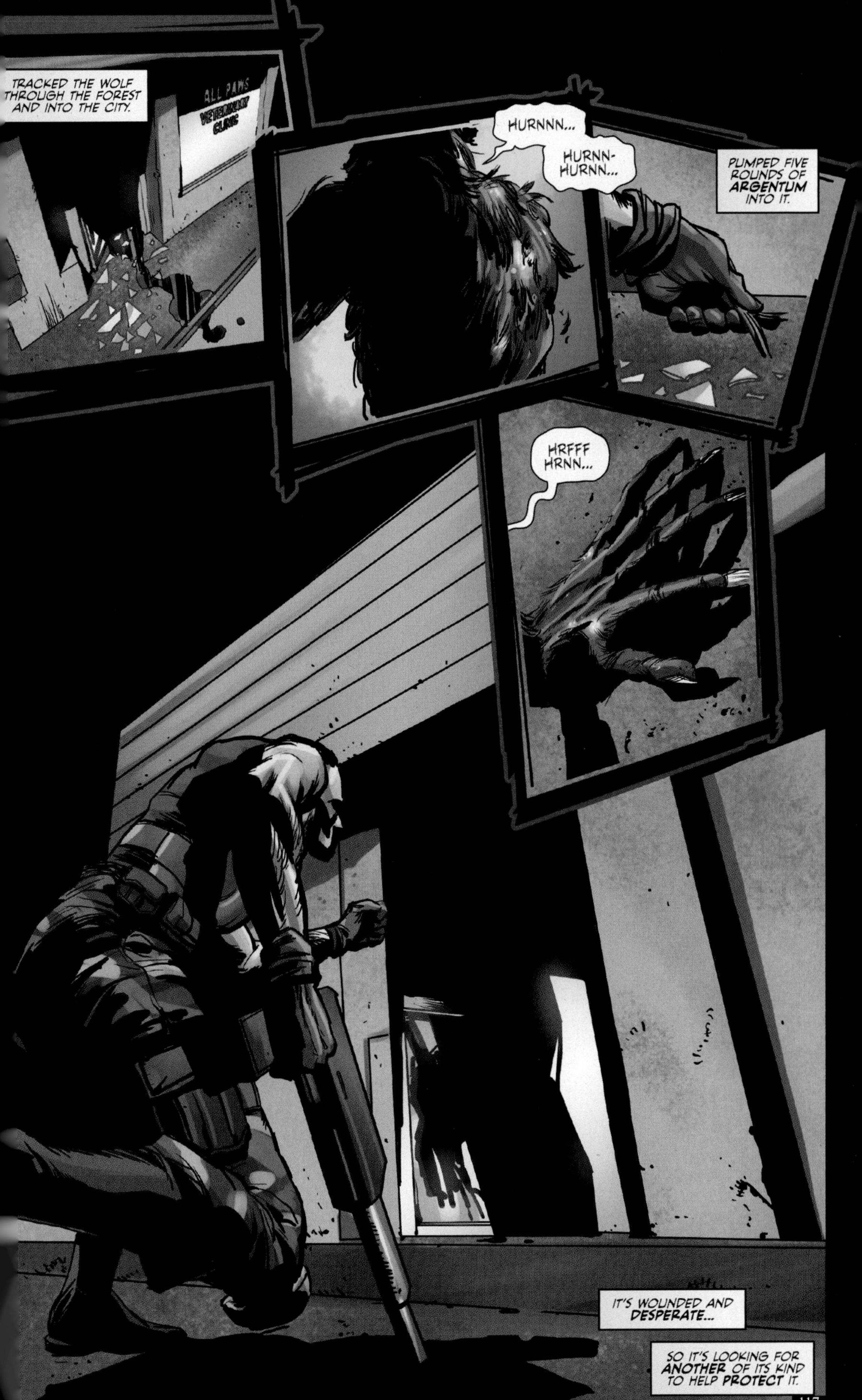

TRACKED THE WOLF THROUGH THE FOREST AND INTO THE CITY.
ALL PAWS
VETERINARY CLINIC
HURNNN...
HURNN-HURNN...
PUMPED FIVE ROUNDS OF ARGENTUM INTO IT.
HRFFF HRNN...
IT'S WOUNDED AND DESPERATE...
SO IT'S LOOKING FOR ANOTHER OF ITS KIND TO HELP PROTECT IT.

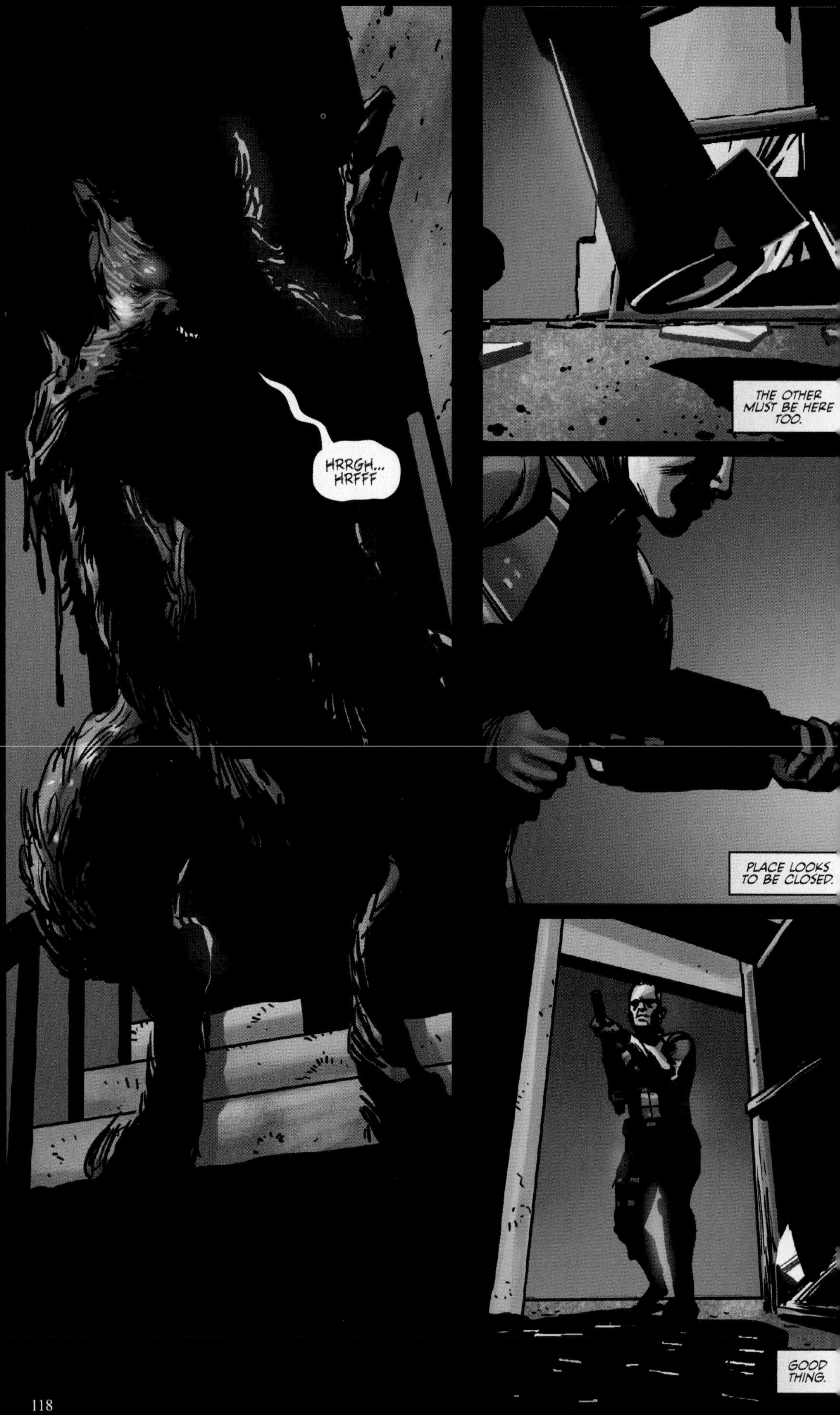
HRRGH... HRFFF
THE OTHER MUST BE HERE TOO.
PLACE LOOKS TO BE CLOSED.
GOOD THING.

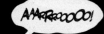

NO NEED FOR ANY *MORE* VICTIMS TONIGHT.

AAARRROOOOO!

DON'T GET *TRIGGER HAPPY,* GUARDS. THE STRAPS WILL *HOLD.*

WHAT--WHAT DO YOU WANT *ME* TO DO?

CONSIDERING YOU'VE DONE NOTHING BUT *COMPLAIN* ALL NIGHT, I THINK YOU'RE FINE JUST STAYING *OUT* OF MY WAY.

I MEAN REALLY, JEFF. YOU ARE WITNESSING SOMETHING *FEW* HAVE EVER EXPERIENCED. THE INITIAL TRANSFORMATION OF A SUBJECT INFECTED WITH THE *LYCAN VIRUS.*

ONE WOULD THINK YOU'D BE MORE *EXCITED.*

GAH! JESUS, RACHEL. THIS IS JUST PLAIN *WRONG!*

THIS IS... WAS A *HUMAN BEING!*

WOULD YOU BE *MORE* COMFORTABLE IF I *LOOSENED* THE *STRAPS* A LITTLE?

SCHOMP

119

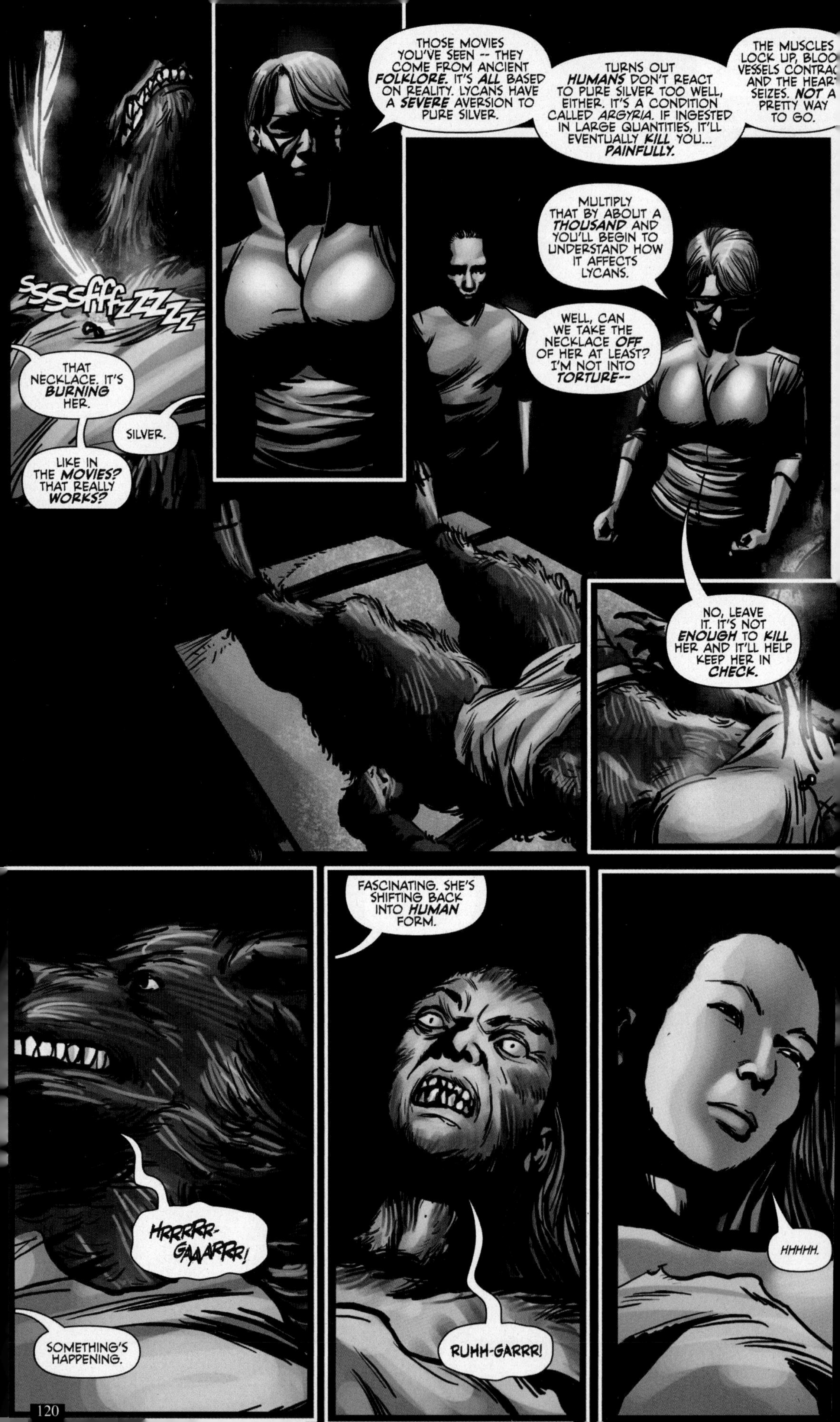

SSSSFFFZZZZZ
THAT NECKLACE. IT'S BURNING HER.
SILVER.
LIKE IN THE MOVIES? THAT REALLY WORKS?
THOSE MOVIES YOU'VE SEEN -- THEY COME FROM ANCIENT FOLKLORE. IT'S ALL BASED ON REALITY. LYCANS HAVE A SEVERE AVERSION TO PURE SILVER.
TURNS OUT HUMANS DON'T REACT TO PURE SILVER TOO WELL, EITHER. IT'S A CONDITION CALLED ARGYRIA. IF INGESTED IN LARGE QUANTITIES, IT'LL EVENTUALLY KILL YOU... PAINFULLY.
THE MUSCLES LOCK UP, BLOO VESSELS CONTRAC AND THE HEAR SEIZES. NOT A PRETTY WAY TO GO.
MULTIPLY THAT BY ABOUT A THOUSAND AND YOU'LL BEGIN TO UNDERSTAND HOW IT AFFECTS LYCANS.
WELL, CAN WE TAKE THE NECKLACE OFF OF HER AT LEAST? I'M NOT INTO TORTURE--
NO, LEAVE IT. IT'S NOT ENOUGH TO KILL HER AND IT'LL HELP KEEP HER IN CHECK.
HRRRRR-GAAARRR!
SOMETHING'S HAPPENING.
FASCINATING. SHE'S SHIFTING BACK INTO HUMAN FORM.
RUHH-GARRR!
HHHHH.

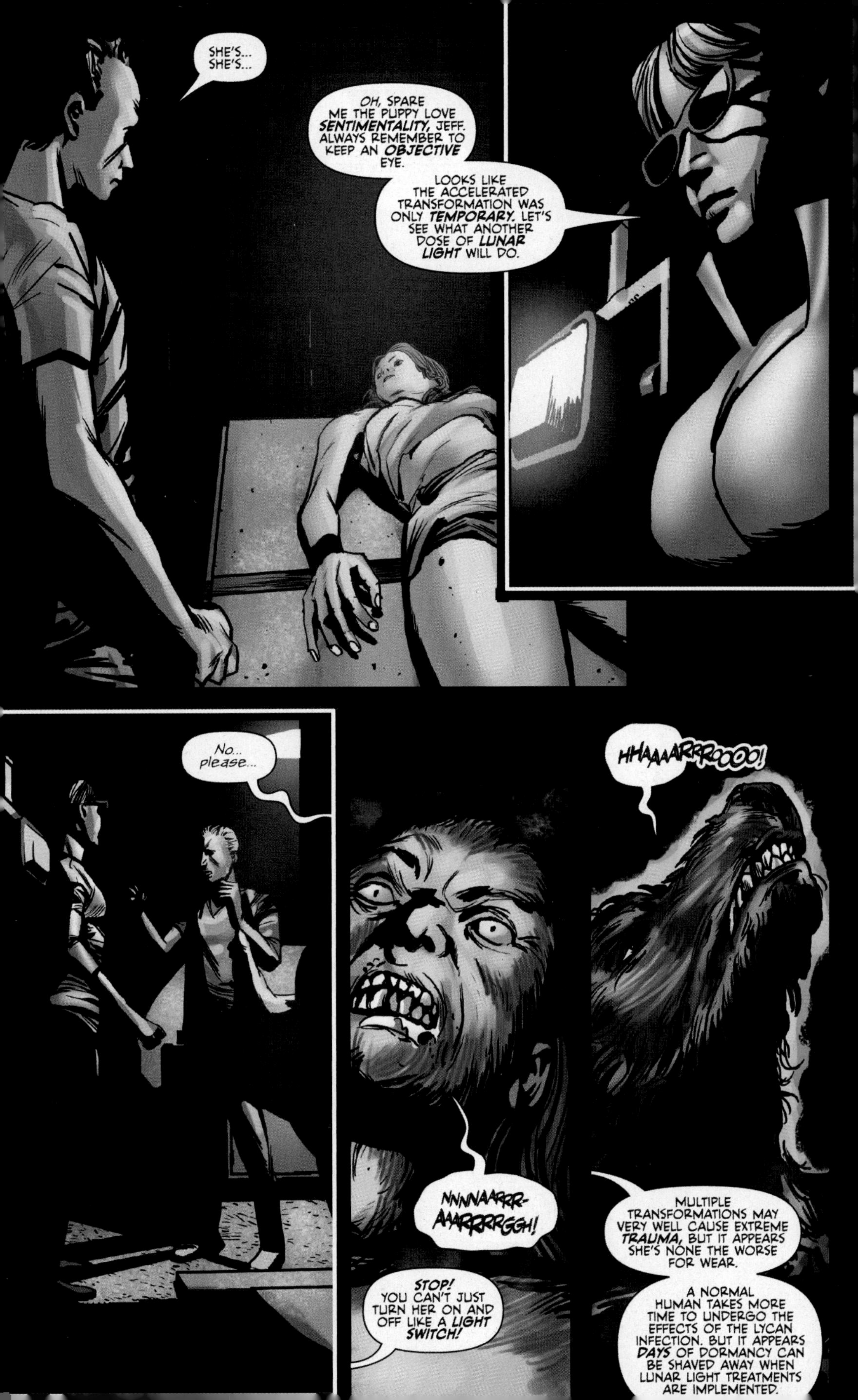
SHE'S... SHE'S...
OH, SPARE ME THE PUPPY LOVE SENTIMENTALITY, JEFF. ALWAYS REMEMBER TO KEEP AN OBJECTIVE EYE.
LOOKS LIKE THE ACCELERATED TRANSFORMATION WAS ONLY TEMPORARY. LET'S SEE WHAT ANOTHER DOSE OF LUNAR LIGHT WILL DO.
No... please...
NNNNAARRR-AAARRRRGGH!
STOP! YOU CAN'T JUST TURN HER ON AND OFF LIKE A LIGHT SWITCH!
HHAAAARRROOOO!
MULTIPLE TRANSFORMATIONS MAY VERY WELL CAUSE EXTREME TRAUMA, BUT IT APPEARS SHE'S NONE THE WORSE FOR WEAR.
A NORMAL HUMAN TAKES MORE TIME TO UNDERGO THE EFFECTS OF THE LYCAN INFECTION. BUT IT APPEARS DAYS OF DORMANCY CAN BE SHAVED AWAY WHEN LUNAR LIGHT TREATMENTS ARE IMPLEMENTED.

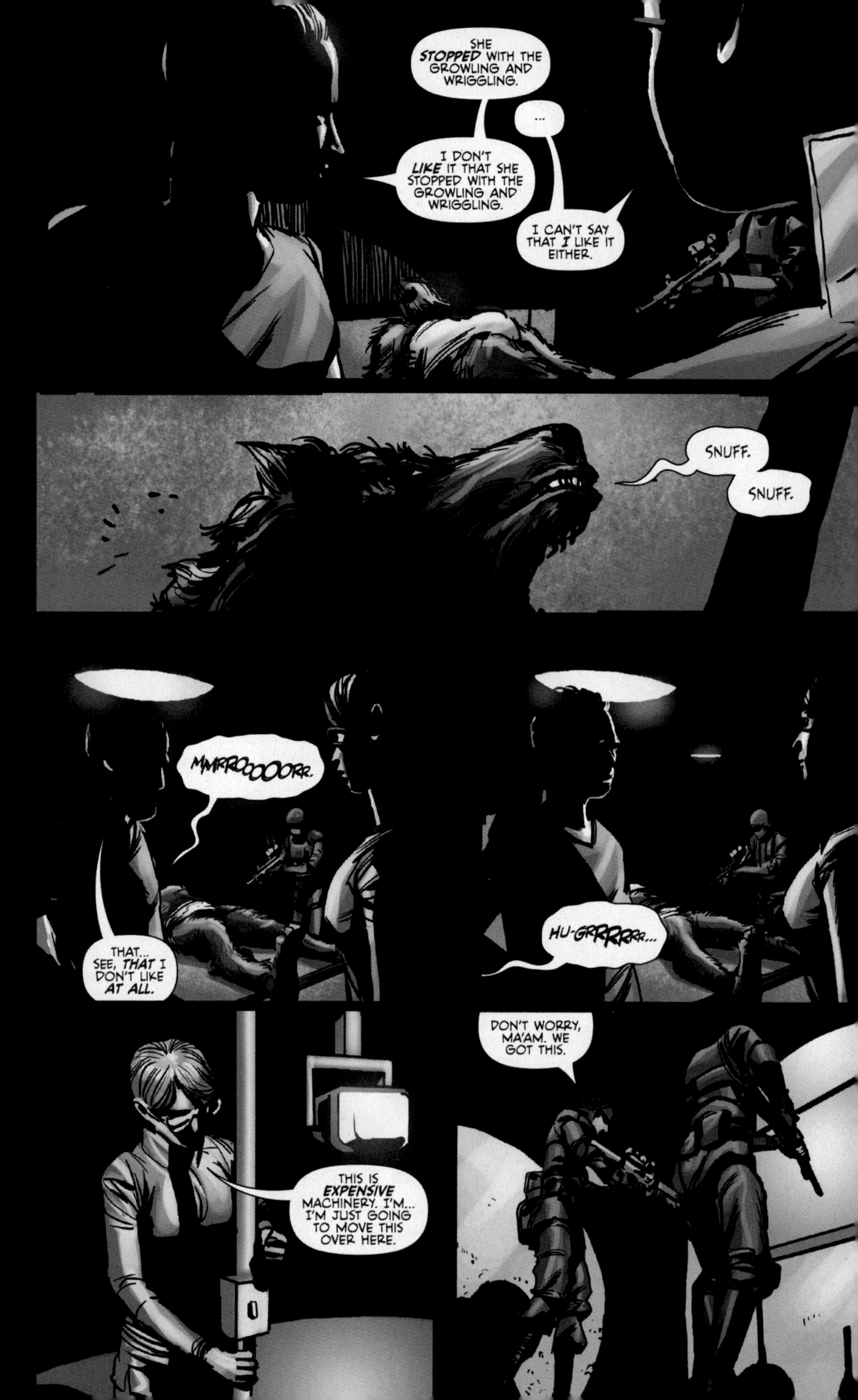
SHE STOPPED WITH THE GROWLING AND WRIGGLING.
I DON'T LIKE IT THAT SHE STOPPED WITH THE GROWLING AND WRIGGLING.
...
I CAN'T SAY THAT I LIKE IT EITHER.
SNUFF.
SNUFF.
MMRROOOOORR.
THAT... SEE, THAT I DON'T LIKE AT ALL.
HU-GRRRRRR...
THIS IS EXPENSIVE MACHINERY. I'M... I'M JUST GOING TO MOVE THIS OVER HERE.
DON'T WORRY, MA'AM. WE GOT THIS.

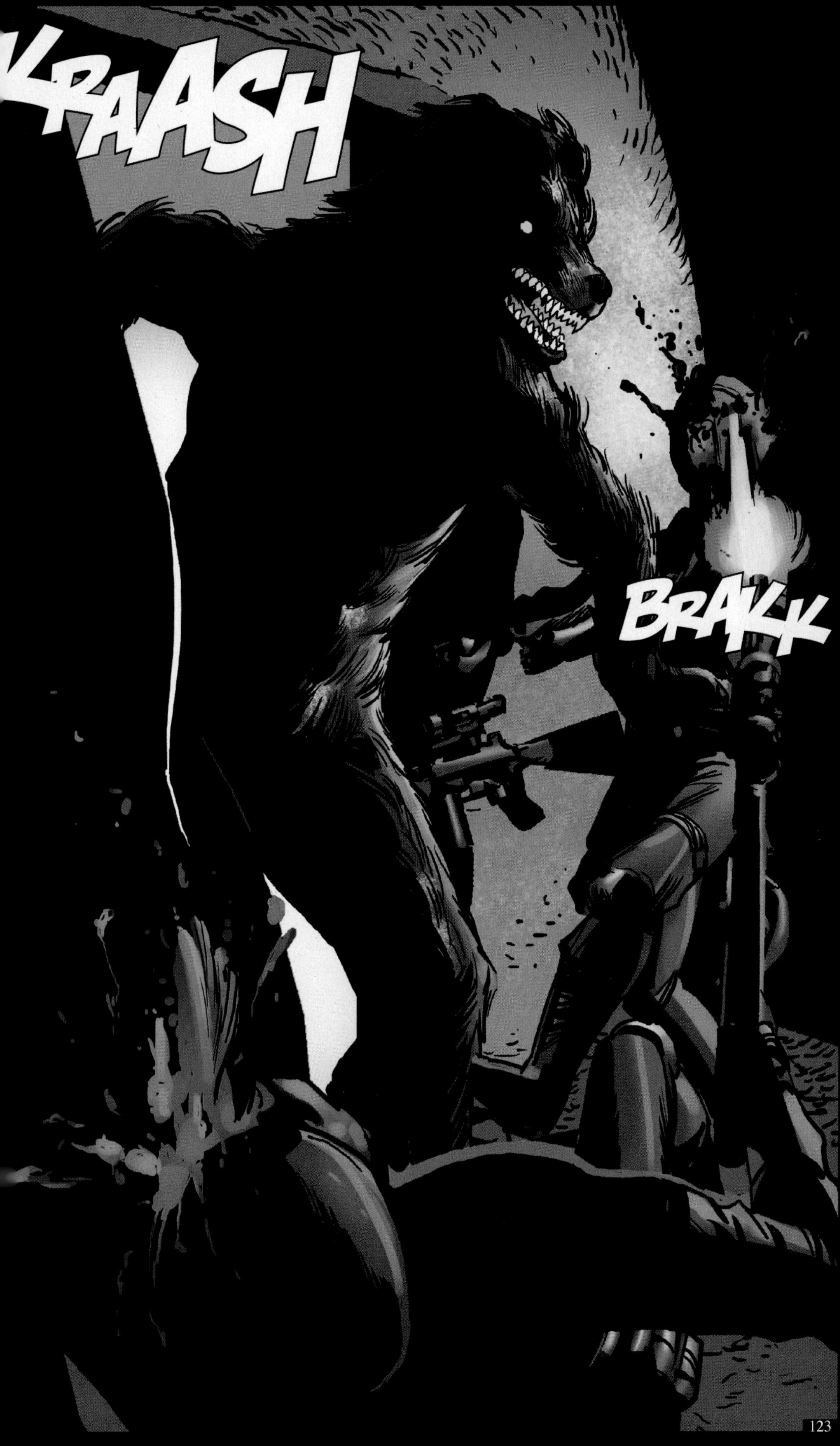
KRAASH
BRAKK

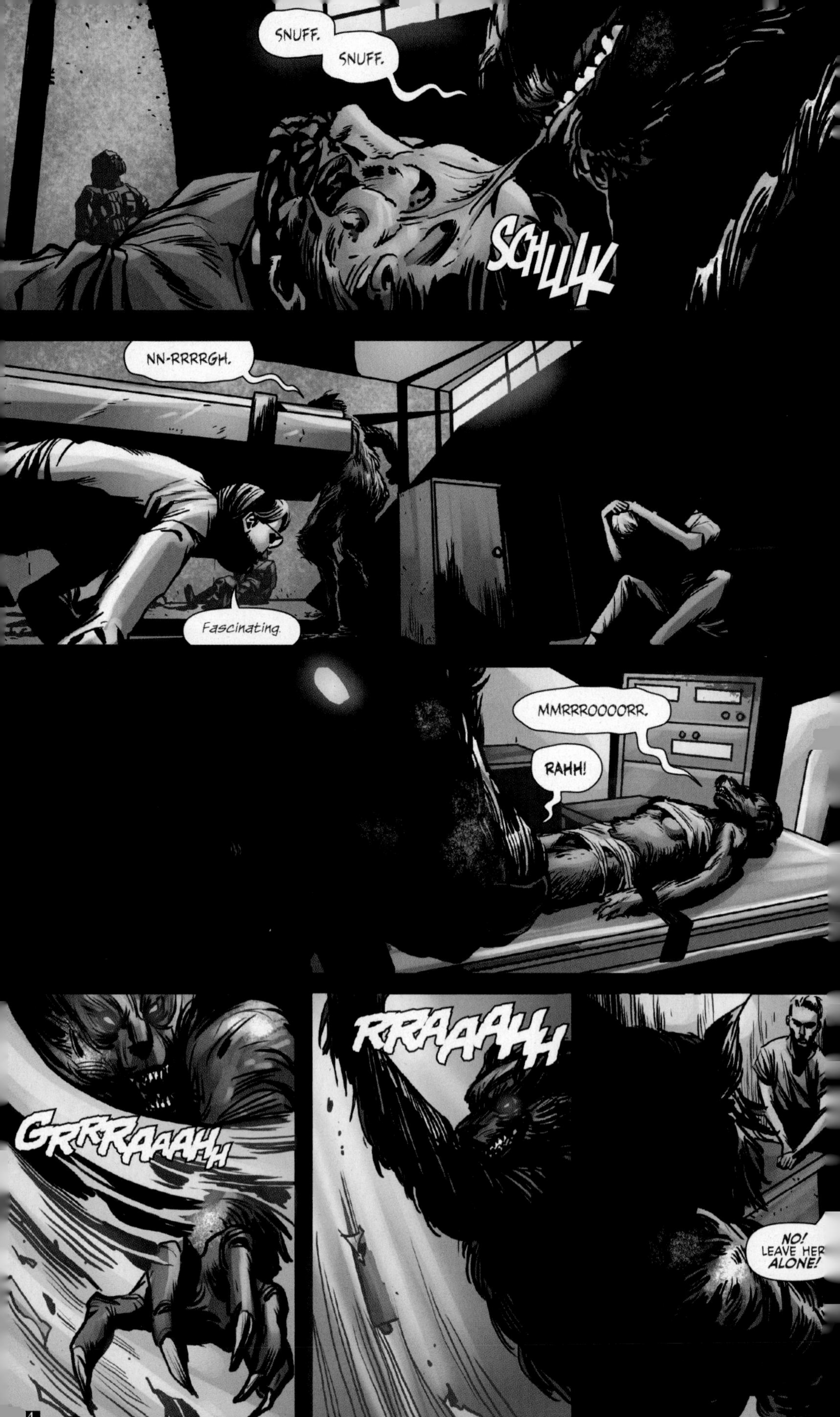
SNUFF.
SNUFF.
SCHLLLK
NN-RRRRGH.
Fascinating.
MMRRROOOORR.
RAHH!
GRRRAAAHH
RRAAAHH
NO! LEAVE HER ALONE!

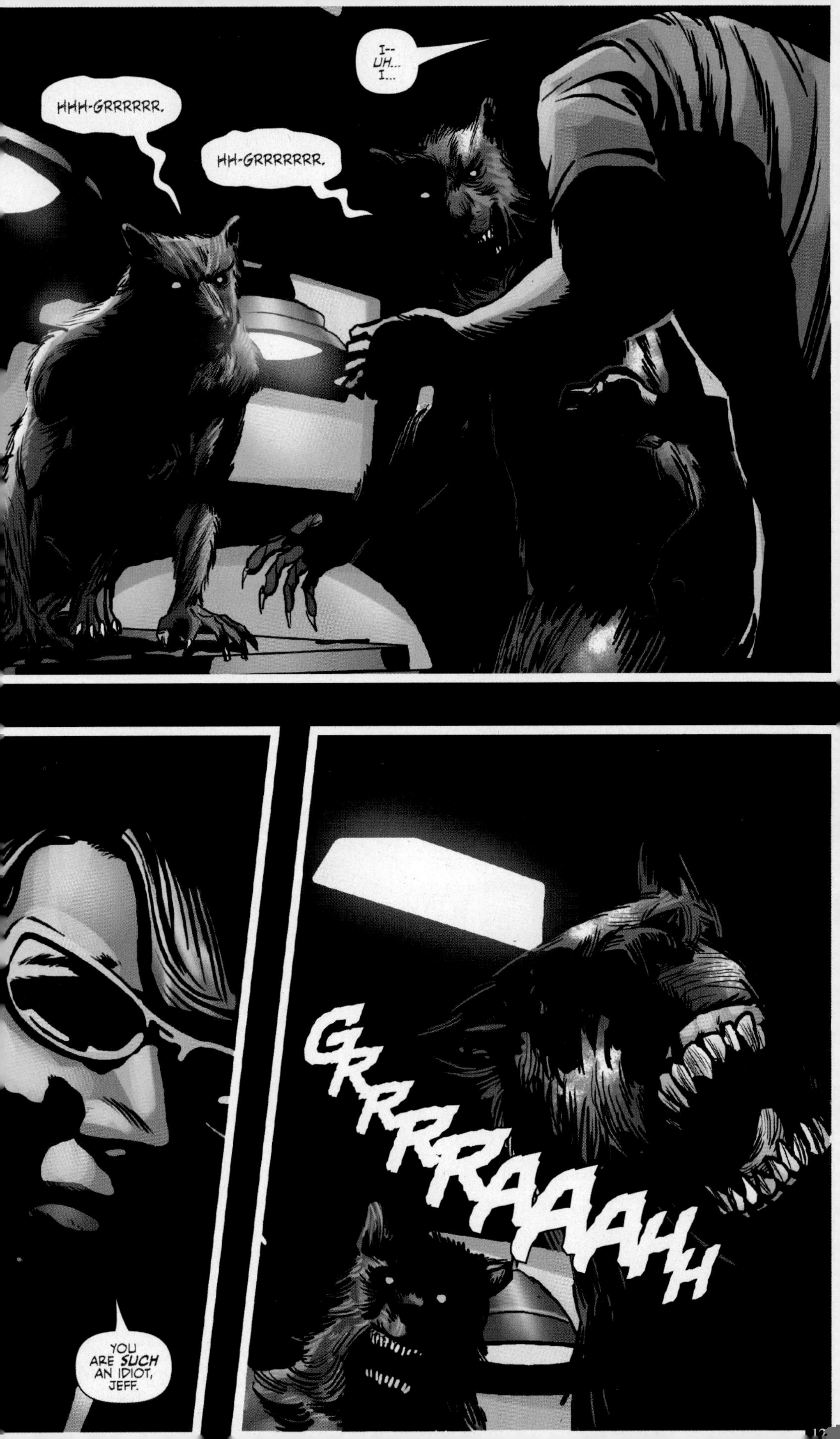
HHH-GRRRRRR.
I--
UH...
I...
HH-GRRRRRRR.
YOU ARE SUCH AN IDIOT, JEFF.
GRRRRAAAAHH

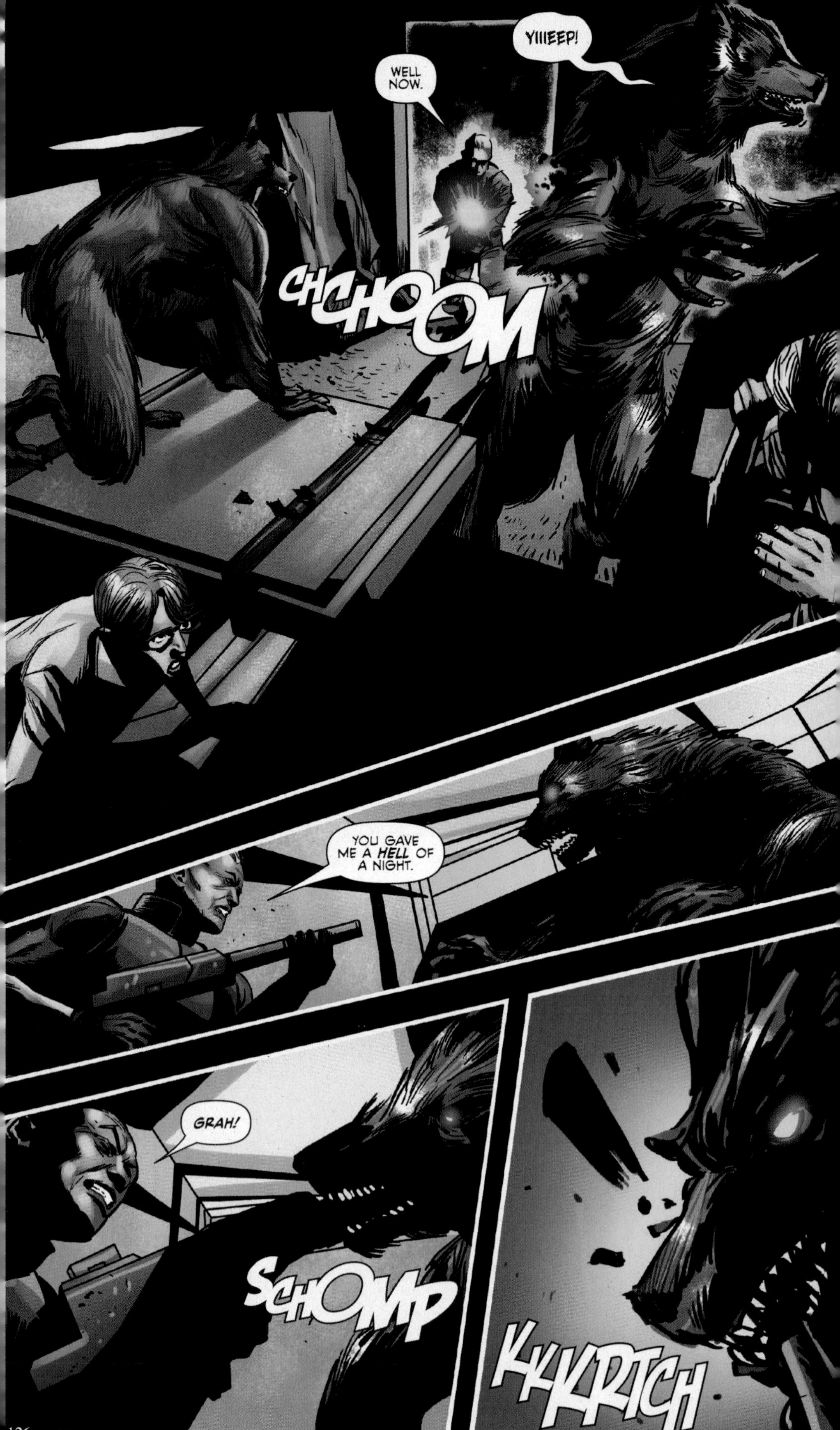
WELL NOW.
YIIIEEP!
CHCHOOM
YOU GAVE ME A HELL OF A NIGHT.
GRAH!
SCHOMP
KKKRITCH

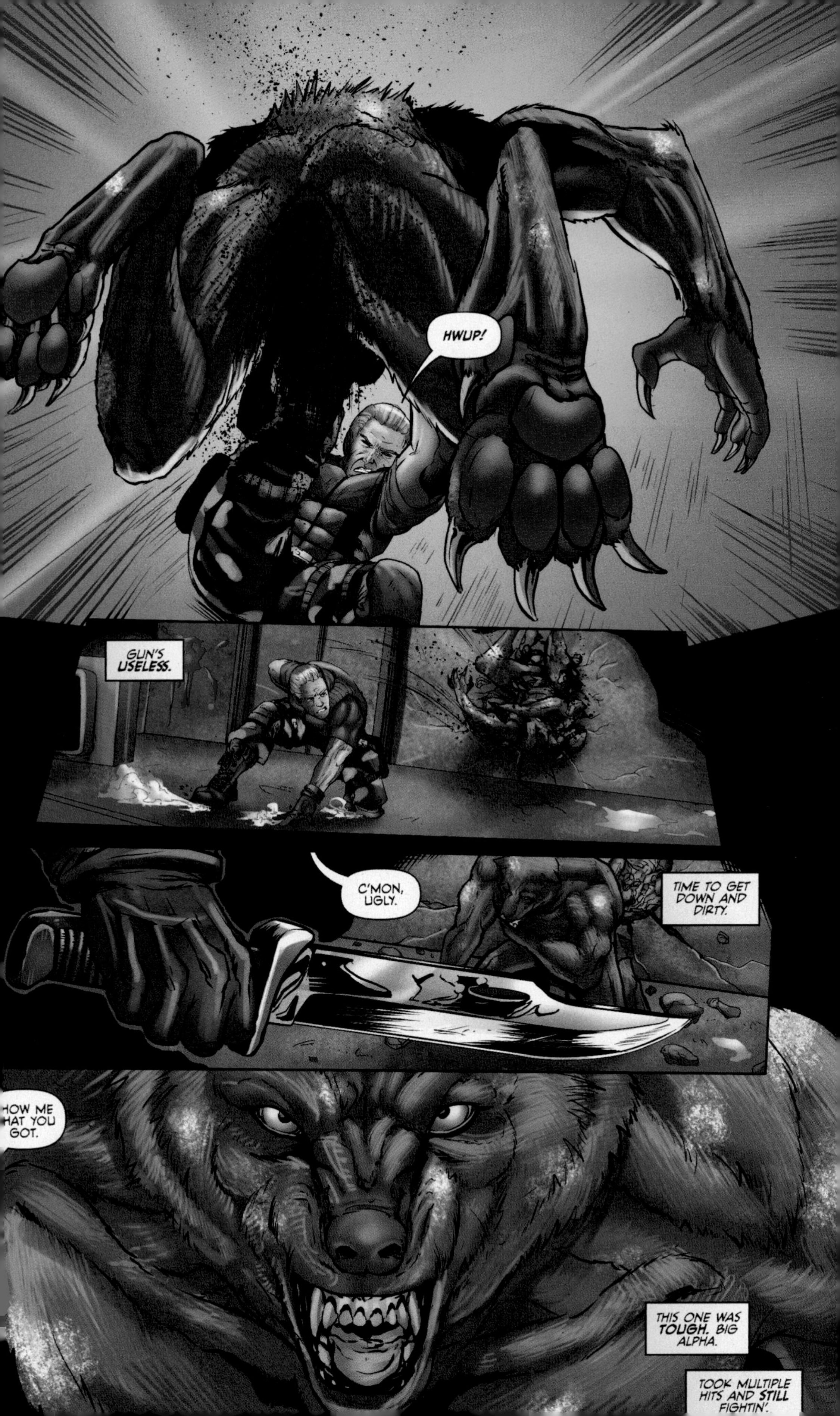
HWUP!
GUN'S USELESS.
C'MON, UGLY.
TIME TO GET DOWN AND DIRTY.
HOW ME HAT YOU GOT.
THIS ONE WAS TOUGH. BIG ALPHA.
TOOK MULTIPLE HITS AND STILL FIGHTIN'.

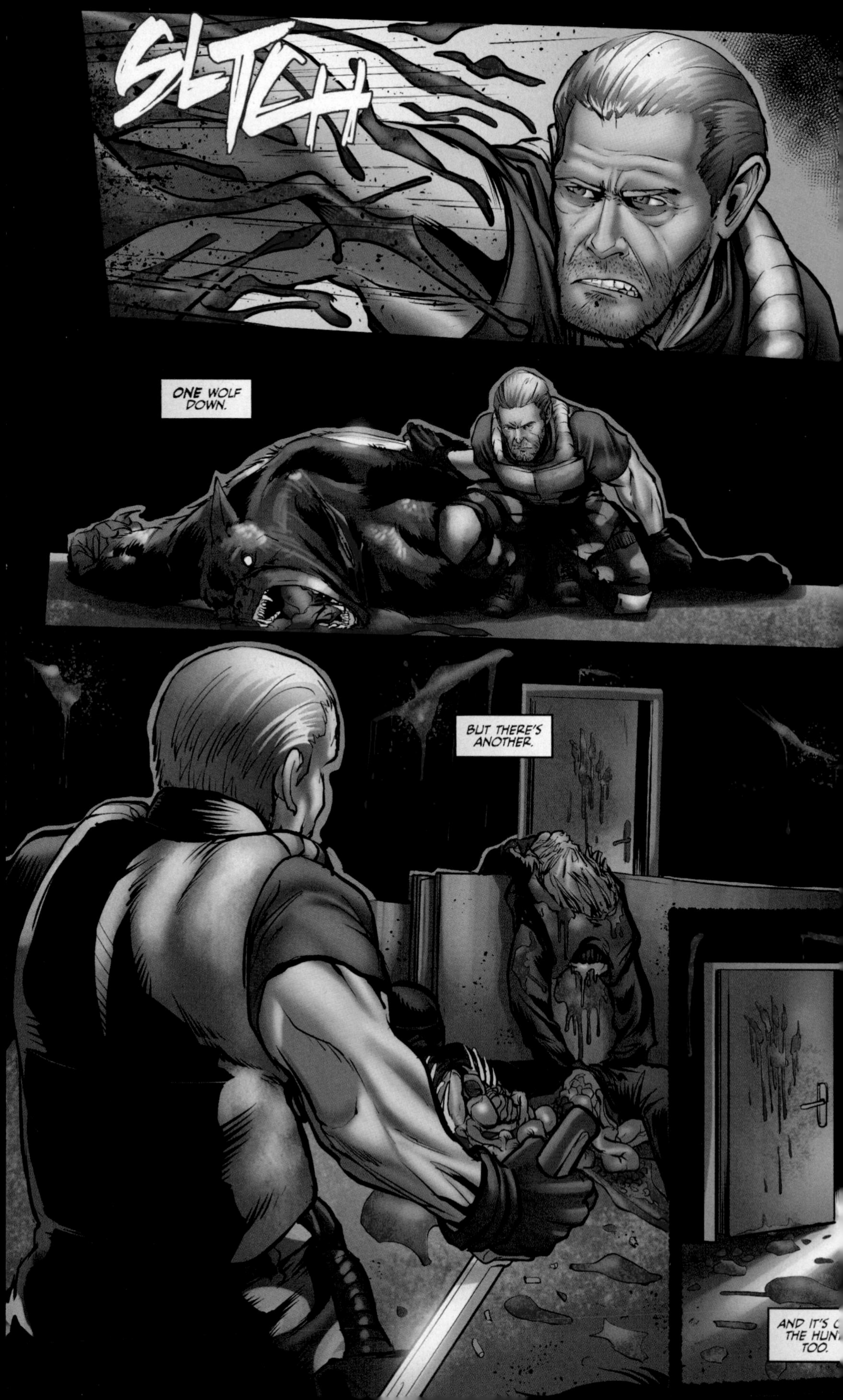
SLTCH
ONE WOLF DOWN.
BUT THERE'S ANOTHER.
AND IT'S
THE HUN
TOO.

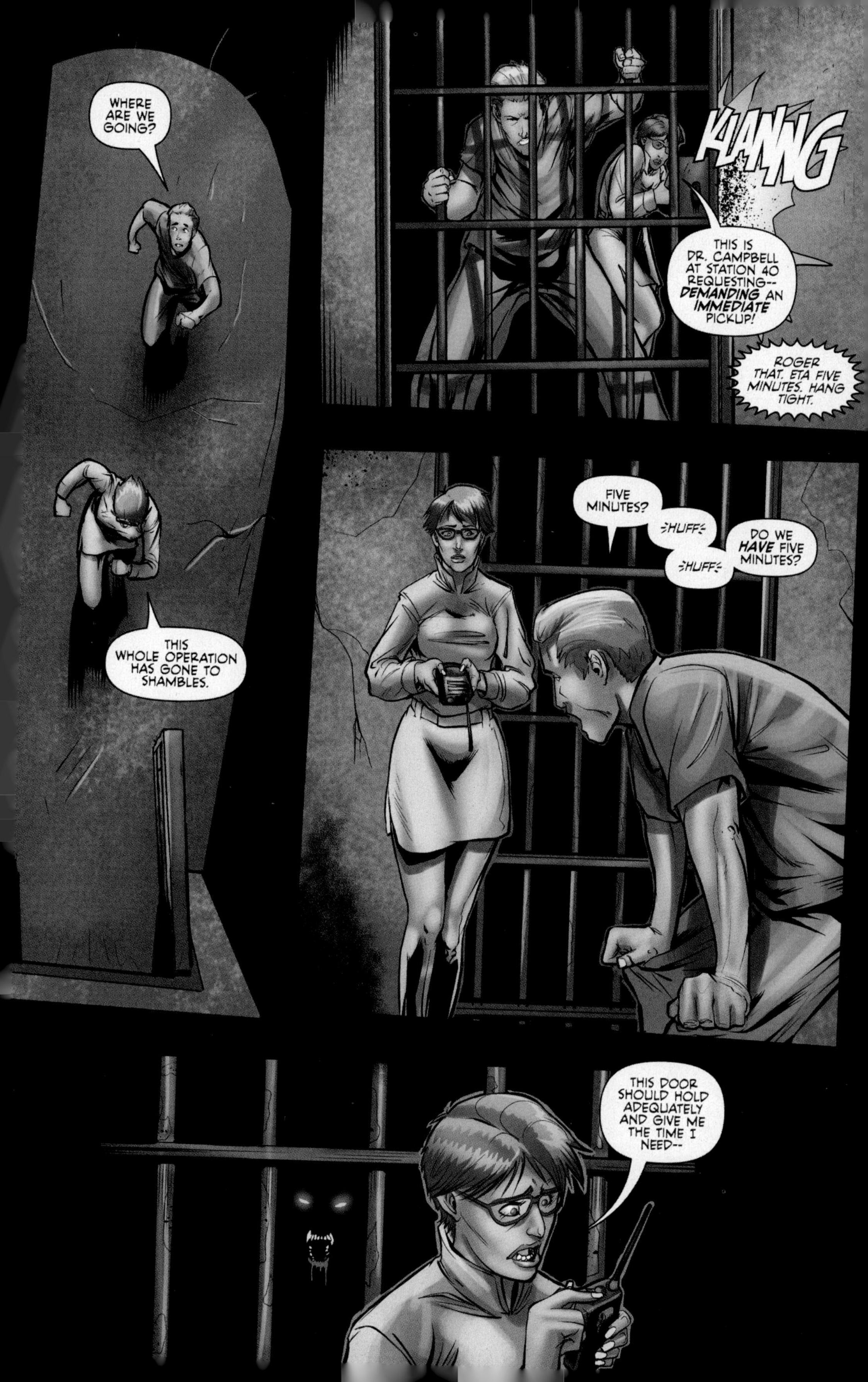
WHERE ARE WE GOING?
KLANNG
THIS IS DR. CAMPBELL AT STATION 40 REQUESTING-- DEMANDING AN IMMEDIATE PICKUP!
ROGER THAT. ETA FIVE MINUTES. HANG TIGHT.
THIS WHOLE OPERATION HAS GONE TO SHAMBLES.
FIVE MINUTES?
HUFF
HUFF
DO WE HAVE FIVE MINUTES?
THIS DOOR SHOULD HOLD ADEQUATELY AND GIVE ME THE TIME I NEED--

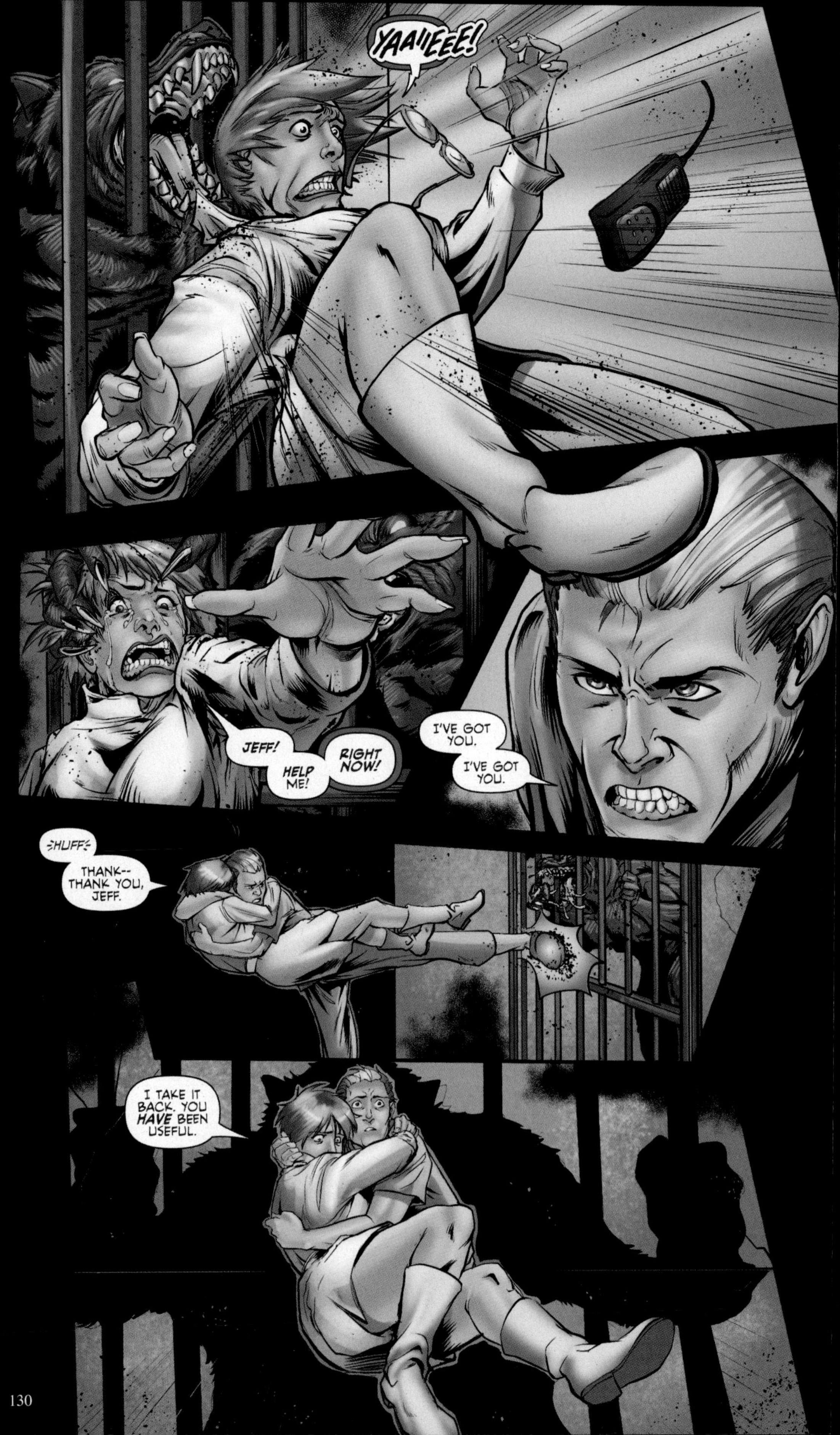
YAAIIEEE!
JEFF!
HELP ME!
RIGHT NOW!
I'VE GOT YOU.
I'VE GOT YOU.
HUFF
THANK-- THANK YOU, JEFF.
I TAKE IT BACK. YOU HAVE BEEN USEFUL.

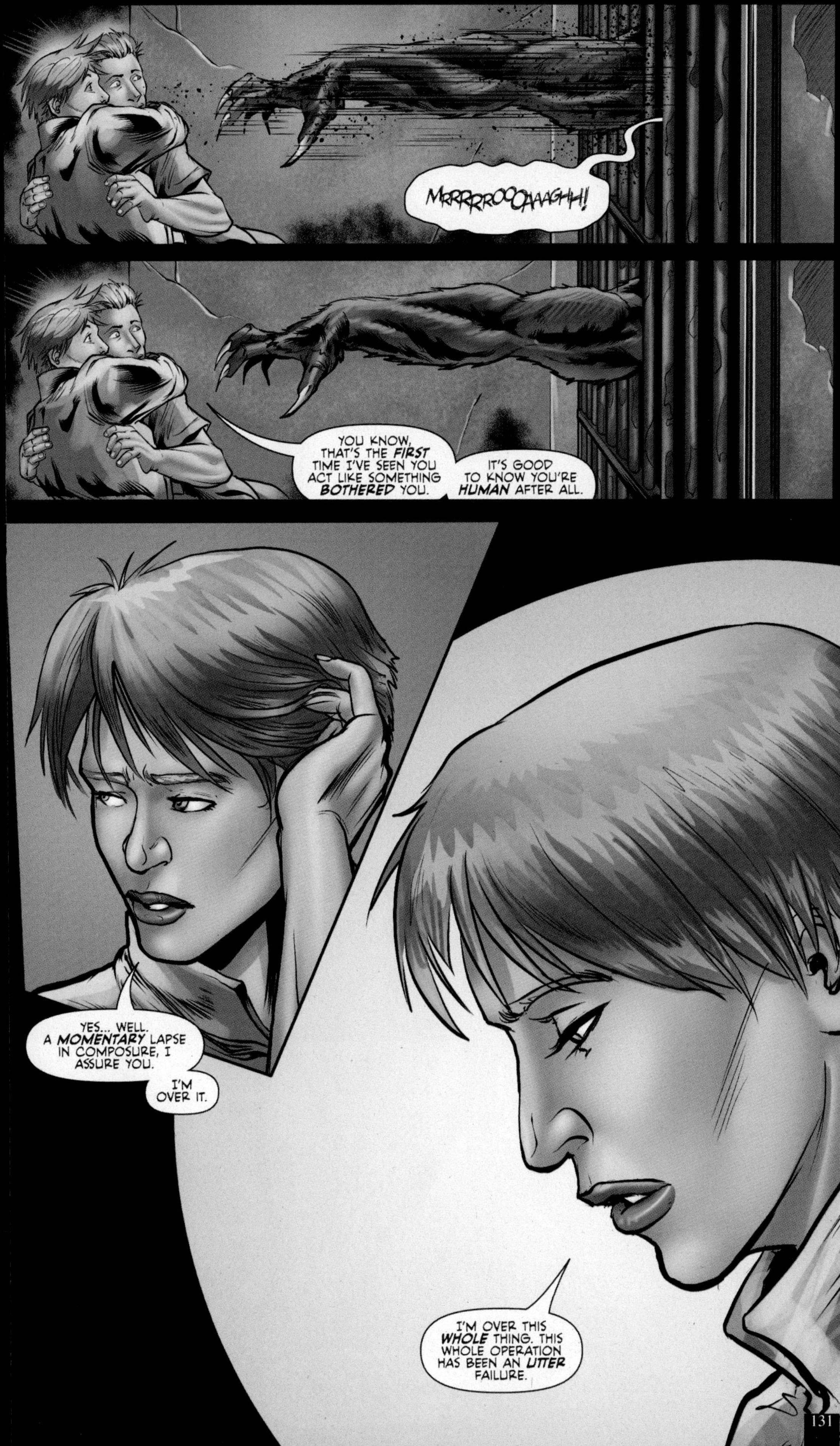
MRRRRROOOAAAGHH!
YOU KNOW, THAT'S THE FIRST TIME I'VE SEEN YOU ACT LIKE SOMETHING BOTHERED YOU.
IT'S GOOD TO KNOW YOU'RE HUMAN AFTER ALL.
YES... WELL. A MOMENTARY LAPSE IN COMPOSURE, I ASSURE YOU.
I'M OVER IT.
I'M OVER THIS WHOLE THING. THIS WHOLE OPERATION HAS BEEN AN UTTER FAILURE.

MAYBE IT'S NOT A *COMPLETE* FAILURE.

LET ME... LET ME TRY TO *TALK* TO HER.

TO THAT YOUNG GIRL INSIDE. THAT SWEET YOUNG GIRL. SOMEWHERE IN THERE, I *KNOW* SHE *STILL* EXISTS. I WANT TO APPEAL TO *HER* -- TO REASSURE HER THAT SHE DOESN'T HAVE TO *HURT* ANYONE.

I WANT TO TELL HER THAT WE CAN *HELP* HER. THAT EVERYTHING WILL BE--

RRRRRRAH

GAH!

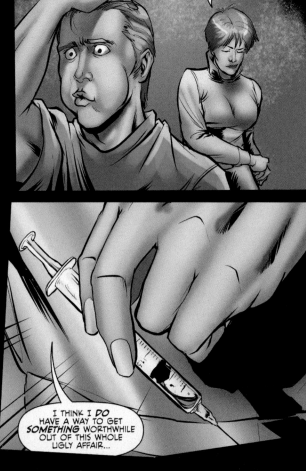

NICE STAB AT POP PSYCHOLOGY, JEFF. I'M SURE THAT SENSITIVE TALK GETS ALL OF THE HEARTS FLUTTERING AT *SCHOOL*, BUT I COULD'VE *TOLD* YOU IT WASN'T GOING TO GET YOU ANYWHERE *HERE*.

I THINK I *DO* HAVE A WAY TO GET *SOMETHING* WORTHWHILE OUT OF THIS WHOLE UGLY AFFAIR...

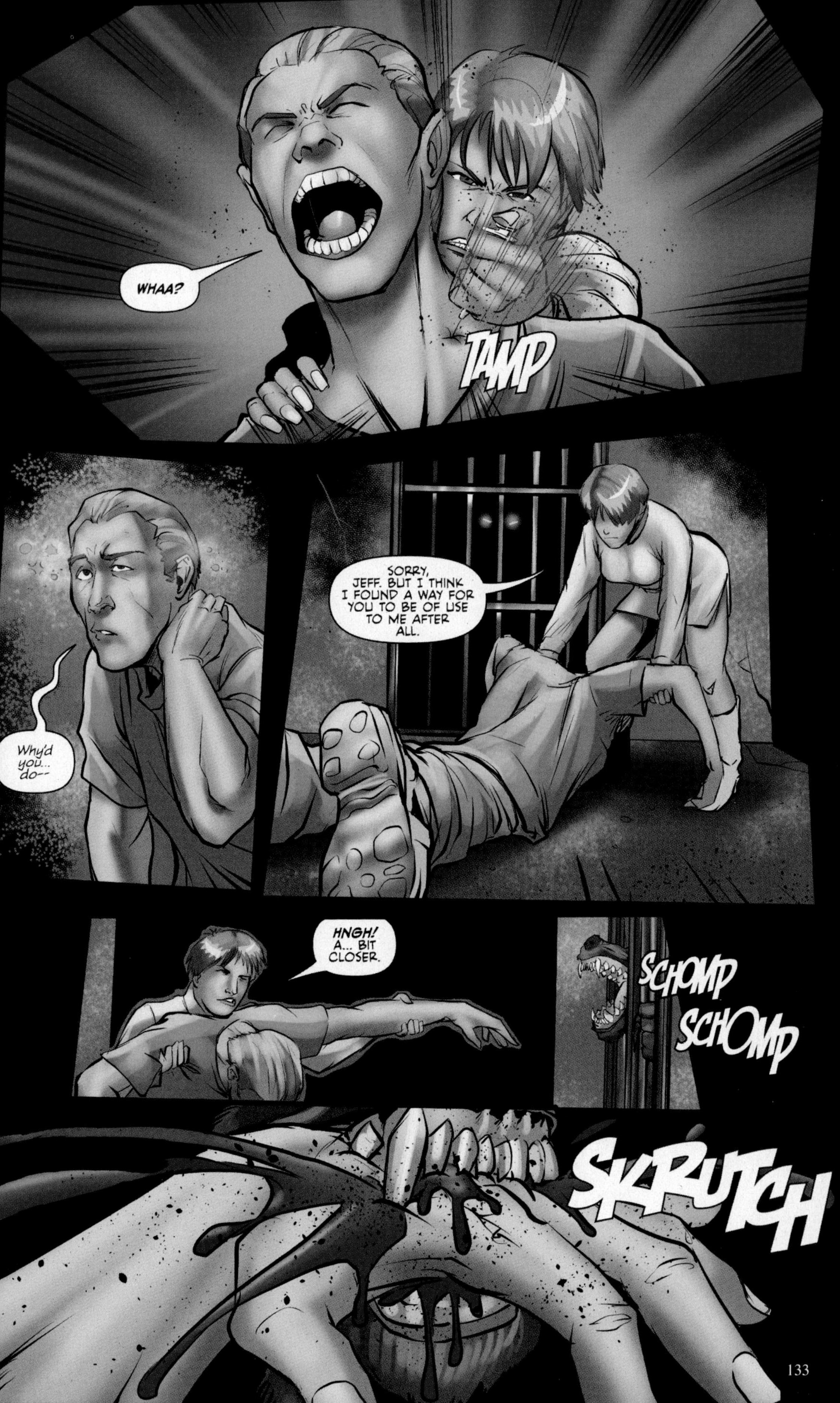
WHAA?
TAMP
SORRY, JEFF. BUT I THINK I FOUND A WAY FOR YOU TO BE OF USE TO ME AFTER ALL.
Why'd you... do--
HNGH! A... BIT CLOSER.
SCHOMP
SCHOMP
SKRUTCH

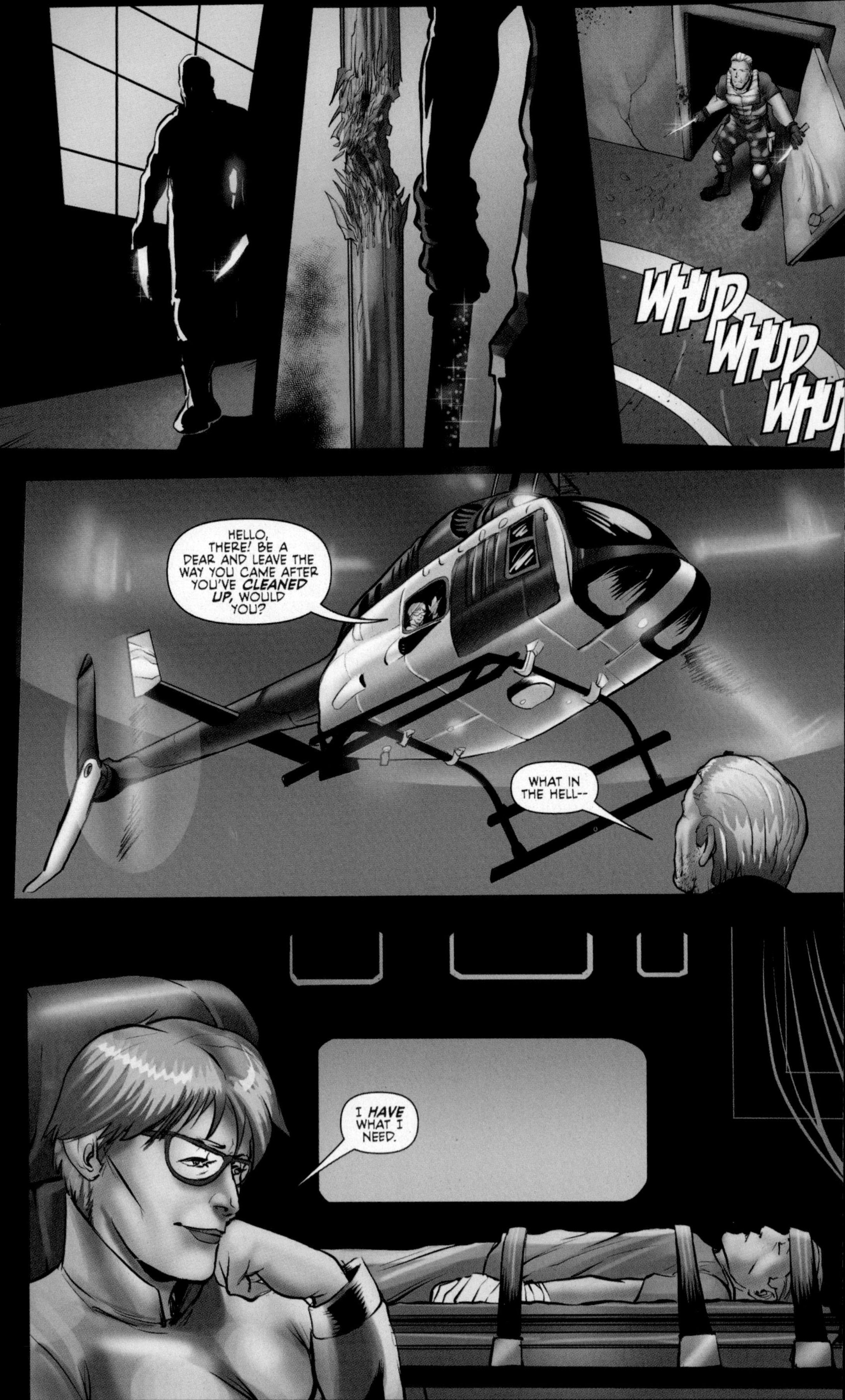
WHUD WHUD WHU
HELLO, THERE! BE A DEAR AND LEAVE THE WAY YOU CAME AFTER YOU'VE CLEANED UP, WOULD YOU?
WHAT IN THE HELL--
I HAVE WHAT I NEED.

...K TO BE LIKE THIS.

HHH-GRRRRR...

BUT HER STORY IS **OVER.** LOOK INTO THE WOLF'S EYES AND YOU'LL SEE IT FOR ALL THAT IT IS.

THERE'S **NOTHING** BUT PAIN, AND RAGE, AND HUNGER IN THERE.

AND IT'S A HUNGER THAT CAN **NEVER** BE FILLED.

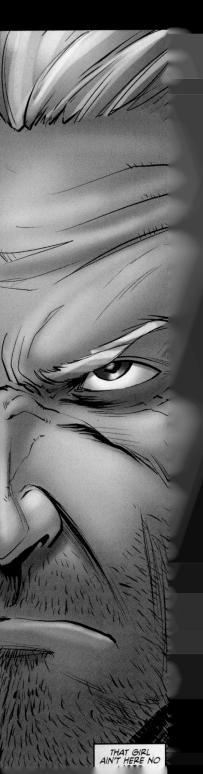

IT'S JUST HER SAD LUCK SHE CROSSED PATHS WITH THE WOLF. HER'S IS A STORY I KNOW **TOO** DAMN WELL.

THAT GIRL AIN'T HERE NO

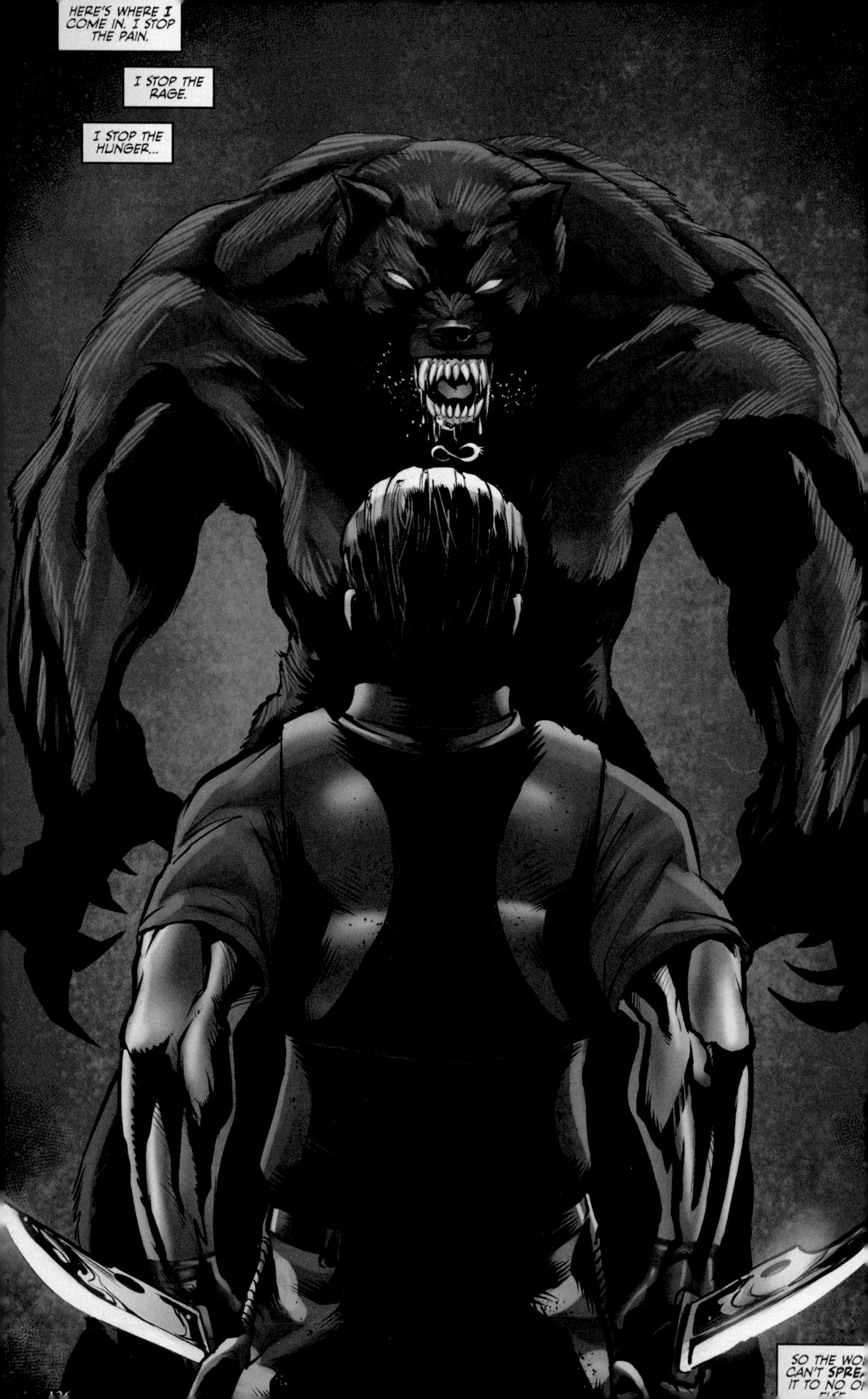
HERE'S WHERE I COME IN. I STOP THE PAIN.
I STOP THE RAGE.
I STOP THE HUNGER...
SO THE WO
CAN'T SPRE
IT TO NO O

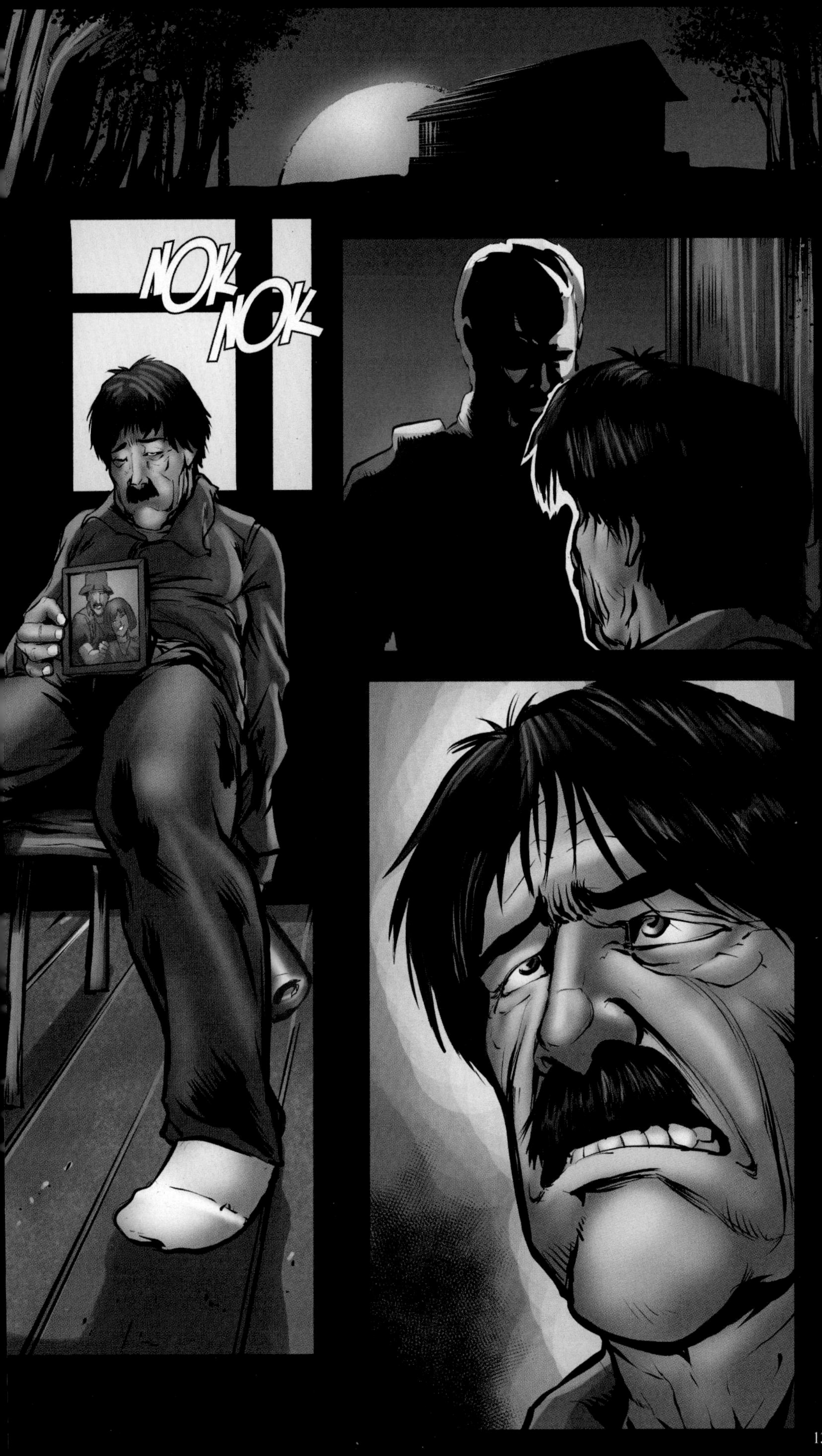
NOK NOK

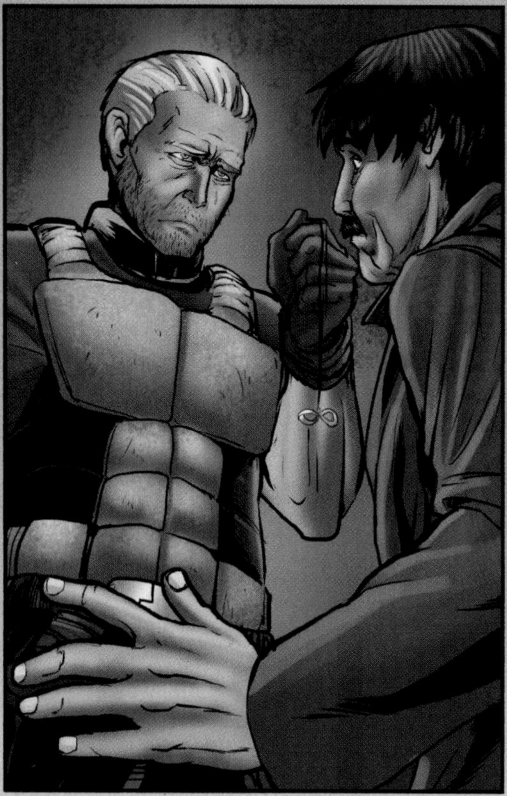

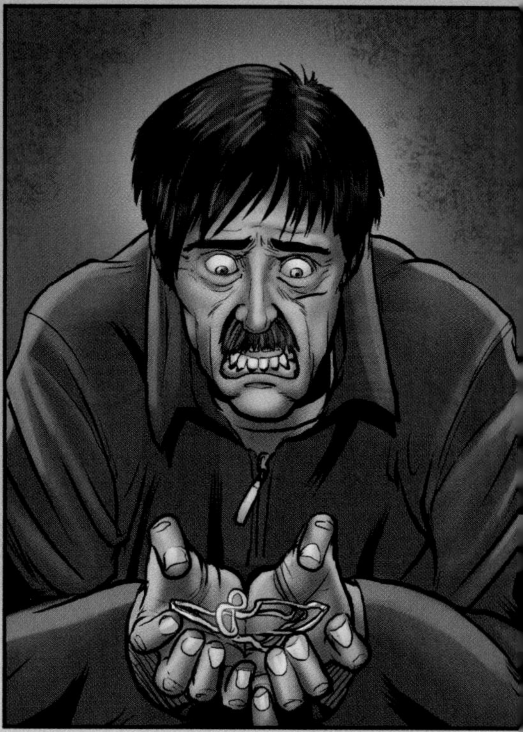

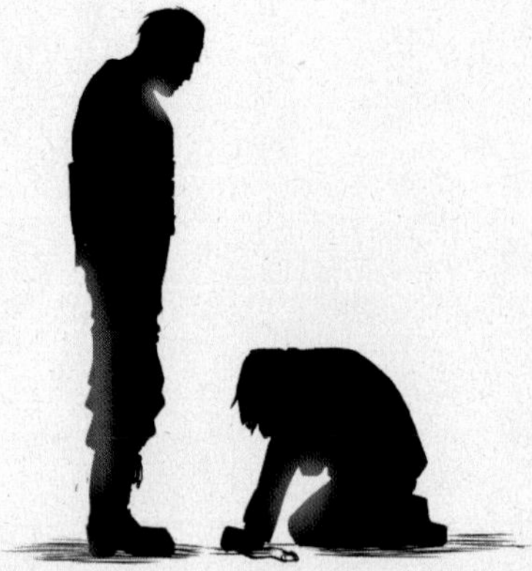

THE EN

Grimm Fairy Tales
presents:

Vampires & Werewolves

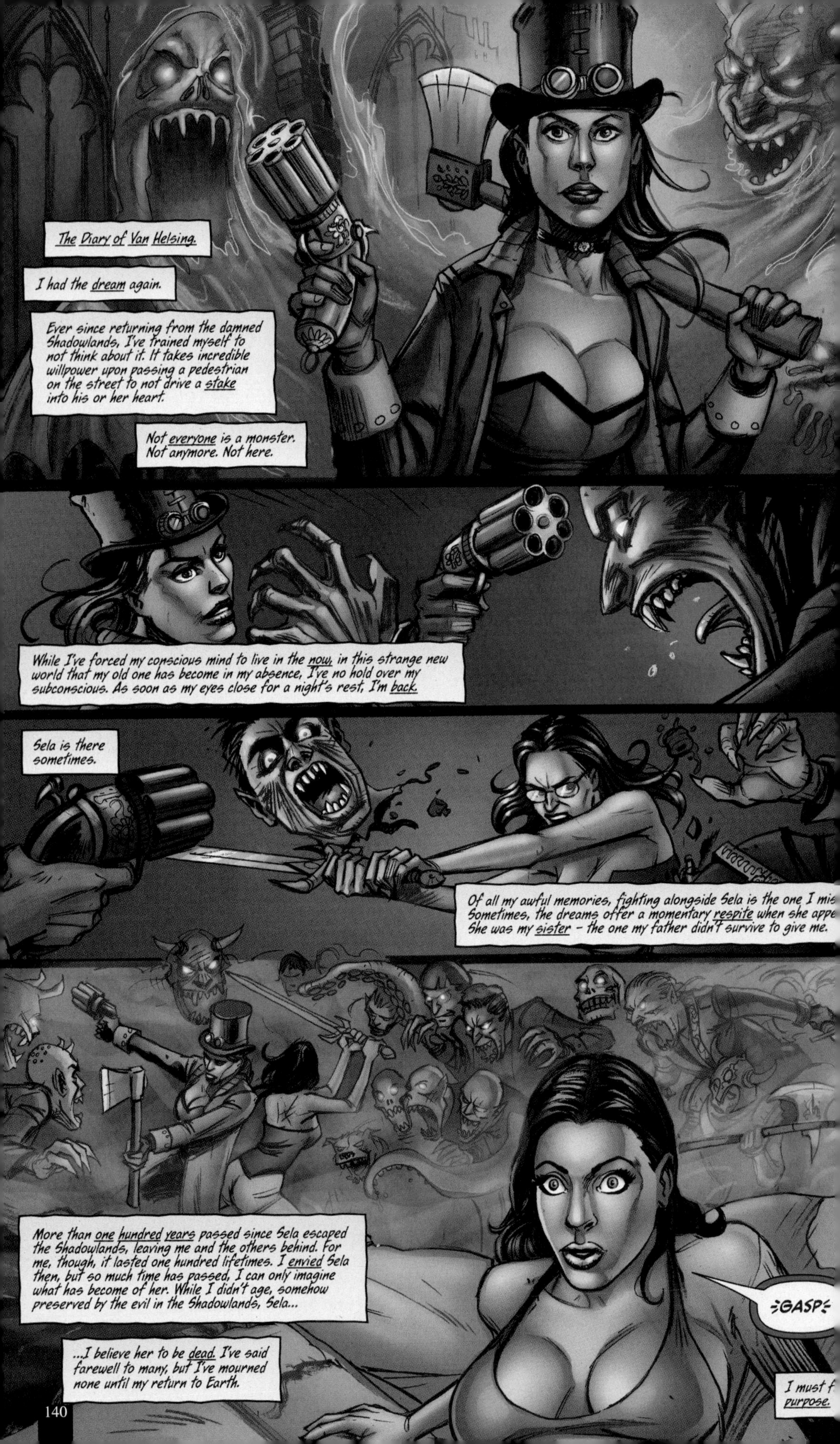
The Diary of Van Helsing.
I had the dream again.
Ever since returning from the damned Shadowlands, I've trained myself to not think about it. It takes incredible willpower upon passing a pedestrian on the street to not drive a stake into his or her heart.
Not everyone is a monster. Not anymore. Not here.
While I've forced my conscious mind to live in the now, in this strange new world that my old one has become in my absence, I've no hold over my subconscious. As soon as my eyes close for a night's rest, I'm back.
Sela is there sometimes.
Of all my awful memories, fighting alongside Sela is the one I mis
Sometimes, the dreams offer a momentary respite when she appe
She was my sister - the one my father didn't survive to give me.
More than one hundred years passed since Sela escaped the Shadowlands, leaving me and the others behind. For me, though, it lasted one hundred lifetimes. I envied Sela then, but so much time has passed, I can only imagine what has become of her. While I didn't age, somehow preserved by the evil in the Shadowlands, Sela...
...I believe her to be dead. I've said farewell to many, but I've mourned none until my return to Earth.
GASP
I must f
purpose.

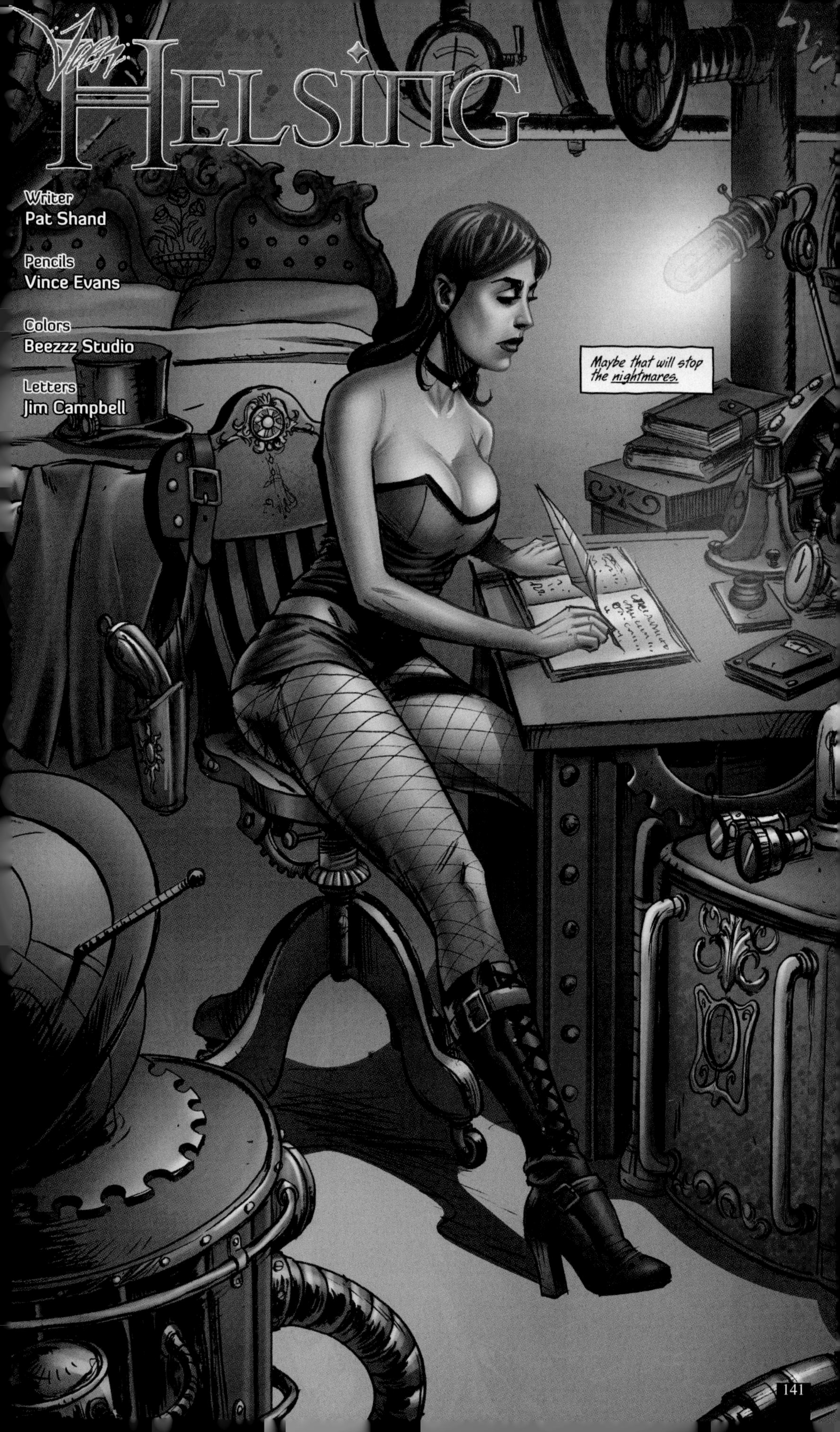
Van Helsing
Writer
Pat Shand
Pencils
Vince Evans
Colors
Beezzz Studio
Letters
Jim Campbell
Maybe that will stop the nightmares.

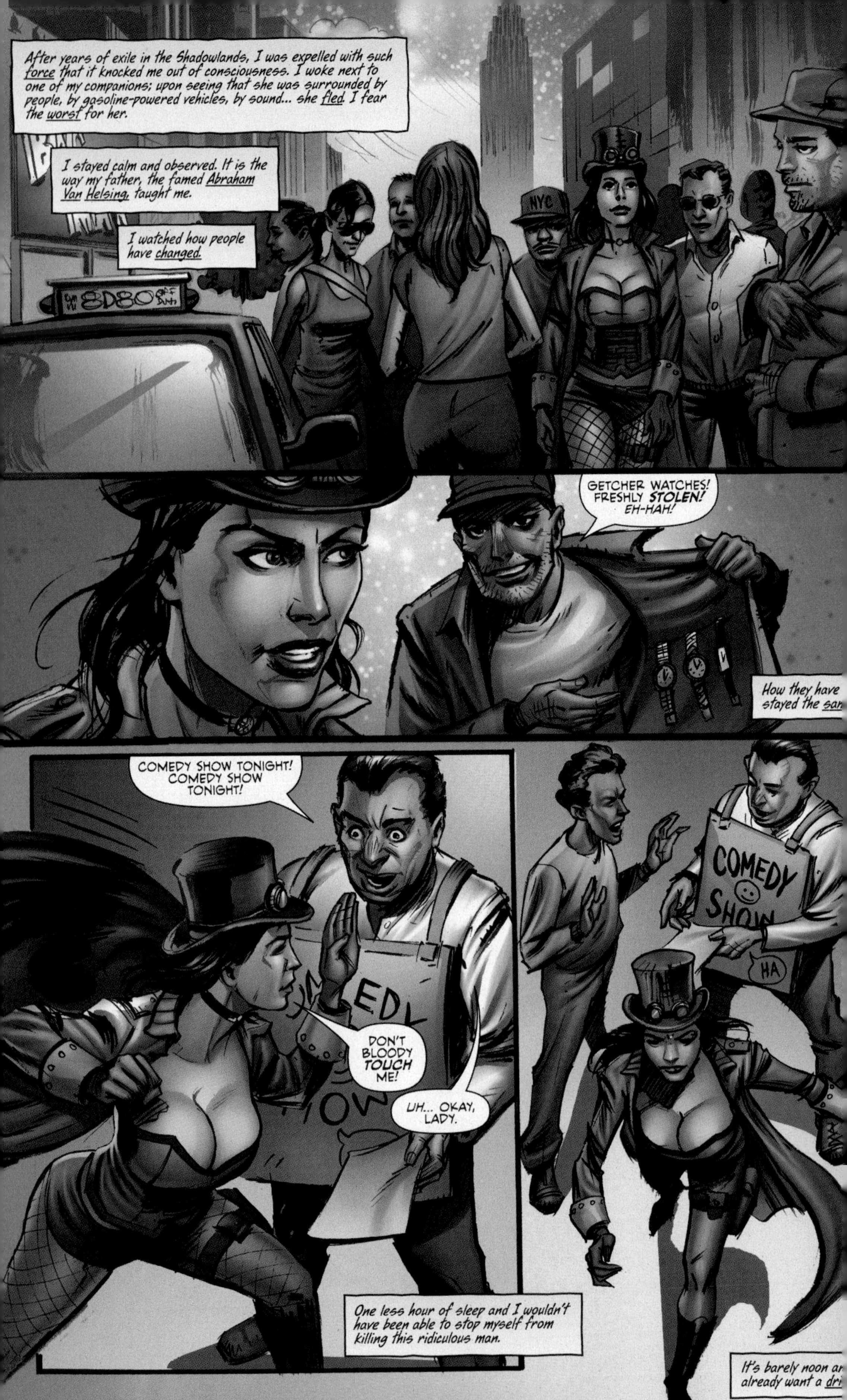

After years of exile in the Shadowlands, I was expelled with such force that it knocked me out of consciousness. I woke next to one of my companions; upon seeing that she was surrounded by people, by gasoline-powered vehicles, by sound... she fled. I fear the worst for her.
I stayed calm and observed. It is the way my father, the famed Abraham Van Helsing, taught me.
I watched how people have changed.
8D80
NYC
GETCHER WATCHES! FRESHLY STOLEN! EH-HAH!
How they have stayed the san
COMEDY SHOW TONIGHT! COMEDY SHOW TONIGHT!
DON'T BLOODY TOUCH ME!
UH... OKAY, LADY.
One less hour of sleep and I wouldn't have been able to stop myself from killing this ridiculous man.
COMEDY SHOW
HA
It's barely noon ar already want a dri

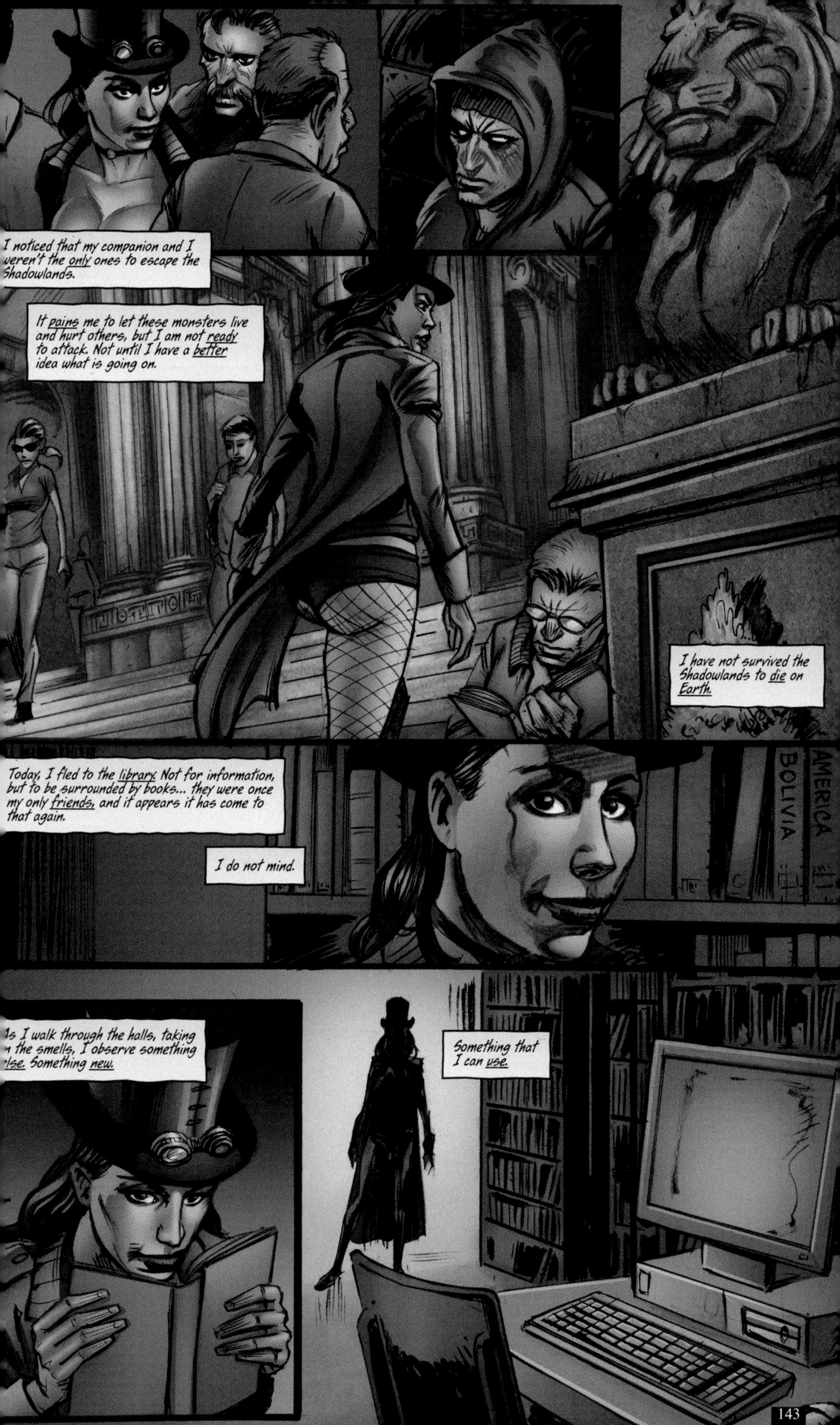

I noticed that my companion and I weren't the only ones to escape the Shadowlands.
It pains me to let these monsters live and hurt others, but I am not ready to attack. Not until I have a better idea what is going on.
I have not survived the Shadowlands to die on Earth.
Today, I fled to the library. Not for information, but to be surrounded by books... they were once my only friends, and it appears it has come to that again.
I do not mind.
BOLIVIA
AMERICA
As I walk through the halls, taking in the smells, I observe something else. Something new.
Something that I can use.

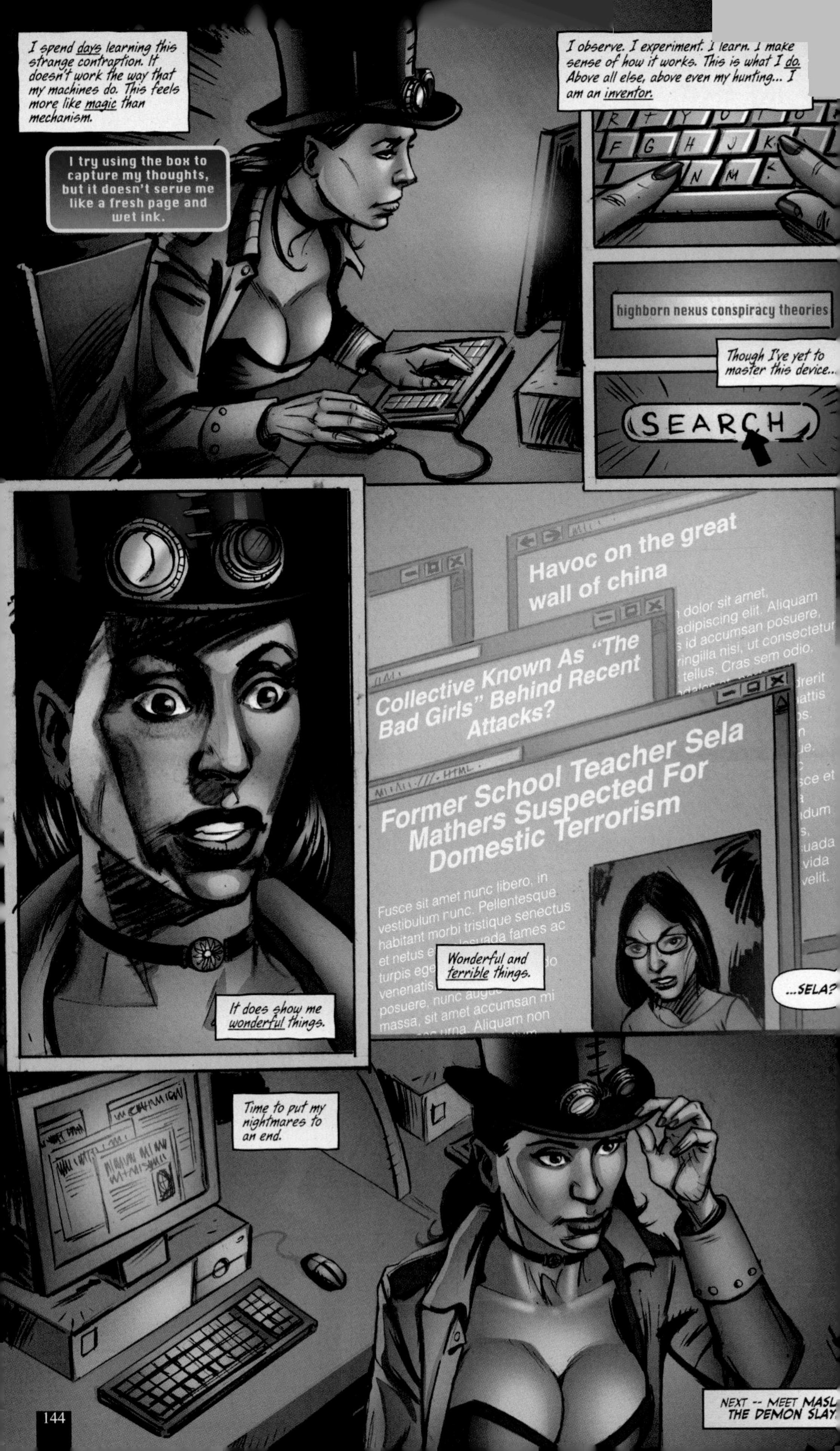

I spend days learning this strange contraption. It doesn't work the way that my machines do. This feels more like magic than mechanism.
I try using the box to capture my thoughts, but it doesn't serve me like a fresh page and wet ink.
I observe. I experiment. I learn. I make sense of how it works. This is what I do. Above all else, above even my hunting... I am an inventor.
highborn nexus conspiracy theories
Though I've yet to master this device...
SEARCH
It does show me wonderful things.
Havoc on the great wall of china
Collective Known As "The Bad Girls" Behind Recent Attacks?
Former School Teacher Sela Mathers Suspected For Domestic Terrorism
Fusce sit amet nunc libero, in vestibulum runc. Pellentesque habitant morbi tristique senectus
Wonderful and terrible things.
...SELA?
Time to put my nightmares to an end.
NEXT -- MEET MASL
THE DEMON SLAY

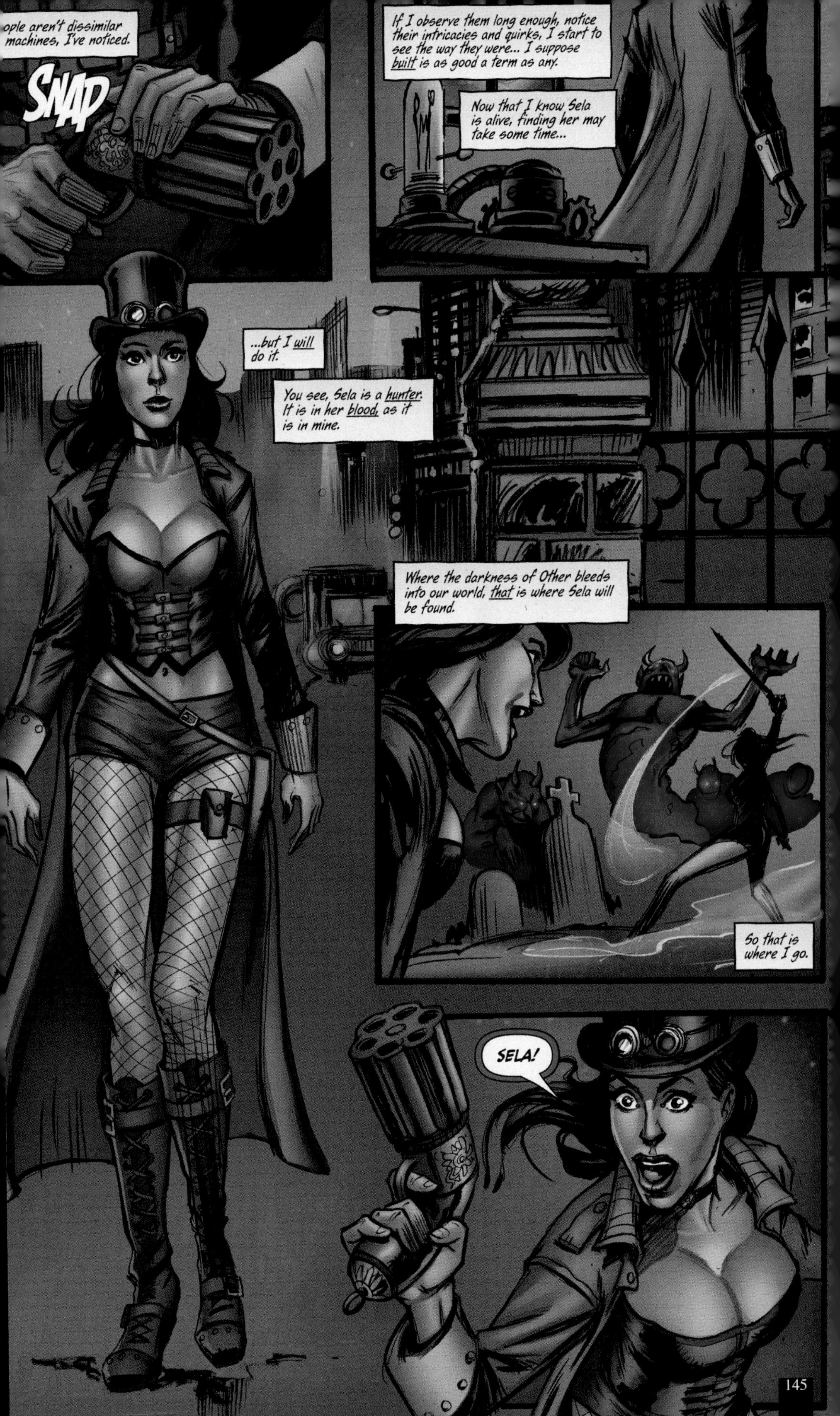
ople aren't dissimilar machines, I've noticed.
SNAP
If I observe them long enough, notice their intricacies and quirks, I start to see the way they were... I suppose built is as good a term as any.
Now that I know Sela is alive, finding her may take some time...
...but I will do it.
You see, Sela is a hunter. It is in her blood, as it is in mine.
Where the darkness of Other bleeds into our world, that is where Sela will be found.
So that is where I go.
SELA!

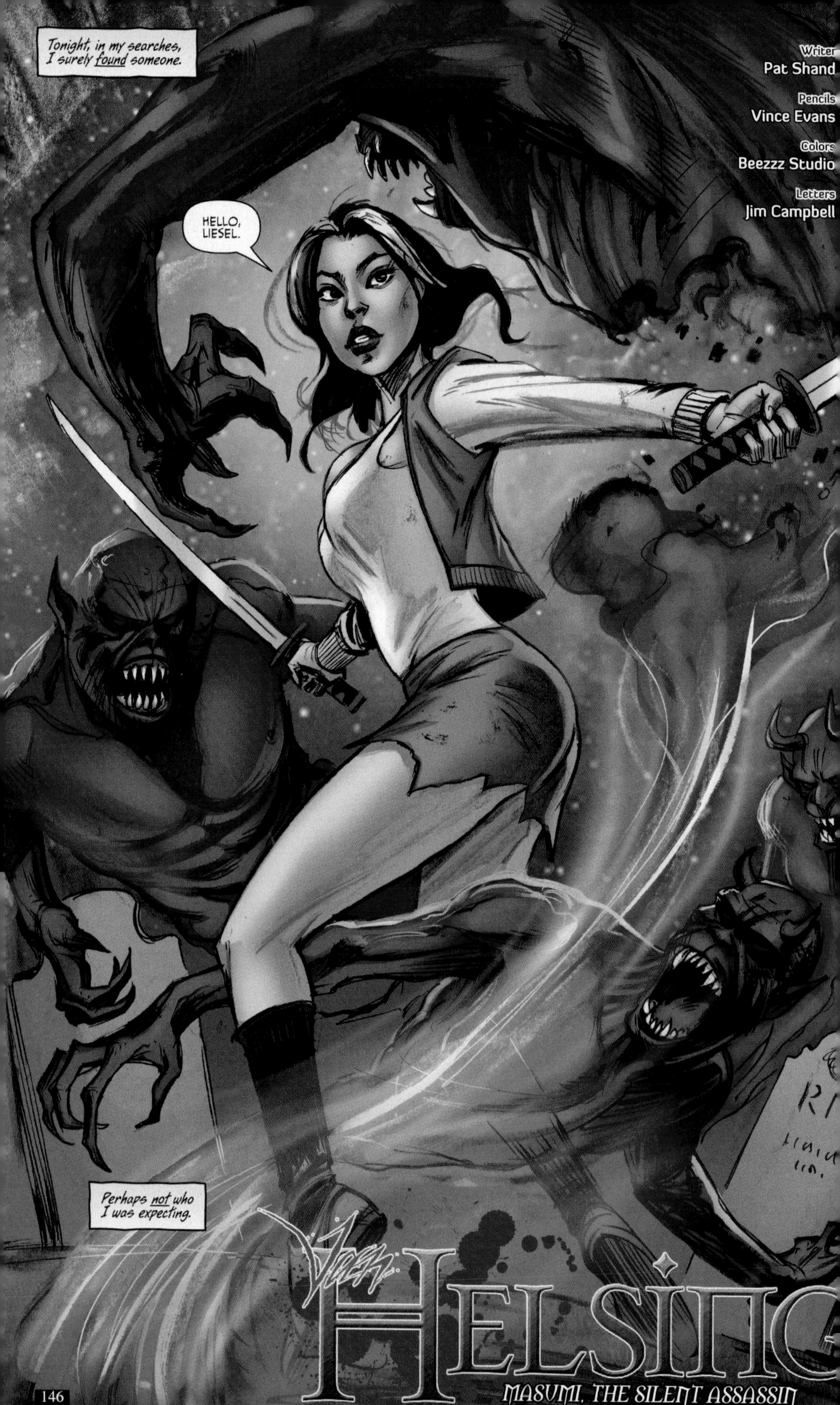
Tonight, in my searches, I surely found someone.
Writer
Pat Shand
Pencils
Vince Evans
Colors
Beezzz Studio
Letters
Jim Campbell
HELLO, LIESEL.
Perhaps not who I was expecting.
Van Helsing
MASUMI, THE SILENT ASSASSIN

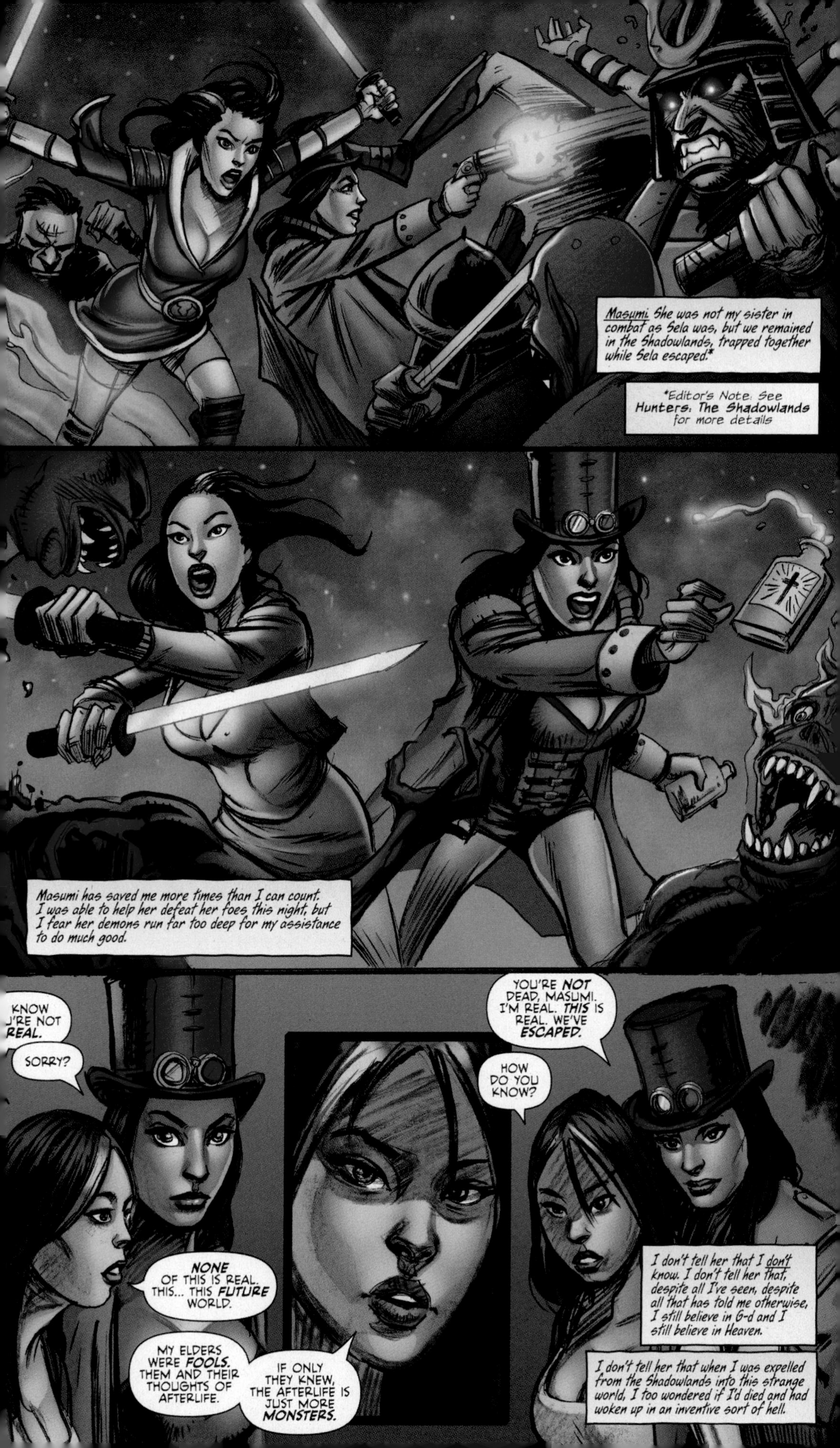

Masumi. She was not my sister in combat as Sela was, but we remained in the Shadowlands, trapped together while Sela escaped.*
*Editor's Note: See **Hunters: The Shadowlands** for more details
Masumi has saved me more times than I can count. I was able to help her defeat her foes this night, but I fear her demons run far too deep for my assistance to do much good.
KNOW 'RE NOT REAL.
SORRY?
NONE OF THIS IS REAL. THIS... THIS FUTURE WORLD.
MY ELDERS WERE FOOLS. THEM AND THEIR THOUGHTS OF AFTERLIFE.
IF ONLY THEY KNEW, THE AFTERLIFE IS JUST MORE MONSTERS.
YOU'RE NOT DEAD, MASUMI. I'M REAL. THIS IS REAL. WE'VE ESCAPED.
HOW DO YOU KNOW?
I don't tell her that I don't know. I don't tell her that, despite all I've seen, despite all that has told me otherwise, I still believe in G-d and I still believe in Heaven.
I don't tell her that when I was expelled from the Shadowlands into this strange world, I too wondered if I'd died and had woken up in an inventive sort of hell.

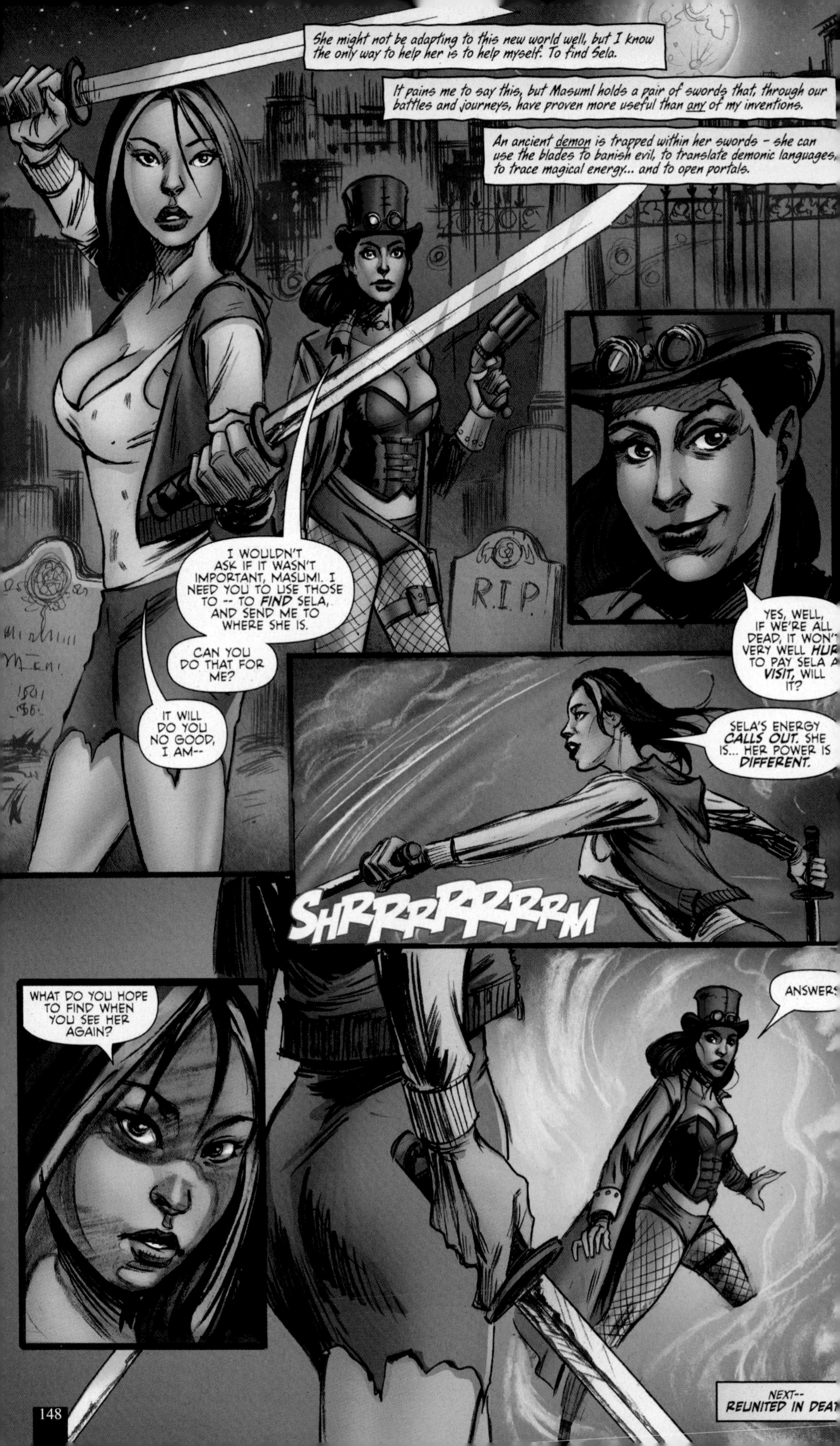
She might not be adapting to this new world well, but I know the only way to help her is to help myself. To find Sela.
It pains me to say this, but Masumi holds a pair of swords that, through our battles and journeys, have proven more useful than any of my inventions.
An ancient demon is trapped within her swords - she can use the blades to banish evil, to translate demonic languages, to trace magical energy... and to open portals.
I WOULDN'T ASK IF IT WASN'T IMPORTANT, MASUMI. I NEED YOU TO USE THOSE TO -- TO FIND SELA, AND SEND ME TO WHERE SHE IS.
CAN YOU DO THAT FOR ME?
IT WILL DO YOU NO GOOD, I AM--
R.I.P.
YES, WELL, IF WE'RE ALL DEAD, IT WON'T VERY WELL HURT TO PAY SELA A VISIT, WILL IT?
SELA'S ENERGY CALLS OUT. SHE IS... HER POWER IS DIFFERENT.
SHRRRRRRRM
WHAT DO YOU HOPE TO FIND WHEN YOU SEE HER AGAIN?
ANSWERS
NEXT-- REUNITED IN DEAT

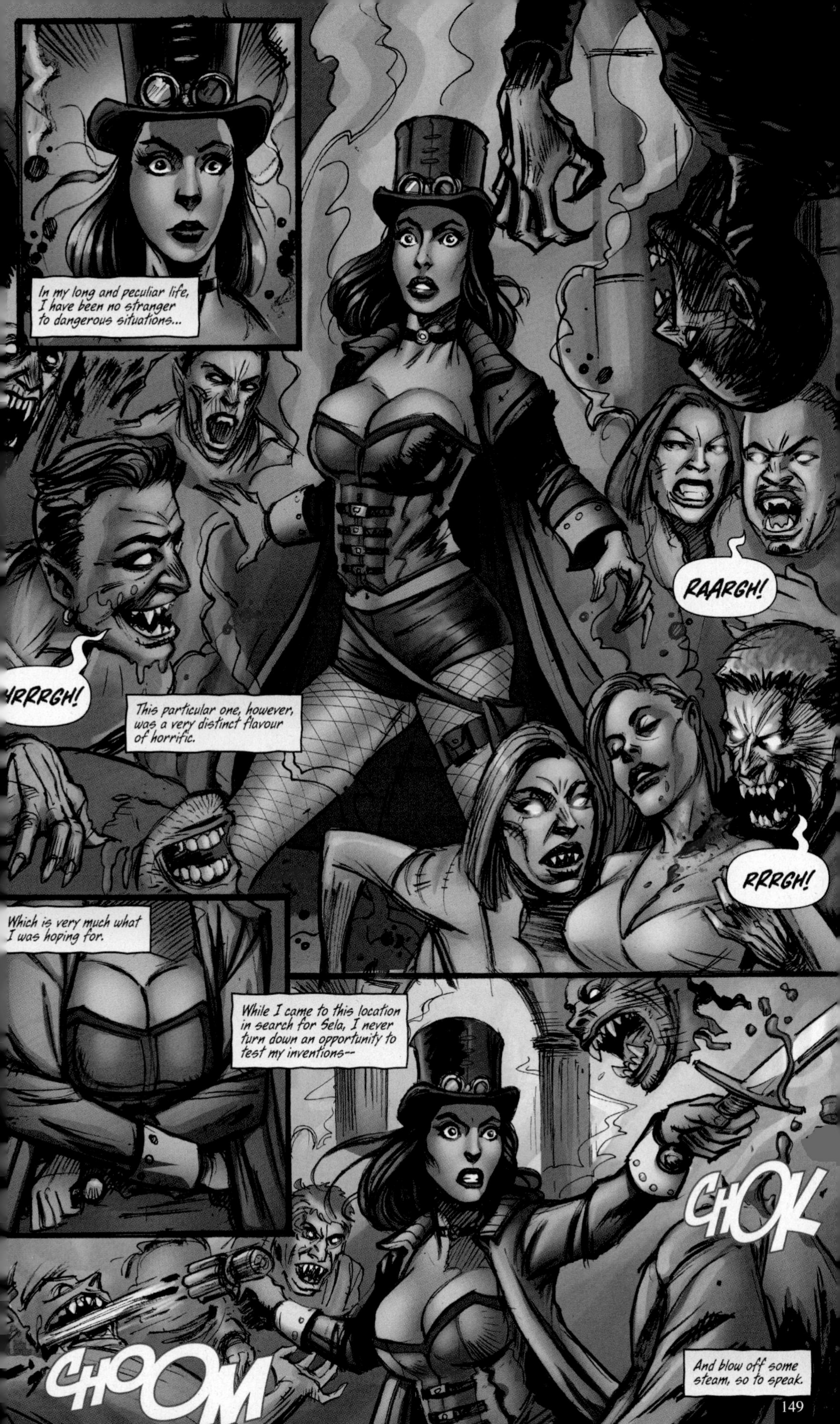

In my long and peculiar life, I have been no stranger to dangerous situations...
RAARGH!
HRRRGH!
This particular one, however, was a very distinct flavour of horrific.
RRRGH!
Which is very much what I was hoping for.
While I came to this location in search for Sela, I never turn down an opportunity to test my inventions--
CHOK
CHOOM
And blow off some steam, so to speak.

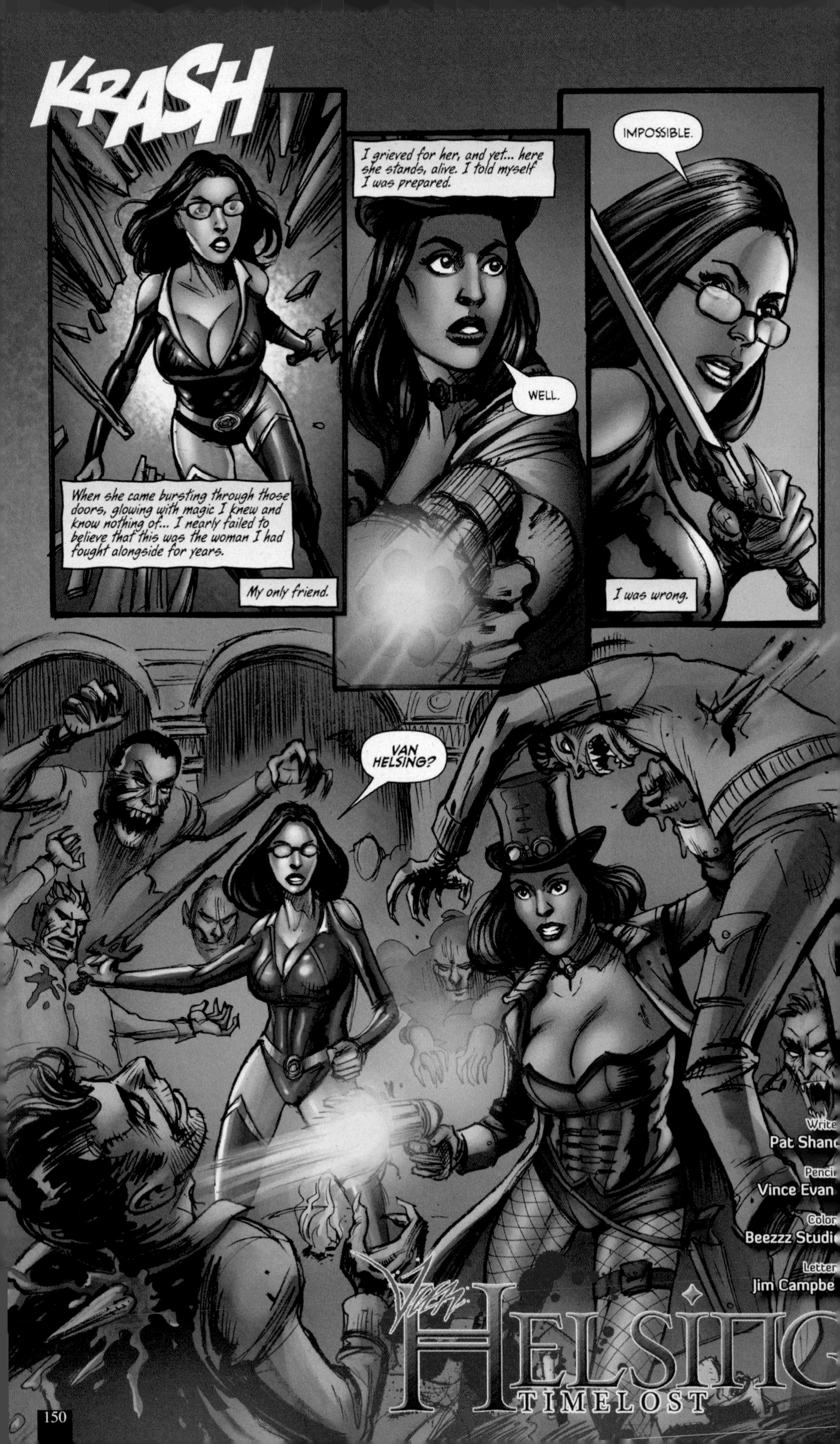
KRASH
When she came bursting through those doors, glowing with magic I knew and know nothing of... I nearly failed to believe that this was the woman I had fought alongside for years.
My only friend.
I grieved for her, and yet... here she stands, alive. I told myself I was prepared.
WELL.
IMPOSSIBLE.
I was wrong.
VAN HELSING?
Write
Pat Shan
Penci
Vince Evan
Color
Beezzz Studi
Letter
Jim Campbe
TIMELOST

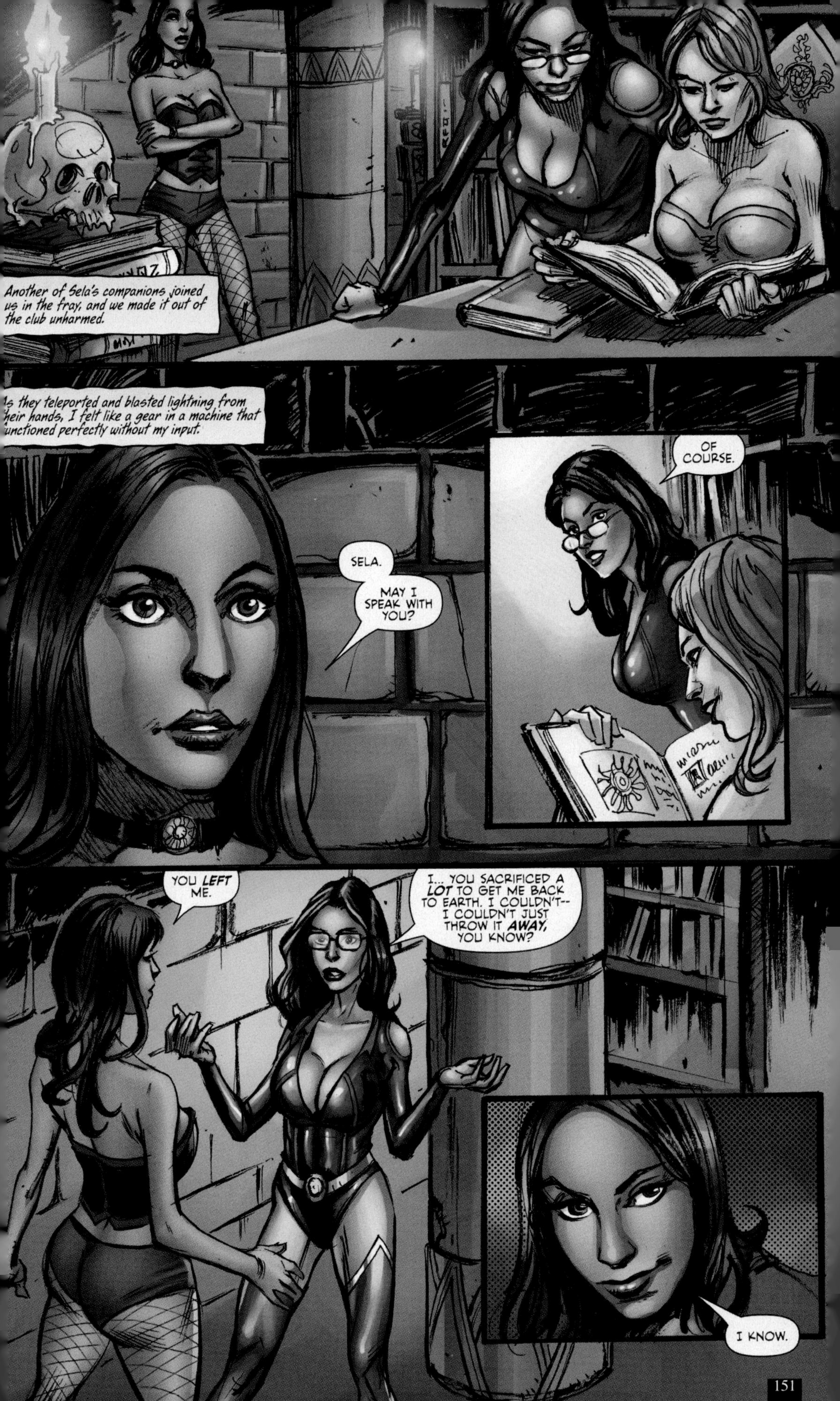

Another of Sela's companions joined us in the fray, and we made it out of the club unharmed.
As they teleported and blasted lightning from their hands, I felt like a gear in a machine that functioned perfectly without my input.
SELA.
MAY I SPEAK WITH YOU?
OF COURSE.
YOU LEFT ME.
I... YOU SACRIFICED A LOT TO GET ME BACK TO EARTH. I COULDN'T-- I COULDN'T JUST THROW IT AWAY, YOU KNOW?
I KNOW.

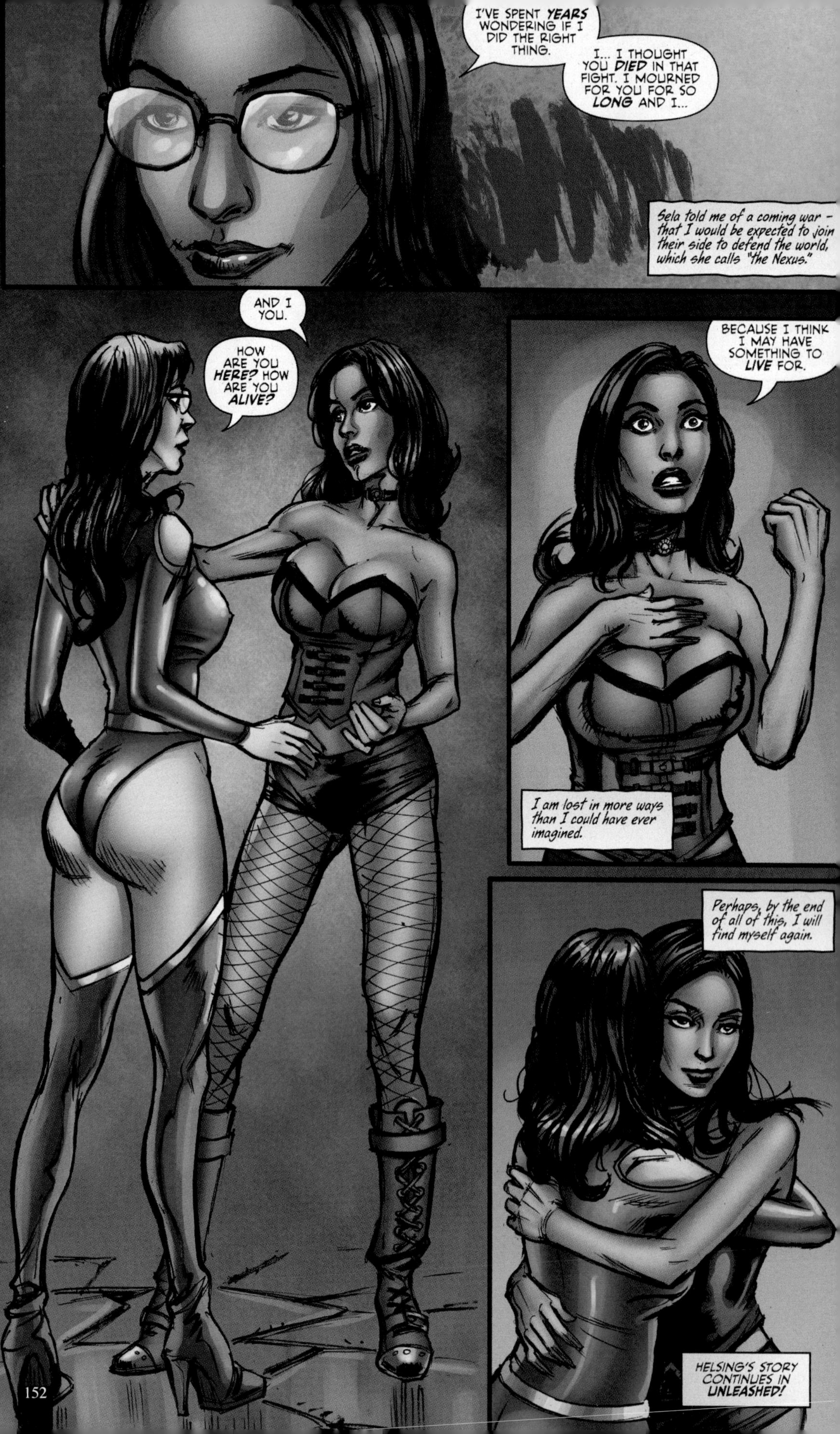
I'VE SPENT YEARS WONDERING IF I DID THE RIGHT THING.
I... I THOUGHT YOU DIED IN THAT FIGHT. I MOURNED FOR YOU FOR SO LONG AND I...
Sela told me of a coming war - that I would be expected to join their side to defend the world, which she calls "the Nexus."
AND I YOU.
HOW ARE YOU HERE? HOW ARE YOU ALIVE?
BECAUSE I THINK I MAY HAVE SOMETHING TO LIVE FOR.
I am lost in more ways than I could have ever imagined.
Perhaps, by the end of all of this, I will find myself again.
HELSING'S STORY CONTINUES IN UNLEASHED!

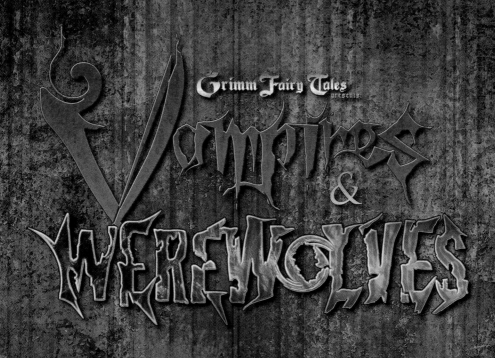

Grimm Fairy Tales
presents:

Vampires
&
WEREWOLVES

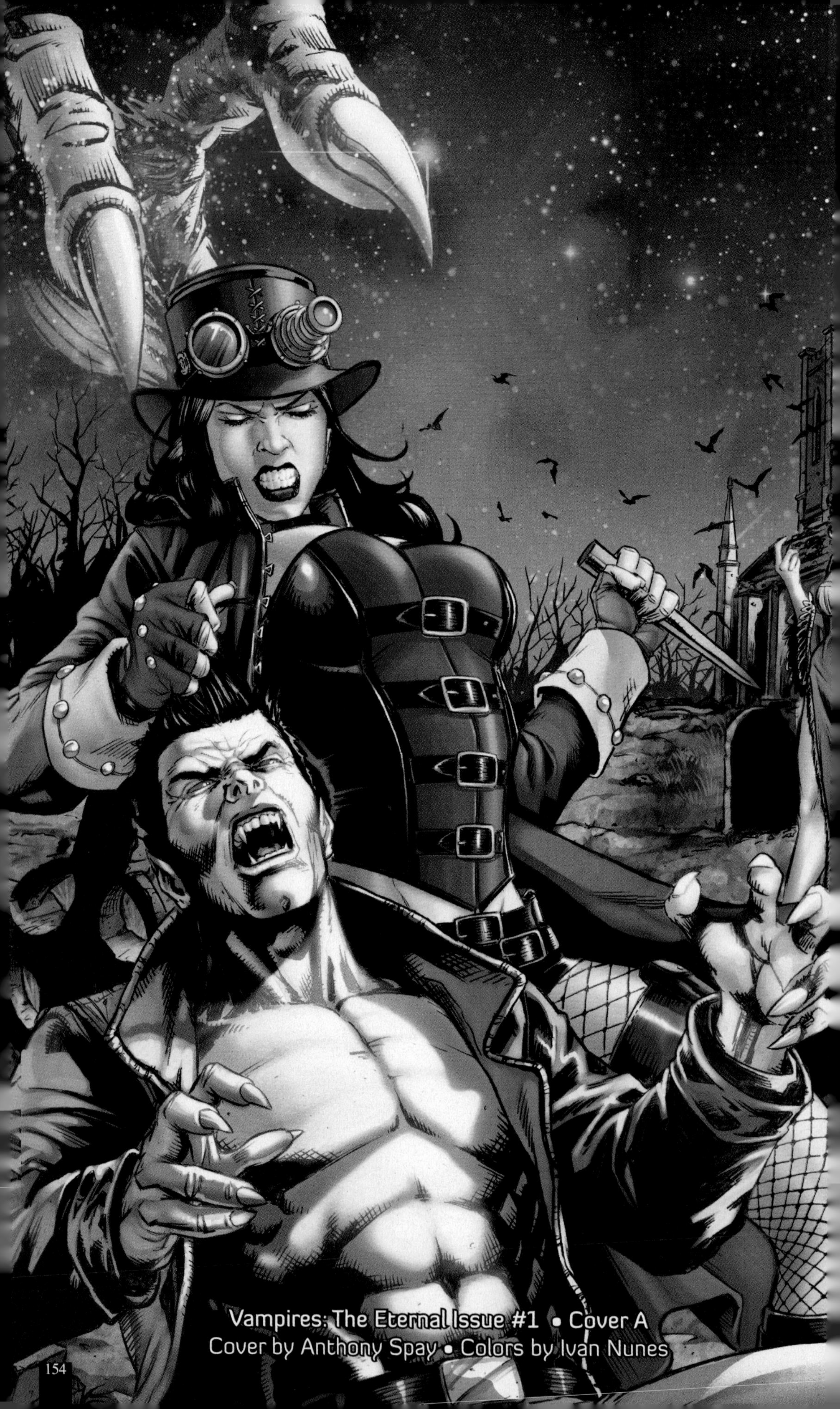

Vampires: The Eternal Issue #1 • Cover A
Cover by Anthony Spay • Colors by Ivan Nunes

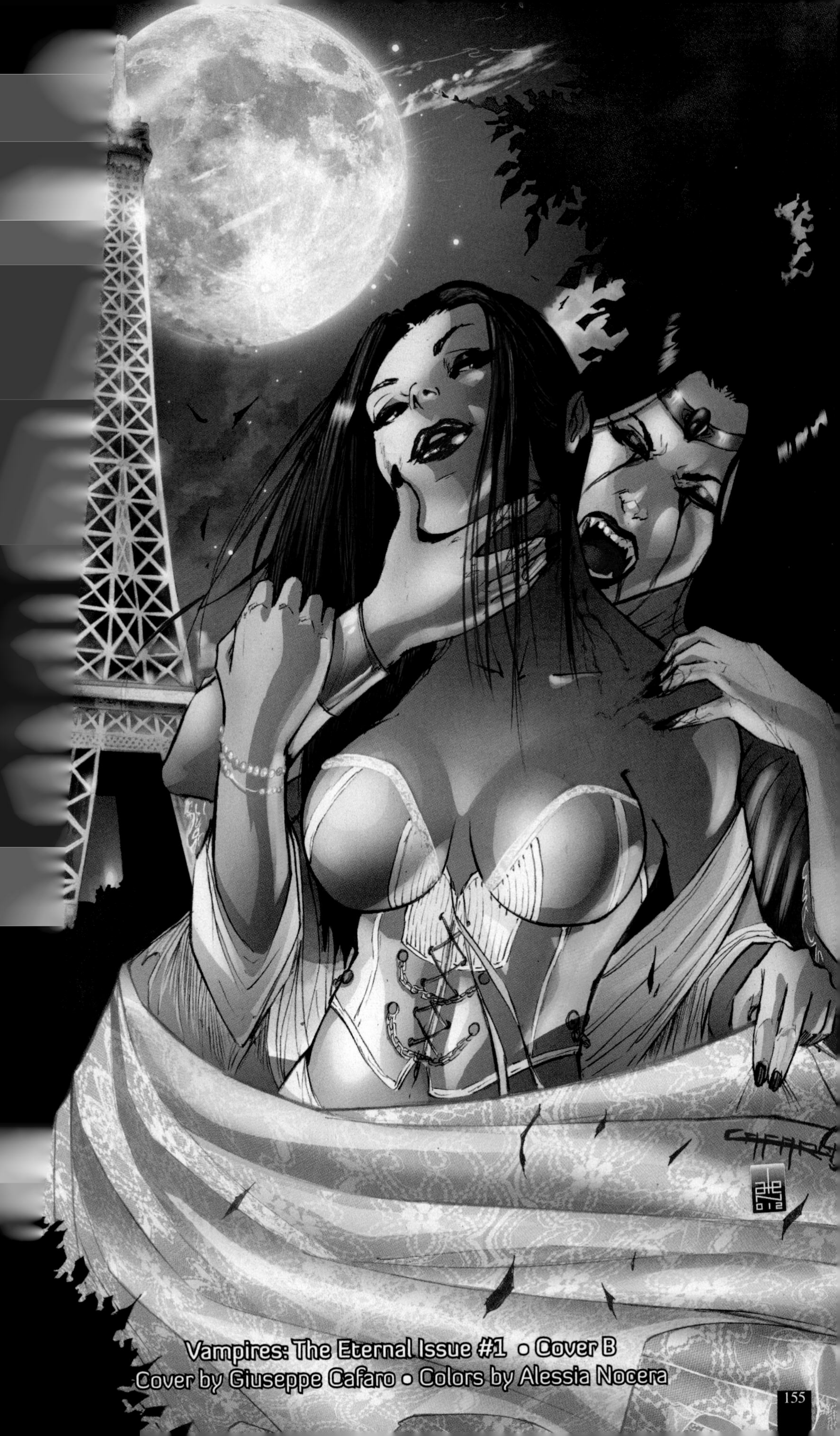

Vampires: The Eternal Issue #1 • Cover B
Cover by Giuseppe Cafaro • Colors by Alessia Nocera

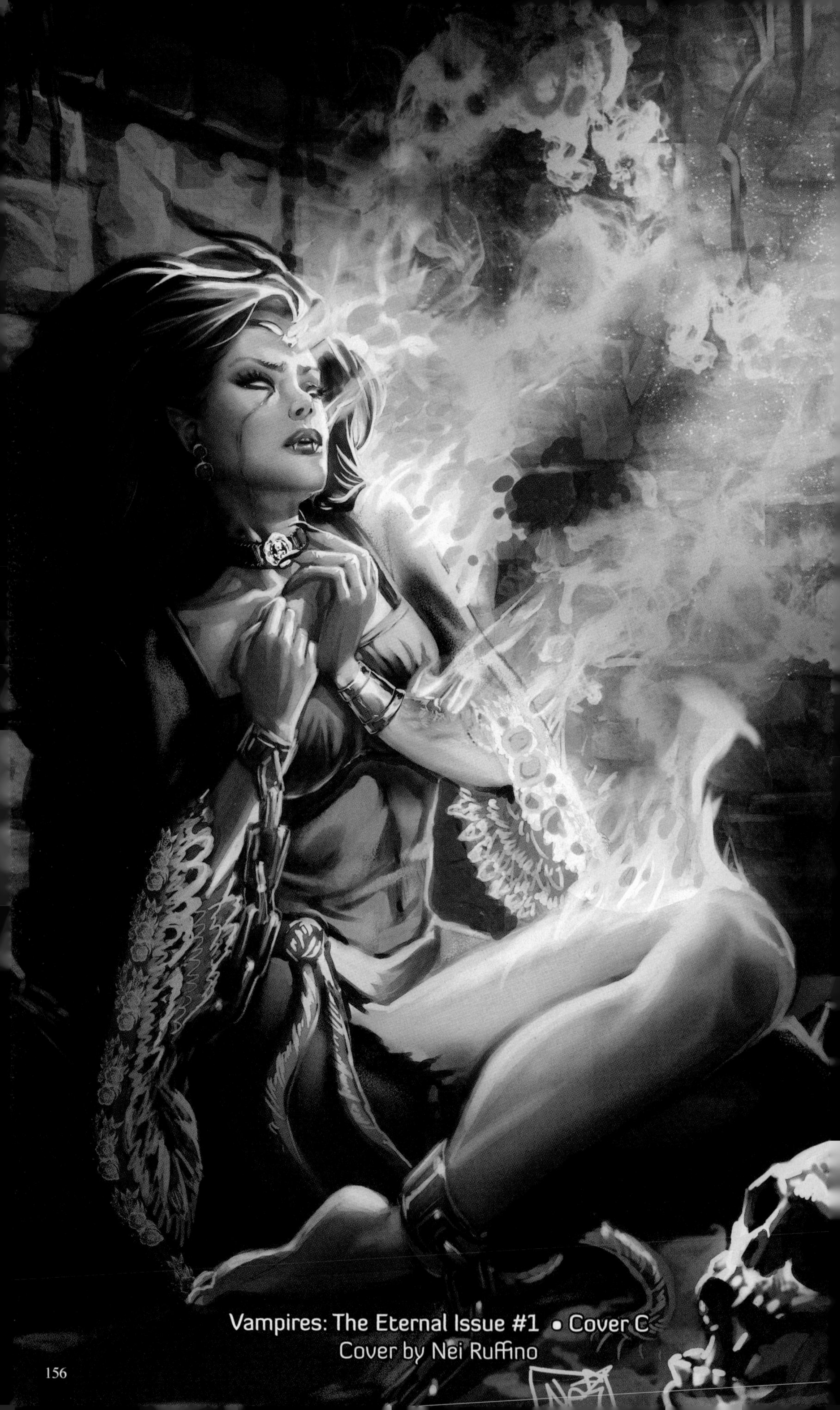

Vampires: The Eternal Issue #1 • Cover C
Cover by Nei Ruffino

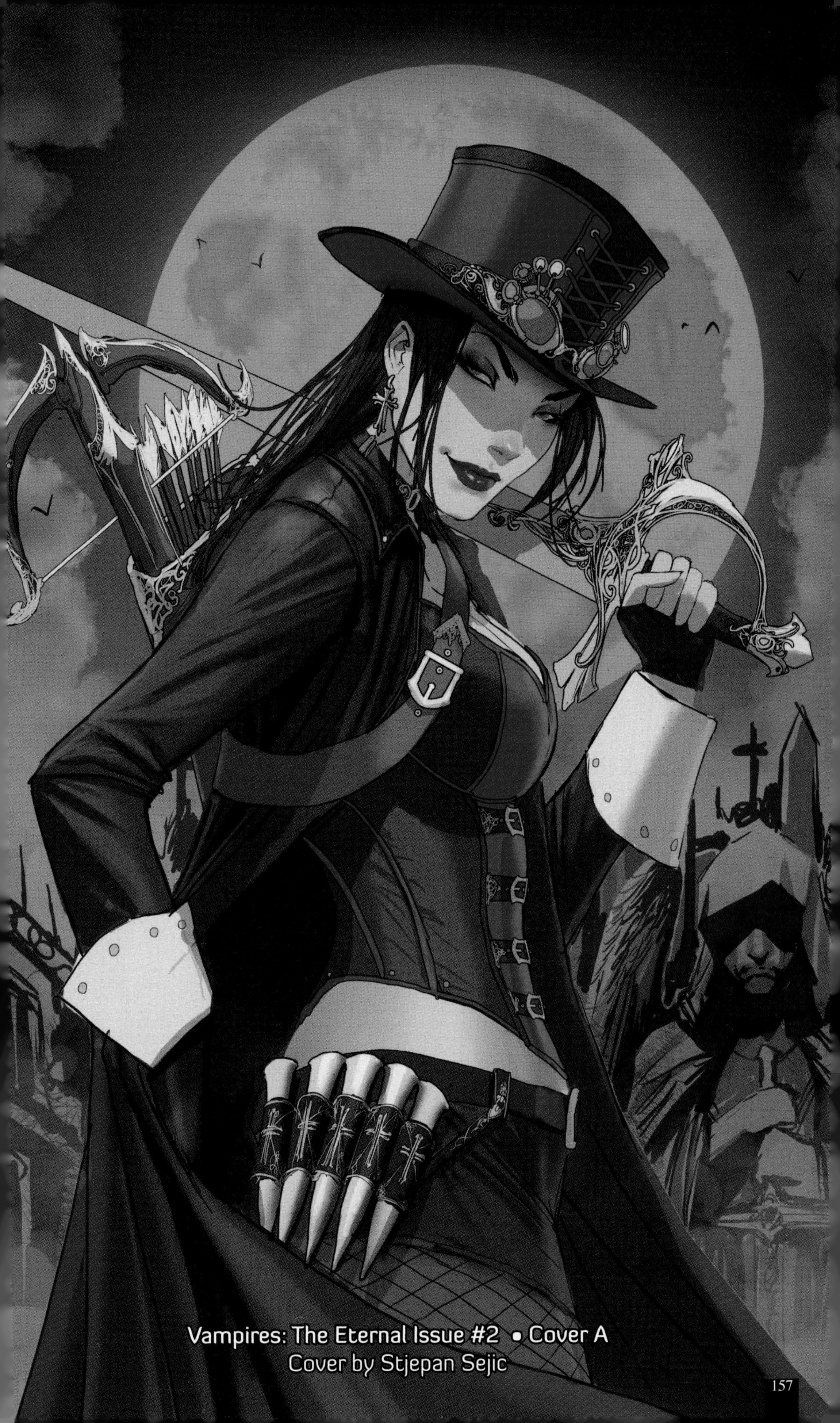

Vampires: The Eternal Issue #2 • Cover A
Cover by Stjepan Sejic

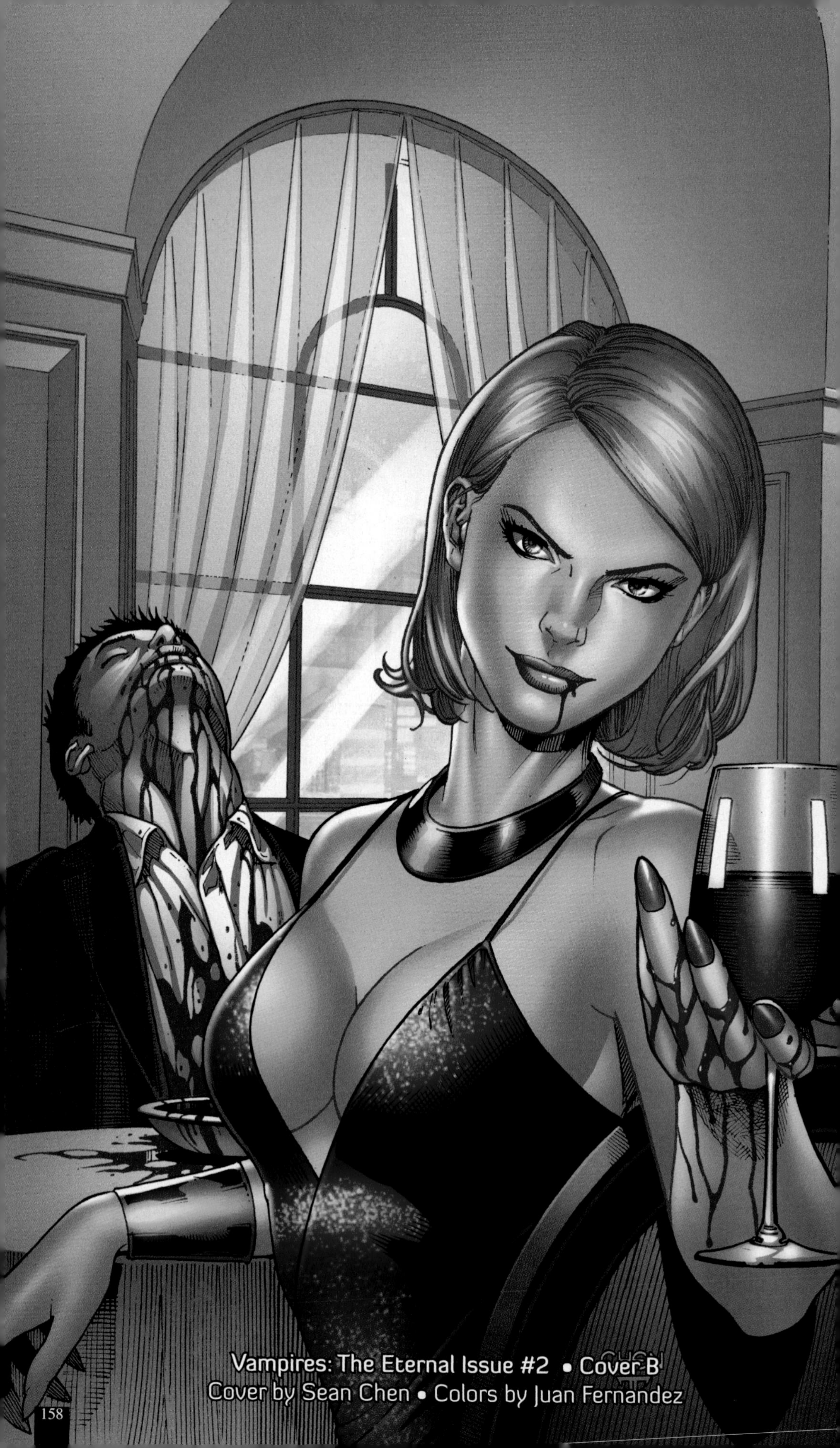

Vampires: The Eternal Issue #2 • Cover B
Cover by Sean Chen • Colors by Juan Fernandez

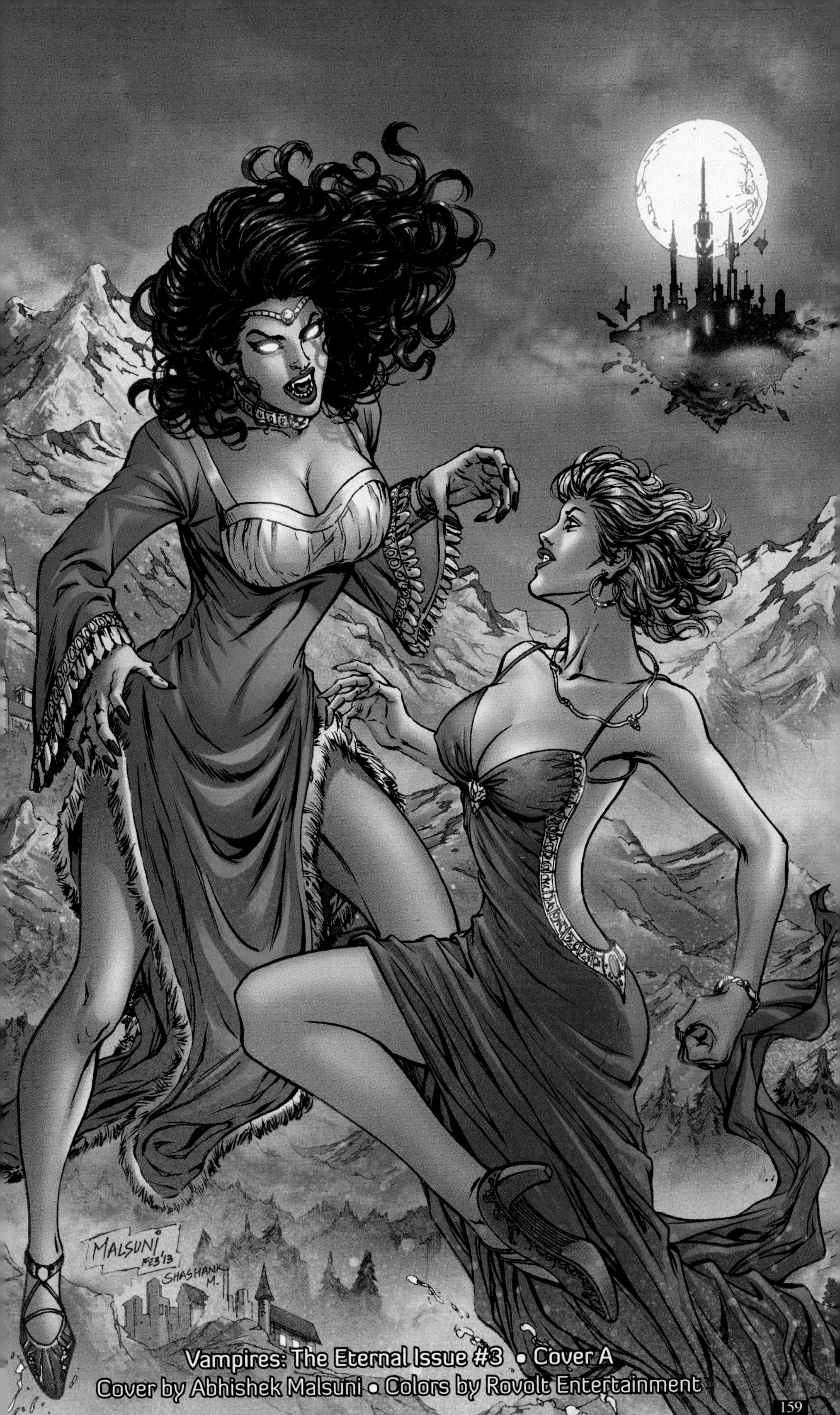
MALSUNI
FEB'13
SHASHANK M.

Vampires: The Eternal Issue #3 • Cover A
Cover by Abhishek Malsuni • Colors by Rovolt Entertainment

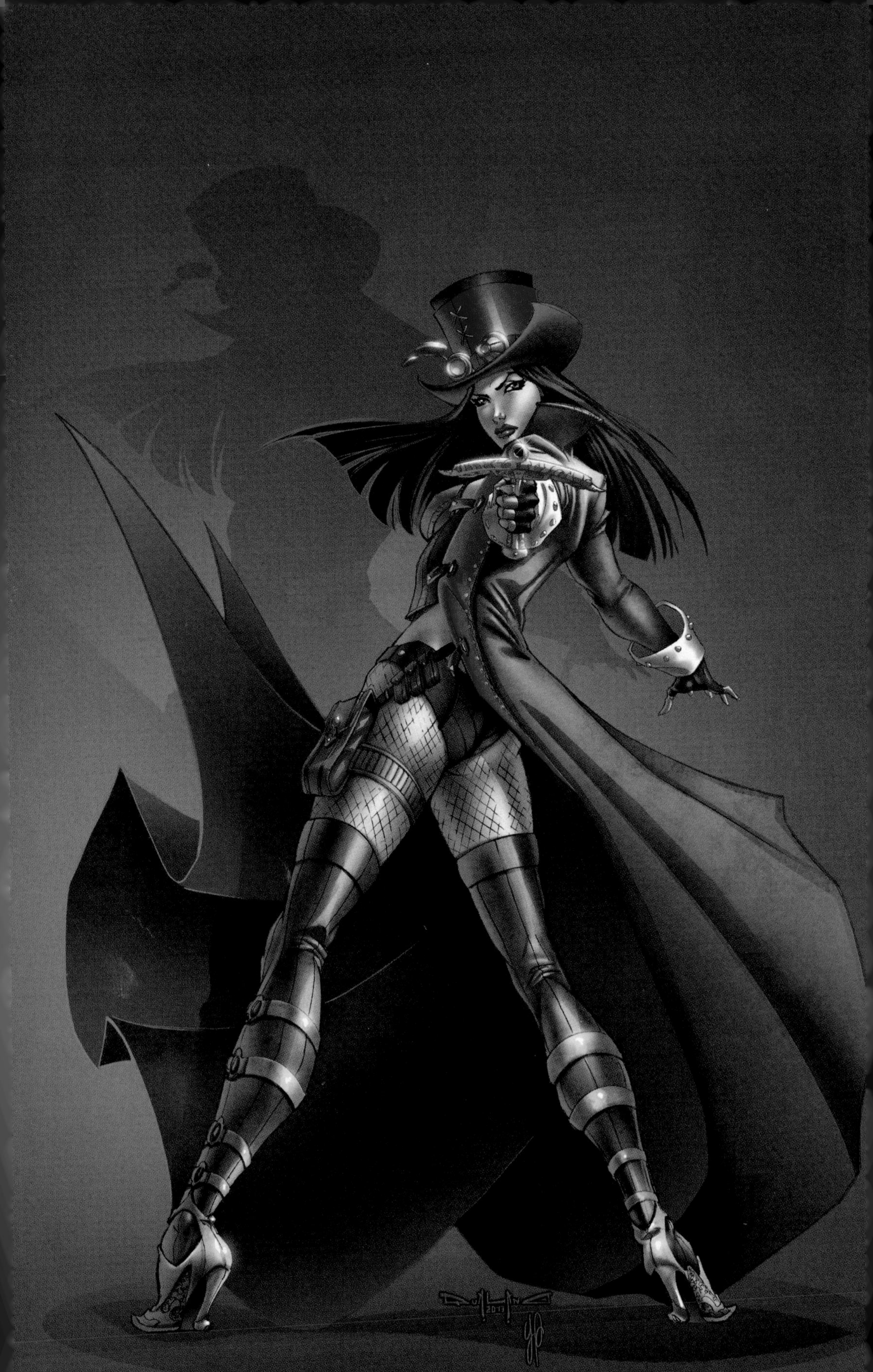

Vampires: The Eternal Issue #3 • Cover B
Cover by Pasquale Qualano • Colors by Ylenia Di Napoli

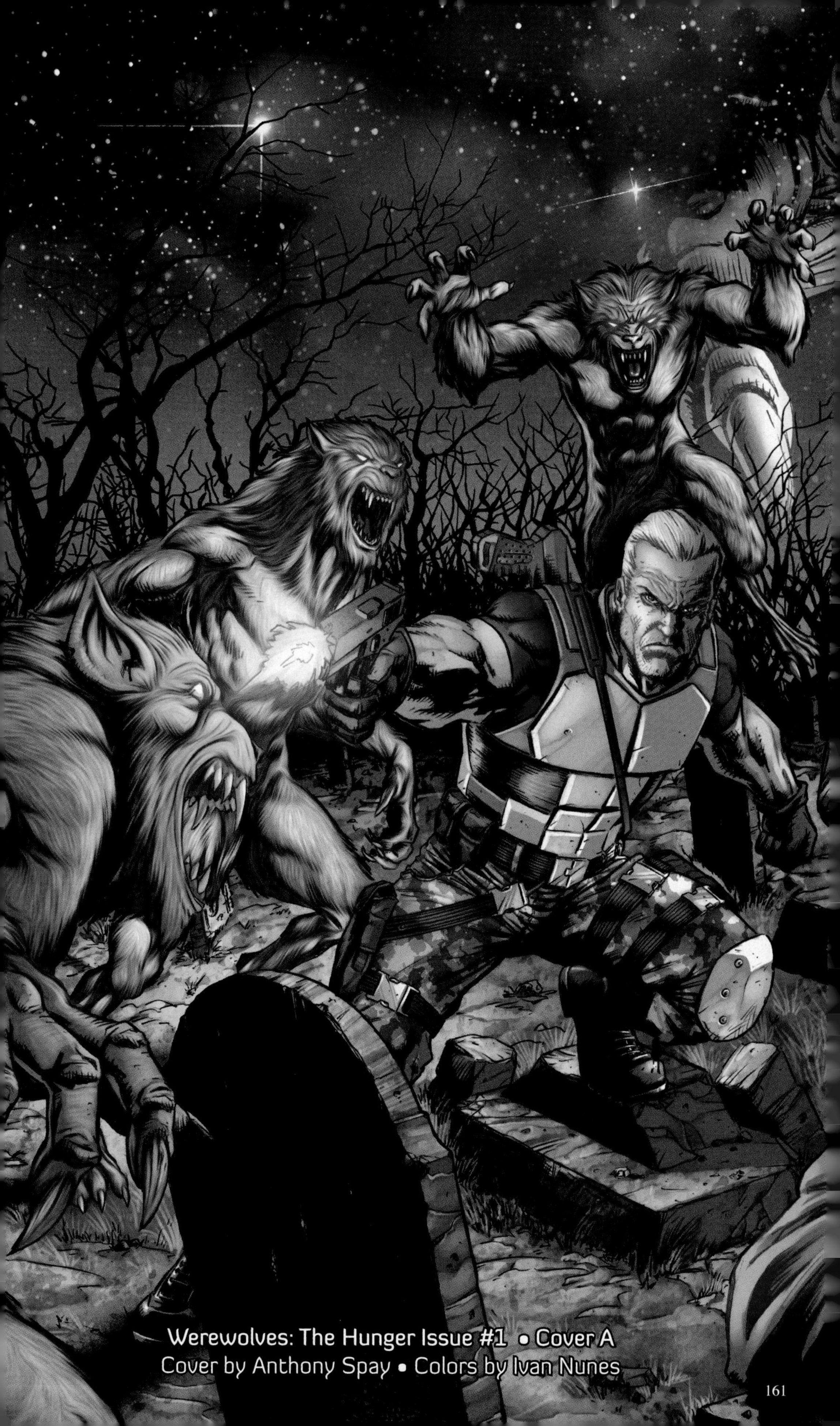

Werewolves: The Hunger Issue #1 • Cover A
Cover by Anthony Spay • Colors by Ivan Nunes

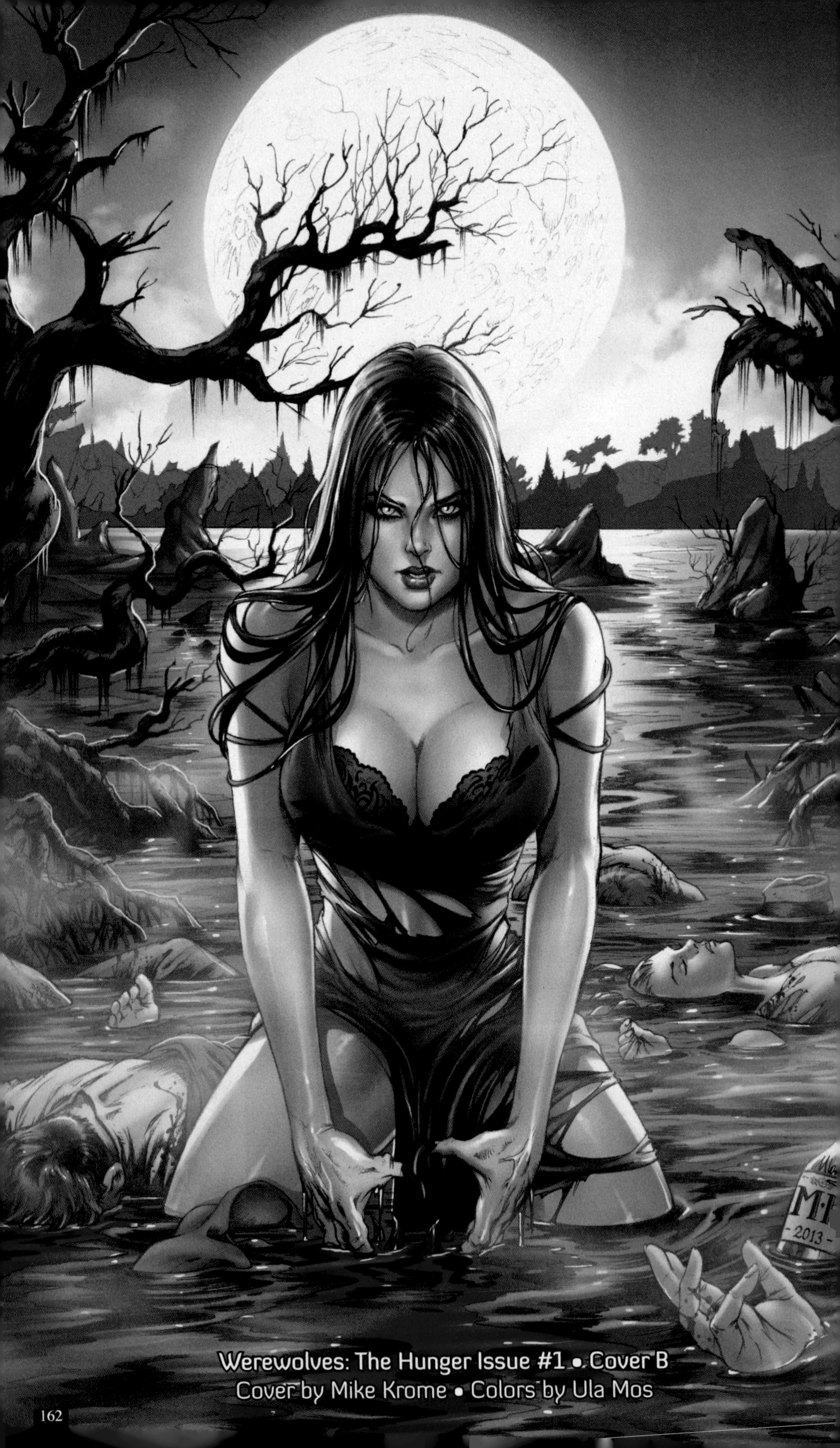

Werewolves: The Hunger Issue #1 • Cover B
Cover by Mike Krome • Colors by Ula Mos

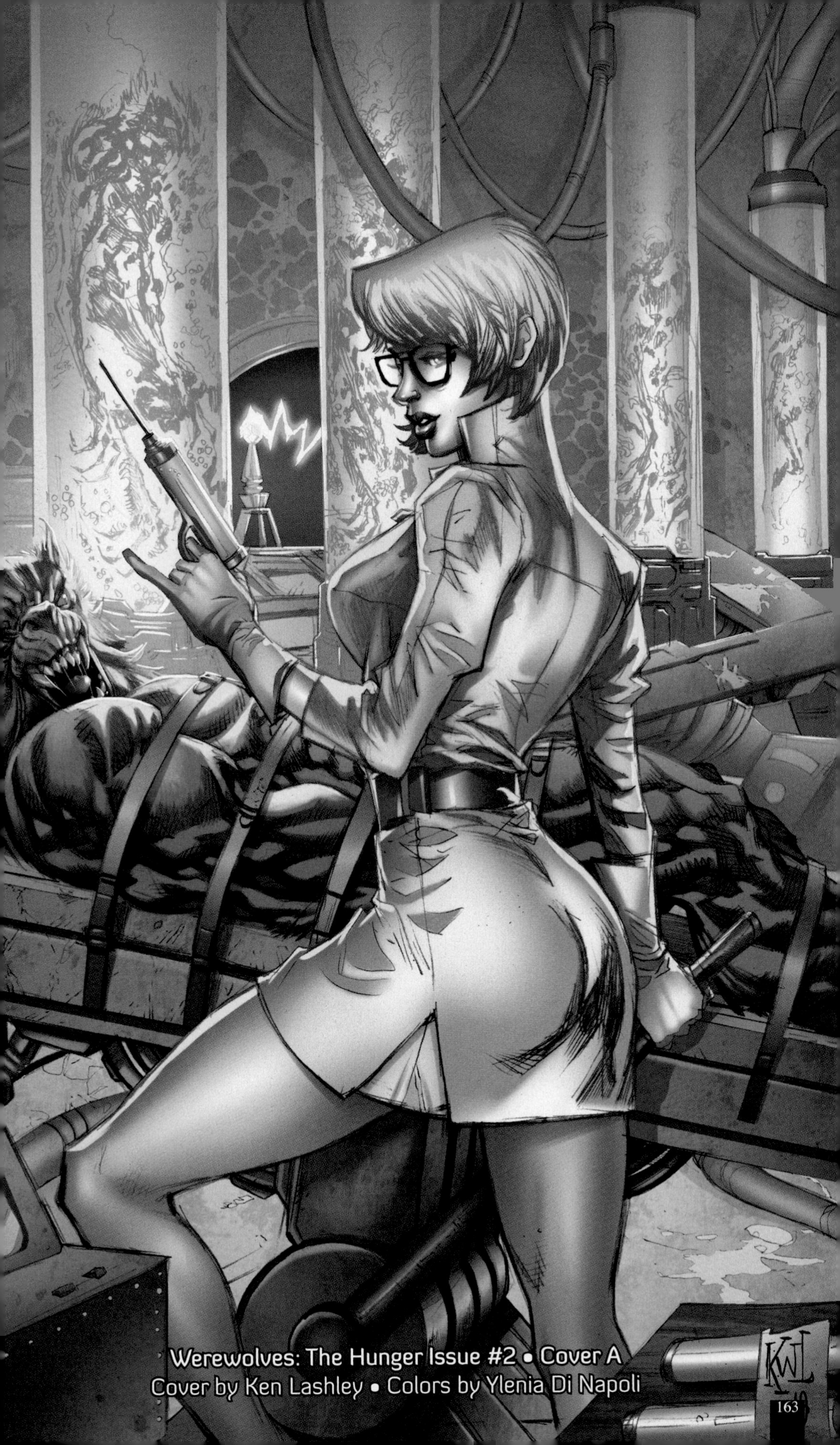

Werewolves: The Hunger Issue #2 • Cover A
Cover by Ken Lashley • Colors by Ylenia Di Napoli

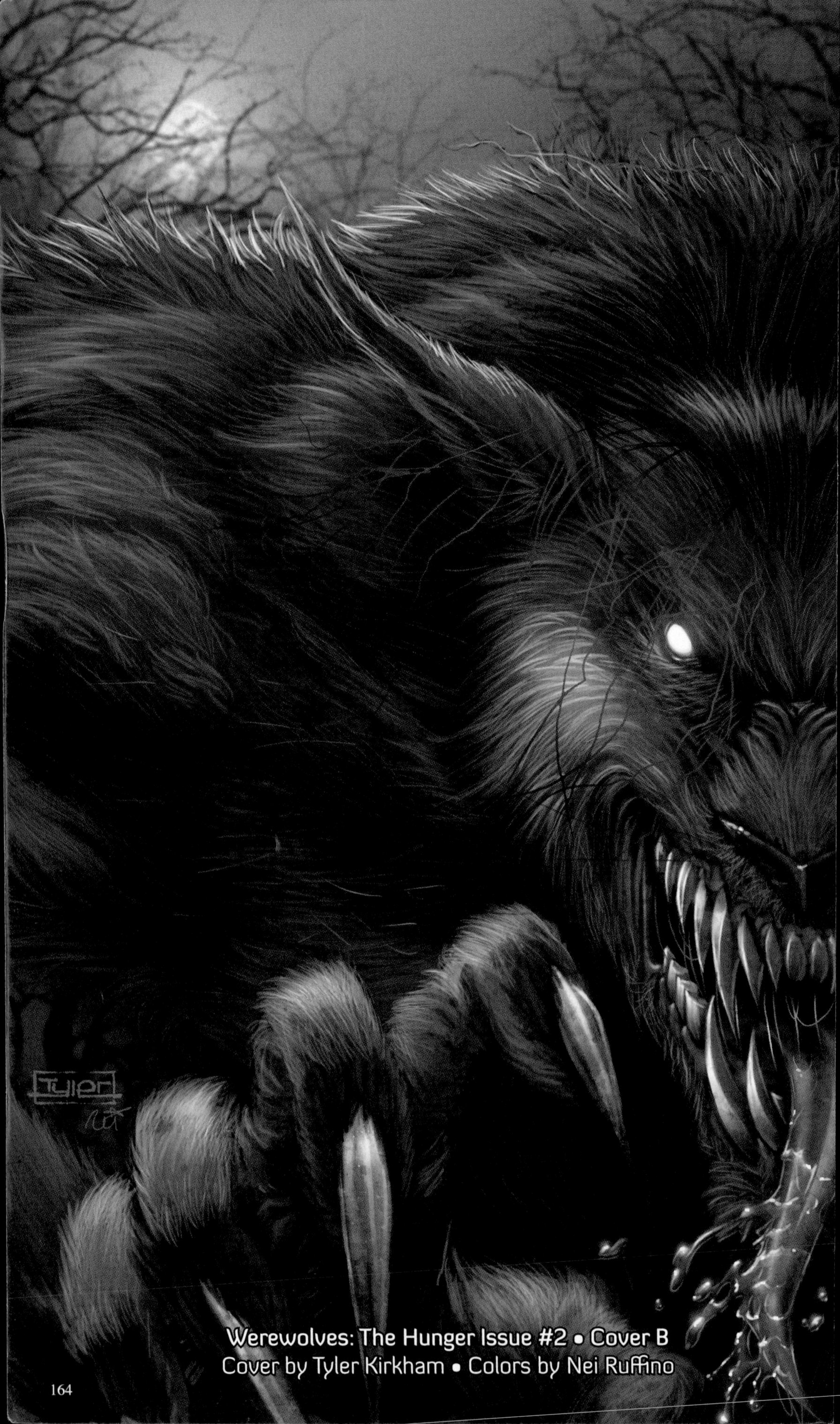
Tyler

Werewolves: The Hunger Issue #2 • Cover B
Cover by Tyler Kirkham • Colors by Nei Ruffino

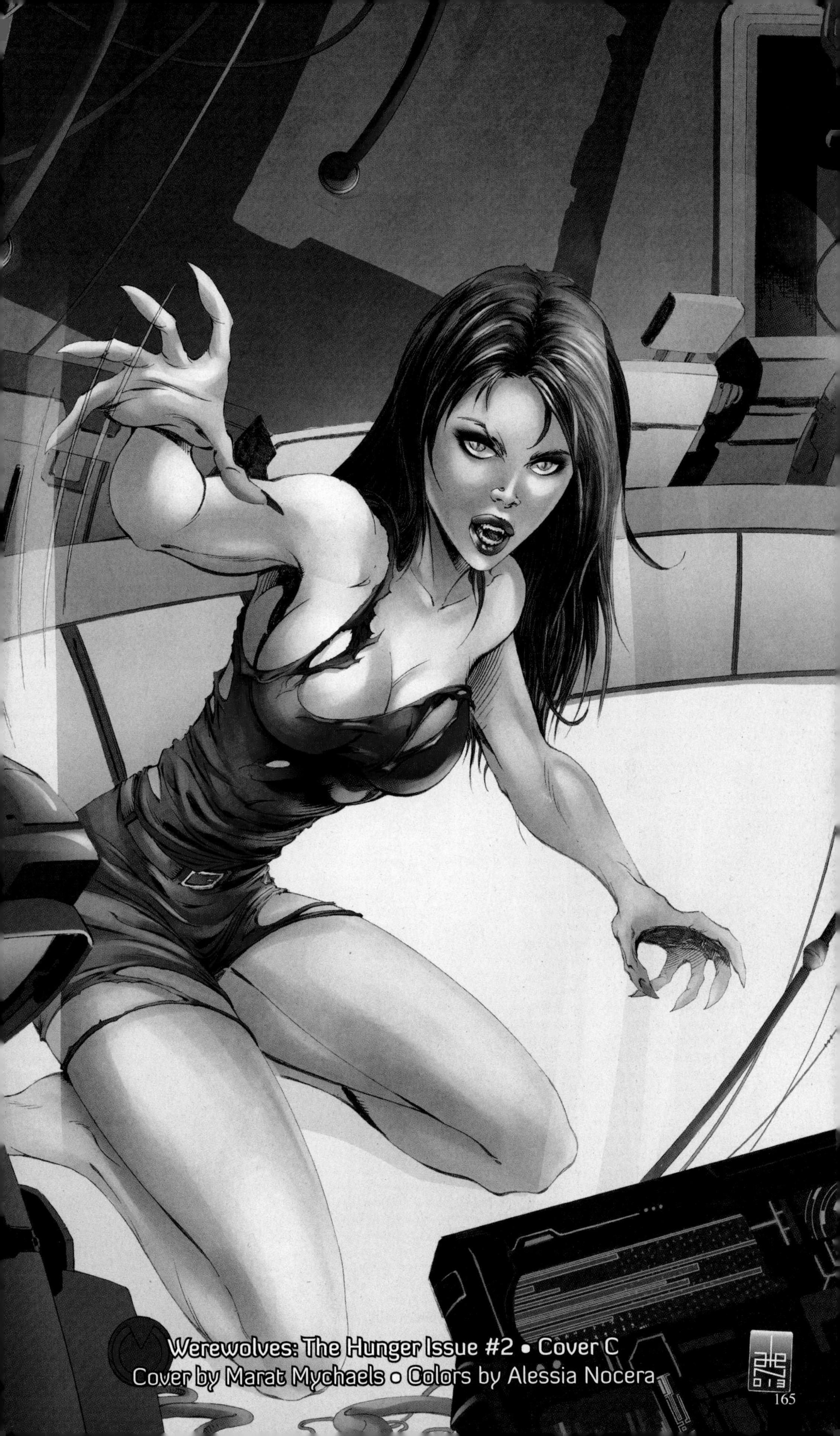

Werewolves: The Hunger Issue #2 • Cover C
Cover by Marat Mychaels • Colors by Alessia Nocera

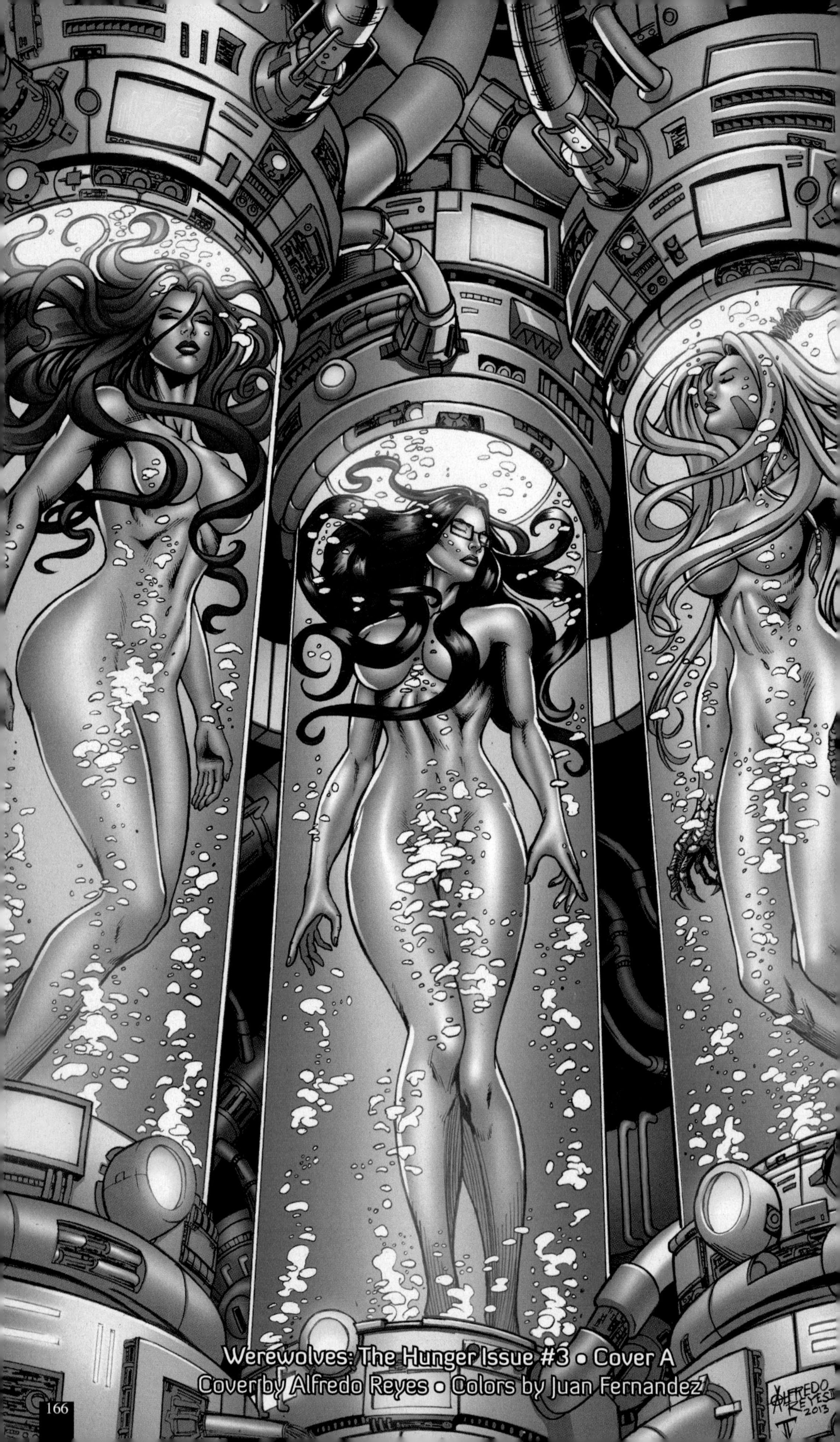

Werewolves: The Hunger Issue #3 • Cover A
Cover by Alfredo Reyes • Colors by Juan Fernandez

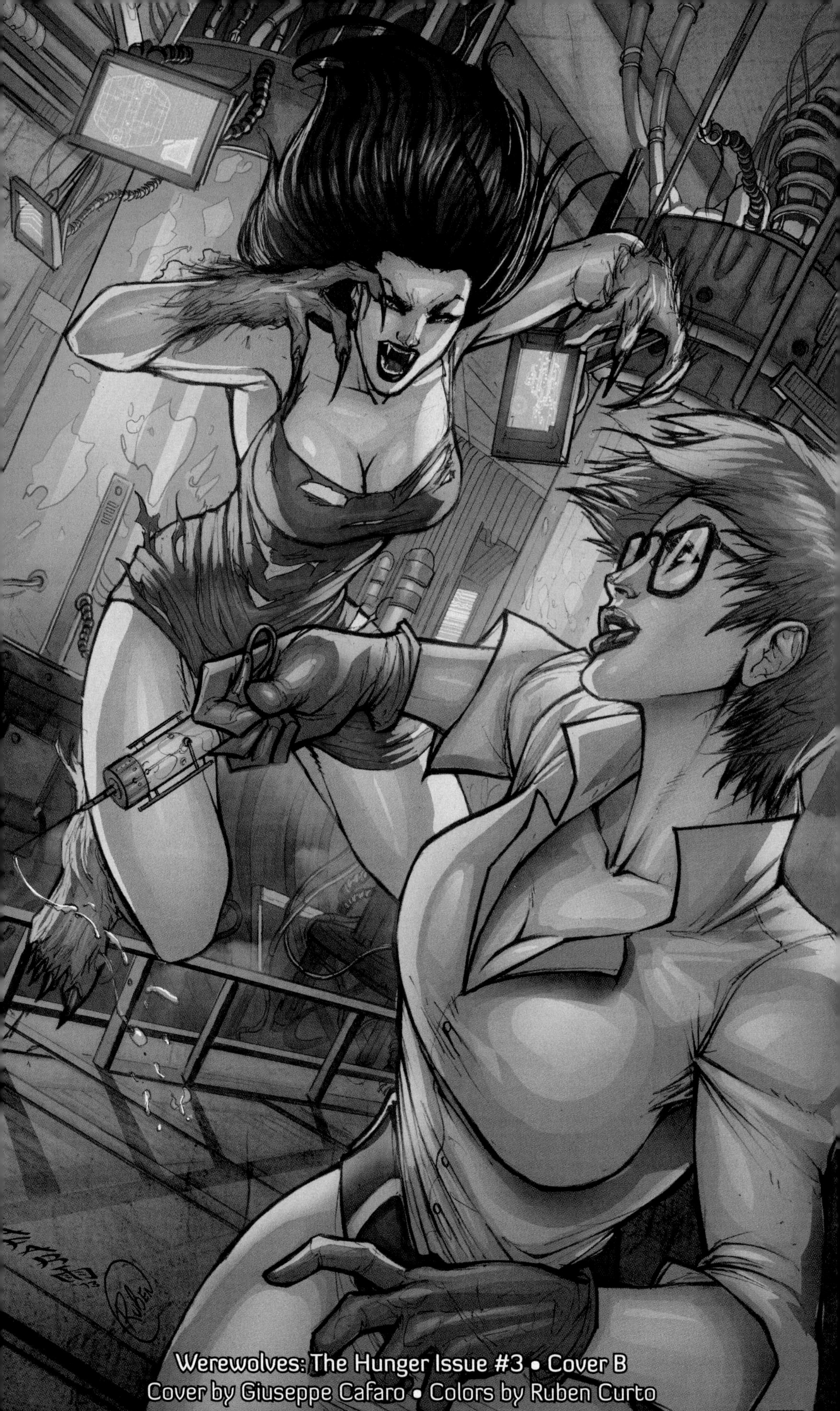

Werewolves: The Hunger Issue #3 • Cover B
Cover by Giuseppe Cafaro • Colors by Ruben Curto

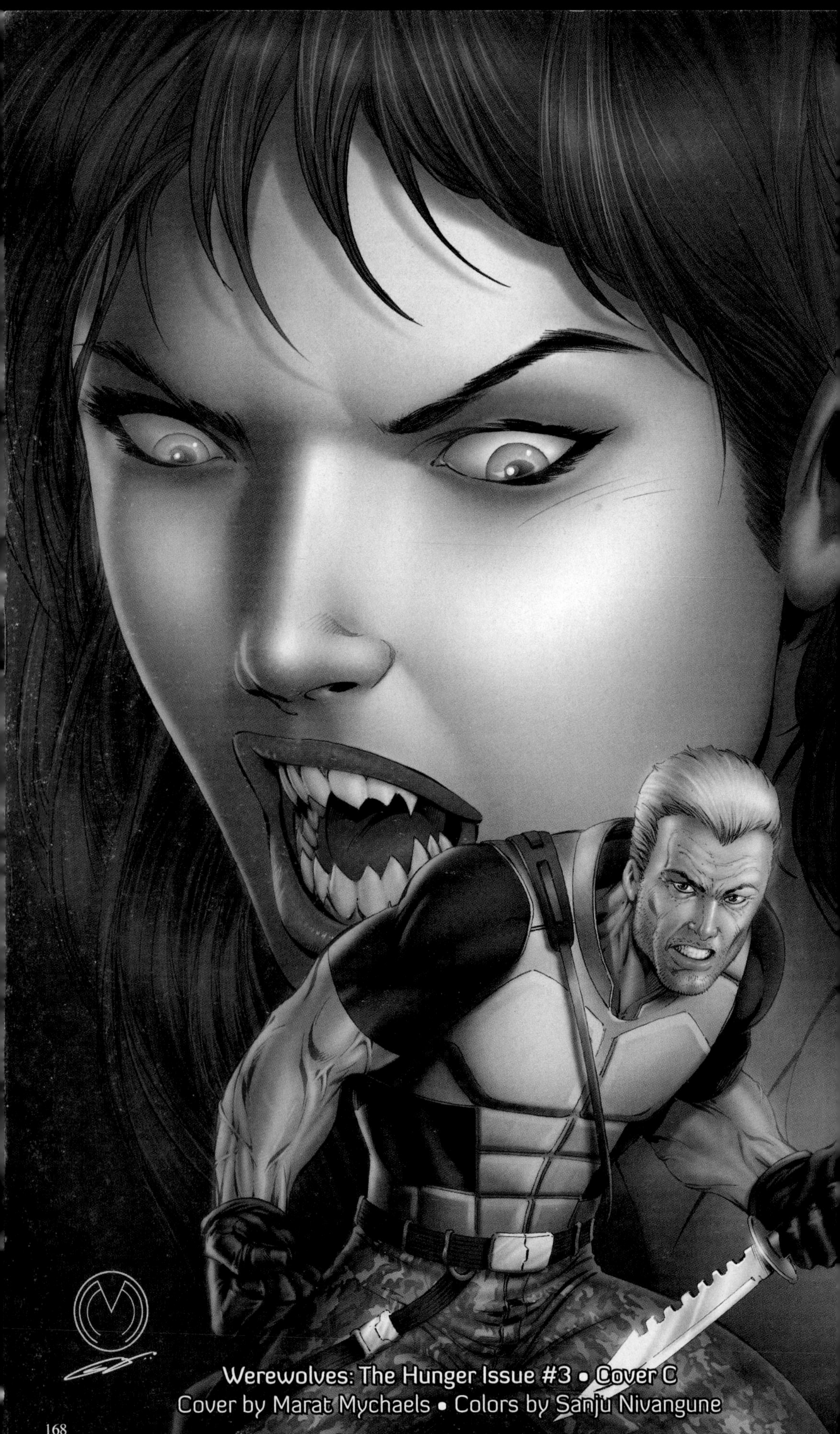

Werewolves: The Hunger Issue #3 • Cover C
Cover by Marat Mychaels • Colors by Sanju Nivangune